TRANSGRESSIONS: CULT
Volume 59

MW01592607

TRANSGRESSIONS: CULTURAL STUDIES AND EDUCATION

Cultural studies provides an analytical toolbox for both making sense of educational practice and extending the insights of educational professionals into their labors. In this context *Transgressions: Cultural Studies and Education* provides a collection of books in the domain that specify this assertion. Crafted for an audience of teachers, teacher educators, scholars and students of cultural studies and others interested in cultural studies and pedagogy, the series documents both the possibilities of and the controversies surrounding the intersection of cultural studies and education. The editors and the authors of this series do not assume that the interaction of cultural studies and education devalues other types of knowledge and analytical forms. Rather the intersection of these knowledge disciplines offers a rejuvenating, optimistic, and positive perspective on education and educational institutions. Some might describe its contribution as democratic, emancipatory, and transformative. The editors and authors maintain that cultural studies helps free educators from sterile, monolithic analyses that have for too long undermined efforts to think of educational practices by providing other words, new languages, and fresh metaphors. Operating in an interdisciplinary cosmos, Transgressions: Cultural Studies and Education is dedicated to exploring the ways cultural studies enhances the study and practice of education. With this in mind the series focuses in a non-exclusive way on popular culture as well as other dimensions of cultural studies including social theory, social justice and positionality, cultural dimensions of technological innovation, new media and media literacy, new forms of oppression emerging in an electronic hyperreality, and postcolonial global concerns. With these concerns in mind cultural studies scholars often argue that the realm of popular culture is the most powerful educational force in contemporary culture. Indeed, in the twenty-first century this pedagogical dynamic is sweeping through the entire world. Educators, they believe, must understand these emerging realities in order to gain an important voice in the pedagogical conversation.

Without an understanding of cultural pedagogy's (education that takes place outside of formal schooling) role in the shaping of individual identity–youth identity in particular–the role educators play in the lives of their students will continue to fade. Why do so many of our students feel that life is incomprehensible and devoid of meaning? What does it mean, teachers wonder, when young people are unable to describe their moods, their affective affiliation to the society around them. Meanings provided young people by mainstream institutions often do little to help them deal with their affective complexity, their difficulty negotiating the rift between meaning and affect. School knowledge and educational expectations seem as anachronistic as a ditto machine, not that learning ways of rational thought and making sense of the world are unimportant.

But school knowledge and educational expectations often have little to offer students about making sense of the way they feel, the way their affective lives are shaped. In no way do we argue that analysis of the production of youth in an electronic mediated world demands some "touchy-feely" educational superficiality. What is needed in this context is a rigorous analysis of the interrelationship between pedagogy, popular culture, meaning making, and youth subjectivity. In an era marked by youth depression, violence, and suicide such insights become extremely important, even life saving. Pessimism about the future is the common sense of many contemporary youth with its concomitant feeling that no one can make a difference.

If affective production can be shaped to reflect these perspectives, then it can be reshaped to lay the groundwork for optimism, passionate commitment, and transformative educational and political activity. In these ways cultural studies adds a dimension to the work of education unfilled by any other sub-discipline. This is what Transgressions: Cultural Studies and Education seeks to produce—literature on these issues that makes a difference. It seeks to publish studies that help those who work with young people, those individuals involved in the disciplines that study children and youth, and young people themselves improve their lives in these bizarre times.

Youth Culture, Education and Resistance

Subverting the Commercial Ordering of Life

Edited by

Brad J. Porfilio
Lewis University, Illinois, USA

Paul R. Carr
Youngstown State University, Ohio, USA

SENSE PUBLISHERS
ROTTERDAM/BOSTON/TAIPEI

A C.I.P. record for this book is available from the Library of Congress.

ISBN: 978-94-6091-178-1 (paperback)
ISBN: 978-94-6091-179-8 (hardback)
ISBN: 978-94-6091-180-4 (e-book)

Published by: Sense Publishers,
P.O. Box 21858,
3001 AW Rotterdam,
The Netherlands
http://www.sensepublishers.com

Printed on acid-free paper

Cover-art by Ginette Boucher

DEDICATION

This book is dedicated to the memory of Joe L. Kincheloe (1950–2008), who lived humanely, inspired many, loved life, and was a good friend.

PRAISE FOR YOUTH CULTURE, EDUCATION, AND RESISTANCE

Youth Culture, Education and Resistance: Confronting Commerialization and Neo-Liberalism continues the important legacy of critical pedagogy by remaining defiant in the face of what seems an unimpeachable foe. There are many positions articulated in this book, and each and every one deserves a hearing. All of the authors are committed to changing the social conditions that racialize, criminalize, pathologize, militarize, and de-skill our youth, who often have little more than opportunities for dead-end, service-oriented jobs once they get through their "corporately-generated high-stakes examinations". Given the daunting task faced by critical educators, it is heartening to see Brad Porfilio and Paul Carr bringing together such a relentlessly creative and courageous group of critical educators, who refuse to give up the struggle to bring social justice to education and the world-at-large, a world increasingly eviscerated of social services on behalf of finance capital.

—Peter McLaren, UCLA (from the Foreword)

Youth Culture, Education and Resistance by Brad Porfilio and Paul Carr is a timely and powerful intervention in contemporary literature on youth, education, and neo-liberalism. Collectively, the authors and editors open up the discussion around young people today, offering us a new and richer language to think about the specific kinds of inequalities young people face today—and how they are being resisted. The topics are as broad as the treatments are deep. We are asked to look beyond an (exclusive) focus on "urban education" towards rural settings as new loci of inequality. We turn our gaze towards white working-class youth in first ring suburbs in the US. We are pushed to de-link questions of nation and culture, turning towards the range of ways young people around the world—from Arab youth in France to young people in the West African country of Burkina-Faso—pick up and deploy hip-hop music to address local concerns. And, of course, we look at the ways young people are resisting their place in this new, brutally realigned world.

—Greg Dimitriadis, University at Buffalo, The State University of New York (from the Afterword)

This book comes at a good time. As various authors in this volume point out, public education in the West has been perverted from Dewey's vision of a progressive engagement with experientially-based learning to transmission-based models that serve corporate, militaristic and imperial purposes. Our youth are increasingly bored and disengaged as citizens, both in and outside of the classroom, while subjected to regimes of testing and curricula processes focused on externally defined objectives and standardized notions of competencies. These tensions have existed for a while, of course. However, what I find valuable about this volume is the way in which the authors look beyond tinkering with the policies of current or outgoing Presidents and Prime Ministers. As this volume emphasizes, the real hope is to be found where it always has been found: in the resistance of youth. Our masters criminalize youth for the same basic reasons that they marginalize and racialize others: to divide and subjugate. I strongly recommend this volume to teachers and academics interested in looking beyond our immediate and localized concerns.

—Douglas Fleming, University of Ottawa

The contributors to this volume present both a theoretically complex analysis of neo-liberalism and the negative consequences for education, and a pedagogically rich portrayal of what is possible possible if we only placed people before profits. Engaging, critical, and ground-breaking.

—David Hursh, University of Rochester

Youth Culture, Education, and Resistance brings together some of the best theoretical and qualitative work currently being done in the field of youth studies and critical pedagogy. It explores the impact of global neo-liberalism—as both policy and cultural practice—in reshaping youth culture; and even more importantly, it reveals how young people today are responding in ways that do not merely reproduce their own domination. The book ultimately leads the reader beyond critique and deconstruction, toward the hope of a radical and creative democratic praxis. The extraordinary set of essays collected in this volume raise fundamental issues of educational theory and practice in the contemporary era. This is a bold, accessible, and timely volume.

—Dennis Carlson, Miami University

ACKNOWLEDGMENTS

This book is dedicated to Joe L. Kincheloe, who has been sorely missed since his untimely death in late 2008. Although we had known Joe for a few years, he had a profound impact on our intellectual, personal, and professional development. Joe's passion for learning and commitment to transforming schools and society came across in his intellectual work, and it inspired us, and many others, to become open to new ideas, new approaches to conducting research, and new ways of teaching. We also found Joe to be genuinely concerned with the growth and development of practitioners and scholars who recently entered the world of criticality. He was happy to spend time to help launch intellectual projects, conduct guest lectures, support candidates for positions in the academy, and befriend scholars who came under fire in academic circles for challenging the intellectual or social *status quo*. Finally, Joe had an incredible zest for life, which was contagious. He enjoyed playing music as much as he enjoyed having dinner with his colleagues, family, and friends. He lived every day to its fullest. It is with great pleasure that we can say that Joe was truly a model academic, pedagogue, and, especially, a freind.

We would like to thank Peter McLaren for his unwavering support of our scholarship and cultural work. Not only does he inspire us to reflect critically upon how neo-liberal globalization impacts social life in First World and so-called *Third World* regions, he provides us with the theoretical insights, courage, and language necessary to image how the cultural manifestations generated by youth can lead us to build a society predicated on democracy, love, freedom, and equality. We would also like to thank Greg Dimitriadis for proving us with the intellectual platform to critically examine the cultural manifestations proffered by youth and their educators within various social contexts across the globe.

Brandi Stillman, a student at Youngstown State University, was extremely helpful in providing some technical support, as well as the team in the Instructional Technology Center, including the Director, Mohamed Jadun, and Matthew Sprankle, Donald Masny, and Adeel Abbas. We would also like to thank Ginette Boucher, a good friend and artist from Montreal, for the wonderful art-work on the cover (Ginette can be reached at gin.boucher@videotron.ca).

We are also both very grateful for the support we have received from our families, and, in particular, our partners, Shannon and Gina.

Brad J. Porfilio and Paul R. Carr

TABLE OF CONTENTS

PETER MCLAREN

FOREWORD

For the past two decades critical educators, their imaginations fired by the templates of John Dewey, Paulo Freire, Che Guevara and others, have raised the hope that they would bring with them a new era of radical reform. This once refulgent hope flickers much more dimly today than it did during those heady years when critical pedagogy became the most shining jewel in the diadem of educational reform. As usual, the battle for educational reform was—and still is—between the liberals and the conservatives, and more recently between the liberals and the far-right. The revolutionary or critical left has never had the same power to change educational policy as the far-right. Much of that has to do with the foofaraw made by the right when critical educators speak out about pro-choice, or the death penality, or global warming, or the debate between developing nations and the developed nations, or crimes committed by Chevron-Texaco against indigenous populations in the Ecuadorian Amazon, or the wars in Iraq and Afghanistan, or especially when capitalism is criticized as a constitutive social relation of exploitation. When socialism is even hinted at as an alternative to capitalism, the right becomes apoplectic. And given that the corporate media sides with the far-right on protecting capitalism from any serious threat, or heavy-handed criticism, U.S. citizens have never been able to discuss publicly, and seriously, alternatives to a capitalist future.

Mainstream liberal educators have tried over the last twenty years to palliate the worst effects of the neoliberal order it has helped to unleash when it made the choice of remaining, at best, politically tepid in the face of this relentless capitalist juggernaut. While the liberal left is changing its tune somewhat in the face of the worst crisis of capital the country has seen since the Great Depression, it has allowed esurient far-right demagogues, talk-show media pundits and the RepublicanParty to continue to stalk the land with its anti-socialist, free market philosophy spewed forth in the most virulent psuedo-populist rhetoric imaginable, and in so doing has given them unmolested space to titivate their reputations as stalwart guardians of the 'Real America'.

While the far-right media machine continues to serve as an 'amen chorus' to neoliberal social policy, effecting a political gaucherie of the most repugnant kind, liberals, in their studied refusal to challenge capital head-on (instead of focussing on capital's excesses), have assured that this present era will end up another dark and barren patch of history. Their whispered pleas to reform and not abolish capital have helped assure inequalities will continue to persist and the social division of labor will not be seriously redrawn.

Today world capitalism is trying to re-establish itself in transnationalized formations, since its current forms are virtually unsustainable. In other words, the transnational capitalist elites are seizing opportunities to use military force to protect their markets and create new ones. In fact, a more dangerous threat than individual acts of terror today are the multifarious contradictions internal to the system of world capitalism. Throughout its history, U.S. capitalism has tried to survive in times of crisis by eliminating production and jobs, forcing those in work to accept worse conditions of labor, and seizing opportunities that might arise in which the public would support military action to protect what the United States defines as its vital interests. One of the major mechanisms used by the ideological state apparatus to prevent a legitimation crisis over the necessity of global capitalism is the school. Students are taught to believe that if capitalism falters, democracy is doomed. But, as Marx argues, capital is an historically produced social relation that can be challenged (most forcefully by those exploited by it). A renewed engagement with and challenge to capital by means of critical revolutionary pedagogy fibrillates our social imagination, which largely has been flatlined since the ascendary of Ronald Reagan and Margaret Thatcher and their successful assault on Keynesian welfare state capitalism. Meszaros has argued that capitalism's functional division of labor is horizontal and is potentially liberating because it partakes of a socially viable universality–the harmonisation of the universal development of the productive forces with the all around abilities and potentialities of freely associated individuals. However, it is the vertical dimension of capitalism and its hierarchical division of labor that constitutes capital's 'reproductive horizon' and 'command structure,' ensuring that living labor is subsumed by dead labor and that capital's productive developments remain containable by the imperative of surplus labor accumulation. This results in the structural/hierarchical subordination of labor to capital. In other words, this creates a permanent structural crisis within capitalism in contrast to what some believe are only periodic, conjunctural crises. Now when we talk about the transnational capitalist class, new forms of imperialism, and the like, we need to see this in terms of the theory of the state that educators work with.

For lack of better terms, there exists left-liberal critical pedagogy, liberal critical pedagogy, conservative critical pedagogy, and variants of each of these. And as both an adjuvant to, and critic of, these versions of critical pedagogy, you have revolutionary critical pedagogy that some of us, myself included, have been trying to develop. These are very rough terms, of course, and there are probably better terms. The crucial point here is that these approaches to pedagogy have implicit or explicit views of the state. Critical pedagogy in the United States is overwhelmingly liberal, and converges, unintentionally in most instances, with neoliberal ideology, policy and practice. In general, it views the state as the "social state" (here I shall borrow some terms from Tony Smith) where symbolic and moral philosophy is the systematic expression of the normative principles of the Keynesian welfare state. In other words, it is a version of the state that offers wage labor as the normative principles of modern society. Some conservative and even liberal-centrist educators take a neoliberal state as the norm, which we could call the entrepreneurial state— in which generalized commodity production requires a world market and they follow Hayek's principle that capital's law of value in the abstract must be followed. Some left liberal educators look to create a new model of the state which could be called an "activist state" (again, borrowing these terms from Tony Smith) that is based, in large part, on the work of Polyani, and includes methods of aggressive state intervention into its industrial policy. International capital still predominates in this model, and there will be an inevitable government and global trade dependence on international capital. Of course, those who govern the activist state desire to place government restrictions on its rules and regulations for attracting global investment capital. So there is a concerted attempt to lessen the worst and most exploitative aspects of the state. Then again, you have some left-liberal educators who prefer the concept of the "cosmopolitan state". This model is largely derived from the work of Habermas, where forms of global market governance can prevail that is intra-national rather than national; here there is a focus on the development of a global civil society. Well, I don't ascribe to any of these models. I believe it is impossible to manage democratically wage labor on a global scale by placing severe restrictions on global financial and derivative markets.

What about the question of property ownership of the mass means of production. Nathalia Jaramillo and I spoke a few weeks ago at IMPA-Industrias Metalúrgicas y Plásticas Argentina, where 172 workers make aluminum products, such as cans, foils and wrappers. How would the cosmopolitan state help these workers? Yes, there would be a stress on greater democratic control of the economy by those who lack access to capital, but it would still support wage labor—and Marx has shown us that wage labor only "appears" to include an equal exchange. Workers sell their capacity to labor to an employer who is able to extract a higher value from the worker than the worker's means of surviving. How could a global state founded upon wage labor work? It is, in my mind, impossible to build a socialist state based on nationalized property because, as Peter Hudis has pointed out, capital can exist as a social form of mediation even in the absence of private ownership. Well, of course, there are other models, such as market socialist models. Some of them incorporate a commodity market within a system of democratically self-managed and worker-run industries. I am not denigrating these more progressive models; some of them have good ideas and are much better than the neoliberal state model that has now international reach.

So basically, let me break the situation down in these two fundamental terms. We need to understand two basic and competing visions of globalization. Let me begin with the first version, that we could call civil societarian. For instance, if we believe that we have witnessed a qualitative transformation of capitalism, beginning in the post-World War II era, a transformation that is grounded in information-based technology and automation, that has basically marginalized manufacturing and productive capital, and if we believe that finance capital flows effortlessly across national boundaries, and if we believe that we have an information or knowledge economy of immaterial labor where productive capital and the working classes are becoming increasingly irrelevant to social transformation, and that the nation state is powerless, then you will probably ascribe to some kind of civil societarianism—putting one's faith in civil society, in NGOs and in the new social movements—because you probably believe that civil society or the public sphere is at least partially autonomous from the state and the market. But such a position ultimately facilitates the privatization of former state-run services, and represents a turn from the global to the local for public funding of social service projects, as John Holst and others have argued. However, I take another position. This position maintains that we have not arrived at the end of the nation state (although we should de-reify the nation state and not assume a nation state-centric position) but that the world has been divided into the global proletariat and working class, and the working-class and the peasantry are at the forefront of anti-neo-liberalism struggles. This view maintains that the fundamental contradictions of our time are not external relations such as the local versus the global, but contradictory relations internal to the process of capitalism itself, contradictions that manifest themselves through the long history of vertical and horizontal expansions of capitalism.

So instead of ascribing to the civil societarian position which utilizes a limited reproductive praxis (where one merely tries to better one's position as an individual or a group within a dialectical relation) I ascribe to a critical revolutionary praxis where one understands the internal relations of capital and struggles to overcome them, to transcend them by means of creating a world where value production ceases to exist. But the question we need to ask is: How do you abolish value production, wage labor? We need to go beyond state intervention into the economy, since this is not socialism. State intervention into the economy doesn't prevent value-producing labor, alienated labor. In fact, capital is a social relation of abstract labor, and it is precisely capital as a social relation that must be transcended. Of course, this is the challenge for all of us. To go up against the ideological state apparatuses (that also have coercive practices such as non-promotion and systems of privilege for those who follow the rules) and the repressive state apparatuses (that are also coercive in that they secure internal unity and social authority ideologically via patriotism and nationalism) is not an easy task. There are disjunctions and disarticulations within and between different social spaces of the superstructure and we must work within those, in spaces of the legal and ideological systems that can be transformed in the interests of social and economic justice.

The struggle is multi-pronged. Let me say that I do not think the civil societarian position is useless. It can do much good. And I do not think we should juxtapose the civil societarian position against the critical revolutionary position. We should take a dialectical approach. Dialectics is not about juxtaposition or "either-or" but about mediation or "both-and". So we can use them both. But the main point I have been making is that we need to be guided by a larger social vision that does not assume the state and civil society are autonomous. Let's face it, civil society is part and parcel of state apparatuses. We fool ourselves if we think there is a strong autonomy in civil society. So the larger vision takes into consideration the social totality, the way capitalism has permeated all spheres of social life, including civil society or the public sphere. This mandates that we need to create a social universe outside of capital's value form. Anything short of this will not bring about emancipation. Revolutionary critical pedagogy strives for the abolition of capital as a social relation. This is the major difference between my position and that of many other critical educators. Now if you change the economic basis of production, will this change our behavior as social beings? The evolutionary biologists seem to being saying no, that there wouldn't be much change. While people might still be inclined to further their self-interest, that doesn't seem much of an excuse to jettison the search for a socialist or ecosocialist alternative to capitalism. Although it might be possible to get better therapy for the persistence of rampant self-interest in a socialist society, given that the world of capital seems to have been invaded by what Barbara Ehrenreich in her book, *Bright-Sided: How the Relentless Promotion of Positive Thinking has Undermined America,* calls "positive psychologists"— those therapists who are out to claim a market share in our corporate world, selling happiness (on the bizarre concept of a 'positive social science') to corporations eager to increase employees' optimism, health, and ability so that they can perform their jobs more efficiently and without complaint, since managed care providers and insurance companies have turned against traditional pathology-oriented psychotherapy because it's too 'negative' (meaning too expensive).

Youth Culture, Education and Resistance: Confronting Commerialization and Neo-Liberalism continues the important legacy of critical pedagogy by remaining defiant in the face of what seems an unimpeachable foe. There are many positions articulated in this book, and each and every one deserves a hearing. All of the authors are committed to changing the social conditions that racialize, criminalize, pathologize, militarize, and de-skill our youth, who often have little more than opportunities for dead-end, service-oriented jobs once they get through their "corporately-generated high-stakes examinations". Given the daunting task faced by critical educators, it is heartening to see Brad Porfilio and Paul Carr bringing together such a relentlessly creative and courageous group of critical educators, who refuse to give up the struggle to bring social justice to education and the world-at-large, a world increasingly eviscerated of social services on behalf of finance capital. The real protagonist in this book is, of course, youth, and youth-led initiatives in the face of the havoc of capitalism—what the editors refer to as "bootstrap capitalism". The contributors to this work are closely aligned with youth, youth culture, and youth movements that are not only resisting the blandishments of neoliberal capital and policies and actively resisting them, but also searching for alternatives to the social relations that continue to hold the United States hostage to a dream swindled and a vision betrayed.

BRAD J. PORFILIO AND PAUL R. CARR

1. THE NEO-LIBERAL SOCIAL ORDER, YOUTH AND RESISTANCE

INTRODUCTION

This introductory chapter provides a framework and background to understand the political, economic and social forces behind the intense suffering and oppression experienced by citizens in a globalized world at today's socio-historical juncture as well as the concomitant damage inflicted upon the environment and other ecological species. We attempt to capture how the current manifestation of capitalism—neo-liberalism—is responsible for generating, arguably, a child-hating environment, one that is antithetical to fostering the social, physical, emotional, and intellectual well-being of children. This chapter also suggests how, despite the stark social and economic realities that exist in the age of "disaster capitalism" (Klein, 2007), some of the cultural manifestations and cultural work generated by youth, both inside and outside of educational institutions, have the propensity to serve as sites of resistance to, and transgression from, the commercial ordering of life. Specifically, the contributors of this volume get beyond the socially degenerative portraits continually generated by corporate leaders, politicians, and right-wing fundamentalist religious zealots, who often characterize youth as violent, lazy, aberrant, or disaffected social animals, individuals who ought not only be contained by the state by force, repression and intimidation, but also ought to be blamed for their own as well as the world's suffering and misery (Giruox, 1997, 2009a; Carlson, 2005). It is ironic that those who characterize youth as pathological or as the source of social problems are the same individuals who have the power to implement policies and practices, within socio-political and economic outlets, that perpetuate the very conditions causing the prevalence of social maladies as well as the social and economic dislocation of youth.

Through their own engagement with youth in K-12 classrooms, through their work with youth in various informal learning spaces (Haworth, this volume; Dimitriadis & Weis, 2008), through their critical analysis of youths' cultural manifestations and social activism, which are often part of broader counter-hegemonic social movements, the contributors in this book, individually and collectively, clearly demonstrate that many of today's "border youth" are socially-aware, civic-minded citizens who possess the critical capacity and courage not only to confront the institutions, arrangements, and policies fueling inequity in their communities, schools, and in other socially-mediated environments, but also hold the determination to forge collective movements predicated on challenging the classist,

B. J. Porfilio and P. R. Carr (eds.), Youth Culture, Education and Resistance:
Subverting the Commercial Ordering of Life, 1–18.
© 2010 Sense Publishers. All rights reserved.

racist, misogynist, and able-bodied status quo. Following the line of research generated recently by transformative scholars who are committed to characterizing youth in a more socially-generative light, as critical agents capable of challenging institutional failure in schools, their communities and the wider society (Ginwright, Nogurera, & Cammartoa, 2006; Dolby & Rizvi, 2008; Giardina, & Donnelly, 2008), the contributors take us inside K-12 classrooms to pinpoint how youth function as stewards of social and personal transformation through the creation of youth-led initiatives that are designed to bring awareness to, and the excavation of, social inequalities, such as racism, sexism, and homophobia. Further, they elucidate numerous alternative narratives generated by youth through music, photographs, and other forms of technology, which speak to the forces causing over-policing within racialized and impovershied communities, consumerism, environmental degradation, militarism, and poverty, and highlight how the neo-liberal agenda in schools is pushing minoritized youth to engage in various forms of resistance strategies for the purposes of empowering their ethno-cultural, racial, or class-based communities, seeking to maintain a sense of empowerment within debilitating educational structures. Finally, the contributors suggest how the current economic crisis provides critical educators with the opportunity to cross age, class, race and intellectual boarders to build a movement of solidarity with youth and other progressive colleagues in academia with a view to engendering cultural work capable of subverting the corporate and military hijacking of childhood, schooling, and other socially-mediated activities unfolding across the global landscape. Ultimately, to not engage in such a struggle would signal a further acquiescence for diverse peoples and interests outside of the power structure in the face of deleterious hegemonic forces that diminish the possibility of a vibrant democracy in and through education (Kincheloe, 2008; Lund & Carr, 2008).

The Rise of Neo-liberalism and its Impact on Youth

Over the past thirty years, transitional corporations, many Western politicians, captains of industry and others enmeshed in neo-liberal expansion have been on a relentless quest to commodify all social life (Hill, 2003). Stressing the virtues of the market-place within education has had the effect of further distancing communities and societies from accessing power, reducing educational debates to functionalist aims, scores and rankings (McLaren, 2007; Kincheloe, 2007). Although most political pundits and news reporters do not make reference to the term in the mainstream media, neo-liberalism is the most dominant doctrine influencing the unfolding of events across the globe. According to Piven, (2007, p. 13) the doctrine is behind the creation of policies and practices that led to "the deregulation of corporations, and particularly financial institutions; the rollback of public services and benefits programs; curbing labor unions; 'free trade' policies; and wherever possible the replacement of public programs with private markets." To implement pro-capitalist policies and corporatist logics that strengthen their interests, corporate leaders have utilized communication technologies, military forces, and international associations, which have coalesced to form a *de facto* world government, with the World Bank, the International Monetary Fund, and the World Trade Organization forming the center-piece (Chomsky, 1999; Giroux, 2004; Klein, 2007; Porfilio & Malott, 2008). This "any means necessary approach" to propagate policies, practices and knowledge designed to control labor power and extract the world of its resources has exponentially intensified suffering and pain inflicted on large swaths of the world's population, while concomitantly concentrating the ruling elite's wealth and power. For instance, Hill's (2008, p. 41) analysis of the impact of neo-liberal policies and practices on so-called "First World" and "Third World" regions underscores how the poor have gotten poorer, demonstrated by middle-income and low-income workers having to work even harder for the past decade to keep the same standard of living. "They (have) suffered pay cuts, union curbs, and a slashed social wage—a sundered social support and survival network of services, provisions and benefits. In contrast, billionaires live in 'Richistan'."

Children, across various social contexts, have experienced significant suffering from an ever-increasing corporate and militaristic ethos impacting the decisions formulated by the world's government and corporate leaders. For instance, with the globalization of culture being based upon market-forces, consumption, and a "survival of the fittest" mentality, youth in North America are not viewed by the state, corporate-leaders, or most citizens as valuable social investments who symbolize "the promise of a better world" (Giroux, 2009a, p. 289), but, rather, are often considered as disposable, violent commodities who do not deserve to be provided social entitlements, such as health care, housing, an adequate education system, and public facilities, such as parks, playgrounds, and libraries, which are some of the essential building blocks for positioning the next generation to become critical, caring, engaged citizens. Critical educators and other concerned social actors must consider the elite's desire to privatize childhood, social entitlements, and other elements of life, along with their desire to use violence and intimation to solve social problems, tantamount to a war on youth. This agenda is responsible for fostering an economic, political, and cultural context for children that is "intolerable and unforgiveable" (Grossberg, 2007, p. 95).

For instance, the current economic crisis, spurred by market-driven decisions and the US's financing of a fanatical "war against terror", is causing more and more families with children in the US to live out of their vehicles, makeshift housing, such as tents, boxes, caves, and boxcars, and moving in and out of homeless shelters (National Coalition for the Homeless, 2008a, 2008b). The impact of the crisis on youth becomes even more telling when considering that 1 in 50 US children are homeless, and about half of all school age children in the US who are "experiencing homelessness have problems with anxiety and depression and 20% of homeless pre-schoolers have emotional problems that require professional care" (National Center on Family Homelessness, 2009). Moreover, Grossberg (2007) underscores how an "epidemic of violence" is plaguing youth at today's historical juncture:

> The U.S. infant mortality rate is higher than that of any industrialized nation in the world. More importantly, 75% of all violent deaths (including homicide, suicide, and firearms-related deaths) of children in the industrialized world

occur in the United States. The suicide rate for kids under the age of fourteen is double the rate of the industrialized world...And while it is hard to get statistics, it appears that for every violent and sexual offense committed by kids, there are three such crimes committed by adults against kids. (p. 97)

Youth in North America, particularly minoritized, youth of color, are also frequently living amid blighted and over-policed urban communities, where they are subject to police harassment and surveillance as a matter of routine. The normative prevalence of the White population to impose an official narrative of color-blindness, predicated on individualism, materialism and merit, further alienates and obfuscates critical pedagogical work that challenges hegemonic forces that are antagonistic to meaningful social justice critical multiculturalism (Carr & Lund, 2007, Kincheloe, 2008). The state not only has egregiously placed blame on youth for the pejorative social conditions pervading urban spaces, but has also criminalized social issues, such as poverty, homelessness, and violence (Giroux, 2004a; Giroux, 2004b; Kozol, 2006). This has led to the creation of a prison-industrial complex, in which communities that have been negatively impacted by de-industrialization, corporate downsizing, and neo-liberal globalization, turn, ironically, to the source of their problem—corporate leaders—to build juvenile detention centers and prisons in order to secure jobs for its citizens, which most often comes at the expense of minoritized youth of color, who are, ultimately, forced to live, at an increasingly younger age, life in confinement (Giroux, 2009a). Dixon (2007) captures the deleterious impact of the state's policy of incarcerating and criminalizing more Black youth for the past thirty years:

America leads the world in numbers of prisons and prisoners, and African Americans, though only one eighth of its population, make up nearly half the locked down...America's malevolent social policy of racially selective mass incarceration is so ubiquitous, so thoroughly part of its statutes, courts, its law enforcement apparatus and traditions that it's hard to believe it was enacted in a single generation, since the ending, about 1970 of the black Freedom Movement. But as late as the 1960s whites, not blacks, were the majority of the nation's prisoners. Since 1970 the U.S. prison population has multiplied about sevenfold, with neither a causative or accompanying increase in crime, and without a public perception that we are somehow seven times safer.

The present level of mass incarceration and its deleterious effects for decades to come upon the black work force, on economic and health outcomes, on culture and family formation are facts of African American life that seem to demand a political response, a concerted and long-term effort to change these awful public policies, much like that called forth by lynching and legal segregation.

Unfortunately, rather than functioning as cultural sites capable of guiding youth to reflect upon what forces give rise to oppression in their schools and communities,schools function as mere appendages of the state, the criminal justice system, and the business world in an age of "bootstrap capitalism." The corporate and militaristic takeover of schools in North America has further debilitated the intellectual development of youth, promulgated policies and practices that criminalize youth, and forced many students to disengage from the schooling process. Youth are frequently pushed out of schools, left to engage in criminal activities, to search tirelessly to secure dead-end, service-oriented jobs, to join the US's imperialistic forces, or to perpetuate the school-to-prison pipeline (Casella, 2008; Farahmandupr, 2008; Kozol, 2006). For instance, many urban schools across in the US, plagued by the state contracting its economic support of education, are unsafe, unsanitary, dilapidated, racially segregated and overcrowded institutions, where ill-equipped educators implement "drill and kill" methods of instruction. While many urban teachers are committed, engaged and focused on the needs of the students, others often make students remain silent and passive in their classrooms in the hope that they pass a battery of corporately-generated high-stakes examinations. These assessments tie students' test scores to the amount of funding schools receive from the state, and can also determine whether schools are taken over by the state or by corporate entities, or whether teachers and administrators lose their jobs or endure other sanctions, such as being ostracized by parents or other community members for not performing as well as "competing" (often well-funded and Whitewashed) academic institutions. Kozol speaks clearly to how NCLB (No Child Left Behind Act, 2001) is responsible for the vast implementation of draconian classroom teaching methods and standardized assessments, which hinder the intellectual, social, and emotional growth of Black and Latino(a) youth:

> At a moment when black and Hispanic students are more segregated than at any time since 1968 (in the typical inner-city school I visit, out of an enrollment that may range from 800 to 4,000 students, there are seldom more than five or six white children), NCLB adds yet another factor of division between children of minorities and those in the mainstream of society. In good suburban classrooms, children master the essential skills not from terror but from exhilaration, inspired in them by their teachers, in the act of learning in itself. They're also given critical capacities that they will need if they're to succeed in college and to function as discerning citizens who have the power to interrogate reality. They learn to ask the questions that will shape the nation's future, while inner-city kids are being trained to give prescribed answers and to acquiesce in their subordinate position in society. (Arran, 2007)

This debilitating environment for youth is further magnified when youth, particularly poor youth and youth of color, are criminalized by zero-tolerance policies. Over the past decade, youth across the US are considered suspects as they arrive on school property. Typically, certain types of youth are scanned by metal detectors, searched by public and private security forces, and kept under constant surveillance through video cameras and other forms of technology (Casella, 2008; Giroux, 2004a). They are also frequently suspended, humiliated or expelled for any range of activities, illustrating, again, how the US's "get tough on crime policy" is considered the panacea for solving social problems affecting youth. Clearly, it would not be in the best interests for proponents of market-driven social reforms to engage in a serious "analysis of the systemic failure to provide safety and security for children through improved social provisions" (Giroux, 2009b). For example, youth have been suspended by school officials if they believe students will hinder the schools' performance on standardized exams, if schools do not want to undertake the "hard work of exercising critical judgment, trying to understand what conditions undermined school safety, and providing reasonable support services for all students, and viable alternatives for troubled ones" (Giroux, 2004b), or due to overt racist attitudes held by school officials in relation to students of color.

This disturbing trend in criminalizing youth in schools overlaps with the reality that US military recruiters have been afforded the unbridled authority to cajole poor youth and disaffected youth of color into the military. With the passage of the NCLB (*No Child Left Behind* Act) in 2001, the US military has been permitted to recruit students in the confines of classrooms as well as being afforded access to students' contact information. Goodman (2009) shows how the US government uses this venue as a conduit to find additional information so that the military target youth who have little social (and cultural) power in educational circles and, therefore, might, incorrectly, believe that the military is the only option for social or economic mobility:

> In the past few years, the military has mounted a virtual invasion into the lives of young Americans. Using data mining, stealth websites, career tests, and sophisticated marketing software, the Pentagon is harvesting and analyzing information on everything from high school students' GPAs and SAT scores to which video games they play.

Therefore, there has been a seismic shift in relation to how schools function in the age of neo-liberalism in the US, and, presumably, to varying degrees, elsewhere as well. Instead of holding to the ideal that educational institutions ought to be "valued for its role in developing political, ethical, and aesthetic citizens and personal growth" (Hursh, 2000), schools are, contrary to Dewey's (1916/1997) vision of progressive, engaged and experiential education, functioning as corporate and military breeding grounds. They can, as a consequence, generate insidious teaching and learning practices that treat students as objects, employ technology and security officials to control and contain youths' bodies and minds, and call on military officials to secure more bodies to advance the US's "permanent war on terror." (McLaren, 2007). Neo-liberal schooling is responsible for an increasing number of youth disengaging from the formal (and formative) educational process, for youths' increased presence in juvenile detention centers or prisons, for youth joining the military without reflecting critically on the personal and societal ramification of their choices, and for youth remaining silent as to what forces are oppressing them and the majority of global citizens (Porfilio & Malott, 2008).

Within the wider social world, youth are not only viewed increasingly as objects by corporate leaders who attempt to inculcate youth in hegemonic ideologies of consumerism, individualism, and intolerance, but as a lucrative market to secure wealth for the corporate world. Corporate leaders realize children and their caregivers spend their excess of dollars to amuse themselves, whether it is through MTV, the Internet, the gaming world, the Western music industry, Hollywood, or the consumption of a myriad digitized texts and goods to embody the supposedly 'cool' lifestyles of Western pop icons (Muehlenberg, 2002; Schor, 2004). Shrewdly, they exploit unjust social conditions facing youth to their advantage. Since many youth face the prospect of working dead-end, service-oriented jobs, lend their time and some of their income to help their families remain economically and socially solvent, and face (as illustrated above) a dehumanizing environment in schools as well as stark conditions in their communities, they are apt to fill social and emotional voids through many "teaching machines," such as computers, television, video games, and music. These are the very sites that condition youth to become loyal to specific brands and products. (Kellner, 1997; Macedo & Steinberg, 2007). Giroux (2009c) spells out with precision the "culture of consumption" that has been propagated by corporate business leaders and the marketing industry for the past thirty years, and how this culture has become hyper-intensified over the course of the last decade:

> Subject to an advertising and marketing industry that spends over $17 billion a year on shaping children's identities and desires, American youth are commercially carpet-bombed through a never-ending proliferation of market strategies that colonize their consciousness and daily lives. Multibillion-dollar corporations, with the commanding role of commodity markets as well as the support of the highest reaches of government, now become the primary educational and cultural force in shaping, if not hijacking, how young people define their interests, values and relations to others.

Moreover, corporate leaders also realize they do not need to focus their energy on using media and schools to produce compliant workers in North America. They continue to outsource labor to less "developed" countries, and have instituted the processes of automation, integration and networking, which have resulted in massive erosion, deskilling and the gradual alienation of work for many (Millar, 1998). As a result, they have accentuated marketing strategies and media campaigns, which have the power to attract more youth to their products or services. This type of entertainment runs counter to the process of political literacy required to allow disenfranchised youth to critically understand, dissect and alter realities that may not be to their advantage (Carr & Thésée, 2008).

Certainly, the influx of corporate ideologies, arrangements and practices to so called "Third World" regions has not improved the quality of life for working-class citizens or children. According to Parenti (2007), the globalization of capitalism to the social context outside of Western countries has allowed Western business leaders to take "over the lands and local economies of Third World peoples, monopolize their markets, depress their wages, indenture their labor with enormous debts, privatize their public service sector, and prevent these nations from emerging as trade competitors by not allowing them a normal development." Children across these contexts are often without food, clothing, and shelter and must toil in unsafe conditions so as to produce goods and services for corporate conglomerates, such as Nike and Disney, which often sell the very goods and services they commodify childhood in every corner of the globe. They also serve as "child soldiers" who are not provided an education that can lead to personal or social transformation. "According to Global March against Child Labor, a third of all children don't make it through the first five years of primary school, the minimum needed for basic literacy. And more than 100 million throughout the world never attend any primary school. As a result, today there are more than 140 million illiterate young people in the world" (Leyva & Leyva, 2004). Globalization is not a neutral prospect, and to crystallize it to mean gainful employment in the US or other Western countries is to belittle the interdependent and nefarious relationships that are established with peoples around the world, often resulting in entrenched, systemic racism, military conflict and visceral poverty (Chossudovsky, 2003; Macedo & Gounari, 2007).

Although the social and economic conditions make it arduous for youth to raise their opposition to the commercialization and militarization of their lived experiences, to the proliferation of global poverty and child labor, to the continuation of Western imperialism and hegemony, and to the demeaning media-driven portraits that characterize them as anti-intellectual criminals who lack any redeeming qualities, some youth are critically aware of the policies, practice, and institutions that oppress children, foster injustice, and perpetuate social inequalities. As a result, they channel their frustration, marginalization and/or opposition to the neo-liberal social order into cultural artifacts, research projects, and social-justice initiatives that can bring awareness to the forces thatbreed oppression as well as to movements that can build a more just and decent social world. In the past, critical scholars in the field of cultural studies and the sociology of education have provided us with portraits of working-class youth who function as critical agents inside of working-class schools. These youth chose to formulate "counter school cultures" in opposition to the cultures promoted by the state and their teachers. They realized that being successful in school only provided a glimmer of hope that they would transcend their class status in an economic system built on the marginalization of most working-class peoples. Consequently, they engaged in behaviors that ultimately led to the reproduction of their class status (McLeod, 1987; McRobbie, 2000; Willis, 1977).

The importance of documenting how youth are consciousness of the reality that schooling has little redeeming value for many within a capitalist-dominated system, since landing a middle-class occupation is often linked to having established connections in the working world rather than based on one's academic record and lived experience. However, researchers, policy makers, and educators must also unearth other forms of youth resistance that not only illuminate youth being cognizant of the constitutive forces that mediate social relationships in schools as well as the relationships between themselves and other working-class peoples across the globe, but also capture how youth are channeling their critical insights into outlets and initiatives that can subvert the structures, policies and practices fueling oppression, hate, and inequity evident with intricate social relations characteristic of today's society. This is where the contributors to this book begin their examination of neo-liberalism, youth culture and resistance.

The chapters in this volume are divided into three sections. In the first section, Carolyn M. Shields, David Requa, Kevin Gosine, Carl E. James, Julie Gorlewski, David Alberto Quijada Cerecer, and Darren E. Lund, and Maryam Nabavi pinpoint the impact of corporatist policies and practices on youth and their teachers in K-12 classrooms as well as the forms of resistance that youth take up to denounce the institutions, policies, and practices perpetuating inequalities and injustice inside and outside of schools. Several of the contributors also document how youth have found fissures amid this commercialized context to implement social-justice initiatives that are intended to provide emancipatory spaces to reflect upon how the neo-liberal agenda is perpetuating oppression inside and outside of their learning communities as well as to develop collaborative movements designed to unearth structural barriers and unjust practices that are causing oppression in youths' social worlds. In the second section, Darius Prier, Brad J. Porfilio, Shannon M. Porfilio, Touorouzou Herve Some, Curry S. Malott, Robert Haworth, Katie Johnston-Goodstar, Alma M. O. Trinidad, and Aster S. Tecle examine the various alternative learning spaces that youth traverse, along with the cultural artifacts that youth consume, produce, and distribute, which give them the outlets to reflect upon what gives rise to injustice and social inequalities in their social circles, in their communities and in the wider society. Several of the contributors also capture how youth are resisting the neo-liberal social order by developing collective movements predicated on bringing awareness to, as well as the excavation of, policies, practices and structures generating an unjust global world order on the structural axes of class, race, gender, sexuality, and age. The contributors map how resistance takes "place in numerous sites and settings with and in-between multiple texts" (Dimitradis & Weis, 2008, p. 335, as cited in Haworth in this volume). In the final section, Michael O'Sullivan and Paul R. Carr and Gina Thésée address the connection between neo-liberalism and education, seeking common ground for diverse interests inside and outside of the formal school experience. O'Sullivan suggests that the financial collapse of late 2008 has brought the world into a post-neo-liberal age, where there has been some discrediting, in both political and academic circles, of the neo-liberal doctrine that has intensified suffering, oppression, and misery for citizens across the globe for over the past thirty years, and Carr and Thésée round out the book with an interrogation of how political literacy is affected and countered by neo-liberal hegemony.

Section 1: Neo-liberal Schooling, Youth, and Resistance

In the first chapter of this section, "Minoritized youth, cultural capital, and the (micro) policy context of schooling," Carolyn M. Shields and David Requa provide a critical document analysis of the NCLB (*No Child Left Behind*) policy legislation, and examine the lived experiences of Latino migrant students, who move between Illinois and Texas during the school year, in order to illustrate how corporatist forms of schooling, "with a heavy emphasis on testing, forces (minoritzed) students to conform to a system that seems largely irrelevant to their daily lives and ill-designed to provide them with educational opportunities of quality."

By employing Bourdieu's theoretical insights in relation to how schools perpetrate the marginalization of impoverished youth and youth of color, the authors also reveal how hidden power relations in schools mask the numerous ways these institutions are complicit in Latino migrant students' lack of educational attainment. Here they show how schools fail to meet the migrant students' particular needs:

> For example, these migrant students like many of their peers, verbalize ambitious career goals; nevertheless, their understanding of how society and schooling are structured is severely limited by their parents' lack of formal schooling as well as their limited awareness of any possible counselling or academic guidance offered by either school. They seemed to believe it to be "normal" that they should have difficulty making and sustaining friendships or good relationships with teachers. They saw nothing particularly unusual in their need to live apart from their families.

The authors also show that youth embody a passive form of resistance towards schools and the economic system, which make it difficult for them to succeed academically or to help secure a living wage for their families. The Latino migrant students have internalized that it is "normal" not to be provided the intellectual and social support needed to meet their personal and career goals. The authors conclude their chapter by offering several suggestions for thwarting the neo-liberal agenda in schools and in the wider society.

In the second essay in this section, "Racialized students resisting: Hindrance or asset to academic success," Kevin Gosine and Carl E. James cull the extant literature surrounding the strategies marginalized youth employ to gain a sense of empowerment in schooling structures that are openly hostile to the 'Other.' The authors demonstrate clearly that commercialized values and an individualistic ethos work to deflect educators and other citizens from seeing unjust practices and institutional inequalities making it difficult for minoritzed students to succeed in schools. In turn, this reifies "the perception that differences in educational outcomes for racialized group members are attributable to the cultural deficiencies that minority students bring to the classroom." To gain a sense of empowerment in schools, minoritized youth typically implement two strategies of resistance:

1. striving for academic success while maintaining a commitment to their ethno-racial community; and
2. 'opting out' of the system which could take a form of, among other behaviors, dropping out of school, limiting school attendance (or being truant), being unconcerned with punctuality, challenging teachers, being disruptive in school and classes, and/or choosing to participate in school primarily through athletic endeavors.

Although the youth resistance strategies do not directly confront the neo-liberal agenda, according to the authors, educators and activists can work with students' knowledges in relation to how they view schooling and social inequality, and can fold students' "social justice desires" into a movement to promote equity and social justice in schools and in society. In the next entry in this section, "White working-class high school students and resistance to neo-liberalism," Julie Gorlewski provides anecdotes from her grade 11 English classroom, which is located in an inner-ring suburb in New York, populated by White working-class high school students. She illustrates how neo-liberal policies, through the implementation of high-stakes examinations and standardized curricula, have ensured that teachers in working-class schools have feelings of "disempowerment, demoralization, and deprofessionalization," as they recognize the standardization of teaching and learning produce a feeling of frustration, anxiety, and insecurity amongst their students. Teachers also are alienated because they recognize that "working-class public schools, social languages and language arts practices that diverge from academic or 'standard' English tend to be treated as deficient, and students are often silenced on the basis of their modes of expression rather than the quality of their ideas." She documents how the dialogic, transformative pedagogies that she implemented broke down students' resistance towards two content areas: poetry, and the college entrance exams. Her students' resistance became a resource to recognize the value of poetry and to get beyond viewing higher education as purely a means to securing gainful employment. She concludes her reflective essay with the belief that teachers have the ability to use dialogic, transformative pedagogies to "challenge existing neo-liberal power relations to channel the resistance that Foucault asserts is a perpetual constituent of power. True dialogue offers the possibility to facilitate solidarity between working-class students and their teachers."

In the fourth chapter in this section, "Every day education: Youth rethinking neo-liberalism by mapping cultural citizenship and intercultural Alliances," David Alberto Quijada Cerecer challenges the reader to get beyond looking at youth as consuming subjects who are preoccupied merely with obtaining one of the few dead-end and service-oriented jobs that exist in many communities, or are focused on buying commodities to satisfy their market-driven wants, impulses. This detached gaze views youth as subjects who occupy the desire and critical insights "to advocate for social justice as civil rights for others". Through his ethnographic research in a high school setting, he documents how a group of working poor, urban youth of color engages in "cultural citizenship practices to forge intercultural alliances across communities by facilitating diversity workshops for other youth in school settings". Specifically, the Youth Dismantling Oppression (YDO) project illustrates the critical insight and determination that his minoritzed participants hold in relation to using art and performance to build intercultural alliances for the purpose of positioning "themselves collectively in society as cultural citizens, who demonstrate civic and social engagement, build community, and take action in relation to racism, sexism, and homophobia through everyday conversations and engagement." Quijada concludes the chapter by arguing that this political form of education and critical form of citizenship have the power to forge a society that embraces "equity, civil rights and full democratic participation for others."

In the final chapter in this section, "Renewing youth engagement in social justice activism," Darren E. Lund and Maryam Nabavi provide readers with data from a research project they launched in the Prairie region of Western Canada, seeking to capture how teachers and students, despite teaching and learning amid socio-political structures that downplay the persistence of systemic inequalities as well as the need to unearth the forces generating hate and hostility in schools and in the wider society. From their conversations with youth aimed at "form(ing) and sustain(ing) coalitions and collaborative projects" in schools that are dedicated to eliminating racism, the researchers determined the motivation for youth joining coalitions to eliminate racism, and the challenges they faced from their peers in putting into place social-justice initiatives, and, further, documented an overriding skepticism related to how they were not being taken seriously by adults who engaged in similar social-justice activities. Despite the obstacles and resistance their participants faced pertaining to the implementation of cultural work within schools, the authors conclude that the anti-racism work designed by the students can serve as a pedagogical guidepost to others who hope to formulate similar social-justice initiatives in schools "to resist the neo-liberal agenda and the positioning of students as consumers in a market economy."

Section II: Informal Education, Youth and Resistance

In the first chapter in this section, "Hip-hop as counter-public space of resistance for Black male youth," Darius Prier documents how the neo-liberal hegemony in schooling, de-industrialization, over-policing of urban communities, and the elimination of social entitlements in urban contexts have merged together and are responsible for many Black male youths' "investments in the counter-spaces such as hip-hop". Drawing on Stephen Haymes' (1995) critical pedagogy of urban struggle, Prier illustrates how hip-hop has provided an outlet for "the voices, narratives, and experiences of Black people, who often struggle to construct and affirm their identities within neo-liberal urban spaces emptied of economic opportunities by neo-liberal reforms." Next, Prier takes up three discursive genres of hip-hop, and captures how Black youth identities have been situated by the various social and economic forces influencing life in contemporary urban contexts: social and politically conscious rap, *gangsta* rap, and commercial rap music. The pedagogical exemplar has the potency to guide scholars, schoolteachers, and researchers to use hip-hop to achieve transformative ends in classrooms and in urban communities. Prier states:

> ...hip-hop as form of popular culture can offer knowledge that is of necessity for teachers and students who are concerned with the moral and political ends of education and schooling in relationship to forms of injustice and inequality. It is also of importance for educators who seek alternative curricular and pedagogical spaces that open up new dialogical and material spaces for urban youth to resist oppression.

In the second chapter of this section, "Hip-Hop Pedagogues: Youth as a Site of Critique, Resistance, and Transfomation in France and in the Neo-liberal Social World," Brad J. Porfilio and Shannon M. Porfilio pinpoint the constitutive forces behind *banlieue* youth appropriating critical elements of hip-hop culture, which were generated by disaffected Black and Latino(a) youth in the US in the late-1970s, to speak directly to the unjust realties they experienced with the onslaught of neo-liberal policies and get "tough on youth" practices impacting their home countries, the

French *banlieue*, and other contexts such as schools. Next, the authors highlight their critical analysis of hip-hop artists' music to show how the depth and level of critique has heightened, as France as well as other global communities have become further militarized, commercialized and impoverished through the implementation of a spate of neo-liberal practices. Finally, the authors conclude their chapter with an examination of the artists' cultural work. They show how the trajectory of the movement has broadened over the past decade to include other critical youth and citizens who are rallying against the corporate and militaristic takeover of the globe. The hip-hop pedagogues' cultural work provides insight to scholars, schoolteachers and other concerned citizens in relation to how they can engage in similar social movements, which are designed to foster social justice and equity in their schools, their communities and in other globalized contexts. They show that:

> In addition to their music, many hip-hop intellectuals have joined other activists, organizations, and countercultural movements to free the globe from institutional oppressions and to generate new social and economic structures that are in line with fostering the needs of humanity and respecting the ecological world. Many of the artists utilize the stage to create a sense of solidarity among minoritized peoples and activists from the dominant culture, to bring awareness to salient issues affecting French society as well as the global community and to raise money for and support of political and social organizations fighting neo-liberal policies and practices.

In the next essay in this section, "Popular music and neo-liberal globalization in Burkina Faso: Counter-hegemonic possibilities and limits of a youth movement," Touorouzou Hervé Somé analyzes the lyrics of several genres of music generated by the youth of Burkina Faso: Blacksomania, Takiborsé (or interchangeably, Takborsé), and the hip-hop movement. He evaluates their potential to engage the citizens in this country to challenge neo-liberal globalization and the country's entrenched political hierarchy. Hervé Somé shows that several artists are very critical of the impact of neoliberlism on the peoples of Burkina Faso and in other communities across Africa. For instance, he argues that rap has been a transformative culture for the youth in Burkina Faso, a critical space where youth express their awareness, outrage and opposition to neo-liberal policies gutting social entitlements in their communities, bludgeoning their communities' value systems, and privatizing their health care system and other sectors of society. He states:

> Today, hip-hop is a powerful movement in Burkina. Rap, more generally hip-hop, is shaping a new destiny for the Burkinabé music...It is arguably the case that hip-hop music speaks to the idiom of (youths') daily lives. For sure, the socio-economic conditions in the late 1990s had not attained the degree of squalor, which now prevails as neo-liberal globalization gains has commodified life in Burkina Faso.

The author concludes the chapter by arguing that it would be shortsighted to think all of youths' cultural formations have the potential to bring awareness to the destructive path of neo-liberalism by demonstrating how Takiborsé music, for example, promotes "materialism that boils down to advancing uncritical consumerism. A new trend observed in Burkina Faso is the conspicuous exhibition of luxury items, from high fashion, clothing, glittering jewelry, and super-expensive personal effects, items that are totally out of reach for the commoner."

In the third chapter in this section, "Anarcho-punk: Radical experimentations in informal learning spaces," Robert Haworth orients the reader to the aims of the anarcho-punk movement through a self-reflexive narrative of how he became involved in the punk scene during the early-1980s. As a privileged member of the White, middle-class world, punk rock provided him a critical window to "learn about political movements in El Salvador, Reaganomics and the ill effects of trickle-down economics explicitly through punk lyrics. Punk songs became stories or vignettes of the ugliness of capitalism and US imperialism". Based on his experience in the punk movement, he critically assesses whether various manifestations of the movement have the power to lead us beyond the corporate malaise to engender a social system predicated on meeting the social and emotional needs of all citizens. He argues that in the contemporary era anarcho-punk is a venue to resisting co-optation by corporate executives. This movement is also effective because it lends a layered "political and cultural critique of capitalism and a willingness to develop non-statist communication and actions that take place and evolve in situated and sometimes temporary communities". Haworth concludes the essay by explicating how critical scholars, teachers, and teacher-educators can also "connect or build an affinity" with youth in informal learning spaces, such as anarcho-punk. "Anarcho-punk offers just one of many outside informal learning spaces where youth engage in discussions about the world beyond capitalism. More importantly, these spaces create moments where subjects may communicate and act within these re-imagined communities"

In the next chapter in this section, "Using God to turn off the radio: Punk rock and the complexities of human resistance," Curry S. Malott argues that right-wing politicians use religion to squash opposition movements forged by youth during the 1980s. The ruling elite uses rhetoric configured by Christian fundamentalists to place blame on working-class peoples and youth for the social problems, such as teen suicide and gang violence, stemming from structural inequalities, the gutting of social entitlements, and de-industrialization. Malott underscores the absurdity of the fundamentalist Christian movement when he states the dominant American mythology of people's economic success being "informed by a version of the Protestant work ethic that explains the accumulation of wealth as God's reward for those who have been *good* Christians—and a good Christian in this context is one who uncritically works hard for the bosses and is intolerant of any ideas or values that differ from those held by the conservative right." Next, he provides a specific example of how elite leaders have used laws and police officials to scare youth away from movements that offer a challenge to neo-liberal hegemony. They went directly after Jello Biafra, who was noted nationally for his alternative political views and political projects. The author concludes the chapter with a critical analysis of the lyrics of punk rockers, providing readers with empowering alternative narratives. Youth use this cultural medium to courageously vocalize their critical insights of the elite's use of religion to promote intolerance, to fuel war, to embrace individualism, and to demonize radical youth and their cultural manifestations, such as punk rock.

In the final chapter in this section, "Critical pedagogy through the reinvention of place: Two cases of youth resistance," Katie Johnston-Goodstar, Alma, M.O. Trinidad and Aster S. Tecle share their findings from two-community-based youth programs. The first case study, which started in 2006, involved the first author, urban Native American youth and community members. The pedagogy for the project "investigated environmental injustice in an urban community with Native youth". The participants used a participatory-action research methodology—Photovoice— in order to encourage youth to "take pictures of their world, to tell the stories of their visual investigation through narratives and to critically engage those stories, in praxis for social change". In the end, the project not only positioned students and community members to become critically aware of the injustices wrought be neo- liberalism in their community, but also nudged them to recognize community strengths "by centering Indigenous theories of place, education and justice. It also served to connect youth participants and encourage commitment and action on behalf of their communities and knowledges." The second project, Youth Organic Farm, "is a social movement to develop a comprehensive plan and sustainable local food system by educating youth, fighting hunger, improving health and nutrition, and being part of the growing organic agricultural industry." This project is located in a rural area in Hawai'I, and the community "mirrors the political, economic, social, and cultural barriers facing today's minoritized, rural families and youth." The authors document how the project was instrumental in engaging youth in a critical praxis of their lived world. The youth "became actively involved with community issues, gained "awareness of injustices that exist in their community," and developed "an identity of resistance" to the forces causing oppression in their community. The authors conclude the chapter by showcasing the value of critical Indigenous pedagogy of place and participatory action research in terms of guiding minoritized youth and communities to become agents of change "who critically respond to and resist neo-liberalism and cultural hegemony from an Indigenous standpoint."

Section III: Post-Neo-Liberalism, Youth and Resistance

In this section, Michael O'Sullivan writes a chapter arguing that "the dramatic meltdown of the global financial system in 2008" has provided the impetus to discredit neo-liberal capitalism. He believes critical transformative intellectuals have been afforded the perfect opportunity to "offer a fundamental challenge to the policies, practices, and ideologies of contemporary globalized consumer capitalism". O'Sullivan also claims workers and intellectuals alike must build on the political movement generated by youth in the US, who spearheaded the election of President Obama, if the state is to "adopt progressive post-neo-liberal policies, a platform to serve the interests of the social base that elected him and not reward the traditional corporate hegemony, as the administration is doing with its multibillion dollar bailout (AKA stimulus)." The author also argues that teachers and teacher-educators have the responsibility in this new era to guide young people to have a critical understanding in relation to how knowledge is produced, how "their worldviews and their values are socially constructed," and how they can work collectively with others to build "a democratic movement for social change." The essay concludes by examining the role critical literacy ought to play in K-12 schools during the post-neo-liberal age. The author believes that "using the skills and perspective associated with critical literacy," along with "values of participatory democracy, social justice, and ecological balance," will provide the pedagogical ingredients to broaden students' identities in relation to how their world functions and the role they must take to ameliorate it.

In the concluding chapter to this book, Paul R. Carr and Gina Thésée examine the notion of political (il)literacy emanating from the formal education process. They interrogate how neo-liberalism can stimulate a teaching and learning deficit that tacitly and explicitly works to establish a benign acceptance of political, economic and socio-cultural hegemonic forces that serve to eviscerate the advent of meaningful transformation in and through the formal education process. Borrowing from Freire (1973/2005) and Kincheloe (2008), they discuss how identity, lived experience and (inequitable) power relations shape the educational context, and advocate for a more salient foray into knowledge construction (and a critical reflection of epistemology) as a mode of building a more just, and democratic, educational experience. Further, they question how accountability is used to marginalize the marginalized, and also how educational policy-making avoids, omits and/diminishes the political reasons for poor educational performance. In addition, they target how education is formulated, and question how fundamental issues, such as political literacy, democracy and critical engagement, can be purposefully neglected by the overseers of formal education. In their conclusion, they provide two models for interrogating political literacy, which also attempt to promote a more equitable and transformative model of education for all peoples.

REFERENCES

Arrant, M. (2007). Kozol on hunger strike to protest NCLB. Retrieved from http://comments fromleftfield.com/2007/09/kozol-on-hunger-strike-to-protest-nclb

Carlson, D. L. (2005). Hope without illusion: Telling the story of democratic educational renewal. *International Journal of Qualitative Studies in Education, 18*(1), 21–45.

Carr, P. R., & Lund, D. E. (Eds.). (2007). *The great white north? Exploring whiteness, privilege and identity in education.* Rotterdam: Sense Publishers.

Carr, P. R., & Thésée, G. (2008). The quest for political (il)literacy: Responding to, and attempting to counter, the neo-liberal agenda. In B. Porfilio & C. Malott (Eds.), *An international examination of urban education: The destructive path of neo-liberalism* (pp. 173–194). Rotterdam: Sense Publishers.

Casella, R. (2008). Security, pedagogy, and the free-market approach to "troubled youth." In B. Porfilio & C. Malott's (Eds.), *The destructive path of neo-liberalism: An international examination of urban education* (pp. 63–80). Rotterdam: Sense Publishers.

Chomsky, N. (2008). *The essential Chomsky* (A. Arnove, Ed.). New York: The New Press.

Chomsky, N. (1999). *Profit over people: Neo-liberalism and global order.* New York: Seven Stories Press.

Chossudovsky, M. (2003). *Globalization of poverty and the new world order.* Montreal: Centre for Research on Globalization.

Dewey, J. (1916/1997). *Democracy and education: An introduction to the philosophy of education.* New York: Free Press.

Dimitriadis, G., & Weis, L. (2008). Globalization and multi-sited ethnographic approaches. In C. McCarthy, A. S. Durham, L. C. Engel, A. A. Filme, & M. D. Giardina (Eds.), *Globalizing cultural studies: Ethnographic interventions in theory, method, and policy* (pp. 323–342). NewYork: Peter Lang.

Dixon, B. (2007). *A leaderless community.* Retrieved from http://www.tompaine.com/print/a_leaderless_community.php

Dolby, N., & Rizvi, F. (Eds.). (2008). *Youth moves: Identities and education in global perspective.* New York: Routledge.

Farahmandpur, R. (2008). Imperialism, global capitalism, and noeliberlism: Critical pedagogy in the age of empire. In B. Porfilio & C. Malott's (Eds.), *The destructive path of neo-liberalism: An international examination of urban education* (pp. 3–22). Rotterdam: Sense Publishers.

Freire, P. (1973/2005). *Pedagogy of the oppressed.* New York: Continuum.

Hill, D. (2008). Class, 'race', and neo-liberal capital. In B. Porfilio & C. Malott's (Eds.), *The destructive path of neo-liberalism: An international examination of urban education* (pp. 41–62). Rotterdam: Sense Publishers.

Klein, N. (2007). *The sock doctrine: The rise of disaster capitalism.* New York: Metropolitan Books.

Kozol, J. (2006). *The Shame of the Nation: The restoration of apartheid schooling in North America.* Pittsburgh: Three Rivers Press.

Ginwright, S., Noguera, P., & Cammarota, J. (Eds.). (2006). *Beyond resistance! Youth activism and community change: New democratic possibilities for practice and polices for America's youth.* New York: Routlege.

Giroux, H. A. (2004a). *The terror of neo-liberalism: Authoritarianism and the eclipse of democracy.* New York: Paradigm Publishers.

Giroux, H. A. (2004b). Class causalities: Disappearing youth in the age of George Bush. *A Journal of Academic Labor, 6*(1). Retrieved from http://www.henryagiroux.com/online_articles.htm

Giroux, H. A. (2009a). *Youth in a suspect society: Democracy or disposability?* New York: Palgrave Macmillan.

Giroux, H. A. (2009b). *Locked out and locked up: Youth missing in action from Obama's stimulus plan.* Retrieved from http://www.alternet.org/rights/127460/locked_out_and_locked_up:_youth_missing_in_action_from_obama's_stimulus_plan/

Giroux, H. A. (2009c). *Commodifying kids: The forgotten crisis.* Retrieved from http://www.truthout.org/040309J

Giroux, H. A. (1997). *Channel surfing: Race, talk and the destruction of today's youth.* New York: Palgrave Macmillan.

Goodman, D. (2009). A few good kids? *Major Jones Magazine.* Retrieved from http://www.Mother jones.com/politics/ 2009/09/few-good-kids

Grossberg, L. (2007). Cultural studies, the war against kids, and the re-becoming of U.S. modernity. In N. K. Denzin & M. D. Giardina (Eds.), *Contesting empire globalizing dissent: Cultural studies after 9/11* (pp. 231–249). New York: Paradigm Publishers.

Hill, D. (2003). Global neo-liberalism, the deformation of education and resistance. *Journal for Critical Education Policy Studies, 1,* 1. Retrieved from http://www.jceps.com/?pageID=article&articleID=7

Hursh, D. (2000). Neo-liberalism and the control of teachers, students and learning: The rise of standards, standardization and accountability. *Cultural Logic, 4*(1). Retrieved from http://clogic.eserver.org/4-1/hursh.html

Kellner, D. (1997). Critical theory and British cultural studies: The missed articulation. In J. McGuigan (Ed.), *Cultural methodologies* (pp. 12–41). London: Sage.

Kincheloe, J. L. (2008). *Critical pedagogy: Primer.* New York: Peter Lang.

Levya, Y., & Levya, J. (2004, April 21). *A day to remember children across the globe.* Retrieved from http://www.progressive.org/media_814

Lund, D. E., & Carr, P. R. (Eds.). (2008). *"Doing" democracy: Striving for political literacy and social justice.* New York: Peter Lang Publishing.

Macedo, D., & Steinberg, S. (2007). *Media literacy: A reader*. New York: Peter Lang.

Macedo, D., & Gounari, P. (2006). *The globalization of racism*. Boulder, CO: Paradigm.

McLaren, P. (2007). *Life in schools: An introduction to critical pedagogy in the foundations of education*. Boston: Pearson Education, Inc.

McRobbie, A. (2000). *Feminism and youth culture* (2nd ed.). New York: Routledge.

Macleod, J. (1987). *Ain't no makin' it: Aspirations and attainment in a low-income neighborhood*. New York: Westview Press.

Millar, S. M. (1998). *Cracking the gender code: Who rules the wired world?* Toronto: Secondary Story Press.

Muehlenberg, B. (2002). Targeting our children: Merchants of cool. *The Australian Family, 24*, 24.

National Center on Family Homelessness. (2009). *State report card on child homelessness: America's youngest outcasts*. Retrieved from http://www.homelesschildrenamerica.org/pdf/rc_full_report.pdf

National Coalition for the Homeless. (2008a). *Homeless families with children: NCH Fact Sheet #12*. Retrieved from http://www.nationalhomeless.org/publications/facts/families.html

National Coalition for the Homeless. (2008b). *How many people experience homelessness? NCH Fact Sheet #2*. Retrieved from http://www.nationalhomeless.org/publications/facts/How_Many.pdf

Parenti, M. (2007). *Mystery: How wealth causes poverty in the world*. Retrieved from http://www.commondreams.org /views07/0216-30.htm

Piven, F. F. (2007). The neo-liberal challenge. *Contexts, 6*(3), 13–15.

Porfilio, B., & Malott, C. (Eds.). (2008). *The destructive path of neo-liberalism: An international examination of urban education*. Rotterdam: Sense Publishers.

Schor, J. (2004). *Born to buy: The commercialized child and the new consumer culture*. New York: Scribner.

Willis, P. (1977). *Learning to labour: How working-class kids get working-class jobs*. New York: Columbia University Press.

SECTION I:
NEO-LIBERAL SCHOOLING, YOUTH, AND RESISTANCE

CAROLYN M. SHIELDS AND DAVID REQUA

2. MINORITIZED YOUTH, CULTURAL CAPITAL, AND THE (MICRO) POLICY CONTEXT OF SCHOOLING

Fifteen-year-old José spent this past summer, as he had since he was 12, trudging through a hot, dusty corn field in Illinois, cutting the tassels off seed plants by hand so that the next year's corn crop would have just the right characteristics. His workday began, as usual, at 5 a.m. when he boarded a school bus to take him to the fields; it ended 12 hours later when he started home, covered with corn pollen and dust, to shower and change his clothes before heading off again to catch the bus for the summer migrant program at the local high school.

The home to which he returned was a decrepit, three-story factory building, with kitchen facilities only available to residents of the first floor. Unfortunately José's family lives upstairs, so they must use one of the grills in the yard for their food preparation. There are no refrigerators; ice chests hold whatever should be kept cool in the blistering summer heat. To shower, he must take his turn at a "gang" shower down a hallway. The facility serves a full floor of residents.

José's parents, undocumented workers from Texas, are particularly anxious that he attend the summer program designed to assist him educationally. To please them, as well as to advance his personal goal of creating a better life for himself, José agrees to participate. The reality, however, is that, exhausted from the day's grind and unfamiliar with his classmates or the program structure, he only attends 3 or 4 of the 19 summer sessions. When he does attend, his day ends with another bus ride home, this one at 9 pm, giving him time to grab a few hours sleep before the routine begins again.

Most years, José is still working in the fields when school starts in Illinois. He stays in the fields for the first two weeks of the school year because he and his family need the money. His father is now working in Texas; but his mother's work, bagging and sorting seed corn, lasts into October, about a quarter of the way through the school year. José's family then packs up a truck and drives back to Texas where he enters school again, taking his Illinois grades and partial credits, and hoping to "make up" what he needs to be able to graduate in Texas in order to receive a high school diploma.

It is obvious, as described in this portrait of a young migrant worker, that the transient lifestyle of José[1] and the almost 900,000 other migrant agricultural workers in the United States under the age of 18 (see Méndez, 2005) poses significant

B. J. Porfilio and P. R. Carr (eds.), Youth Culture, Education and Resistance: Subverting the Commercial Ordering of Life, 21–39.

challenges to those wishing to attain high school graduation. Moreover, Mehta and colleagues (2000, p. vii) report that the median income of US farm worker families in the 1990s remained below $10,000 a year, and that more than half of their minor children did not live with their parents. Further, they report that 85% of migrant workers have less than a high school education, with the average being about six years of schooling; many are functionally illiterate. Huang (2002, p. 6) states that more than one third of the children of migrant workers fall behind academically or drop out of school.

INTRODUCTION

In this chapter, we examine the experiences of Latino migrant students as illustrative of the ways in which the policy context of American schools neglects, ignores, and marginalizes many groups of students whose lived experiences are distinctly different from the White middle-class norm. The transient nature of migrant students' lives makes the challenges they face particularly poignant but not necessarily very different from those faced by many other students (African American, Indigenous, some immigrant groups) whose lived experiences are disregarded in today's educational policy frameworks. Here, we provide a critical analysis of how current policies structure educational experiences in ways that often create barriers to students' academic achievement. We argue that the current neo-liberal policy framework (Giroux, 2005), with its heavy emphasis on testing, forces students to conform to a system that seems largely irrelevant to their daily lives, and is ill-designed to provide them with appropriate and quality educational opportunities. Further, we examine the ways in which solutions to student failure tend to place blame and the onus for change on individual students, teachers, and even schools, rather than on the system itself.

Given that the January 8, 2002, version of the *Elementary and Secondary Schools Act* (ESEA), now commonly known as *No Child Left Behind* (NCLB), has likely become the best known, most lauded, and most critiqued education bill in recent US history, it provides an appropriate and relevant focal-point for this examination. We explore the experiences of migratory students in the light of some tenets of the NCLB policy framework to better understand how the micropolitical context of education affects the experiences and opportunities of minoritized[2] students. We sought to understand the nature of their resistance (if any), and to identify ways in which the detrimental impact of neo-liberal schooling policies could be challenged to create educational environments that are more inclusive of, and responsive to, students, minoritized by virtue of their race, ethnicity, social class, gender, sexual orientation, or religious persuasion.

The chapter draws primarily on the NCLB legislation and policy documents widely available on the Internet. To supplement this information, we conducted interviews with five migrant students and three White school administrators who, like the majority of administrators who serve migrant students in Illinois, reflected the privileged norms of the US middle class. The interviewed students were randomly selected from a group of students whose primary residence is in Texas, but who, like José, had spent their summer in Illinois and were enrolled for the fall 2008 term at an Illinois high school. They were asked questions about possible challenges their migrant status posed for school success and how they thought educators might help them to achieve their goals. The administrators, who comprised a small, convenient sample, were asked about their perceptions of the constraints and problems that NCLB poses for minoritized youth, and, importantly, how educators might overcome these difficulties.

In our first section, we introduce students' comments as background to our analysis and critique of the NCLB legislation. Here, we note an overwhelming sense of resignation and even capitulation to existing norms of schooling. We then present a brief, critical overview of NCLB as reflective of some ways in which the policy context imposes conformity to middle-class norms as well as reproducing the current inequitable status quo. We argue that rather than providing support for the distinct needs of children, the overall effect of the Act, with its neo-liberal overemphasis on managerialism, surveillance, and control to the exclusion of more meaningful considerations of the needs of students, is to deny both mainstream and migratory students' opportunities for school success.

We believe that Bourdieu's (1997) work on reproduction, including his discussion of habitus, fields, legitimation, and, especially the concept of symbolic violence, provides a strong heuristic framework for understanding the impact of current policies on the schooling experiences of all minoritized students, including the Latino migrant students studied here. In the final part of this chapter, we use the lens of social and cultural reproduction to examine, in more detail, how the micro-political policy context of American high schools negatively influences minoritized students' opportunities for academic success, and, at the same time, constrains their life chances beyond school. We conclude with some implications that may encourage educators to resist the dominant policy trends of this decade, and to improve schooling for migrant students, and, by extension, other minoritized groups as well.

The Student Perspective

In this section we present, largely through the words of migrant students we interviewed (in italics the first time they are mentioned), a picture of how our interviewees respond to and navigate their experiences, including their social relations, their schooling experiences, and their career goals.

José, unlike his more reserved peers, is both friendly and outgoing. He is quick to describe his discomfort with peers in Texas who "josh" and tease him, by calling him "Mexican"; ironically, he also uses this term in a pejorative sense when talking about a fellow migrant student in Illinois, *Teresa*, age 15. José says the apartment building in Illinois where her family stays has many people her age, but that she has only one friend there. Perhaps this is due to a medical condition that prevents her from working in the fields with other students, requiring her to spend her days babysitting. In Texas, she says, she has many friends, and the rest of her family, including her two older brothers (one has long ago dropped out of school; the other is in jail). *Reyna* relates that it is "hard to make friends" when you transfer from school to school, but tells of counsellors advising her to attend college far away from home, outside of Texas. Both Reyna and her cousin *Dorena* had still been working in the fields when school started, and had to enroll after other students had been together in classes for nearly two weeks.

Although they agree that friendships are difficult to maintain because of their transiency, others are more concerned about family. Dorena, for example, lives in Illinois with her aunt, having left her family behind in Texas, near the Mexican border, to facilitate her summer employment. Most, as is typical for migrant students, are living apart from some immediate family members. José lives in Illinois with his mother, grandmother, and four brothers, while his father and a younger brother remain in Texas. He explains that he works hard to earn money. However, since he supports a younger sibling, he does not always have enough money left for lunch and sometimes feels hungry.

> I send money to my little brother in Texas. He does much better than me. He's smart, way smarter. I'm paying private school for him. I sent over $9,000 up there. He's my brother and he wants to learn a lot so I send it to him.

These students tended to see themselves in terms of the labels often imposed on them, as "migrant students" or "Mexicans"—labels that serve to reinforce their awareness that educators often do not expect them to attain the necessary academic standards to graduate from high school, let alone proceed to college or university. Despite these perceptions and the difficulties of their daily lives, the students generally expressed ambitious academic and life goals but little awareness of how to achieve them. Teresa, for example, indicated that despite her health problems, her goal was to become a Border Patrol agent—a law enforcement position with which she was familiar on a daily basis, and one that she perceived to be highly respectable. She insisted that she was well aware of the work an agent does, and wanted to be able to make decisions about who is permitted to enter the country. Reyna explained that her goal is to be a pediatrician, a goal she believed would require her to complete "about four years after high school." Dorena, her cousin, plans to be a lawyer, but was unable to tell us whether or not she had passed all her courses the previous year. Despite having failed to earn most of his freshman year credits, José was determined to be the first in his family to finish high school. He explains that he has two cousins born the same day and year, and that the three of them have the same goal; they also plan to go into business together.

> I am good at math. I like to use my brain a lot. I like cartoon design, animation, I'm so good at that ... I want to do animation very well because one of my cousins wants to do computer design. We want to build games but he cannot draw so he tells me if I draw for him, we could do a company together. He would do all the design on the computer and I do all the drawings and the other one, the third cousin, he makes stories... We're so good at that. We did a movie. Our own movie...only we never finished it because it takes a lot of money.

Here, José's statement that he wants to go to college but is unaware that one can actually study graphic arts and design, once again highlights the disconnect between his enthusiasm and ability and the lack of guidance he has received with respect to attaining his career goals. Overall, we found considerable dissonance between these students' goals for the future and their naiveté about what is necessary to graduate from high school or to pursue their desired careers.

Dorena, the girl who wanted to be a lawyer, reported that she had little difficulty moving between Texas and Illinois, and considered her "B's" and "C's" to be good grades—certainly a reality given her circumstances, but unlikely to permit her access to her chosen career. José expressed a desire to both further his goals and maintain his culture and family traditions. He reports that, in spite of a history of fighting and school suspension, he still plans to go to college. His wealthy uncle (rich due to his connection with drugs) promised José that he would financially support his future studies; at the same time, he says agricultural work is his "tradition," so even if he finished college, he "would always come back to corn." *Jorge*, on the other hand, has simply given up doing work in school. He says he wants to earn a better living than his migrant worker parents but he steadfastly refuses to do any homework or accomplish anything his teachers ask of him. He attends solely because his parents require him to be in school. This passive resistance is leading directly to the likelihood of his being pushed out of high school.

Dorena and Reyna explained that when they return to Texas, they take the grades they have achieved with them, and immediately join the classes already underway in their home schools. Dorena explains that "the teachers just give you review sheets for what they have been doing," and that she just does them in class, choosing not to take advantage of the tutoring available through her homeroom teacher. Reyna told us the same thing but observed: "They just give me the classes, and they give me a lot of homework." Reyna is frustrated trying to get her extra work done because she has chores at home, including caring for her sisters, ages 1 and 3. As a result of her responsibilities, she participates in no school activities, a choice that, once again, makes maintaining friendships, and an attachment to the school, difficult. Prior to the Texas state-wide tests that ultimately determine school success, teachers provide review sheets and offer extra study sessions, opportunities in which neither girl participates; nor do they do additional homework, believing instead that they can be successful simply by following directions, and working as they are told. Yet, Dorena's admission that she is "not sure" whether she passed all her classes the previous year reveals, once again, the lack of help provided to these students to understand and negotiate the system.

Bourdieu's sociological lens of reproduction helps us to understand how the forces in the wider society contribute to what appears to be an untenable situation for these and many other students. In fact, as Swartz (1997) argues, Bourdieu and Passeron (1997) introduce the concept of symbolic violence in which situations appear to be legitimate by "concealing the power relations" that impose legitimacy. For example, these migrant students, like many of their peers, verbalize ambitious career goals; nevertheless, their understanding of how society and schooling are structured is severely limited by their parents' lack of formal schooling as well as their limited awareness of any possible counselling or academic guidance offered by either school. They seemed to believe it to be "normal" that they should have difficulty making and sustaining friendships or good relationships with teachers. They saw nothing particularly unusual in their need to live apart from their families.

Although these students seem to accept, without overt rebellion, these elements of their daily existence that severely limit their future choices and opportunities, we interpret them to be examples of symbolic violence perpetrated both by society and by its educational institutions. Moreover, we argue that the micropolitical framework, with its heavy emphasis on test-taking, reporting, and uniform standards, serves, in fact, to weed out students, ignoring their social realities and neglecting to make them aware of the nature of the "schooling game." The problem is exacerbated as educators are already so overwhelmed by the need to raise test scores that they fail to recognize the impact of the neo-liberal context on these or other minoritized students. In general, as we present in the next section, their needs are far from central to the reform agenda of NCLB, and consequently, far from the radar of most educators struggling to meet their statutorily defined minimum accountability demands.

The Policies of NCLB

Our contention is that, for the most part, students from other than White upper-and middle-class families continue to be marginalized in neo-liberal policy contexts, exemplified by *No Child Left Behind.* Moreover, we acknowledge that, although the policy space may be dominated by the NCLB policies that we examine here, other national, state, and local policies also impinge on the ability of administrators and teachers to conceptualize teaching in broad and meaningful ways and to create welcoming, inclusive spaces in which students truly have the opportunity to learn.

Within the 670 pages of the NCLB statute is an exhaustive list of provisions for the various federally funded "Title" programs, with the Title I provisions, purportedly designed to address students of poverty and their additional need for resources, comprising approximately one third of the whole document. Within each section, there are multiple additional programs and provisions. Part C of Title I of the Act, for example, requires each state to develop a comprehensive plan to ensure that "migratory children will have an opportunity to meet the same challenging State academic content standards and challenging State student academic achievement standards that all children are expected to meet" [(sec. 1306,(a)(1)(C)]. Other titles extend the focus beyond students: for example, Title II addresses teacher quality, while Title IV focuses on school drug and violence prevention programs.

Despite the intent of Part C of Title I of NCLB to ensure additional measures be taken to support the schooling of migratory youth, it appears that in most cases the student experience is constrained, and largely defined, by a crowded policy space in which there is a singular emphasis on standards as exemplified by testing and test scores. For the most part, there seems to be little room for spaces in which students may negotiate and (re)construct identities so that they become mature and reflective citizens, able to participate in meaningful ways in what Green (1999) calls a deep concept of democracy "that expresses the experience-based possibility of more equal, respectful, and mutually beneficial ways of community life" (p. vi). In general, as we examined the tenets of NCLB, Bourdieu's constructs resonated in the background. The more we probed the Act, the more we became aware of the ways in which the current US policy framework legitimates and reproduces the status quo and, in so doing, also permits ongoing, sustained, and symbolic violence to be perpetrated on youth on a daily basis. Bourdieu and Passeron (1997) state that:

> Every power to exert symbolic violence, i.e. every power which manages to impose meanings and to impose them as legitimate by concealing the power relations which are the basis of its force, adds its own specifically symbolic force to those power relations. (p. 4)

It must be acknowledged, however, that symbolic violence has actual and material consequences related to narrowing students' life choices and chances. In other words, the force of symbolic violence is not simply symbolic, but actual as well.

A closer look at some of the provisions of the Title I section illustrates some ways in which it imposes a set of power relations that perpetuate reproduction and legitimation of the status quo as well as symbolic violence. The stated purpose of this section, known as Title I: Improving the Academic Achievement of the Disadvantaged is:

> to ensure that all children have a fair, equal, and significant opportunity to obtain a high-quality education and reach, at a minimum, proficiency on challenging State academic achievement standards and state academic assessments.

To accomplish this goal, among other provisions, the Act includes the mandate to close "the achievement gap between high and low performing children, especially the achievement gaps between minority and nonminority students, and between disadvantaged children and their more advantaged peers" (1001.a.3), and to hold schools, local educational agencies, and States accountable (1001.a.4). It responds to a capitalist agenda by providing grants to schools that use packaged programs (Reading First, Early reading, etc.) to improve literacy. States are required to submit comprehensive plans demonstrating their "challenging academic content standards and challenging student academic achievement standards" to serve as a benchmark for the education of all children (regardless of home language or identified special need). States are also required to provide an overview of their standards for meeting "adequate yearly progress" (AYP), and the sanctions and rewards, bonuses and recognition they will provide to ensure compliance. Additionally, Title I includes a stringent timeline, requiring that by 2014 all students within each sub-group (economically disadvantaged students, students from major racial and ethnic groups, students with disabilities, and students with limited English proficiency) "will meet or exceed the State's proficient level of academic achievement."

The above account of the importance of all students and all sub-groups meeting AYP demonstrates the difficulty of offering a unique and flexible program for migrant and other minoritized students. The provision for students to transfer does not ensure they will receive a better, more culturally responsive education; rather, the addition of supplemental educational services is most often fulfilled by private contractors and outside tutors who focus entirely on attaining the desired outcomes on standardized tests. At the end of the year, the school must provide evidence that migrant students (and other minoritized groups) have attained the same level as their peers—"regardless of identified special need." NCLB lacks any provision for addressing the different needs of various students and instead, evaluates them all by one uniform standard. This helps to account for the practice, reported by Reyna and Dorena, of having to jump into classes in Texas, where their classmates are, without any specific attention being paid to what they may have learned in Illinois. Apparently, there is no room for individualization when benchmarks and standards must be met.

Title I requires that each school receiving federal funds "implement an effective means of *outreach* to parents of limited English proficient students *to inform* the parents regarding how the parents can be involved in the education of their children ..." (1468.4, italics mine). José's statement that his mother, an undocumented worker who has lived at least 18 years in the US, is afraid to come into the school, demonstrates the need to carefully consider the lived realities of parents. If the goal is better communication, it must be a two-way interaction, not one that focuses on informing parents about how they can support the school, but one that also emphasizes learning *from* parents about their unique perspectives and needs. The Act is severely limited for this group of students whose parents are unwilling or unable, or understandably afraid to participate in school life.

A careful examination of the legislation for its understanding of culture is revelatory. Culture is recognized in sections of the legislation as pertaining exclusively to educational, cultural, apprenticeship, and exchange programs for Alaska Natives, Native Hawaiians, and their historical whaling and trading partners in Massachusetts—a limitation that implies somehow that no other cultures warrant recognition or attention in public schools. There is no explicit discussion in the 670 pages of the Act related to the need to incorporate students' home languages or cultures or to take account of multiple perspectives or various materially different lived experiences. It is little wonder that our student respondents had been so conditioned to believe schooling was simply about doing the assigned work, preparing for, and taking tests, that they could hardly suggest changes in school policy or practices that might help them learn. Once again, in NCLB, there is no recognition of the extensive bodies of literature related to culturally responsive pedagogy (Cummins 1989; Ladson-Billings, 1995; Shields, 2008) or anti-oppressive education (Dei, 2002). In fact, ignoring the home cultures and hence the social and cultural capital brought to school by these students comprises a form of violence often called color-blind racism (Bonilla-Silva, 2006), a phenomenon sometimes addressed as contributing to the lack of achievement of minoritized students (Freeman, 2005; Shields, 2003).

Perhaps in part because of the lack of attention to students' backgrounds, traditions, or cultural needs, the interviewed students had learned to think about schooling primarily in terms of their own individual responsibility. José told us, for example, that he used to fight because others told him that was how he gained respect. Now, he says, "I don't fight. I always think about school. I look to my own self. I had other people controlling my life. It was not me it was other people." He expressed the hope that taking responsibility would result in fewer suspensions and a greater likelihood of school success. Despite the positive change in his attitude, we are struck with the fact that neither he, nor his peers, attribute any of their social or academic difficulties to elements of schooling itself. Jorge's assertion that he wanted to succeed, even though he was often truant and failed to do his assigned homework, was expressed as another example of individual responsibility.

Nowhere in our data did our student respondents identify the fact that the very structures and cultures of schooling and the pedagogy and curricula to which they were exposed might fail them. Yet, this does not suggest that our students were unaware of inequity in the wider society. José was clear about the historical inequity in this country when he asserted, in a somewhat convoluted argument:

> This is Mexico and this is USA (draws with fingers). We just draw this little line to get to here. You all ... crossed the whole ocean and we just crossed this little land and you call us wetbacks. It's not fair.

He recognized the inequity of White immigrants easily gaining legal status, while so many Mexicans, quite nearby, are often barred from access. We believe this is another illustration of how overemphasis on statewide tests and conformity to prescribed curriculum exclude discussion of students' insights in relation to the marginalization of their ethnic group within schools and the wider society. The dominant perspective is so legitimized that, although students may question the ways in which their ethnic group have been historically constructed, many of them seem unprepared (or at least unwilling) to extend any critique to the norms of schooling itself. Yet, with the words of the students ringing in our ears, we wonder why José's perception is not front and center. He was clear that his favorite teacher was "messing with his brain" to make him think. He said that when he got to Illinois, he thought he could "blame all schools" because in his previous class,

> they used to judge people ... They said, "You're Mexican, you cannot do all of these things. They josh people. So I thought, "forget about school." Then I started knowing people and I started doing better and better. Here the teachers don't give up on us and don't let us get away with anything.

For José, as for many other students, disaffection with schooling came as a result of teacher perceptions and attitudes—a reflection of what many scholars have identified as the need to reject deficit thinking and to support the learning of all students (Shields, Bishop, & Mazawi, 2005; Valencia, 1997). Likewise, the successes he experienced came largely as a result of relationships formed by caring educators whose encouragement facilitated some academic success. Unfortunately, too few educators, perhaps due to the arduous nature of teaching amid overcrowded classrooms and preparing students for a battery of standardized examinations, foster these relationships, opting instead (likely without being aware of it) to support the stem that perpetuates symbolic violence on many students.

Widgets, Fungibility, Reproduction, and Symbolic Violence

Based on the above summary of some of the provisions of NCLB, it is easy to understand why one superintendent from a district that houses a large migrant population, explained that he thinks there is a "great attempt to over-simplify people generally, students specifically, to widgetize them, to make them fungible items as opposed to individuals." He continued: "I think the policy framework, often because of its rigidity and lack of taking into account differences acts as a sorting process, because those who don't fit within the patterns that are dictated get filtered out ... NCLB sets a single standard and says this is what success is and what isn't." The implication, he suggested, is that schools in middle and upper-class areas are going to perform well, and "lower income schools that fit less well into the single pattern...are not going to perform as well."

The superintendent was clear: It is possible to push the requirements of NCLB to one side so as to make student learning a chief priority. To be sure, he still met the requirements of the law, for example, inviting students daily to say the Pledge of Allegiance or permitting military recruiters (as mandated) to come into the school. But he had begun to think differently about education, acknowledging that "when our goal in having students in school is to make them like us, that does violence" to children. He added that, unfortunately, he believes that it is the goal of many teachers to say, "I'm a middle class White person and that's what you should aspire to be; you should aspire to have my characteristics, and my traits, and my culture."

High Standards and Pedagogical Conformity

Extensive research literature stresses the need to hold high standards and expectations for all children (Alexander, Entwisle, Bedinger, 1994; Marzano, 2004; McKown & Weinstein, 2008; Murphy, Weil, Hallinger, & Mitman, 1982). Unfortunately, too often, high standards are equated with test scores. Schools often have with little or no goals beyond test-taking, and have no understanding that standards may be high but do not need to necessarily be the same for all. Critical theoretical perspectives must challenge and inform the ways in which practitioners and policy makers interpret the focus on high standards. For example, there is a persuasive body of literature related to critical pedagogy (see for example, Freire, 1990; Giroux, 2005; McLaren & Kincheloe, 2007; Macedo, 1995) that addresses the need for pedagogy that understands that some "differences make a difference" (Bateson, 1972). Such approaches emphasize the need to incorporate the lived experiences of students and to acknowledge that no curriculum is neutral. This literature suggests that a school culture that is not only dissonant from that of the home but that tends to devalue and negate home culture is insensitive and counterproductive (see for example Cummins 1989; Ladson-Billings, 1995; Ryan, Chandler, Samuels; 2007; Shields, 2008). Here, the underlying rationale is that when all students feel included and can see themselves reflected in the school curricula, and when they can bring their own lived experiences to make sense of the formal curricular topics (Grumet, 1995), they will ultimately achieve the greatest possible academic success. Perhaps because this literature is sometimes wrongly perceived to be unscientific, to lack an empirical base, to be too ideological, or even threatening to the status quo, it is not incorporated in any way into the thinking reflected in the tenets of NCLB.

Other dominant trends in research come from such theoretical perspectives as critical race theory (Bell, 1987; Parker & Villalpando, 2007), critical feminism (Brady & Kanpol, 2000), anti-oppression (Dei, 2002; Dillard, 2007), or cultural and multicultural studies (Banks, 2008; Delpit, 1990; Sleeter, 2003)—all of which address the need for educators to attend to issues related to race, ethnicity, home language, poverty, advantage, ability/disability, gender and sexual orientation, and so forth. These theories, as well, emphasize the importance and validity of multiple perspectives, of encouraging students to learn through dialogue and critique instead of from drill and (s)kill strategies or programs proclaimed to be "best practice" in which everyone is treated the same. Once again, these perspectives are ignored in NCLB.

A third, extensive body of literature addresses the need for democratic education, which calls on educators to attend to patterns of systemic inequalities in the historic development of citizenship rights—injustices that are still present at today's historical moment (see for example Barber, 2001; Green, 1999; Giroux, 2005; Torres, 1998; Shields, 2009). Yet, once again, there is little attention paid to any of these salient factors in NCLB or in the micro-political contexts of US schools in the 21st century. Indeed, the focus on identifying a single standard that all children must attain and the requirement that all students from whatever circumstances pass the same test, regardless of socio-cultural differences or physical and emotional dissimilarities, are manifestations of the superintendent's notion that patterns of injustice are neglected in the pedagogical work of today's schools.

The cycle is ferocious. The NCLB requirement that all sub-groups meet an identical standard leads to blame—blame on the part of the rest of the school and wider community when, because of a specified sub-group, the school fails to meet its annual goal. Conversations reported by our administrator respondents include comments like, "If it weren't for that group of kids..." or "we shouldn't have to try to prepare African American students for college." Students are believed to be "substandard" in some way if they have not previously passed state tests; they are then forced to stay at noon hour or after school for extra tutoring, the implicit message being that they are not smart enough to learn what is necessary in the normal five hours of schooling. Then, if their sub-group does not achieve the arbitrary state standard, they are blamed for school failure. It is little wonder that the process narrows the options of minoritized students, pushes them out of school, and actually leads to a situation in which the same social groups are soon over-represented in the criminal justice system. Here, the issue is not that standards should be lowered for minoritized students; rather we argue that all students should be held to high academic standards, but they should not be widgetized (see for example, Shields, 2009). There is no pedagogical rationale for assessing all students in the same way, at the same time, on a single standardized measure as required by NCLB. Indeed, each of these requirements is illustrative of the ways in which neo-liberal policies and practices can, and generally do, work against the ability of these migrant students to succeed.

Dominance and Reproduction

Bourdieu and Passeron (1997) argue that educational systems perform two fundamental functions: (1) they reproduce the dominant culture (cultural reproduction); and (2) they reproduce the power relations between the groups or classes that comprise society (social reproduction) (Pajak & Green, 2003, p. 395). These notions of dominant culture, cultural reproduction, and power relations are notably missing from most practical discussion of the micro-political context of today's schools, and of attendant issues of curriculum and pedagogy. Moreover, we would argue that unless educators and policymakers acknowledge the explanatory power of these concepts for understanding how and why many reform efforts fail and for thinking differently about educational institutions in the 21st century, schools will continue to sort and select students on the basis of largely unconscious assumptions about ability, achievement, and success.

It is for this reason that Bourdieu's (1977) sociological focus on fields, *habitus*, and types of capital provides an important starting-point for analyzing how the policy context we have examined here reflects broader attitudes and values of the wider society. In introducing the concept of fields, Bourdieu identified education (along with other areas such as the state, church, political parties, and the arts) as a "relatively autonomous" site of struggle with its own internal logic in which "those occupying dominant positions will necessarily adopt defensive and conservative 'conservation strategies' in order to preserve their status" (Swingewood, 1998, p. 92). Moreover, as sites of struggle, fields are structured, in part, through an "unequal distribution of the forms of capital pertinent to them; forms of capital whose possession and definition are precisely the objects of the aforementioned struggles" (Crossley, 2003, p. 44).

The dominant actions, policies, and relations within each field have developed over long periods of time, through what Bourdieu (1997) calls *habitus*—the system of traditions, rules, and practices that have come to be interpreted as normal through their arbitrary legitimation of certain forms of capital (and their denial of the legitimacy of other forms).

> Habitus tends to generate all the 'reasonable' and 'commonsense' behaviors (and only those) which are possible within the limits of these regularities, and which are likely to be positively sanctioned ... At the same time...it tends to exclude all 'extravagances' ('not for the likes of us'), that is, all the behaviors that would be negatively sanctioned because they are incompatible with the objective conditions. (p. 55–56)

Hence, the ways in which we have come to think about schooling, governance, achievement, accountability, and so forth are reflected in the policy framework discussed earlier, but without any recognition that they represent arbitrary forms of legitimation of certain approaches and delegitimation of others. Indeed, if we accept Bourdieu's explanation, it becomes obvious that educators themselves are often unaware of how *habitus* constrains both thought and action with respect to how we might do schooling differently. This may help to explain the ideology that pervades the normative practices of schooling, an ideology that devalues migrants (and other minorities). When the rightness of this ideology is unquestioned, the concomitant assumption is that the minorities must adjust but that the dominant structures do not need to change. This supports the practice, for example, of reintegrating migrant students into regular classes, already underway, without providing structural modifications for this large group of students.

Legitimized Cultural Capital

Even more detrimental to the possibility of school success for minoritized youth is the fact that *habitus* legitimizes certain kinds of cultural capital and rejects others. Bourdieu (2004) explains that within any field, several kinds of capital operate simultaneously: economic, social, and cultural capital. He explains that cultural capital is capital that manifests itself as dispositions of the mind and body, as cultural goods such as books and instruments, and in institutionalized states such as educational qualifications. Social capital is made up of "social obligations and connections which are also, under certain conditions, convertible into economic capital" and may also be "institutionalized in the forms of a title of nobility" (p. 47). An understanding of these forms of capital makes it possible to understand Bourdieu's notion of social reproduction and his conceptualization of the school's role in this process. Bourdieu (2004) argues that too often we ignore "the contribution which the educational system makes to the reproduction of the social structure by sanctioning the hereditary transmission of cultural capital" (p. 17) and the fact that "the scholastic yield from educational action depends on the cultural capital previously invested by the family" (p. 17).

For the most part, educators seem to believe migrant students' familial cultural capital is confined to their hard work in the cornfields. Despite the insistence of our student respondents that their parents want them to get a better education and "make something of themselves," their schools apparently fail to offer the necessary guidance and support that might help them to develop realistic plans. Apart from José's contention that his drug-involved uncle will support his college education, none expressed any clear idea of what it would take to get to college, or of the time or cost involved. In a very real way, these students have a vision but no concept of the means to attain that vision. Schools must take the responsibility here to go beyond offering test-taking skills; they must assist students to navigate the paths to post-secondary education—paths that value the social and cultural capital of schooling more than that of their homes.

The role of the family is particularly important to Bourdieu's understanding of how capital is reproduced and explains the dissonance often experienced by children and youth between what has been taught and valued at home and what is valued at school. Bourdieu believes that child-rearing is "primary pedagogical work"—in other words, children's first opportunity to develop cultural capital and to learn cultural mores occurs in the home. However, as Herr and Anderson (2003) explain, there is often a "disconnect between the cultural capital they obtain through child-rearing (primary pedagogical work) and cultural capital implicitly valued in formal schooling and the mass media" (p. 418). Picking up Bourdieu and Passeron's (1997) concept of symbolic violence, Herr and Anderson go on to state:

> Moreover, the disconnect, because of its very invisibility, has the potential to powerfully "exert symbolic violence" to children whose capital may have high value at home, but be little valued in contexts of schooling. It is incumbent on us to recognize how this disconnect has not only been nurtured by historical inequities in citizenship, but is perpetuated by their persistence in society at large. (p. 418)

Here, then, is the explicit connection between the foregoing discussion of the micropolitical context of schooling in the US and the ongoing lack of achievement of migrant and other minoritized children in school. When the child's culture is not valued at school, it is not obvious how additional tutoring, test preparation, or increased pressure to attain certain standards on tests will overcome the disconnect. As indicated at the beginning of this chapter, there is strong evidence (related to the persistent achievement gaps, the drop-out statistics for migrant youth and youth from other visible minority and impoverished families), that such policies and practices are ineffective.

Symbolic Violence

What makes this situation even more critical are the assertions by Bourdieu and Passeron, that:

> educators are all directly implicated in: (a) committing acts of symbolic violence against students by imposing the arbitrary culture of dominant groups, and (b) perpetrating a conspiracy that maintains the illusion that education and schooling provide an avenue for lower classes to attain upward social and economic mobility. (summarized by Pajak & Green, 2003, p. 396)

Pajak and Green assert: "this misrecognition of education's role in perpetuating inequities, we propose, could very well be partly responsible for thwarting needed reform" (p. 396). The issue is not that any individual educator (or group of educators) is consciously imposing practices that thwart the achievement of certain groups of children; rather, that failing to understand the power mechanism of social reproduction supports the invisible and unconscious nature of the neo-liberal "conspiracy"—one educators as well as policy makers must begin to address.

This misrecognition of education's legitimizing role may also explain why minoritized students often appear acquiescent and accepting of the norms and structures of schooling. The only forms of resistance they have learned and that appear permissible (conditioned and sanctioned by the habitus of schooling) are those that are passive rather than active, requiring individual rather than collective action. Our respondents have been conditioned to take the responsibility for their own educational difficulties and bear the blame for their educational failures rather than to consider that the school or school system bears any responsibility for the violence that destroys dreams or thwarts achievement.

Herr and Anderson (2003) studied not only symbolic violence but the ways in which student violence is often framed in educational organizations through such interventions as anti-bullying or conflict resolution programs. They argue that we too often "focus on behaviour as if it were independent of its socio-historical context" and state that this approach is "embedded in a narrow psychological paradigm that limits solutions to classroom or organizational interventions" (p. 429–430). This insight is telling, given the number of incidents recounted by our student-respondents of getting into fights, being in trouble, and being suspended from school. In each case, they and the educators dealing with the situation simply addressed their individual behavior, without consideration of the ways in which migrant students were constructed and addressed by their classmates or even, as José indicated earlier, by some of their teachers. With Herr and Anderson (2003), we believe that the lack of attention to the needs of both individual students and minoritized groups of students is, indeed, a form of violence. To redress this violence, educators and policy-makers must address the socio-historical contexts of schooling that continue to perpetuate the historic inequities in citizenship found in society at-large, for these inequities support the *habitus* of schooling that actually does violence to many children.

Conclusion

The foregoing analysis has elucidated the large rhetorical gap between a mythical education system in which no child is left behind and the actual situation in which many children do not succeed—even in meeting the basic academic standards required by the state. More significant, however, is the fact that the negative micro-political context of schooling reflects rather than challenges elements in the wider society that create environments in which violence is perpetrated on students. Students bring to their schooling experiences the violence of the material situations of poverty and low levels of education forced upon their families by the nature of their work and an immigration policy that too often forces them to maintain a low profile as "illegals." As educators fulfil the sorting and selection required by legislation, the violence is continued and exacerbated through the assumptions inherent in this sorting mechanism, and, perhaps most importantly, in terms of the constraints placed on students in their development as reflective, contributing human beings.

Bourdieu's theory of change is explanatory with respect to the continuation of social inequality. First, it draws attention to the advantages (in the form of social, economic, and cultural capital) bestowed upon children of dominant families. Second, it subverts the myth of meritocratic schooling in which individual aptitude alone is the determinant of success. It thus helps educators to understand why educational change is so difficult and, at the same time, why it is necessary to take a broad system approach (rather than a psychological or programmatic one) if we want to institute reforms that have the potential to truly effect change in educational outcomes. Finally, it offers a wake-up call to action. As Herr and Anderson (2003) state:

Just as Bourdieu's theory of symbolic violence involves many forms of capital and many sites of oppression that occur on multiple levels, altering

> relations of domination will require struggle on many fronts, including, both the critical pedagogical action of committed teachers who understand how symbolic violence operates, and large-scale political struggles. (p. 431)

If we are to enjoin the struggle to promote equity and social justice in schools and in the wider society, we must first recognize that change will not result primarily from the use of additional resources, more certified teachers and administrators, additional parent information, new instructional support or test preparation programs, or better discipline policies, although these are certainly all important components of efforts to achieve greater equity. Meaningful change cannot depend solely on policies or programs but must start with recognition of the ways in which schools reproduce the inequities of our wider society. To overcome the persistent (and often stifling) habitus of today's schooling will also require educators to value the diverse cultural capital of minoritized students and to build strong and positive relationships with them. It is time for educators to take up this *habitus* of activism—to challenge the current neo-political political policies that reduce all children to widgets and fungible commodities, and to affirm their differences. Unless educators better understand how the dominant (largely White) middle-class capital has become accepted as the norm, how it operates to advantage some and continues to dis-advantage others, we will constantly grasp at reform initiatives that are individualistic and inherently disconnected from the main systemic problem. Too often, the current policy climate develops strategies to redress individual student failure by rejecting or retooling "defective widgets." Too often, educational policymakers fail to understand or take account of the underlying ideologies and practices that support current inequitable systems.

The policy context of today's schools constructs not only migrant students, but many others who are marginalized by reason of race, color, home language, religious perspective, sexual orientation, and so forth, as problems, as deficient widgets, thereby narrowing not only their individual opportunities for success, but inhibiting the creation of a healthy democratic citizenry as well. Because the policy context of NCLB is so all encompassing, so punitive, and so "high-stakes," it has become the touchstone for all activities in local schools. As adults capable of undertaking and understanding the foregoing analysis, we must change the current policies that convince children and youth that they are, alone, responsible for their failures. We must recognize that within the *field* of education there are those who dominate and those who are dominated, those whose cultural capital is valued and those whose capital is not—and take immediate steps to ensure that schools affirm and include different kinds of cultural capital. We can no longer ignore the ongoing failure of education to help all children achieve the goals of knowledge acquisition, individual freedom, and collective responsibility, thereby continuing to label and blame them for the systems' shortcomings. We must make the system more inclusive and more responsive.

We must not mistake acquiescence for engagement, nor interpret student disengagement, lack of "discipline", or academic failure simply as indications of lack of motivation. Instead, as Ogbu (2008) might suggest, we must recognize that these may be the only forms of resistance they have learned, and indeed, in this era of conformity and control, in some cases, the only forms of resistance available to them. Instead, we must find ways to "set them free." Our argument is that we must start by challenging policies that reinforce conformity and replace them with policies that foster cultural understanding, creativity, and critical thinking. We must disrupt the current violence that the micro-politics of schooling inflicts on youth. We must ensure that the educational organizations of which we are a part create policy communities and spaces in which youth are freed from acts of symbolic violence and in which they are supported to achieve their goals of a better future for themselves, and indeed, for the society in which they will later participate as adults.

QUESTIONS FOR REFLECTION

1. The chapter identifies some ways in which symbolic violence is imposed on minoritized students. In what ways do you see students subjected to symbolic violence in your school setting?
2. In what ways may a student express resistance in your context? What is the institutional response to student resistance?
3. How has NCLB affected the way students (especially minoritized students) are treated in your school? Does it narrow the curriculum? Affect the recognition of various forms of students' cultural capital? Permit alternate kinds of assessment? Discourage a focus on preparation for achieving career goals, etc.?

NOTES

[1]   This and all other names of students are pseudonyms.
[2]   We use the term minoritized, rather than the more common word minority to indicate the process by which those who are not members of the dominant middle class power group are ascribed characteristics of subordinate groups, whether or not they are in the actual numerical minority in a given school or community. For example, Spanish-speaking students may be in the numerical majority in their Texas schools, but because the curriculum, rules, tests, and processes of schooling are still those of the predominantly White middle class, one could appropriately refer to them as minoritized.

REFERENCES

Alexander, K. L., Entwisle, D. R., & Bedinger, S. D. (1994). When expectations work: Race and socio-economic differences in school performance. *Social Psychology Quarterly, 57*(4), 283–299.
Banks, J. A. (2008). Diversity, group identity, and citizenship education in a Global Age. *Educational Researcher, 37*(3), 129–139.
Barber, B. R. (2001). An aristocracy of everyone. In S. J. Goodlad (Ed.), *The last best hope: A democracy reader* (pp. 11–22). N San Francisco: Jossey-Bass.
Bateson, G. (1972). *Steps to an ecology of mind.* Chicago: University of Chicago Press.
Bell, D. (1987). Neither separate schools nor mixed schools: The chronicle of the sacrificed Black schoolchildren. In D. Bell (Ed.), *And we are not saved: The elusive quest for racial justice* (pp. 102–122). New York: Basic Books.
Bonilla-Silva, E. (2006). *Racism without racists: Color-blind racism and the persistence of racial inequality in the United States.* Lanham, MD: Rowman and Littlefield.
Bourdieu, P. (2004). The forms of capital. In S. J. Ball (Ed.), *The RoutledgeFalmer reader in sociology of education* (pp. 13–29). New York: RoutledgeFalmer.

Bourdieu, P., & Passeron, J.-C. (1997). *Reproduction in education, society and culture*. Thousand Oakes, CA: Sage.

Brady, J. F., & Kanpol, B. (2000). The role of critical multicultural education and feminist critical thought in teacher education: Putting theory into practice. *Educational Foundations, 14*(3), 39–50.

Crossley, N. (2003). From reproduction to transformation: Social movement, fields and the radical habitus. *Theory, Culture, & Society, 20*(6), 43–68.

Cummins, J. (1989). Empowering minority students: A framework for intervention. In N. M. Hidalgo, C. L. McDowell, & E. V. Siddle (Eds.), *Facing racism in education* (pp. 50–68) Cambridge, MA: Harvard Educational Review Reprint Series 21.

Dei, G. S., et al. (2002). *Moving the margins: The challenges and possibilities of inclusive schooling*. Toronto: Canadian Scholars' Press Inc.

Delpit, L. D. (1990). The silenced dialogue: Power and pedagogy in educating other people's children. In N. M. Hidalgo, C. L. McDowell, & E. V. Siddle (Eds.), *Facing racism in education*. Reprint Series No. 21 ed. Cambridge, MA: Harvard Educational Review.

Dillard, C. B. (2007). Research as resistance: Critical, indigenous, and anti-oppressive approaches. *Qualitative Research, 7*(2), 271–272.

Freeman, E. (2005). No child left behind and the denigration of race. *Equity & Excellence in Education, 38*(3), 190–199.

Freire, P. (1990). *Pedagogy of the oppressed*. New York: Continuum.

Giroux, H. A. (2005). The terror of neo-liberalism: Rethinking the significance of cultural politics. *College Literature, 32*(1), 10–19.

Green, J. M. (1999). *Deep democracy: Diversity, community, and transformation*. Lanham, MD: Rowman & Littlefield.

Grumet, M. R. (1995). The curriculum: What are the basics and are we teaching them? In J. L. Kincheloe & S. R. Steinberg (Eds.), *Thirteen questions* (2nd ed., pp. 15–21). New York: Peter Lang.

Herr, K., & Anderson, G. L. (2003). Violent youth or violent schools? A critical incident analysis of symbolic violence. *International Journal of Leadership in Education, 6*(4), 415–433.

Huang, G. G. (2002). What federal statistics reveal about migrant farmworkers: A summary for education. ERIC Digest. ED471487. Retrieved from http://www.eric.ed.gov/ERICDocs/data/ericdocs2sql/content_storage_01/0000019b /80/1a/a1/bc.pdf

Ladson-Billings, G. (1995). But that's just good teaching! The case for culturally relevant pedagogy. *Theory into Practice, 34*(3), 159–165.

Macedo, D. (1995). Power and education: Who decides the forms schools have taken, and who should decide? In J. L. Kincheloe & S. Steinberg (Eds.), *Thirteen questions*. New York: Peter Lang.

Marzano, R. J. (2004). *Building background knowledge for academic achievement: Research on what works in schools*. Alexandria, VA: ASCD. Retrieved from http://www.ascd.org/portal/site/ascd/template.chapter/menuitem.5d91564f4fe4548cdeb3ffdb62108a0c/?chapterMgmtId=9427a2948ecaff00VgnVCM1000003d01a8c0RCRD&printerFriendly=true

McLaren, P., & Kincheloe, J. (Eds.). (2007). *Critical pedagogy: Where are we now?* New York: Peter Lang.

McKown, C., & Weinstein, R. S. (2008). Teacher expectations, classroom context, and the achievement gap. *Journal of School Psychology, 46*(3), 235–261.

Méndez, T. (2005, February 15). Changing school with the season. *Christian Science Monitor*. http://www.csmonitor.com/2005/0215/p11s01-legn.html?s=rel

Mehta, K., Gabbard, S. M., Barrat, V., Lewis, M., Carroll, D., & Mines, R. (2000). *Findings from the national agricultural workers survey (NAWS), 1997–1998: A demographic and employment profile of United States farmworkers*. Washington, DC: U.S. Department of Labor (ERIC Document Reproduction Service No. ED 446 887). Retrieved from www.eric.ed.gov/ERICDocs/data/ericdocs2sql/content_storage_01/0000019b /80/16/9c/97.pdf

Murphy, J. F., Weil, M., Hallinger, P., & Mitman, A. (1982). Academic press: Translating high expectations into school policies and classroom practices. *Educational Leadership, 40*(3), 22.

NCLB. (2002). *No Child Left Behind, PL 107–110.* Retrieved from http://www.ed.gov/policy/elsec/leg/esea02/107-110.pdf

Ogbu, J. U. (2008). *Minority status, oppositional culture, & schooling.* New York: Routledge.

Pajak, E., & Green, A. (2003). Loosely coupled organizations, misrecognition, and social reproduction. *International Journal of Educational Leadership in Education, 6*(4), 393–413.

Parker, L., & Villalpando, O. (2007). A race(cialized) perspective on education leadership: Critical race theory in educational administration. *Educational Administration Quarterly, 43*(5), 519–524.

Ryan, K. E., Chandler, M., & Samuels, M. (2007). What should school-based evaluation look like? *Studies in Educational Evaluation, 33*(3/4), 197–212.

Shields, C. M., Bishop, R., & Mazawi, A. E. (2005). *Pathologizing practice: The impact of deficit thinking on education.* New York: Peter Lang.

Shields, C. M. (2003). Dialogic leadership for social justice: Overcoming pathologies of silence. *Educational Administrative Quarterly, XI*(1), 111–134.

Shields, C. M. (2009). *Courageous leadership for transforming schools: Democratizing practice.* Norwood, MA: Christopher-Gordon.

Sleeter, C. E., & Grant, C. A. (2003). *Making choices for multicultural education: Five approaches to race, class, and gender.* New York: John Wiley & Sons.

Swartz, D. (1997). *Culture and power: The sociology of Pierre Bourdieu.* Chicago: Chicago University Press.

Swingewood, A. (1998). *Cultural theory and the problem of modernity.* New York: St. Martin's.

Torres, C. A. (1998). *Democracy, education, multiculturalism.* Lanham, MD: Rowman & Littlefield.

Valencia, R. R. (Ed.). (1997). *The evolution of deficit thinking.* Washington, DC: Falmer.

KEVIN GOSINE AND CARL E. JAMES

3. RACIALIZED STUDENTS RESISTING

Hindrance or asset to academic success?

INTRODUCTION

An ongoing concern of marginalized[1] youth and their parents is the failure of schools—i.e. educators, administrators and counsellors—to acknowledge the lived experiences they bring into their schooling and educational process as well as the hidden forms of oppression that variously shape their lives and life chances. As such, they often resist schooling structures that minimize their experiences stemming from social differences (James, 2007; Pon, 2000; Yosso, 2005), and they resist claims made by educators and others that individuals are the sole designers of their own successes and/or failures, a claim premised on the ideology of individualism and meritocracy. Moreover, when the issue of inequality based on race is broached, the hegemonically-informed response is that some ethno-racial groups, particularly Blacks, lack the appropriate cultural capital (knowledge, skills, abilities, social networks, and role models) necessary to achieve academic and occupational success (Codjoe, 2001; Yosso, 2005). This cultural deficit explanation erroneously informs the ways in which many educators interpret academic disengagement and resistance on the part of marginalized students. Students, in turn, perceive the meritocratic explanation to be a myth, and, in response, strive to demonstrate that their racial identification is not a liability but provides them with the resilience needed to confront the daily, often alienating, routines of school. Researchers in Canada and the US have demonstrated that, in many North American schools, marginalized youth experience a school culture that contributes to their sense of alienation caused by, among other things, being profiled by teachers based on ethno-racial identification as well as being academically labelled and streamed—processes that serve to narrow their educational and career options (e.g., Codjoe, 2001; Dei et al, 1997; Henry, 1998; Milner 2007). Their experiences, histories and the cultural capital that they bring to their schooling process are unacknowledged in the curriculia, especially by teachers who show little or no respect for them (Dei et al, 1997; Lee, 2006). In a context, then, where the emphasis is based on an individualistic, meritocratic ethos that plays down inequalities based on group differences, it is not surprising that schooling for marginalized students would be full of conflict and resistance. The ideology of individualism, rendered increasingly pronounced in recent years by a neo-liberal hegemony that emphasizes individual responsibility and subordinates social justice concerns to market needs, underlies the structural aspects of schooling that serve to alienate many marginalized and racialized students.

B. J. Porfilio and P. R. Carr (eds.), Youth Culture, Education and Resistance:
Subverting the Commercial Ordering of Life, 41–56.

The Asian (including South Asian) 'model minority' stereotype embedded within North American schools, for example, is underpinned by this value system of individual achievement (James, 2007; Lee, 1994; 2006; Lorenzo et al, 2000). This discourse characterizes Asian Americans and Asian Canadians as quiet, hardworking, intelligent students who play by the rules and excel in mathematics and the sciences, thereby personifying the ideology of individualism embedded within schools. This stereotype, as well as those that pertain to other ethno-racial groups, inform the ways in which educators interact with those they teach as well as the expectations they form for different groups of students. Furthermore, the implication of the model minority discourse is that other minorities and immigrants can overcome a history of racism and oppression if, like Asians, they demonstrate a hard work ethic and self-reliance (Lee, 1994, 2006; Pon, 2000). This stereotyping of Asian students, which is embedded within the institutional processes of schools, creates a situation (however inadvertently) in which one group of students is seen as 'fitting in' and meeting the expectations of the system while other groups are stigmatized as less equipped to do so (James, 2007). Such aspects of schooling culture serve to institutionalize racial inequality within the educational system, thereby alienating students from certain racialized groups, many of whom feel that they are trying to achieve their aspirations within a system that offers little respect and recognition for their lived experiences, believeing they have little control over their academic careers.

In this chapter, we discuss how marginalized students negotiate and navigate the oppressive structures of schooling with a determination to claim voice within school spaces, confront negative racial stereotypes, and transcend the hegemonically-imposed boundaries or limitations associated with their ascribed raced, gendered, and classed identities. Drawing on North American educational literature that has examined youth's resistance to the oppressive educational processes they experience, we discuss two resistance strategies employed by marginalized students in navigating schooling environments: 1) striving for academic success while maintaining a commitment to their ethno-racial community; and 2) 'opting out' of the system which could take a form of, among other behaviors, dropping out of school, limiting school attendance (or being truant), being unconcerned with punctuality, challenging teachers, being disruptive in school and classes, and/or choosing to participate in school primarily through athletic endeavors.[2] We conclude with a discussion of the potential of a social justice approach to education to build on the cultural capital and social justice desires that are inherent in the resistance strategies of marginalized students. Before doing so, in the section that follows, we reflect on the ethos of individualism, which operates in schools to thwart students' attempts to culturally and fully engage with school. Using Yosso's (2005) concept of "community cultural wealth," we contend that marginalized students' strategies of resistance represent a counteraction to the ethos of individualism that devalues their communities, which they see as important to their navigation of the racializing and marginalizing structures of schools. Their resistance is reflective of their assertion of entitlement to an education that is premised on democracy, equity, social justice and the recognition of their cultural values and learning needs.

Our reference-point in this discussion is the Canadian context where multi-cultural education, informed by the Federal Multicultural Policy of 1971, has been implemented in schools in an effort to promote the retention of ethno-cultural heritage of students, thereby claiming to accommodate diversity within schools (Lund, 2006). However, based on the notion of building inter-group harmony through an appreciation of cultural differences, and in a schooling context informed by an ethos of individualism, multicultural education has done little else than provide cultural programs and supplemental pedagogical materials designed to encourage attitudinal changes at the individual level (Lund, 2006). As such, the needs, concerns, issues, interests and aspirations of marginalized students have remained unaddressed by multicultural education (James, 2007). Critics charge that Canadian multicultural approaches to addressing diversity fails to identify and address explicitly racism and other forms of oppression, while implicitly supporting assimilation to the dominant culture and (however inadvertently) reinforcing the notion of certain minority ethno-racial groups as "Other" by constructing their cultures as static and bounded entities that originate from elsewhere (Gosine, 2002; James, 2007; Lund, 2006; Walcott, 1997). As a result, the vast majority of marginalized students have found multicultural educationto be, at best, irrelevant as they struggle to negotiate educational systems that fail to reflect their lived experiences or accommodate their interests and aspirations (James, 2007).

Individualism and Community Cultural Capital

A middle-class hegemony emphasizing discourses of marketization, consumerism, and individualism predominates in North America (e.g., Banks, 1997; Bellah, et al, 1985; Reay, 1998). This individualistic ethos is embedded within North American structures of schooling. Reay (1998) characterizes this phenomenon as:

> [t]he current orthodoxy of individualistic self-realization represents the almost universal acceptance of middle-class perspectives in society, which have replaced the collectivist inclinations of earlier eras among working-class groups (p. 263).

According to Reay (1998), hegemonic middle-class individualism is perpetuated in a large part by "a media controlled by middle-class interests and the prevalence of individualistic discourses of consumerism across society" (p. 263). Bellah et al. (1985) further contend that, while the middle-class emphasis on personal success has had a fragmenting effect on American society (i.e., people find themselves largely isolated in their attempts to achieve personal success), it also serves as a form of integration (or "pseudo integration," as the authors cynically charge), as people "can at least recognize [their] fellows as followers of the same private dream" (p. 281). This individualistic ideology has been made more salient in North America in the last decade by the rise of neo-liberalism as well as a corporate ethos, which have bolstered the notion of individual responsibility alongside the simultaneous stigmatization of government intervention, non-profit public organi-zations, and democratic institutions (Giroux & Giroux, 2004; Lund & Carr, 2008;

Porfilio & Malott, 2008). In the prevailing neo-liberal climate, "private interests trump social needs, and economic growth becomes more important than social justice" (Giroux & Giroux, 2004, p. 250).

The concept of meritocracy constitutes a pillar of this pervasive individualistic middle-class culture. Meritocracy is an ideology that stresses that individuals, irrespective of their differences, are provided equality of opportunity and as such, are able to compete and attain their aspirations based on the efforts they put into doing so. It is held that treating everyone the same constitutes fairness (Henry & Tator, 2006; James & Taylor, 2008). In the meritocratic view, unfettered individual competition is a natural and desirable mechanism for distributing rewards and entitlements. Inequality and hierarchy, then, are accepted as inevitable as well as healthy for the functioning of society (Fleras & Elliott, 2003). This meritocratic emphasis on equal opportunity can be contrasted with an equality of outcome perspective, which concentrates on the egalitarian distribution of goods and services for members of traditionally disadvantaged groups (Fleras & Elliott, 2003). North American society is considered meritorious even as White middle-class values as well as corporate desires, logics, and practices dominate. So the failure of working-class (or 'underclass') and certain racialized community members to participate fully in the society and attain success is attributed to deficiency on their part (Reay, 1998; Yosso, 2005). Differential or unequal outcomes, then, is seen as the natural result of individuals' efforts insofar as the society is understood to be constructed as meritorious and equal. This view of inequality deflects attention from its structural causes, such as the systemic racism and sexism that are embedded in the society's dominant institutions, including in schools. Instead, individuals are viewed as having engineered their own success or failure (see Elliot & Fleas, 2003; Henry & Tator, 2006; Lund & Carr, 2008; Porfilio & Malott, 2008).

According to Hill (2003, p. 1), the neo-liberal demands of local and international capital have resulted in schools world-wide taking on an increasingly "anti-egalitarian" character. The invasion of capital into the educational sphere has diminished the capacity of schools, once considered power institutions which provide outlets to make sense of the causes of oppression, to address issues of social justice in a meaningful way (Hill, 2003; Lund & Carr, 2008). The neo-liberal, individualistic, and meritocratic ideology that is ingrained within schooling structures deflects attention from institutionalized inequalities, thereby reifying the perception that differences in educational outcomes for racialized group members are attributable to the cultural deficiencies that minority students bring to the classroom (James, 2007; Yosso, 2005). The individualistic ethos of the school system stands in sharp contrast to the collectivist orientation of many racialized communities (Li, 2001; Yosso, 2005). In North America, the experience of institutional racism results in the adaptation of a protective and empowering "minority ideology" on the part of many racialized groups (Li, 2001, p. 481). In response to their experiences of alienation and marginalization, members of racialized groups develop collective strategies of coping and resistance.

Yosso (2005) argues that the individualistic emphasis within North American education prevents educators from fully recognizing and harnessing the strategies and assets that racialized students bring to the classroom from their respective homes and communities. According to Yosso (2005) racialized young people bring various forms of cultural capital—aspirational, linguistic, familial, social, navigational, and resistant—to their schooling situation. She refers to these dynamic and inter-related forms of capital as "community cultural wealth," which is "an array of knowledge, skills, abilities and contacts possessed and utilized by Communities of Color to survive and resist macro and micro-forms of oppression" (p. 77). Aspirational capital, Yosso (2005) writes,

> is the ability to hold on to hope in the face of structured inequality and often without the means to make such dreams a reality. Yet aspirations are developed within social and familial contexts, often though linguistic storytelling and advice … that offer specific navigational goals and challenge (resist) oppressive conditions (p. 77).

Resistant capital refers to "those knowledges and skills fostered through oppositional behavior that challenges inequality … and is grounded in the legacy of resistance to subordination exhibited by Communities of Color" (Yosso, 2005, p. 80). Such resistance seems necessary if marginalized youth are to successfully navigate or "maneuver through institutions not created with Communities of Color in mind" (Yosso, 2005, p. 80).

The various forms of cultural wealth are illustrative of marginalized students' capacity to utilize their familial and community socialization and connections as resources in order to navigate various structural obstacles that threaten their academic success. So rather than emphasizing ways in which members of ethno-racial communities are culturally 'deficient,' schools need to harness and build on their community cultural wealth in ways that heighten students' level of engagement with their academic needs, interests, expectations and aspirations. Our discussion, therefore, attempts to highlight the forms of community cultural wealth that are inherent in the various strategies employed by marginalized youth to navigate schooling environments perceived to be White-normed and exclusionary.

Exercising Resistance, High Aspirations, and Entho-racial Consciousness

While many marginalized students exercise resistance to the racist aspects of schooling by opting out of the system, research demonstrates that some of these youth view the achievement of academic success as a vehicle for fighting racism and constructing a positive ethno-racial identity. These studies suggest that a salient racialized identity and a corresponding sense of commitment to an ethno-racial community can facilitate the achievement of mainstream success ideals, as students are motivated to use the school's individualistic ideology of hard work and personal achievement as a means of elevating the position of the ethno-racial groups with which they identify (James & Taylor, 2008; Lee, 1994).

In the case of African Americans and Canadians, research argues that 'successful' Blacks view personal success and the advancement of Black people as a collectivity as going hand-in-hand (Edwards & Polite, 1992; Gosine, 2008; James, 1997; James & Taylor, 2008). It has been found that many Black university students and professionals view a strong Black identity as empowering and, therefore, insist on maintaining a sense of connectedness with other Blacks (Gosine, 2008; James, 1997; Miller, 1999). In his exploration of socialization, self-concept, and career aspirations of urban Black high school students in Canada, James (1991) found that Black youth tend to hold high career aspirations, despite having to grapple with the debilitating effects associated with living in a society that privileges Eurocentric ideals and perpetuates injustice against racialized groups.

In order to realize these aspirations, James' (1991) research participants expressed a staunch belief in hard work, often expressing the need to work harder than their White counterparts. Related to this, the youth expressed a strong belief in education and the importance of having the 'right attitude'—in other words, the sense that nothing can stop them from achieving what they want. While the youth express an awareness of racial discrimination, this is not seen as a barrier. Instead, it is perceived as an "obstacle" or "hurdle" that can be overcome if one has the right attitude and possesses the appropriate qualifications. Hence, in the context of living in a racist society where Blackness is negatively represented, the Black youth attempt to construct a positive Black identity centered on education, hard work, and perseverance. Black youth not only viewed hard work and education as important for achieving individual success but also see them as essential for disproving prevailing negative stereotypes of Blacks.

In his ethnographic study of a Toronto high school, Yon (2000) details the experiences of an anti-racist and anti-sexist student organization that called itself the African Queens. Consisting of 10 female students, all of whom except one identified as Black, this organization was founded for the purpose of "consciousness-raising and mutual support around issues related to race and gender" (Yon, 2000, p. 106). According to Yon, there was evidence that the members were performing better academically as a result of the support provided by the group. In the spirit of consciousness-raising, the Queens held sessions where members recited poetry and read short stories designed to affirm their cultural identity and a sense of Black pride. Internal disagreements and divisions ultimately forced the African Queens to break up but the formation of such groups illustrates the sorts of initiatives taken by marginalized students within North American high schools to assert their identities, earn recognition, and provide positive role modeling (Dei et al, 1997; Yon, 2000).

In a 1999 study, Yon solicited the reactions of two groups of high school students to the 1994 Isaac Julien film *The Darker Side of Black*. The film is described as one that problematizes the notion of Blackness as a homogeneous or essentialized identity, portraying instead the complexities, conflicts, and discontinuities within the community (Yon, 1999). Yon noted the largely negative reaction to the film on the part of the mostly Black student audience, whom he saw as grasping for a salient and cohesive Black community, one that can be easily differentiated from its racial Other. The students viewed efforts to complicate essentialized notions of Blackness as detrimental to efforts to build such a community. "'[D]ifference within,'" writes Yon (1999, p. 638), "is ironed over by the desire for valid representations and positive images of community that would allow coherence, solidarity, and recognition within and at the same time from outside." While Yon sees such quests for narrow, essentialist identities as problematic, given the threat posed to intra-communal difference and individuality, he recognizes this phenomenon as a natural response on the part of minority youth to living in a context where they are negatively constructed and marginalized.

Although potentially stifling by placing discursive constraints on identity construction-related agency, a strong ethno-racial identity and associated sense of community can play an important role in the lives of marginalized young people (Gosine, 2008; Yon, 2000). In addition to being psychologically empowering, feeling that one is part of a strong ethno-racial community provides minority youth with valuable peer support, which has been found to be crucial to the academic success of marginalized students (Dei et al, 1997; Miller, 1999; Yon, 2000; Yosso, 2005). Many racialized students see ethno-racial identity and related initiatives (such as mutual-aid groups) as instrumental to their academic success, as this identification provides them with the sense of community and support needed to navigate educational institutions perceived as White-centred and hostile.

Research demonstrates that Asian students also view high educational attainment as the most valuable weapon in the fight to ameliorate racism. Lee (1994) conducted an ethnographic study in a Philadelphia high school in which she found that some Asian students, mostly those born in the US, used high educational accomplishment as a mechanism for directly combating racism. Although these students did not believe educational attainment to be as strongly correlated with equality of opportunity as the hegemonic meritocratic ideology suggests, they saw education as a means of equipping or enabling them to fight racism and other forms of inequality more effectively. These students spoke out against the model minority stereotype, but ironically embodied this racialized discourse in striving for educational success as a means of resisting racism (Lee, 1994).

Familial expectations of academic and occupational success along with deep sense of responsibility to their families propel many marginalized students to hold high aspirations. For instance, in a study that explored the educational expectations of second generation South Asian males, Johal (2002) reported on the significant role the family played in the aspirations that the youth set for themselves because, as one participant remarked, South Asian parents "often live their dreams through their children," and are concerned with "how the family will look" (p. 87; see also Varghese, 2006). In this regard, as one respondent noted, everybody grows up with the "idea of... going to university or working at a specific job" (Johal, 2002, p. 87; see also Bhatti, 1999; Handa, 2003).

Concerned about the disruptive behaviors of South Asian students in her suburban Canadian high school, teacher Lisa Varghese, explained that while such behaviors were contrary to the essentialized construction of these students as 'quiet, hard-working, pleasant and academically successful', these very behaviors represent the students' reaction to their lack of support from, and expectations of, teachers and parents. She observed "it seems that these youth are resorting to negative behaviour in order to gain some sense of power and status (p. 125). And she concludes:

To a certain extent they might have in them the good, obedient, intelligent South Asian characteristics, but they have the desire to smoke, hang out and bum around with their friends and do other not-so-productive activities which are frowned upon. South Asian adolescent males are simply trying the best way they know how to figure out who they are and how they fit in as strong, proud South Asians in Canadian society" (Varghese, 2006, p. 120).

In a study of the expectations of Chinese parents who recently immigrated to Canada, Li (2001), found that they held on to a minority ideology that viewed educational accomplishment as a means of combating racism. The parents had high expectations for their children, with this achievement ethos reflecting traditional cultural values, a desire for a better life, a quest for excellence, and a means of challenging the perceived disadvantage that comes with their minority racialized status. Success, then, was not only an individual accomplishment for second-generation Chinese Canadian students but a collective accomplishment that benefited their family, community, and the larger society. In addition to living up to traditional Chinese values that place great value on education, parental emphasis on educational accomplishment stemmed from the belief that minority children have to be "better and stronger than the white majority" in order to achieve and live well in the face of institutional racism (Li, 2001, p. 487). Hence, as noted earlier, in many cases a strong racialized consciousness seems necessary to help facilitate academic success.

For many marginalized youth living within a Eurocentric context, then, it would appear that a sense of obligation prevails where individual success is linked to the collective goal of empowering and honoring their communities. (Gosine, 2008; James, 1997; James & Taylor, 2008; Li, 2001). Indeed, many academically successful marginalized youth are spurred to achieve in part by a desire to fight racism and improve the plight of the ethno-racial groups with which they identify. Many Black Canadian youth, for example, have shown a determination to prove something to the dominant society regarding the capabilities and aptitudes of Black people as well as a long-term sense of commitment to an imagined Black 'community' (Gosine, 2008; James, 1991, 1997). Disturbed by hegemonic cons-tructions of Blacks as people who are intellectually less capable than other racially demarcated groups and therefore not fit for various high profile middle-class pursuits, many successful Black Canadians are driven by a desire to succeed in order to challenge such perceptions and provide positive role models for young Black Canadians.

Research (e.g., Gosine, 2008; James, 1997) demonstrates that the means employed by most individuals to improve the plight of the Black community—namely the promotion of educational and occupational attainment through Black self-help organizations, mentoring, and role modeling—are very much shaped by the dominant, middle-class ideology that emphasizes individual initiative while playing down the structural obstacles embedded in Canadian institutions. As James (1991) observes, many marginalized youth "seem to believe that they cannot succeed if they operate outside the cultural norm of Canadian society" (p. 108–9), and their solution to navigating hostile schooling environments is to adopt a collectivist ethos and develop strategies to "play by the whites' games better than the whites do" (p. 109).

For youth who identify strongly with an imagined ethno-racial community perceived as marginalized within the Canadian context, a racialized sense of identity can cushion them against the isolating, individualistic value system of middle-class culture that is embedded within schooling cultures (Gosine, 2008). For many Black North American youth, an involvement with Black student organizations and a desire to serve as role models and counteract negative racial stereotypes provides them with a sense of belonging, giving meaning to their lives (Gosine, 2008; James, 1997). A salient ethno-racial identity, then, can serve to counter the seclusion often associated with middle-class individualism. For many people with a strong racialized identification, academic achievement is not an end in itself, but a means of elevating a given ethno-racial community as a whole. As Bellah et al (1985) observe in a more general context, people such as this "evince an individualism that is not empty but is full of content drawn from an active identification with communities and traditions" (p. 163).

As much as academically successful marginalized students feel a largely rewarding sense of commitment to an imagined ethno-racial community, they also experience considerable stress from taking on a racialized "burden of representation," that is, the (agency-constraining) burden that falls on racialized people to represent their race (Gosine, 2008; see also Yon, 2000). This burden arises in part from the essentialist way in which certain racialized groups, such as Blacks, are constructed by the dominant society, as within-group diversity is rendered invisible to the point where members of a given ethno-racial group are viewed as interchangeable. Given dominant essentialist constructions of Blackness, for example, the hegemonic perception is that almost any Black person can reasonably represent the values, perceptions, aptitudes, and aspirations of Blacks in general, and many Black people accept this burden out of a sense of commitment to a perceived Black community (Gosine, 2008). The weight of this responsibility can be especially pronounced for high-achieving young Black individuals who specialize in White-dominated subject areas and professions with few Black people—a situation that heightens their sense of visibility as racialized subjects. A second phenomenon that contributes to this strain in the lives of racialized students is their location between membership in a marginalized social group to which they feel a sense of commitment, and their participation in educational systems that largely emphasize individualistic achievement. The pressure associated with balancing a collective sense of commitment with individualistic aspirations can create a unique sense of tension in the lives of marginalized students. Yon illustrates this point throughout his 2000 ethnographic study, particularly when he talked with a young Black Canadian woman named Margaret (a pseudonym), a politically active former member of the defunct African Queens who described the frustrations she experiences living within hegemonic categories of Black and woman, which she sometimes finds confining and oppressive. In a moment of counter-hegemonic defiance, Margaret declared, "bust being Black and bust being a woman. That is a form of oppression because you are limited in those two little notches" (Yon, 2000, p. 93). At other points, however, Margaret readily invoked these identity categories, particularly in the context of the anti-racist and anti-sexist activism in which she participates, illustrating the complex and often conflicted nature of her identity.

The strategy of combining high aspirations with a strong ethno-racial identification contains elements of resistance to schooling structures experienced as alienating or, at best, irrelevant. This form of cultural wealth is undoubtedly illustrated in the capacity of marginalized students to utilize their ethno-racial identities as a source of empowerment in order to maintain aspirational capital and navigate various structural obstacles that threaten their academic success. Through initiatives such as organizing ethno-racial self-help groups in schools, marginalized students draw on peer and other social networks that provide them "both instrumental and emotional support to navigate through society's institutions" (Yosso, 2005, p. 79). Marginalized young people have the ability and desire to work collectively to challenge inequality and pursue social justice. They bring resources to the classroom that can be harnessed and nourished by educators who themselves possess a commitment to social justice and critical pedagogy.

While some students respond to their marginalization by combining high aspirations with a strong racialized consciousness, others respond to educational systems that fail to meet their needs by opting out of the system in order to preserve a healthy racialized identity. Both resistance strategies represent a means of negotiating the assimilating, homogenizing, and alienating aspects of North American educational systems.

Resisting by Being Disruptive and Opting Out

Another strategy employed by many marginalized students who experience frustration negotiating oppressive and alienating educational structures involves opting out of the schooling system, which includes leaving school before graduating or engaging in acts of defiance while remaining in school. While many educators are inclined to attribute such actions to immaturity or a lack of cultural capital on the part of certain groups of students, such behaviors represent a dimension of community cultural wealth, that is, resistant capital, which for some youth represents a means of preserving a healthy racialized identity in the face of an educational system that devalues and fails to effectively accommodate them. Holding the perception that their lived experiences have been shaped to a significant degree by racism, resisting by opting out represents rejecting the individualistic achievement ideology emphasized within schools which suggests that one's goals can be achieved through hard work and determination, regardless of social differences.

The concept of resistance among marginalized youth was brought to prominence in the US by Fordham and Ogbu (1992), who argued that a collectivist, counter-hegemonic ethos prevails within the African American community that is not conducive to achieving success within a capitalist context that emphasizes individual initiative. Employing evidence from qualitative, in-depth interviews with students from an inner-city Washington, DC high school, these investigators argue that African American students constructed an oppositional sub-culture in which virtually everything associated with the dominant White culture is rejected, including the pursuit of mainstream (i.e., White) ideals of success such as academic achievement. Instead, students developed an oppositional stance based on "a sense of collective identity or sense of peoplehood in opposition to the social identity of white Americans because of the history of oppression to which they have been subjected at the hands of the dominant society" (p. 290). In this regard, they developed an oppositional cultural frame of reference that consists of "devices for protecting their identity and for maintaining boundaries between them and white Americans" (p. 290). Fordham and Obgu argue, then, that the failure to succeed academically on the part of many African American youth can be explained as a form of resistance to school systems and a larger society perceived to be racist. Writing on African Canadian youth, Dei et al (1997, p. 240) note:

> For Blacks living in predominantly non-Black societies, race can be said to have primary significance in the construction of individual and collective social identities. Race can create a specific vantage point for resistance and the development of an oppositional identity.

Researchers have used the term resistance to explain why Black Canadian youth lag behind other racially-defined students in academic performance and achievements (Dei et al, 1997; Ibrahim, 2000; Solomon, 1992). Dei et al (1997), for example, challenge the conventional understanding of the term 'drop out.' Contrary to the hegemonically informed understanding of a school drop out as someone who made a personal decision to leave school due to individual deficiencies, Dei and his colleagues argue that dropping out is a gradual process facilitated by an interplay of out-of-school factors as well as school-related experiences. They point out that the institutional structures and processes of schooling in Canada lead Black students to disengage from the system. Aspects of the school culture that serve to alienate Black students include low teacher expectations, differential treatment of Black students, conflict with school officials who are perceived as not respecting Black students, a lack of curriculum content that explores Black history and experience, and academic labelling and streaming that limit the future career possibilities of Black students. These issues not only serve to alienate Black students but also contribute to their feelings that they have little in the way of guidance, support, or control over their academic future. Dropping out, then, is seen as an act of empowerment—a form of resistance against a Eurocentric system that restricts the agency of Black students and prevents them from developing a positive racial identity (Dei et al, 1997; see also Solomon, 1992).

Dei et al. (1997) also report that students felt their identity to be "stifled" within the school system, which was perceived as devaluing their culture while emphasizing conformity with Anglo-Canadian norms and behaviors. In the face of such assimilative pressures, and in the absence of a critical, anti-oppressive pedagogy to help them situate their experiences and challenges within a wider, structural context, students who leave school before graduating feel they had little choice if they wish to preserve their self-esteem as well as their racial and ethnic identities. Students who stayed in school despite structurally induced experiences of alienation would demonstrate resistant capital by often flagrantly defying school policies. Such defiance takes a number of forms, such as adopting a particular type of attire (Black male students, for example, may roll up their pantlegs and shirt sleeves, wear earrings, necklaces, baseball caps, and bandannas, and decorate their school uniforms with accessories and logos representing various consumerist status symbols) and speaking in a contrived African-American form of English (Ibrahim, 2000). These dress and language patterns represented strategies to assert their presence, voice, and identity as well as to demonstrate to school authorities and the rest of the student population their sense of agency and power (James, 2007).

This form of resistance is not unique to Black students, as Asian youth have been shown to resist the model minority stereotype by opting out of the system in various ways. In reflecting on his elementary school and high school experiences in Canada, Pon (2000) recalls how he and his Chinese peers were enthused by the opportunity to work with non-Chinese students, which they saw as a chance to show off their superior math skills. Pon and his friends appreciated the grade six mathematics teacher who paired them with the non-Chinese students, as they took this as a recognition on the part of the teacher of their superiority as students. The model minority stereotype, and the pressure of living up to it, would ultimately come to trouble Pon and his peers as they progressed in school, however. Pon tells of a Chinese friend, Jason, who responded to his mathematics teacher's erroneous assumption that he was good at math by skipping classes, ultimately inviting his peers to join him. His peers cheered a resultant confrontation between Jason and the teacher, an altercation they viewed as somewhat liberating.

Similarly, in the US, Lee (1994) found Asian students from poor and working-class backgrounds, particularly Southeast Asian refugees, displayed opting out forms of resistance in response to adverse schooling experiences and the model minority stereotype. These students, or 'new wavers', did not see school as the avenue to a successful future, and flouted their disdain for academic achievement. They refused to conform to the rules prescribed for academic success, as they would find ways to circumvent school rules and pass their courses while doing as little work as possible. They actively resisted the model minority stereotype, which they felt constructed Asians as "nerds" and prevented them from achieving popularity among peers (Lee, 1994, p. 422). Also fuelling new wavers' resistance was their social experiences within the school, as they were looked down upon by other Asian students and seen by teachers as Asian students who "went wrong" (Lee, 1994, p. 425). Problems with both Asian and non-Asian peers as well as their mistrust of teachers encouraged many Southeast Asian students, or new wavers, to reject the school system and spend most of their time socializing among themselves (Lee, 1994).

In all, deprived of the opportunity to learn in a context that enables them to understand and contextualize their experiences, thereby channelling their resistance in a politically productive fashion, resistance for some students takes the form of opting out. This helps them achieve culturally-prescribed ideals of success. Such resistance or navigational strategies represent efforts to maintain some self-esteem within educational structures that provide differential opportunities, a reality that stands in sharp contrast with the dominant liberal democratic ideology that schools purport to embrace.

Conclusion

In this chapter, we have argued that the oppressive aspects of schooling are underpinned by an individualistic ethos that trumpets the existence of equality of opportunity while denying the lived experiences of young people from traditionally marginalized groups. This individualism results in a failure to highlight the initiative, resources, capital and other community-based assets that students bring to classrooms, and, as such, deflects educators' attention from utilizing these assets in the teaching/learning processes. A critical approach to education would help to counter this individualistic ideology to better reflect the lived experiences of minority students, and empower them to work collectively toward social change. The approach recognizes that schools are sites of power imbalances and contestation; they generate different and unequal opportunities for student participation. Moreover, it illuminates the reality that students' educational successes and challenges are not merely attributable to their cultural and/or individual deficiencies relating to race, ethnicity, class, gender, language, and nativity but, significantly, reflect social inequalities systemically woven into the fabric of the larger society. Power differences are highlighted, as are the hegemonic discourses and educational processes within schools that marginalize, oppress, and silence students (James, 2007). Critical education combines traditional academics with social justice activism in order to raise students' consciousness with respect to anti-oppression themes (Lund, 2006; see also Lund & Carr, 2008; Westheimer & Kahne, 1998).

We identified two ways in which marginalized youth tend to adapt to the oppressive and alienating schooling structures. Some resist (or at times they resist) the oppressive experience within the educational system and society at-large by constructing a defensively-situated minority identity that, in turn, shapes their educational expectations and career aspirations. The adaptation of such a defensively-situated minority mentality tend to lead to two forms of resistant behavior: Opting out of the system or embracing mainstream, culturally prescribed academic and career aspirations partly as a means of uplifting the minoritzed group. In the case of students who opt out of the system, the school's meritocratic achievement ideology is viewed as invalid, and is rejected; for other students, who maintain strong racialized identifications, despite their awareness of institutional racism, this individualistic ethos is embraced as a means of elevating their ethno-racial communities. These two modes of navigating school are by no means mutually exclusive, as more than one may be employed strategically at different moments by marginalized youth struggling to find a place within alienating schooling environments.

Critical education initiatives can help to harness the community cultural wealth of marginalized students by raising their awareness of the structural forces that affect their lives and engage them in what Lund (2006) sees as social justice initiatives. This, in turn, would heighten the relevancy of schooling for these students, and enhance their sense of belonging in their academic programs. With a critical and democratic emphasis in education, then, the raw, distracting critical consciousness exhibited by students who opt out of the system, or the structurally-induced frustrations that spur young people to abandon any sense of racial consciousness in order to navigate the system, could be channelled into different and more productive ways. Such an approach to education as, for example, an Afrocentric school program for students who underperform in the existing school system would contribute to the creation of a system that acknowledges (rather than eliminate or assimilate) differences, creates equitable opportunities, raises consciousness, and empowers young people by steering the community cultural wealth that they bring to the classroom toward participatory democracy.

QUESTIONS FOR REFLECTION

1. Discuss how the ideology of individualism informs dominant explanations for racial differences in educational outcomes in North America? Also address how racial differences intersect with class, ethnicity, immigrant status, gender, etc. to inform educational outcomes.
2. The authors claim that multicultural education as implemented in Canadian schools has failed to meet the needs, interests and aspirations of racialized students. With reference to your understanding and/or observation of multicultural education in your context, do you find this to be the case? Discuss.
3. Describe the two strategies of resistance marginalized youth employ to navigate schooling structures that they find alienating or oppressive. Give examples of your experience of each form of resistance and illustrate how each of these strategies relate to the ideology of individualism.

NOTES

[1] When we employ the adjective 'marginalized', we refer to groups or categories of people who historically have been pushed to the societal periphery and largely denied full participation in the political and social realm, therefore resulting in many of these groups falling victim to material inequality (see Young, 1990).

[2] The strategy of resistance that marginalized students adopt is inevitably influenced by the ways in which various statuses such as race, ethnicity, gender, class and nativity intersect in their lives (Gosine, 2002; James, 2007; Waters, 1994). A young person growing up in a middle-class context, for example, might more readily embrace the individualistic ethos of the broader society and be better positioned to pursue academic success within the current mainstream educational system than someone from a lower working-class environment (Dei et al, 1997).

REFERENCES

Banks, J. (1997). Multicultural education: Characteristics and goals. In J. A. Banks & C. A. M. Banks (Eds.), *Multicultural education: Issues and perspectives* (pp. 3–31). Boston: Allyn & Bacon.

Bellah, R. N., Madsen, R., Sullivan, W. N., Swidler, A., & Tipton, S. M. (1985). *Habits of the heart: Individualism and commitment in American life*. New York: Harper & Row.

Bhatti, G. (1999). *Asian children at home and at school*. New York: Routledge.

Codjoe, H. (2001). Fighting a 'public enemy' of Black academic achievement: The persistence of racism and the schooling experiences of Black students in Canada. *Race, Ethnicity and Education*, 4(1), 343–375.

Dei, G. J. S., Holmes, L., Mazzuca, J., McIsaac, E., & Zine, J. (1997). *Reconstructing 'drop-out': A critical ethnography of the dynamics of Black students' disengagement from school*. Toronto: University of Toronto Press.

Edwards, A., & Polite, C. K. (1992). *Children of the dream: The psychology of Black success.* New York: Doubleday.

Fleras, A., & Elliott, J. L. (2003). *Unequal relations: An introduction to race and ethnic dynamics in Canada.* Toronto: Prentice Hall.

Fordham, S., & Ogbu, J. U. (1992). Black students' school success: Coping with the burden of "acting white". In J. J. Macionis & N. V. Benokraitis (Eds.), *Seeing ourselves: Classic, contemporary, and cross-cultural readings in sociology* (pp. 287–303). Englewood Cliffs, NJ: Prentice Hall.

Giroux, H. A., & Giroux, S. S. (2004). *Take back higher education: Race, youth, and the crisis of democracy in the post-civil rights era.* New York: Palgrave Macmillan.

Gosine, K. (2008). Living between stigma and status: A qualitative study of the social identities of highly educated Black Canadian adults. *Identity: An International Journal of Theory and Research, 8*(4), 307–333.

Gosine, K. (2002). Essentialism versus complexity: Conceptions of racial identity in educational scholarship. *Canadian Journal of Education, 27*(1), 81–100.

Grayson, J. P. (1999). *The student experience at York University: The effects of income, race, and gender over four years.* Toronto: Institute for Social Research, York University.

Handa, A. (2003). *Of silk sari and mini skirts: South Asians girls walk the tighrope of culure.* Toronto: Women's Press.

Henry, A. (1998). " Speaking up" and "speaking out": Examining "voice" in a reading/writing program with adolescent African Caribbean girls. *Journal of Literacy Research, 30*(2), 233–252.

Henry, F., & Tator, C. (2006). *The color of democracy: Racism in Canadian Society.* Toronto: Nelson, Thomson Ltd.

Henry, F., & Tator, C. (1994). The ideology of racism—"democratic racism." *Canadian Ethnic Studies, 26*(2), 1–14.

Hill, D. (2003). Global neo-liberalism, the deformation of education and resistance. *Journal for Critical Education Policy Studies, 1*(1).

Ibrahim, A. (2000). 'Whassup Homeboy?' Black/popular culture and the politics of 'curriculum studies'. In G. J. S. Dei & A. Calliste (Eds.), *Power, knowledge, and anti-racism education: A critical reader* (pp. 57–72). Halifax: Fernwood.

James, C. E. (1991). *Making it: Black youth, racism and career aspirations.* Oakville, ON: Mosaic Press.

James, C. E. (1997). Contradictory tensions in the experiences of African Canadians in a faculty of education with an access program. *Canadian Journal of Education, 22*(2), 158–174.

James, C. E. (2007). Negotiating school: Marginalized students' participation in their education process. In G. F. Johnson & R. Enomoto (Ed.), *Race, racialization, and antiracism in Canada and beyond* (pp. 17–36). Toronto: University of Toronto Press.

James, C. E., & Taylor, L. (2008). 'Education will get you to the station': Marginalized students' experiences and perceptions of merit in accessing university. *Canadian Journal of Education, 31*(3), 567–590.

Johal, R. S. (2002). *The world is ours: Second generation South Asians reconcile conflicting expectations.* Unpublished MA Thesis, Faculty of Education, York University, Toronto.

Lee, S. J. (1994). Behind the model minority stereotype: Voices of high and low achieving Asian American Students. *Anthropology and Education Quarterly, 24*(4), 413–429.

Lee, S. J. (2006). Additional complexities: Social class, ethnicity, generation, and gender in Asian American student experiences. *Race, Ethnicity and Education, 9*(1), 17–28.

Li, J. (2001). Expectations of Chinese immigrant parents for their children's education: The interplay of Chinese tradition and the Canadian context. *Canadian Journal of Education, 26*(4), 477–494.

Lorenzo, M. K. (2000). Social and emotional functioning of older Asian American adolescents. *Child and Adolescent Social Work Journal, 17*(4), 249–303.

Lund, D. E. (2006). Addressing multicultural and anti-racist theory and practice with Canadian teacher activists. In D. E. Armstrong & B. J. McMahon (Eds.), *Inclusion in urban educational environments: Addressing issues of diversity, equity, and social justice* (pp. 255–274). Greenwich, CT: Information Age Publishing.

Lund, D. E., & Carr, P. R. (Eds.). (2008). *Doing democracy: Striving for political literacy and social justice*. New York: Peter Lang.

Miller, D. B. (1999). Racial socialization and racial identity: Can they promote resiliency for African American adolescents? *Adolescence, 34*, 493–501.

Milner, H. R. (2007). African American males in urban schools: No excuses—teach and empower. *Theory into Practice, 46*(3), 239–246.

Pon, G. (2000). Beamers, cells, malls, and cantopop: Thinking through the geographies of Chineseness. In C. E. James (Ed.), *Experiencing difference* (pp. 222–234). Halifax: Fernwood.

Porfilio, B., & Malott, C. (Eds.). (2008). *The destructive path of neo-liberalism: An international examination of education*. Rotterdam: Sense Publishers.

Reay, D. (1998). Rethinking social class: Qualitative perspectives on class and gender. *Sociology, 32*, 259–275.

Solomon, P. (1992). *Black resistance in high school: Forging a separatist culture*. Albany, NY: SUNY Press.

Varghese, L. S. (2006). *Finding a "home": Thinking through the issues and complexities of South Asian adolescent conduct in today's greater Toronto area*. Unpublished MA Thesis, Faculty of Education, York University, Toronto.

Walcott, R. (2003). *Black like who?* Toronto: Insomniac Press.

Waters, M. C. (1994). Ethnic and racial identities of second-generation black immigrants in New York City. *International Migration Review, 28*, 795–820.

Westheimer, J., & Kahne, J. (1998). Education for action: Preparing youth for participatory democracy. In W. Ayers, J. A. Hunt, & T.Quinn (Eds.), *Teaching for social justice* (pp. 1–20). New York: Teacher's College Press.

Yon, D. A. (1999). Pedagogy and the 'problem' of difference: On reading 'community' in The Darker Side of Black. *Qualitative Studies in Education, 12*, 623–641.

Yon, D. A. (2000). *Elusive culture: Race, identity and schooling in global times*. New York: SUNY Press.

Yosso, T. J. (2005). 'Whose culture has capital?' A critical race theory discussion of community cultural wealth. *Race, Ethnicity and Education, 8*(1), 69–91.

Young, I. (1990). *Justice and politics of difference*. Princeton, NJ: Princeton University Press.

JULIE GORLEWSKI

4. WHITE WORKING-CLASS HIGH SCHOOL STUDENTS AND RESISTANCE TO NEO-LIBERALISM

INTRODUCTION

The word "suburban" evokes a predictable set of images: sprawling homes surrounded by manicured lawns; sparkling vehicles navigating well-maintained roadways; sunshine splashing on charcoal grills; playgrounds, pools, and porches populated by intact middle-class White families and their Frisbee-catching dogs. If these rarefied representations of suburbia exist, they are most likely located miles from their defining urban centers, in relatively exclusive and often gated-communities inaccessible by public transportation. In contrast, the suburbs adjacent to cities, known as "first-ring" or "inner-ring" suburbs, bear more resemblance to their urban neighbors than their second-or third-ring suburban counterparts. Inner-ring suburbs tend to be populated by poor and working-class families. As socio-economic inequities have increased, disparities between communities have been exacerbated; these disparities are, in the United States, reflected by, and within, public schools.

Neo-liberalism, which "defines society exclusively through the privileging of market relations, deregulation, privatization, and consumerism" (Giroux, 2003, p. 3), has reified existing class relations, reinvigorating the wealth and power of dominant classes and diminishing the wealth and power of working-classes. According to Yates (2007),

Neo-liberal ideology was the dominant classes' response to the considerable gains achieved by the working and peasant classes from the end of the Second World War to the mid-1970s. The huge increase in inequality that has occurred since then is the direct result of the growth in income of the dominant classes, which is a consequence of class-determined public policies such as: (a) deregulation of labour markets, an anti-working-class move; (b) deregulation of financial markets, which has greatly benefited financial capital …; (c) deregulation of commerce in goods and services, which has benefited the high-consumption population at the cost of labourers; (d) reduction of social public expenditures, which has hurt the working-class; (e) privatization of services, which has benefited the richest 20 percent of the population at the expense of the well-being of the working-classes that depend on public services; (f) promotion of individualism and consumerism, hurting the culture of solidarity… Each of these class-determined public policies requires a state action or intervention that conflicts with the interests of the working and other popular classes. (pp. 25–26)

B. J. Porfilio and P. R. Carr (eds.), Youth Culture, Education and Resistance:
Subverting the Commercial Ordering of Life, 57–73.

Neo-liberalism is infused in the United States' economic, political, and socio-cultural conditions. The interests of the working-class have been ravaged by policies associated with neo-liberalism. Increased economic inequities have pilfered the resources and the prospects of working-class families, the types of families who tend to populate first-ring suburbs.

Working-class youth are particularly affected: their families suffer economic strain while institutions (such as public schools) meant to foster the public good are subject to regulatory standardization and reduced funding. Students in public schools serving working-class communities embody class-based cultural dispositions that are perceived as detrimental to academic achievement. Yates (2007) explains:

> The attitude of working-class youth towards school mirrors their parents' ambivalence toward success and work. Schools are oppressive places, and kids naturally rebel against the agents of this oppression: teachers and administrators....From the point of view of the rulers of the economic system, schools have been great successes. Only a few working-class youth are needed to fill the relatively few skilled labour slots in the workplace. The values absorbed by the rest of the working-class boys and girls will fit them very well for the work they will do and make it difficult to blame anyone but themselves for their failure to escape their class. (p. 153)

One way public schools promote reproduction of social class is by reinforcing students' attitudes toward education (Anyon, 1981). The dynamics of social class (and its inherent cultural construction) are rarely acknowledged or explored in schools, making its force largely invisible. Resisting authority is part of the cultural identity of the working-class; in fact, the working-class is predominantly defined *against* Others (e.g., authority figures, people of colour). Because policies of neo-liberalism reflect the new socio-cultural authority, working-class youth represent real potential for resistance to neo-liberalism, resistance that might develop into the type of solidarity necessary to move toward social justice.

In this chapter, I discuss the potential for dialogic pedagogical approaches to ameliorate the deleterious effects of educational reforms grounded in neo-liberalism. I explain the connection between neo-liberalism and standards-based high-stakes assessments, and examine how these assessments affect the educational experiences of students in a predominantly White, working-class, inner-ring suburban high school. Shifting socio-economic dynamics of inner-ring suburbs are considered, as are the power relations inherent in working-class schooling and the relationships between students and teachers in this setting. My own experiences enacting various roles in the research setting (teacher, learning centre director, parent of students, district resident) provide a nuanced set of perspectives. In addition, the potential for tapping student resistance as a means of engagement and empowerment are revealed by two anecdotes from an 11th grade English class. Finally, dialogic, transformative pedagogies are discussed as a means for providing spaces for productive resistance in an effort to seek solidarity between working-class students and their teachers.

Dialogic Pedagogies

To challenge neo-liberalism and tap the potential of working-class culture through solidarity and critical engagement, social class relations must be interrogated through genuine dialogue between students and teachers. Freire (2007/1968) describes true dialogue, in which power relations are explicated and, therefore, ameliorated, as essential to social transformation.

> Dialogue is the encounter between men, mediated by the world, in order to name the world. Hence, dialogue cannot occur between those who want to name the world and those who do not wish this naming—between those who deny others the right to speak their word and those whose right to speak has been denied them. Those who have been denied their primordial right to speak their word must first reclaim this right and prevent the continuation of this dehumanizing aggression....

> If it is in speaking their word that people, by naming the world, transform it, dialogue imposes itself as the way by which they achieve significance as human beings. Dialogue is thus an existential necessity. And since dialogue is the encounter in which the united reflection and action of the dialoguers are addressed to the world which is to be transformed and humanized, this dialogue cannot be reduced to the act of one person's "depositing" ideas in another; nor can it become a simple exchange of ideas to be "consumed" by the discussants. ... Because dialogue is an encounter among women and men who name the world, it must not be a situation where some name on behalf of others. It is an act of creation; it must not serve as a crafty instrument for the domination of one person by another. (pp. 76–77)

Pedagogies that promote dialogue can illuminate cultural dynamics in ways that transform perceived deficiencies into constructive attributes. Dialogue has the capacity to transform relations marked by coercive uses of power into partnerships marked by empathy and solidarity. Since schools incorporate relations of power, resistance is inevitable. Teacher response to resistance, however, can vary. Instead of being perceived as a problem to be stifled and squashed, student resistance can be understood as part of a constructed political reality as well as a critique of neo-liberalism.

Neo-liberal Reform and Standardization

Neo-liberalism has had profound effects on public education. Hursh (2005) explains:

> Neo-liberal governments... desire to reduce funding for education while at the same time reorganizing education to fit the needs of the economy. Because the public might object to cuts in social spending and increasing economic inequality, neo-liberal policy makers have skillfully packaged the reforms to make it appear that they are promoting equality. As I will describe,

they use discourses emphasizing increasing fairness in education, such as 'requiring all students to achieve high standards as measured by objective tests', and opportunity, such as 'leaving no child behind'.

Another way in which neo-liberal governments are able to retain their legitimacy is by blaming schools for the essential injustices and contradictions of capitalism, while they preserve inequalities through other policies such as taxation and reductions in social spending. (p. 5)

In the mid-1990s, New York State[1] anticipated the political movement that has engulfed public schools through the federal legislation entitled *No Child Left Behind* (United States Department of Education, 2003). Portending developments enacted through this legislation, the state's education department implemented common, comprehensive learning standards meant to drive local district curricula. In addition, the state unveiled a plan to attach the standards to mandatory assessments for students, beginning in the area of English Language Arts (ELA).

Consequences for students and educators were significant and comprehensive. In addition to gauging individual student performance, tests at all levels were designed to measure schools' progress towards meeting the state's established standards and to rank schools according to student achievement. Scores and rankings were published and distributed by districts, the state education department, and media outlets; and schools with inadequate scores and unacceptable levels of improvement were threatened with the possibility of being designated as a "School Under Regents Review" (SURR). So-called SURR schools would be required to show rapid, significant improvement on standardized assessments or face state takeover (New York State Education Department, 1999; United States Department of Education, 2003).

Since 2001, students in New York State's public schools must score at least 65% on five Regents[2] exams in order to earn a diploma. Because it removed the lower track, this reform was introduced, and continues to be promoted as "raising the bar" for disadvantaged students. It is clear, however, that mandated Regents examinations have disproportionately deleterious effects on students from backgrounds marked by poverty, as well as those who represent racial and ethnic minorities (Dorn, 2007; Gunzenhauser, 2006; Nichols, 2006; Orfield & Kornhaber, 2001). Standardized assessments exhibit class bias (Finn, 1999; Giroux, 2003). Yet the fact that poor and working-class students tend to perform worse than middle-class students on standardized assessment is ultimately exploited as justification for what amounts to politically and educationally sanctioned social reproduction.

It should be noted that reforms involving high-stakes standardized assessments reinforce social class stratification in that they target—and, therefore, affect—those who participate in public schooling. Families and teachers with the resources to opt out of these testing regimes and their pedagogical implications are able to do so by electing a private educational alternative. Furthermore, it is important to note that while upper classes are not immune from the testing frenzy, students from upper-middle and upper-class backgrounds tend to be exposed to a completely different testing regime (e.g., Advanced Placement [AP] or International Baccalaureate [IB] examinations) which is linked to entrance into certain types of institutions. (Interestingly, AP and IB examinations are linked with rigor and elite rankings among schools. Unlike assessments associated with political reform which are mandated for all public school students, availability of and eligibility for AP and IB examinations tend to be intentionally exclusive.) Of course, public school students whose academic achievements (including test scores) warrant eligibility for more selective institutions are *then* subjected to more rigorous, elite testing regimes. Although the design, purposes and implementation of state tests and AP/IB examinations differ markedly, it is evident that both sets of tests serve as mechanisms of exclusion that serve to limit the opportunities of poor and working-class students who are the predominant constituents of public schools.

Nationally, the trend is toward more standardized, assessment-based curricula (Apple, 2001). The NCLB legislation requires standardized testing from grades 3–11; districts' federal funding is contingent on students' test scores. Federal and state legislation that legitimates testing as the central measure of learning undermines the ability of educational institutions to inspire excellence and achieve social justice. These mandates and the associated consequences have significant effects on how students and teachers experience schooling; in effect, they make the possibility of meaningful dialogue among students and teachers more unlikely than ever as all participants in the public education system strive to meet mandates of reform.

The effects of recent reform policies on public school teachers are significant because the identities teachers construct affect their interactions with students. The roles of teachers are undergoing a profound shift as the pressures of high-stakes tests come to be perceived as "normal." Teachers are experiencing a sense of deprofessionalization as they are re-socialized toward the working-class aspects of their occupation. Since many teachers were raised and educated in working-class communities, their schooling has provided little experience with empowering literacies. Although their backgrounds are predominantly working-class, teachers perceive themselves as having moved beyond the working-class, particularly with respect to education and income.

As teachers' self-perceptions shift toward the middle class, they may define themselves against working-class Others—a group which includes their students and the families in this working-class community. Conservative columnist David Brooks (2005) asserts that escalating economic disparities are affecting social class, particularly regarding education:

> Economic stratification is translating into social stratification. Only 28 percent of American adults have a college degree, but most of us in this group find ourselves in workplaces in social milieus where almost everybody has been to college. A social chasm is opening up between those in educated society and those in noneducated society, and you are beginning to see vast behavioural differences between the two groups.

Economic pressures and increasing income disparities across society are causing Americans to become more competitive as they try to maintain social status, and teachers are no exception to this trend.

The identity construction of students in this setting is complicated when students resist the authority of teachers who perceive themselves as offering opportunities that will improve students' life chances. Teachers' identity construction is further complicated by the fact that their professional identities (which exist, in part, in opposition to working-class Others) hinge on the very performance of their (sometimes resistant) students. It would seem clear that teachers have multi-layered reasons to encourage students to shed aspects of working-class identity that act in opposition to academic achievement. They are liable to embrace students who comply and reject those who resist. Although these dynamics are certainly not new, they are undoubtedly exacerbated by the current political and economic pressures.

Inner-Ring Suburbs, Teachers, and Whiteness

Inner-ring suburban communities are undergoing socio-economic shifts reflected in national metropolitan polarization as families seek to escape substandard urban schools and are able to access affordable housing in school districts such as the one studied here (Orfield, 2002). As Orfield notes, schools are particularly interesting sites for understanding demographic trends. "Schools are the first victim and the most powerful perpetuator of metropolitan polarization. Local schools become socio-economically distressed before neighbourhoods become poor; rising poverty among a community's school children predicts the future of its adults" (p. 3). Teachers in this school view the community as having changed; they perceive this change as "urbanization" and describe it as a loss of middle-class values.

This shift in perception is accompanied by a small but significant shift in racial composition, with the black student population rising from 1.8 percent in 2000 to 5.2 percent in 2005 (*New York State District School Report Card Comprehensive Information Report*, 2007). The community, however, remains predominantly white. Just as the term "urban" tends to be code for "black," the word "suburban" is generally associated with whiteness and with privileges connected to whiteness. Inner-ring suburban communities and their schools, however, complicate essentialist perceptions of race and class, as these suburbs are increasingly populated by people of color. White working-class students benefit from the privileges associated with their race; however, they are disadvantaged vis-à-vis their social class. Certainly, their immediate prospects are enhanced by their whiteness—white students can shift identities in ways that black students cannot. In a predominantly white population, white students do not suffer discrimination; black students certainly do[3]. Moreover, the racial border-patrolling characterized by members of the white working-class has not been diminished by the economic pressures associated with neo-liberalism. Weis (2004) describes the attempts of the white working-class to maintain their race-based privilege in the face of neo-liberal pressures:

> Armed with their whiteness, (working-class) men and women hold together to preserve privilege in an economy that has stripped them of the life they knew....White working-class women join their men to assert the legitimacy and even the necessity of white family space, thus preserving the wages of whiteness, a move that enables this class fraction to continue to differentiate

itself from an increasingly impoverished urban underclass of colour as well as the now more racially/ethnically diverse broader working-class. Collectively asserting whiteness, white working-class men and women, for the moment at least, converge as they work to position themselves for decades to come. (p. 164–5)

It is evident that the white students who constitute the vast majority of this school's student body are privileged by their whiteness (Carr, 2007). Their experiences of schooling, however, provide neither the opportunity to critique the culture which bestows this privilege nor the impetus to unite with their non-white peers to challenge the status quo—the hegemonic structure that benefits only dominant classes. Despite their relative privilege, long-term socio-economic possibilities of working-class white students tend not to be improved by their experiences of schooling.

In general, working-class students are alienated from the content and nature of public schools. They do not relate to the cultural norms—including academic language—that are privileged within public schools. These conditions persist despite the fact that many teachers in the public school under consideration graduated from local public schools and attended area public post-secondary institutions. They often describe themselves as having "working-class" backgrounds. However, teachers' current levels of income and education situate them outside the working-class. They tend to associate more with their new "classmates" in the lower middle-class than with the members of the working-class communities in which they teach. Moreover, teachers are not likely to critique the educational system in which they have become acculturated. Having been successful in the system, teachers naturally perceive the system as effective and have little incentive to support large-scale reform.

Gos (1995) notes that working-class students are expected to compete in an unfair educational climate—one in which their cultural background puts them behind from the start. He states:

Some working-class students can go to college and, with little remediation and a lot of work, be successful. . . . But the percentages are against them and those that do succeed come away from the battle suffering huge losses, most notably a separation from their families and communities—in effect, from their heritage. It is my belief that this carnage can be alleviated.... Teachers in secondary schools are in a position to make the difference. (p. 33)

My place in this school as a teacher, parent, researcher and resident involves transformations of my own identity. I must mediate between the institutional, state-mandated goals of the school and its cultural (including sociolinguistic) norms and the cultural (and socio-linguistic) norms of the students and parents who are the school's constituents. In addition, I must recognize and act on the basis of existing power relationships in order to become an effective educator. To fulfill this role, I seek to understand and speak various social languages and open dialogue among all constituents as potential classmates. One way of doing so, I learned, is attending to students' resistance.

Power and Resistance

Because schools are social institutions, power relations are integral to schooling. Foucault describes power as diffuse, not easily defined or compartmentalized by possessors; in fact, Foucault's description of power precludes its possession at all. Foucault's way of considering power does not centralize its locus; social control is perceived as being created and perpetuated through everyday activities of people within society as they participate in dominant forms of discourse. Power is created and dispersed, then, in a "capillary" manner. Foucault conceives of social control as being regulated through the "regularization" of practices, discourse being a central facet through which control is maintained (Foucault, 1993).

Foucault's conception of resistance as a fundamental component of power relations offers insight into the evolution of social theory. Foucault contends that resistance is a constituting element of any power relationship. That is, a Foucaultian concept of resistance asserts that it is an integral part of power itself:

> Foucault says: "Where there is power, there is resistance, and yet, or rather consequently, this resistance is never in a position of exteriority in relation to power." What he seems to mean is this: because power is not coercive in the sense of direct threat of violence, it must be understood as an asymmetrical set of relations in which the existence of this multiplicity of nodal points or relations necessarily entails the possibility of resistance. (Hartmann, 2003, p. 3)

Resistance, then, can be perceived as either a force to be marginalized (since it cannot be eliminated) or a means of empowerment. A key factor that influences the effects of resistance on schooling involves student-teacher relations.

While cultural correspondence between students and teachers tends to facilitate affirmative educational experiences, disparities between students and teachers with regard to socially constructed aspects of identity can be detrimental to student achievement. In a suburban high school that is predominantly white and working-class, it may appear that teachers and students share relevant cultural characteristics, despite the fact that hidden disparities in social class can create cultural conflict (Bernstein, 1990; Brantlinger, 1993; Wertsch, 1991). Graf (1999) asserts that "to address educational problems at their root, then, we need to start with the enormous gulf that separates the culture and discourse of students from that of teachers" (p. 140). Furthermore, in an educational climate of assessment-based accountability, both teachers and students are alienated from the curricula and resentful of standardized tests. Often, negative feelings connected to this alienation heighten already tense relations of power in classrooms.

Current neo-liberal policies in the United States have resulted in the reinstantiation of working-class aspects of teachers' roles; teachers report feelings of disempowerment, demoralization, and deprofessionalization. However, this phenomenon could provide the motivation for teachers and students to build on their shared working-class interests, offering a means for collective resistance that would minimize alienation and marginalization and enhance the possibility for social justice.

In working-class public schools, social languages and language arts practices that diverge from academic or "standard" English tend to be treated as deficient and students are often silenced on the basis of their modes of expression rather than the quality of their ideas. Moreover, in attempting to offer students access to "upper class" echelons of language (e.g., poetry), teachers may unintentionally alienate students from the power and prestige typically associated with these genres. Teachers may not perceive student resistance to these genres as a reflection of students' culture.

The next sections of this chapter explore a pedagogical journey into the experiences of my students with content areas heavily laden with social class: poetry and the college entrance process. By observing my students' reactions to these two conventionally non-working-class signifiers, I reach into the working-class culture to validate and extend our collective class (room) experiences. By listening, respecting, and responding to cultural norms, I seek to co-construct a classroom where transformations can occur and where resistance can signify the initiation of dialogue and a struggle that results in mutual learning and movement toward liberatory learning and social justice (Freire, 2007/1968).

Resisting Literature

To establish dialogue about language and literature, I began the year with a survey asking students about what they liked and disliked about various literacy-based activities. When asked to list the last book they had read, it was common for students to boast of *never* having completed a book. Unfortunately, our high school curriculum was hardly designed to engage reluctant readers. Reminiscent of devotion to the canon of western literature and dead white males, it included texts such as *Great Expectations, All Quiet on the Western Front, The Great Gatsby*, and *Julius Caesar*. As an English major, I had no difficulty appreciating the value of such texts. As an English *teacher*, however, I could not ignore the effects they had on students' dispositions toward reading.

This year's grade 11 class had been going well. We had explored themes of power and powerlessness in Miller's *The Crucible*, and they had participated in a trial of a key character in *The Great Gatsby*. My students knew that I cared about their experiences and opinions. We had established a classroom community marked by trust and open communication. Their response to my spring plans, therefore, surprised me.

When I introduced the poetry unit, my high school juniors morphed into first graders. Like small children, their responses were immediate and genuine, their revulsion displayed both physically and verbally. "I *hate* it. I never *get* it. Why do we have to *read* that stuff ? " These reactions were so spontaneous and candid as to be rather endearing. It was March, and I had planned to finish the school year with two units: poetry and a college application essay. I had sketched out each of these units and had developed general ideas about my objectives, materials, and assessments. But my students' powerful aversion made me reconsider.

Understanding the cultural and academic dynamics that had resulted in my students' open aversion to school (in general) and poetry (in particular) helped to prepare me for the challenge of facilitating pedagogical transformation through dialogue. The importance of this understanding cannot be overestimated, particularly in the neo-liberal context of high stakes testing and assessment-oriented account-ability. Teachers experience pressure from numerous fronts, and a teacher's initial reaction to student resistance is likely to be defensive and angry. Good teachers are highly devoted to their content and methods. Excellent teachers spend time and energy investing imagination and passion into their lessons. Furthermore, effective teachers care about whether students learn relevant content. When students respond with resistance, it is natural for teachers to feel disappointed, unappreciated, and upset. They may also be anxious about how students' resistance may affect their ability to earn high school credentials, since demonstration of content knowledge is critical to passing mandatory assessments. Despite these very real concerns, it is essential for teachers to reflect on classroom reactions and, even more importantly, those of our students.

"Resistance," on its surface, seems like a simple concept rooted, perhaps, in motivational deficiency on the part of students. The individual and social cones-quences of resistance, however, are complex and unpredictable. Weis (2004) points out that "While ... researchers have chronicled and theorized "resistance," few have taken up the consequences of such 'resistance' over time .... What is possible as collective and/or individual moments of resistance are lived out?" (emphasis in original, p. 180). This question: *What is possible in these spaces of resistance?* reveals an interval of opportunity for teachers. It is in these spaces of struggle that structure and agency are destabilized and we can see our educational and social contexts as in flux (Weis, 2004). This does not, of course, imply that when students complain, teachers ought to capitulate. We must neither ignore nor romanticize resistance; however, we must recognize and respect it (Graf, 1999). I recognized that, in this situation, developing a positive disposition toward literature, in general, and poetry, in particular, was more important than assessing their understanding of literary terminology. If I could help my students develop a disposition to appreciate poetry, I could build a bridge toward cultural capital—a bridge that would not invalidate their own language experiences.

I considered the elements of social class that disempowered these White working-class students in our society (Heilman, 2004). Most of them were outspokenly anti-academic. They wanted good grades (or at least passing grades), but valued neither the learning process nor the knowledge generally associated with good grades. Many students engaged in schoolwork primarily to avoid punishment. Even the highest achieving students saw school participation as "playing a game" whose ends were report card results, which sometimes translated into privileges and opportunities. A traditional poetry unit in which we studied characteristics of poems, read about authors, and explored literary eras might have reinforced some students' ability to analyse poetry according to an academic rubric. However, such instruction would fail to promote critical thought or to engage student resistance.

I considered the possibility that, instead, students might engage with poetry in a personal way, to read poems that they enjoyed, to attain power through and experience pleasure in the genre of poetry.

I imagined students learning to see themselves as readers and writers of poetry. An internet search with this possibility in mind led me to the *Favourite Poem Project* (Pinsky, 1997). Inspired by Pinsky's aims and successes, I spent the first day of this unit reading aloud to the class, sharing poems that I loved, and poems that I did NOT love. I intentionally sought to provide a subjective space for them to dislike poetry, hoping that might open a space for appreciation as well. Agency, it seemed to me, ought to flow in both directions. Next I set students loose on the library's poetry collection. Their first task was to immerse themselves in poetry. Most of my students had never perused a literature anthology, much less a collection of poetry, with the idea of finding something that "spoke" to them, so it took some time for students to take this activity seriously. Several students started by looking for the shortest poems they could find; others looked for taboo words (and, of course, found them). But after the novelty wore off, skimming, reviewing, and really reading poetry—for personal purposes—became acceptable undertakings.

By the end of the third class period, every student had selected and orally interpreted a "favourite poem" for the class. Selections ranged from Silverstein's nonsense verses to war protest poetry. The rest of the unit was equally rewarding. Students wrote their own poems and read them to the class. They responded to one another's work, sharing critiques and compliments. As part of the unit, every student was required to submit one poem to the school's literary magazine. This assignment led to the highlight of the semester when Vern, a student of mine who was also the captain of the \ wrestling team, won second place in the literary magazine's poetry contest. When Vern's name was announced at a school-wide assembly, a series of emotions crossed his face: shock, dismay, and then—most amazingly—pride. By the end of class that day, Vern was signing copies of the school literary magazine in which his poem appeared. He had become, publicly, a poet! And by doing so, he had expanded his "portfolio of experiences"[4] to include poetry (Gee, 2004). I was pleased at the outcome of the Favourite Poetry Project; students no longer held an uncritical perspective of poetry. They had established personal connections with at least one work of poetry and provided public explanations for their choices—empowering activities that do not typify educational norms of working-class schools (Gos, 1995). Their resistance had not blocked effective learning; it had become a lever that enhanced the curriculum. These experiences helped prepare me for my students' reaction to our next unit.

Applications and Aspirations

Reduced funding of public entities has resulted in diminished resources for working-class students. Concrete illustrations of this neo-liberal phenomenon in a working-class school include fewer school counsellors, less available financial aid, and higher tuition costs at public institutions of higher learning. For working-class high school students, the effects are profound with respect to access to higher education.

Working-class students face reduced financial support and higher expenses, and working-class schools have fewer professionals to assist them. As the parent of a high school junior, I was familiar with the rites of passage for college entrance. There are innumerable details to negotiate. Although I understood the anxiety related to this process, the level of stress my students expressed about the college admission process, including the application essay, surprised me. Their reactions reminded me of their initial responses to the word "poetry"—except this time their resistance was laced with fear. They may have hated the idea of poetry, but they were terrified by the prospect of college.

I had intended to spend two or three class periods working with students to complete a sample college application and an essay to accompany it. As I introduced the assignments, however, I asked students to raise their hands if they had signed up for the SAT or ACT test. Students glanced around at each other but avoided eye contact with me. I considered this situation, studying my students as I walked around the room distributing handouts with test sign-up information. Then I asked individuals directly about taking the SAT and ACT. When I approached Margaret, a tall, outspoken, intelligent soccer player, she covered her face with her hands. "I can't do it!" she cried. "I'm so scared!" The intensity and authenticity of her reaction alerted me. At that moment, I understood that my students needed more than a little assistance writing college application essays. They needed a guide, a cultural translator willing to engage in genuine dialogue.

I considered the cultural matters that affect the college application process. One interaction illustrated the need to empathize with the experiences of this working-class population. While I was in the planning stages of this unit, I encountered the parents of one of my son's peers at a local supermarket. I have known these parents since our children (my son and their daughter, Angela) were five-years-old. Angela was an exceptional college candidate. She was a star athlete in three interscholastic sports and a member of the National Honour Society. Her overall average is well into the 90s. Furthermore, Angela is active in the community, coaching soccer and softball and volunteering for her church. Aware of Angela's credentials, I asked her parents about their daughter's college plans. In response, Angela's father shook his head. "It's going to depend on what she can afford. I don't know where it's written that we have to pay for college." He laughed, clearly expecting that I would agree, and then explained that Angela would probably attend the local community college for two years and then transfer, if at that point she has "… figured out what she wants to do." He and his wife agreed that going to college, without a definitive sense of what you were going to do with your education, represented a waste of time and money. This instrumental perspective of education is consistent with working-class culture. His wife picked up the issue of location, stating that Angela was not interested in leaving the area and that she and her husband were pleased about that. "Angela just likes it here. It's comfortable," she finished.

The local community college does not even require a high school diploma for admission; most students who go there have few other options. The conversation— the disparity between achievement and aspirations—haunted me for days. As I reflected, the situation began to make sense. Neither of the Angela's parents had attended college; in this context, community college was an experiential departure. Tuition and financial aid considerations can seem overwhelmingly complex; avoidance is one way of coping. Furthermore, should the parents have explored higher education alternatives to our local public community colleges, it is possible that projected expenses would have matched—or even dwarfed—their annual family income.

The reaction of these parents is consistent with working-class attitudes toward schooling (Gos, 1995; Heilman, 2004; Willis, 1977): Education should be practical; it is a commodity whose value is measured by direct increases in earning power. And proximity to family is significant; why pay room and board when you can stay at home? In addition, working-class parents often feel incapable of providing guidance and assistance. If private college or room and board are unaffordable, it makes sense to denigrate the importance of these opportunities. Heilman (2004) expands on this idea:

> Many working-class people have experienced some of the "hidden injuries of class," (Sennett & Cobb, 1972) resulting in low expectations about their status and chances for success. Rubin (1976, 1994) observed that the working-class families she studied did not have educational role models or access to information concerning college admissions, nor did they try to gain this information because their educated children would be lost to an alien way of life. (p. 76)

I reflected on these issues as I planned the unit. I realized that, even though my native culture was working-class, my portfolio of experiences, especially educational experiences, had altered my perspective. To serve as a transformational educator, I needed to understand, not censure. I developed activities and assessments with this in mind. The general objectives of the unit were to expose my students to the college admissions process with a sense of empowerment and possibility.

First, I acknowledged their fears and concerns. This alone was enlightening. Most of the students believed that "everyone else" (i.e., all the other upperclassmen) was confident, organized, decisive and competent. Providing the opportunity to share misconceptions created a sense of community that students sorely needed in this endeavour. Next, I enlisted the help of a knowledgeable, enthusiastic school counsellor. Then I involved the librarian, who—as the parent of a college freshman—was equally supportive. She offered access to software and the internet as well as personal experience with this process.

I introduced the unit, and then the school counsellor urged students to develop a range of college options and to aim high—beyond where most of them had ever contemplated. Our counsellor demonstrated software to expand students' horizons and stretch their understanding of career possibilities a college could provide. Then he showed them how to use the software to match their interests and strengths to various educational institutions. The librarian directed students to the College Board website, which offers a plethora of resources and college entrance tools. Thus scaffolded, students were free to explore opportunities and options for meeting the goals of the unit.

About half the students engaged in the process immediately, completing interest inventories and conducting thorough, interactive college searches. The rest of the class, however, was listless—still resistant. I circulated among them, sitting with students and trying to determine what factors were impeding their commitment to this task. The primary theme re-emerged: fear. This was no surprise, but the solution was unexpectedly simple. In a pattern that was remarkable to me in its predictability, I found that once their fear was revealed and acknowledged, it diminished. These students, virtually all of whom would, if they enrolled in an institution of higher education, be the first person in their families to attend college, needed to know that their fear was natural—typical—and not a sign that they didn't "belong" in college. As we talked to students, the counsellor, the librarian, and I shared our own experiences. All three of us are white (the entire faculty and staff of this district are white) and were raised in working-class communities much like the one where we teach. In addition, we were educated in public institutions. Although we now have graduate degrees, critical analysis of our own backgrounds enabled us to connect with our students. We had to avoid judgment and establish dialogue in order to provide a transformative educational experience. Together, we debunked myths and clarified processes. And by the end of the hour, the atmosphere of the class had changed from dread to anticipation.

By creating authentic objectives and opening a space for genuine dialogue, my colleagues and I had engaged students in a transformational pedagogical experience. Instead of judging students and their parents as deficient based on student resistance to an activity connected with (presumably desirable) upward mobility, we accepted resistance as part of our classroom's lived experience and used its contextual connections to construct new meanings and possibilities. Through explication and empathy, we had used dialogue to transform their experience of the college admissions process, allowing our working-class students the opportunity to think of themselves as classmates with people outside of their own cultural norms.

Conclusion

Both the poetry unit and the college entrance unit began with an academic, middle-class assumption: that what was being taught was, in fact, obviously worth learning. As a teacher, I believe in the value of poetry and post-secondary schooling. However, the content of my class was altered by the students' reactions—their candid resistance. They were resisting; I had to listen.

Transformative education requires schools to serve as spaces where students and teachers develop learning communities to engage in dialogue and critical analysis of themselves and their societies, ultimately shifting individuals and societies toward social justice (Rethinking Educational Change, 2006). Transformative educational approaches explore and validate cultural diversity, conflict and resistance. For teachers, validating resistance can seem senseless. Neo-liberal reform policies, wherein high-stakes assessments drive instruction and credentialing, leave no space for teachers to accept, much less foster, curricular resistance. Teachers are held accountable for student performance and there is barely enough time to cover curricula that will be assessed by state tests (Nichols, 2006; Dorn, 2007). However, the dynamics of neo-liberalism and the role of schooling in social reproduction provide a broader perspective for educators.

Had one student objected to poetry or complained about the SAT test, I doubt that I'd have changed my plans. But their responses were ubiquitous and universal; these students were telling me—through the language of resistance—about themselves and their culture. By listening to them and collaborating with colleagues, I was able to establish dialogue to create meaningful cultural connections that were inclusive, not exclusive. At the end of each unit, students had begun to reconstruct their identities, as I had mine. Perhaps, through pedagogical transformation, we had facilitated the development of working-class poets and first generation college applicants. Certainly, we had created a classroom culture in which resistance had become an energizing factor, not a divisive force. Students became participants in a dialogue rather than silent resistors. The possibilities of this approach are compelling, especially for working-class students in high school where resistance behaviours foster social reproduction.

A dialogic approach to education is in the best interests of teachers as well. Neo-liberalism has weakened union influence and reduced funding for public institutions. The regulatory effects of NCLB and similar legislation have resulted in demoralization and deprofessionalization of teachers. Historically, members of the white working-class have defined themselves against Others with respect to race and class. This has diminished the ability of the working-class to wield its own power through solidarity. Moreover, neo-liberalism has reinforced disparities in wealth, causing tremendous insecurity among working-class and lower middle-class people who are scrambling to maintain their socio-economic status. If white, once working-class, teachers can look beyond immediate conditions, they will certainly see the value of fostering solidarity with their working-class students—of all races. Despite portfolios of experience that place them (precariously) in the lower-middle class, teachers are ill-served by neo-liberalism.

In the years following the experiences described in this chapter, I have taken on a leadership role in the English department. Since becoming chairperson, I have begun to establish professional dialogue among teachers in order to create safe spaces to consider resistance to standards-based reform initiatives. Together, as a department, we have sought to implement engaging approaches to a summer reading requirement and adopted literature intended to connect with and extend the experiences of our students (including authors with diverse backgrounds and cultural perspectives). Our professional dialogue has also addressed the cultural disparities that exist between students and teachers, particularly in terms of social class and age/generational factors. Through such dialogue, we seek to reconceptualise our students' life experiences as different rather than deficient and to validate their cultural norms as we explicate those of dominant classes.

Engaging students in pedagogical transformation may offer a means to challenge existing neo-liberal power relations to channel the resistance that Foucault asserts is a perpetual constituent of power. True dialogue offers the possibility to facilitate solidarity between working-class students and their teachers.

QUESTIONS FOR REFLECTION

1. In a political climate permeated by demands for assessment-based "accountability", what challenges do teachers face? How can educators simultaneously serve their students, themselves (vis-à-vis their own profession) and the state?
2. Using instructional time to accomplish objectives such as "establish meaningful dialogue" could be perceived as inefficient or non-productive. What factors should teachers consider when planning instruction that is both practical (in an assessment-based political culture) and aimed toward social justice?
3. The pressures of neo-liberalism exacerbate the tensions between students and teachers, often causing teachers to reject students whose failure will reflect on them as professionals. Identify arguments that are essential for teachers to understand in order to maintain a sense of their obligation to students. How might teachers work collectively to develop partnerships with members of their working-class communities?

NOTES

[1] The public school featured in this chapter is located in Western New York.
[2] "Regents" exams are assessments developed, administered, and scored under strict state regulations.
[3] This is revealed by data from a previous study at this setting that involved both school discipline records and student interviews.
[4] Gee (2004) associates social class to a person's "portfolio of experiences." That is, the range, extent, and type of experiences a person has are the basis for the social class to which that person relates.

* Note: Portions of the data in this chapter previously appeared in *Multicultural Perspectives,* and were adapted for use here.

REFERENCES

Anyon, J. (1981). Elementary schooling and the distinction of social class. *Interchange, 12*, 118–132.
Apple, M. (2001). *Educating the "right" way: Markets, standards, God, and inequality.* New York: Routledge-Farmer.
Bernstein, B. (1990). *The structuring of pedagogic discourse.* London: Routledge and Kegan Paul.
Brooks, D. (2005). *The education gap.* The Centre for Student Opportunity. Retrieved from www. CSOpportunity.org
Brantlinger, E. A. (1993). *The politics of social class in secondary school.* New York: Teachers College Press.
Carr, P. R., & Lund, D. E. (Eds.). (2007). *The great white north? Exploring whiteness, privilege and identity in education.* Rotterdam: Sense Publishers.
Dorn, S. (2007). *Accountability Frankenstein: understanding and taming the monster.* Charlotte, NC: Information Age Publishing.
Finn, P. J. (1999). *Literacy with an attitude: Educating working-class children in their own self-interest.* Albany, NY: State University of New York Press.
Foucault, M. (1993). Power as knowledge. In C. Lemert (Ed.), *Social theory: The multicultural and classic readings* (pp. 475–480). Toronto, CA: HarperCollins.
Freire, P. (2007/1968). *Pedagogy of the oppressed.* New York: Continuum.
Gee, J. P. (2004). *Situated language and learning: A critique of traditional schooling.* New York: Routledge.

Giroux, H. A. (2003). *The abandoned generation: Democracy beyond the culture of fear.* New York: Palgrave MacMillan.

Gos, M. W. (1995). Overcoming social class markers: Preparing working-class students for college. *The Clearing House, 69*(1), 30–34.

Graf, G. (1999). The academic language gap. *The Academic Clearing House, 72*(3), 140–142.

Gunzenhauser, M. G. (2006). Normalizing the educated subject: A Foucaultian analysis of high-stakes accountability. *Educational Studies, 39*(3), 241–259.

Hartmann, J. (2003). *Power and resistance in the later Foucault in 3rd annual meeting of the Foucault circle.* Cleveland, OH: Southern Illinois University at Carbondale.

Heilman, E. E. (2004). Hoosiers, hicks, and hayseeds: The controversial place of marginalized ethnic whites in multicultural education. *Equity and Excellence in Education, 37*, 67–69.

Hursh, D. (2005). Neo-liberalism, markets and accountability: Transforming education and undermining democracy in the United States and England. *Policy Futures in Education, 3*(1).

New York State Education Department. (1999). *Description of SURR school groups.* New York State Department of Education. Retrieved from http://www.emsc.nysed.gov/nyc/PDFs/SURRDescr.pdf

New York State District School Report Card Comprehensive Information Report. (2007). Albany, NY: New York State Education Department.

Nichols, S. L. (2006). *Collateral damage: How high-stakes testing undermines education.* Cambridge: Harvard Education Press.

Orfield, G., & Kornhaber, M. L. (2001). *Raising standards or raising barriers.* New York: The Century Foundation Press.

Orfield, M. (2002). *American metropolitics.* Washington, DC: The Brookings Institute.

Pinsky, R. (1997). Favorite Poem Project.

Rethinking Educational Change. (2006). *A vision for transformative education.* Conference Proceedings. 3rd Vittachi Conference, Al Akhaway University, Ifrane, Morocco. Retrieved from http://www.transformedu.org/Conference/Proceedings/AVisionforTransformativeEducation/tabid/70/Default.aspx

Rubin, L. B. (1976). *Worlds of pain: Life in the working-class family.* New York: Basic Books.

Rubin, L. B. (1994). *Families on the fault line: America's working-class speaks about the family, the economy, race, and ethnicity.* New York: HarperCollins.

Sennett, R., & Cobb, J. (1972). *The hidden injuries of class.* New York: Knopf.

United States Department of Education. (2003). Retrieved November 13, 2004, from No Child Left Behind: http://www.ed.gov/nclb

Weis, L. (2004). *Class reunion.* New York: Routledge.

Wertsch, J. V. (1991). *Voices of the mind: A socio-cultural approach to mediated action.* Cambridge: Harvard University Press.

Willis, P. (1977). *Learning to labor: How working-class kids get working-class jobs.* New York: Columbia University Press.

Yates, M. D. (2007). *More unequal: Aspects of class in the United States.* New York: Monthly Review Press.

DAVID ALBERTO QUIJADA CERECER

5. EVERYDAY EDUCATION

Youth Rethinking Neo-Liberalism by Mapping Cultural Citizenship and Intercultural Alliances

Young people participate in social relations; use and invent technology; earn, spend, need, desire, and despise money; comprise target markets while producing their own original media; and formulate modes of citizenship out of the various ideologies they create, sustain, and disrupt (Maira & Soep, 2005, p. xvi).

INTRODUCTION

Today's youth live in a world of ever-expanding transnational and globalized free markets that have generated political decisions that do more than liberalize the economy. Neo-liberal governments have sought to regulate the lives and behaviors of youth and their parents (Rose, 1990). For example, neo-liberal governments discipline parents into parenting practices that advocate for their children's education through consumption, shopping and increased privatization. Youth and childhood have become synomonous with future productivity and profits to invest, which will supposedly lead to a better society (Qvortrup, 2005). Neo-liberalism coupled with corporate curricula and pedagogies have brought economic theories close to home, making enterpreneurialism a normal part of everyday life as reflected in daily discourse, popular culture, and today's consciousness (Grossberg, 2005; Steinberg & Kincheloe, 1997).

Immersed in ideology, neo-liberalism works with conventions of citizenship that resemble strategies invoked by markets such that today's youth learn how to question their individual actions as they make calculated risks to protect their rights (Strickland, 2002). This forging of neo-liberal subjects pushes youth to be more autonomous, encouraging authoritative subjectivities to develop from economic markets that promote greed, individualism, and liberal choices for investors and investments (Mitchel, Marston & Katz, 2003). However, if neo-liberalism has pushed youth to equip themselves with skills and knowledge that demonstrate how they make an "enterprise of themselves" (Apple, 2001), then I ask how do youth undo and rethink the neo-liberal subject that understands human relationships through enterpreneurialism. While "neo-liberal youth subjects" may be socialized as politically independent decisions-makers who act as free moral agents, then what of those youth who work across communities and forge intercultural alliances,

B. J. Porfilio and P. R. Carr (eds.), Youth Culture, Education and Resistance:
Subverting the Commercial Ordering of Life, 75–89.
© *2010 Sense Publishers. All rights reserved.*

as active contributing members of society. What if youths' actions are not measured as "earnable competence" for future individual gains but are, instead, measured as how they advocate for social justice as civil rights for others?

Herein lies the tensions underpinning this chapter's concerns. I begin with the premise that youth are active, contributing members of society, who are not citizens in the making. Discontent with youth as objects of socialization, or as passive consumers of culture who have been constructed as future trajectories who need to be protected or policed until they reach adulthood (Lesko, 2001; Johnson, 2001; James & Prout, 1998), I move to discuss what youth do. Aware of the neo-liberal context that informs the lives of youth, I argue that youth, especially marginalized youth of color, have not been adequately discussed or represented as citizens who care and contribute to society beyond resistence.

In this chapter I draw upon a larger ethnographic study. I discuss how a diverse group of youth participants (ages 15 to 18 years) engage in what I understand to be cultural citizenship practices to forge intercultural alliances across communities by facilitating diversity workshops for other youth in school settings. Participants—a group of working poor, urban youth of color—utilize art and performance to interrogate assumptions underlying their position as youth and their role as citizens. By facilitating and participating in youth-led diversity workshops, participants work across difference and reflect upon their disparate social positions. Involved with a youth empowerment project that I call Youth Dismantling Oppression (YDO), youth participants do more than facilitate diversity workshops as they create alliances across race, class, gender and sexual orientation.

Analysis of data-sets reveals how participants communicate across difference and position themselves collectively in society as cultural citizens, who demonstrate civic and social engagement, build community, and take action in relation to racism, sexism, and homophobia through everyday conversations and engagement. By collectively sharing, critically self-reflecting, stepping out of their comfort-zone, making mistakes, challenging and asking questions of each other, youth participants embody intercultural alliances, and develop a type of everyday social justice education, one that reconstitutes duties and responsibilities associated with being a member of a community. They co-create educative space in and out of school to forge new identities that disrupt traditional definitions of citizenship tied to legal status, patriotic nationalism, age group and individualism (Buckingham, 2000; Maira & Soep, 2005; Lesko, 2001).

I challenge neo-liberal assumptions underlying youths' active contributions and investments in community as something other than individual, self-regulating, autonomous and detached from civic responsibility. Specifically, I discuss how YDO's youth facilitators attempt to create space to forge social justice as everyday education in and through their direct relationship and involvement with race, class, gender and sexuality. The chapter first reviews the relevant literature on youth studies and youth culture, which help connect citizenship and intercultural alliances beyond categories that frame youth in opposition to adulthood. The discussion helps us get beyond the literature put forth by academics who have created placid portraits of youth so as to view youth as active participants in today's society.

The research-setting, participants, and methods are then outlined. I draw upon one ethnographic approach to illustrate how youth interns are mapping citizenship and intercultural alliances to forge social justice as everyday education. The chapter concludes by broadening notions of citizenship to include intercultural alliances, framed by a discussion that explores how cultural citizenship practices emerge in everyday education and are mapped onto the present lives of today's youth.

Re-framing Categories of Youth: Citizenship and Intercultural Alliances

Youth have been constructed as future trajectories that represent a transitional life-stage located somewhere between children's fantasies and adult realities (James, 1986; Sibley, 1995). Framed through biological and physiological stages of development, youth are always growing into adulthood or out of childhood (Schwartzman, 2001). Understood in opposition to adulthood, youth presume a unidirectional state of development that has been described through arbitrary markers of time (Austin & Willard, 1998; Vadeboncoeur & Stephens, 2005). For example, age typically determines when youth can legally drive, consume alcohol, vote, or work. Such age categories presume youth to be developmentally incomplete and irrational human beings who need guidance and protection before legal privileges.

Immersed in socializing discourses, youth are bound within adult-centered institutions (i.e., family, school, legal) that purport to educate them towards adulthood and protect them from the realities of daily life. In this linear developmental context, youth behaviours become easy targets for adults to police. Discipline and protection become normative practices that define youth-adult relationships. Bound in contradictory practices, some youth are marked as deviant, sexually promiscuous, and violent who need discipline and punishment while others, are associated with innocence and purity need protection.

More than undergoing biological changes, youth unquestionably are born into an ideology and a political struggle over the category of youth. The struggle to define youth is shaping today's economic and political conditions. Youth have become the signifier of society's "last and lost" hope (Sibley, 1995) who are "caught in the crossfire of modernity" (Grossberg, 2005). Understood as a social construct, "youth" remain what Cohen (1972) referred to as "today's folk devils." In other words, youth are to posses the alleged power to generate moral panics that do more than call into question their life stage or potential ability to participate fully as rational adults. For example, struggles over youth are immersed in ideologies that secure nation building by policing the boundaries of social order and citizenry (Lesko, 2001; Maira, 2005; Mizen, 2004). Echoing rally cries that nostalgically yearn for a time "when children were children," political platforms continue to advocate, "doing it for the children," despite conservative agendas that strip away legal rights for future citizens, including youth.

Recent scholarship has sought to change the way we understand the lives of youth by applying "citizenship" as a more inclusive transitional social category than adulthood (Pole, Pilcher & Wiliams, 2005; Invernizzi & Williams, 2008). Parallels between youth and adults come in close proximity as transitions toward citizenship are no longer solely marked by age, nationality, birth rights or legal rights to vote but rather by social and economic inequalities (Invernizzi & Williams, 2008; Jones & Wallace, 1992; Coles 1995). Increased privatization and market-driven economies have resulted in labor shifts and increased unemployment that unequally affect youth in society (Miles, 2000). Youth and youth culture are not only targeted by markets, but today's youth are also making more decisions about where they work and how they spend their time and money (Canclini, 2001) No longer excluded from traditional adult economic worlds, today's youth are directly involved with popular culture and markets tied to economic consumption and employment across the globe (Dolby, 2003; Willis, 2003; Schneider & Stevenson, 1999; Milner, 2004).

New global markets have transformed everyday relationships such that citizenship coupled with civic responsibilities and rights look more and more like consumer rights. More specifically, Canclini (2001) describes how citizenship is being reconfigured such that our collective rights and interests are discussed through commodity consumption in the private realm and not as "abstract rules of democracy" (p. 5). In this context, youth developmental models can no longer keep up with consumption as a stage of growth towards independence and citizenship (Pole, Pilcher & Williams, 2005). Today's free market and global capitalism have generated economic conditions that invoke youth as active citizens (not passive or incomplete citizens) to freely consume at the expense of social investment (Strickland, 2002; Maira & Soep, 2005; Dolby & Rizvi, 2008).

Living under tenuous economic conditions have made youth aware of their uncertain futures such that they cannot afford to be passive consumers. Acting as neo-liberal subjects, some youth have adapted market-driven responses that make "right choices" and develop "authoritative dispositions" to acquire skill sets for the purpose of promoting their individual success in society (Demerath & Lynch, 2008). For example, today's affluent student population has sought to weigh the "benefits and costs" of extra curricular activities, community involvement, and service learning as they compete in school and apply to elite higher education institutions. However increasing numbers of youth, especially poor urban youth of color, continue to be marginalized by "rational choices" that replace citizenship, civic responsibility and political empowerment with individualization, zero tolerance, decreased social services, increased militarization and the criminalization of youth (Robbins, 2008; Giroux, 2002).

Rather than upholding citizenship as yet another marker of development that is used to illustrate how youth are socialized into consumption that parallels today's market -driven economy, I move to understand how youth shape and reconstitute citizenship rights and responsibilities to forge social justice for others. By centering the lives of urban youth of color, I ask: How do young people generate opportunities and create educative space to connect citizenship, intercultural alliances and social justice as everyday education?

Citizenship

Youth activism has transformed how society views youth participation in today's global market (Shepard & Hayduk, 2002) and in immigration reform debates (Quijada, 2008a). Such youth-led involvement identifies democratic process outside of birth rights, age, or developmental paradigms (Ginwright & James, 2002). No longer easily subsumed into precise age configurations that solely understand youth as future economic and political trajectories who are passively controlled by adults and institutional structures, today's youth are civically involved and invested in their communities (Ginwright, Noguera & Cammarota, 2006). In some cases these interactions draw upon everyday discourses, experiences and practices that reflect a type of citizenship that is more aligned with daily life than arbitrary markers of time and age (Lesko, 2001; Maira, 2005). For example, Flores and Benmayor (1997) describe a cultural citizenship less invested in legal status and more attuned to forms of activism that advocate immigrant and civil rights not tied to legal citizenship status. How might citizenship exclude a whole range of possibilities that youth create through their own socialization, community involvement and political participation in the real world (Smith, Lister & Middleton, 2005)?

Social Justice and Intercultural Alliances

Recent youth studies have sought to move beyond traditional oppositional strategies of resistance by presenting new political critiques of late modernity by young women (Harris, 2004), queer youth (Driver, 2008), immigrant youth, youth of color, and youth in general (Dolby & Rizvi, 2008; Ginwright, Noguera & Cammarota, 2006). New ways of thinking of how youth organize themselves and build community to collectively address societal concerns collide with every increasing demand for consumption. In this context, cultural production and community-building create new spaces to produce political activity. Similarly, Duncombe (2002) reminds us that cultural resistance develops from "free spaces" that allow for contestation and negotiation to flourish.

Increasing numbers of youth use new technologies to create cyber communities, and develop unregulated communication to politically organize (Loader, 2007). Today's youth are also producing online blogs and/or zines to connect with the global community and promote alternative politicized identities (Schilt & Zobl, 2008). For example, Kenway and Bullen (2008) describe how young cyberflâuners are critically reflecting upon real world conditions and putting forth alternative positions by hijacking multi-media (i.e., culture jamming, cyber-girl websites, etc.), and contesting dominant ideologies (i.e., corporate greed, and gendered stereotypes). This commitment to align and create space is best captured in the following quote by Harris (2004):

> If we understand these spaces providing transient places to take time out and try on new identities and alliances, to network and share ideas and information with other youth away from regulation, they can be imagined as a kind of pre-or even newly figured participatory politics. At the least they can be acknowledged for their ongoing use as rest stops, fissures, places for momentary reflection, and connection (p. 180).

Youth Dismantling Oppression (YDO): Setting, Participants and Methods

The following research-study is based on a larger on-going ethnographic study of youth facilitators and interns who participate in a youth empowerment project I refer to as "Youth Dismantling Oppression" (YDO). YDO is a small, low-budget non-profit organization that supports youth-led performance (i.e., gorilla art or interactive theater[1]), spoken word, critical dialogue, hands-on activities and direct community involvement to talk across difference and build relationships across race, class, gender and sexuality. Originally, the project was designed as a 2-year ethnographic study to describe the experiences of an ethnically diverse group of interns as they moved through high school and facilitated diversity workshops for other youth in school settings. The study continues to grow and evolve to include how the original cohort utilize and transform skills developed as youth diversity trainers to forge social justice in college, graduate school, and/or the workforce. This chapter reports on findings based upon youth interns and facilitators who are in high school.

Central to the project is the diverse youth population that YDO draws upon. YDO brings together an ethnically diverse group of youth who range in age between 14–18 years of age. While youth facilitators self-identify as "activists" who are working-class or "poor," "urban" and either biracial (Black and Latino (a), White and Black), Black or Latina/o, the youth interns who participate in YDO's youth-led diversity workshops cut across gender and self-identify with diverse political affiliations, sexual orientations, and economic social positions.

Data were collected through participant observations, informal interviews and natural-occurring tape-recorded conversations in and out of diversity workshops, while eating, commuting between workshops or on the street while practicing performances with facilitators. Focus groups and individual interviews were conducted with interns and facilitators coupled with naturally occurring tape-recorded conversations between interns as they debriefed their facilitation of diversity workshops. Participants also shared their personal journals with other interns, the YDO staff and the researcher.

What follows is an ethnographic portrait of a diversity workshop, followed by descriptions and exchanges from youth interns and facilitators who participated in this and other youth-led workshops. This event, as in other sessions, represents how participants actively discuss their involvement and facilitation in workshops beyond their role as facilitator or intern in Youth Dismantling Oppression. I discuss how these exchanges generate possible sites to forge social justice and intercultural alliances that may re-articulate membership in society and may challenge neo-liberal conceptions of citizenship.

Youth Making Space to Wiggle and Move into Citizenship: An Ethnographic Snapshot?

Youth facilitators arrived early and set up the classroom's desks into a circle. The Civics teacher, Ms. Holland, had purchased snacks (i.e., cookies, potato chips, and sodas), which she had left on her desk for students and facilitators to eat during the workshop. As students arrived, Anita, one of the four youth facilitators wrote statements (i.e., try it on, no put downs, share space) on the dry-erase board while the other three facilitators (Joel, Brian, and Maria) invited students to have snacks. There would be 15 high school students (mostly 9th and 10th graders) who had volunteered to stay after class for the workshop.

Facilitators began by introducing themselves by first name and by explaining the previously written statements as ground-rules for participation and listening. Joel stated, "Today we are going to talk about oppression and how it affects our community." Anita who sat next to Brian whispered something to Maria. She interrupted Joel as well as the students sitting next to her. Joel ignored Anita by continuing to explain, "Oppression happens to all kinds of people, youth and adults, people of color, the poor, gay and lesbian communities." However when both Anita and Maria uncontrollably giggled, Joel could no longer ignore the disruption. Annoyed, Joel looked directly at Anita and asked, "Why are you laughing?"

The classroom grew silent and one student jokingly said, "Now you're in trouble." Anita without hesitation replied, "It's just that you sound so boring, so old and tired. I thought we were going to bring music and pictures to talk about oppression?" Joel responded, "Yeah, but we didn't bring music because you don't like rap or hip-hop." Anita did not hold back, "It can't just be about what kind of music you like or what music is played on the radio. Most of that stuff is all about pimps, hoochies and hoes, anyways." Joel shouts back, "Who said anything about music on the radio. I'm talking about real beats and rhymes that are political and that talk about me and my community."

Some students unsure by Joel and Anita's exchange fidget with their pencils and squirm in their seats as they wait for Anita to respond. Instead Maria who has multiple piercings and black eyeliner says, "Why is it always about hip-hop? I hate that music and the look that goes with it." Now the classroom grows silent anticipating how Joel will respond to both Maria's and Anita's allegations. Some students look to me, almost expecting I will intervene, but instead I ignore their gaze and act equally startled by the developing conflict.

Brian breaks the anticipation by shouting, "freeze!" as he assumes the role of "narrator" in this improvised scene of "interactive theater." He asks the class, what just happened? Maria, Joel and Anita sit exaggeratedly motionless in their seats. One student explains, "They (Anita and Maria) are bored with him (Joel) talking all grown up and not bringing music to the workshop." Several students are upset over the way facilitators are talking about hip-hop. For example, one student says, "I don't know why they have to talk bad about music, whatever type of music it is—its just music." Still others argue: "Why do girls always think hip-hop is sexist? I think its racist." There's a lot of White folks that listen to hip-hop and they don't even care." My parents are always on my back about what I listen to because they think the music is all the same." Brian attempts to facilitate discussion by encouraging students to talk directly to Joel, Anita and Maria, "Go ahead ask them directly see what they think." Facilitators remain in character as conversation continues to develop between students. One student questions, "Is it the music? What about how it gets bought and sold, isn't that bad?" This encourages another student to say, "Yeah, I agree with Joel, a lot of music doesn't even make it on the radio and so we don't even get to know what's out there."

Some participants look confused, and one participant asks, "When is the workshop going to start?" Still others contribute to the developing conversation by broadening analysis to the production and marketing of music. For example one student asks, "Do you know what it costs to get a record deal and produce an album," while another follows with, "A lot of people don't want to listen to political talk. What sells is the body grinding, booty shaking music." One student describes some of the music he and his friends are producing, "We just burn and cut it up in our garage and it won't ever be played on the radio, but it makes a difference to us." People engage conversation as it moves from personal preference to the marketization of music with specific focus on how race and gender gets shaped in and out of private and public spaces of consumption and production.

Disentangling Broad Contours: YDO, Citizenship, Intercultural Alliance

While participants were new to the workshop and did not know each other, they willingly engage in conversation, take risks, and ask questions despite their differing positions. Participants' exchanges speak more to their collective commitment to engage social issues than to the innovative pedagogical moves that youth facilitators invoke through interactive theater. For example, I have come to understand this emergent process as "talking relationships" that youth collectively produce when afforded opportunity to talk across differences by referencing their active participation in the world (Quijada, 2008b). These co-created "conversational contexts" I discuss as a participatory process of learning constituted in dialogical relations of conflict and coalition that go beyond diversity trainers' paid responsibilities (Quijada, in press). However, how do these frames of analysis make space for youth to wiggle more freely from the constraints of today's citizenship? More specifically, how do youth-led interactions invoke intercultural alliances as a form of social justice and membership in community? What follows is my attempt to map the broad contours of YDO, cultural citizenship, and intercultural alliances. With these general characteristics I move to discuss points of intersection where youth produce everyday education and forge social justice as active members of society.

Youth Dismantling Oppression (YDO)

Youth facilitators are not just duplicating standardized curricula that treat students as passive receivers of information. Instead they create opportunities to critically interrogate real world conditions and improvise possibilities for change. Unlike traditional school based theater productions that rely upon pre-packaged scripts to narrate, perform and actualize a play writer's story, facilitators embody and act out their own life conditions. Their use of interactive theater comes from a place of realness that reflects their life story and encourages sharing. For example, Anita describes how, "Me and Maria had never done this activity before. We were really kind of just going off the top of our heads." But as Maria describes, "It was cool because it made us see what we live in now. What we would live. You know through the opinions of other people who talk and even argue with us." In this way, youth diversity trainers do more than teach diversity or discuss issues underlying oppression. Instead they develop opportunities for youth to discuss their opinions and to struggle collectively with concerns that affect their own communities as well as others' communities.

Both Maria and Anita agree: Workshops are introductions to new conversations that develop when "conversations are open." They encourage "opinionated folks to talk off the top of their heads." Facilitators have witnessed how participants strive to "go a little deeper by expressing another point of view." For diversity trainers, workshops represent more than a set of exercises that lead to outcomes. Instead they are spontaneous educative spaces that are dependent upon collective participation. As Joel describes, "It depends on you guys (the group).... your response whether I would have did something different and how I would have thought about my involvement, you see I'm always learning and trying new things in this group." Facilitators expect people to talk (including themselves), which for Brian is as simple as, "if you got something to say, say it." Brian like the other facilitators realizes that some folks dominate conversation by being overly focused on, "me, me, me I know the answer, I know, I know." Despite their struggle to engage and collectively involve others, they do think it is important to fully participate beyond facilitation.

There is a type of presence and concern underlying youth facilitators' commitment to teach diversity and oppression that reflects how they confront societal concerns. For example, youth facilitators draw from real world experiences, which might include how they consume music but it also includes how their identities and participation in community are reflected in the consumption of music. Facilitators are quick to make themselves vulnerable by bringing oppression close to home and putting it forth to discuss shared inequalities they collectively address. For Joel like the rest of the facilitators this requires "gett(ing) off subject and gett(ing) into something that's real personal to them."

Intersecting Positions: Lola's Everyday Education

YDO is a space where facilitators use body and voice to interact and create opportunities to collectively discuss social concerns. More than pre-fabricated skits, facilitators engage interactive theater through personal experiences they discuss as shared reality. While active discussion over social inequality is in itself an important act of political activity, it is also a co-created space to forge intercultural alliances across difference. This co-created space, albeit temporary and contested, invokes a type of citizenship that questions membership in community rather than accepts a legal or birth right in community. The following represents Lola's reflections weeks after the workshop took place. Her self-reflective process demonstrates movement towards a type of citizenship that strives for collective involvement and works across difference, while it simultaneously grapples with individual privileges.

Lola after the workshop began to question how intersections of race, gender and sexuality operate to construct membership in society. Discontent with how music videos represent her role as a woman, Lola wrote in her journal:

When I think of how I am looked at and put down simply for coming to this world with a certain gender, I feel devastated and angry. I feel taken for granted and classified because of what I am and who I am. However I also

83

feel like I'm being 'downed' for being heterosexual as if I got it easier. I may not be struggling because I'm not gay/lesbian. But I am struggling being an African American young lady trying to be positive and just make it far in this world. What if we all suffer and we all struggle for equality. . . if somebody would define our understanding of what it actually is, 'to have it made' or 'easy,' then maybe we could all realize what rights we all don't have.

Interactive theater and workshops represent more than a one-stop shop to think critically about oppression. Lola discusses her participation in workshops because it reflects her everyday realities. As she describes, "It really wasn't about the music they was talking about. It's about how we talk about ourselves, 'who we are and how we are part of something,' when we talk about stuff like music. Like a lot of people were talking about being Black hip-hop artists or female rappers but then I started thinking about all the other people who are missing. What would they say and how come I'm not talking about them at the workshop." Lola took note of her own biases as she rode the bus home from the workshop. She wrote in her journal:

I don't know why but I felt disgusted by the two men kissing on the bus. It caught me off guard because I know I wouldn't have felt that if they were women. But something else caught me. It was like a strong feeling that I was doing something different and that I was part of something. I really stopped to look. I saw myself. I could see how I was acting. Those two guys and me, we really are part of the same community and yet we don't even talk.

In a different journal entry, Lola writes how "distanced" she felt between people and how stuck she felt because of capitalism:

America has free trade. Anyone can make money in the open market anyway they want. This too means that any one person can own everything and sell everything however they please even if it means creating a monopoly. Capitalism is bad because it means that people will do whatever it takes to make $ or change however much $ they want. Just look at gasoline and electricity in California or what it costs for a gallon of milk.

When I questioned Lola about the journal entry, she explained how stuck she felt because, "I have to do everything by myself. I feel powerless because I'm not supposed to ask for help to be a part of the world, I'm just expected to do it by myself." Lola sought alternatives, "I just want to act with people, you know change my individual thinking so it isn't just about me." More specifically, Lola describes, "I don't want to walk around thinking I'm the only person in the world." In this way, Lola reflected upon her own contradictions as she sought support to question her position in the world. Lola explained, "I know I'm [sic]not supposed to enlighten other people just because I might know something. But I also think its [sic]about sharing what we've learned by describing how we have changed. Yet I don't think it's about being the ultimate crusaders of diversity. It's a tough balance to talk about our differences and to each other but it has to be done."

Lola finds refuge in the sharing of her journal and in poetry. She wrote the following verses for a friend who she could no longer argue with because as she describes, "he's too stuck to talk with." The following verses helped Lola communicate across her frustrations because they described what she saw happening around her world that he could not:

> Jose can you see by the cops flashing lights what so proudly we hailed is so greatly deceiving. Whose big jails and locked bars seem to stop our good fight behind borders we watch while they ignore our great plight. And the rockets red glare. The bombs bursting in air gave proof thru the nite that their fears were still there Jose does our tar spangled banner still wave? For land of the free and the home of the brave.

Lola's reflections reveal her concerns with how to live as a member of a multicultural society. More than acts of resistance, Lola puts forth a reflective process that draws upon her real world relationships to rethink her participation in the world. Rather than draw upon direct involvement, Lola engages with previous conversations and experiences she has had with oppression and diversity to extend one of the workshops' goals. In this context, Lola is able to critically reflect upon her interactions by sharing her journal, questioning her relationship to homophobia, thinking broadly about institutions, and making real world observations that interrogate her position in the world. Through this process we see how Lola's reflections draw upon lived experiences that relate to other members of her community. Equally significant is how her collective effort promotes community building as a necessary part of being a member of community.

Conclusion

I have argued that YDO's participants and facilitators critically invoke everyday education through real life experiences that reflect their participation in the world as active members of society. YDO's interactive theater generates space for youth to not only talk across difference, but to also reflect upon how they might align their differences to forge social justice. More than citizens in the making, youth produce meaning through their everyday experiences to extend what it means to citizens. In this context citizenship is less attributed to one's political affiliation, patriotic duty, or voting experience, but rather directly related to forms of political literacy, civic engagement and social justice that promote equity, civil rights and full democratic participation for others (see Lund & Carr, 2008). As witnessed by Lola's reflections, participants do not necessarily rely upon a mainstream citizenship discourse to emphasize their active political participation or explicit resistance to policy and legislation that shapes their legal rights. Instead citizenship is shaped by everyday education that is revealed in their shared and disparate experiences with marginalization and through social positions that intersect across race, class, gender and sexuality.

Immersed in contradictory discourses that frame youth as active consumers, socially pathological, or in need of adult protection, the participants unconsciously reposition themselves as critically reflective members of society. They draw from lived experiences and put forth ideas to build community that are not anchored in truth claims or in active resistance. Participants demonstrate a type of presence and awareness of real world conditions that they themselves understand to be malleable and debatable, especially as they attempt to locate their position in society. Through this cultural practice, youth participants co-create and support opportunities to critically engage, question and reflect upon societal conditions rather than uphold and legitimize pre-established norms that define what is citizenship or who is a citizen.

Here participants embody "education as a political enterprise" as they develop awareness of power and institutional constraints through critical engagements with each other and as they continue to promote their activist role and participation in the world (Friere, 1973). In this way, participants invoke what Freire (1998) refers to as an "epistemological curiosity" to challenge educational compliance and common sense practices that schooling and other socializing institutions uphold. More specifically, participants demonstrate a commitment to actively engage with differences between and across groups such that their own ideas about society and the marginalized positions they hold are called into question. For example, youth participants demonstrate how they implicitly rethink constructions of youth, re-frame categories of citizenship and co-create space to discuss intercultural alliances beyond consumption in the following ways:

- Participants actively talk across difference and willingly reflect upon their social positions.
- Participants extend conversations that deal directly with race, class, gender and sexuality into their everyday lives and experiment with new affiliations between groups.
- Participants draw upon their shared experiences to interrogate and question their individual social positions.

In this process, YDO's participants embody and enact a type of citizenship whereby responsibilities are collectively shared, accounted for and reflected upon as members of a community. This participation calls into question their social position not as a means to protect their future investments, but rather to collectively endure and struggle over their present conditions. While late modernity encourages today's youth to grow into authoritative subjects who make rational choices or become victims to market-driven decisions, YDO and youth participants temporarily violate and trouble such a protocol. With today's society adhering to practices that myopically believe that markets will solve all, youth participants return to questions of accountability that invoke reflexivity and question their participation and position in the world not in relation to themselves but to others as well. Herein lies a temporary albeit necessary moment to engage a type of citizenship that collectively questions and rethinks the rational choices today's youth has inherited in late modernity. Of concern is how youth engagement and civic participation compete with neo-liberalism and how free-market forces diminish youth participation, action and reflection that promote critical citizenship. Therefore, critical educators, activists, and other concerned must develop pedagogical practices, create educative spaces, and generate research initiatives that promote critical citizenship and the everyday education needed to undo neo-liberalism.

QUESTIONS FOR REFLECTION

1. How might youth empowerment projects support and better incorporate youth led initiatives to forge social justice and rethink cultural citizenship practices?
2. What types of citizenship conversations and/or pedagogical moves develop when youth share their everyday experiences with race, class, gender and sexuality?
3. How might citizenship and intercultural alliances be discussed as a potential site of struggle over neo-liberalism?

NOTES

[1] Gorilla art or interactive theater refers to an improvised performance that primarily relies upon actors' bodies and voices to script a story. The audience is invited to participate and join into the performance.
[2] I use pseudonyms for participants in the study.

REFERENCES

Apple, M. W. (2001). Comparing neo-liberal projects and inequality in education. *Comparative Education, 37*(4), 409–423.
Austin, J., & Willard, M. N. (Eds.). (1998). *Generations of youth: Youth cultures and history in twentieth-century America.* New York: New York University Press.
Buckingham, D. (2000). *The making of citizens: Young people, news and politics.* New York: Routledge.
Canclini, G. N. (2001). *Consumers and citizens: Globalization and multicultural conflicts.* Minneapolis, MN: University of Minnesota Press.
Cohen, S. (1972). *Folk devils and moral panics: The creation of the mods and rockers.* Oxford: Basil Blackwell.
Coles, B. (1995). *Youth and social policy.* London: University College of London Press.
Demerath, P., & Lynch, J. (2008). Identities for neo-liberal times: Constructing enterprising selves in an American suburb. In N. Dolby & F. Rizvi (Eds.), *Youth moves identities and education in global times* (pp. 179–192). New York: Routledge.
Dolby, N. (2003). Popular culture and democratic practice. *Harvard Educational Review, 73*(3), 258–284.
Dolby, N., & Rizvi, F. (Eds.). (2008). *Youth moves: Identities and education in global perspective.* New York: Routledge.
Driver, S. (Ed.). (2008). Queer youth cultures: Performative and political practices. *INTERRUPTIONS: Border Testimony(ies) and Critical Discourse/s.* New York: State University of New York Press.
Duncombe, S. (Ed.). (2002). *Cultural resistance reader.* London: Verso.
Flores, W. V., & Benmayor, R. (Eds.). (1997). *Latino cultural citizenship: Claiming identity, space, and rights.* Boston: Beacon Press.
Freire, P. (1973). *Pedagogy of the oppressed.* New York: Continuum.
Freire, P. (1998). *Pedagogy of freedom: Ethics, democracy and civic courage.* Lanham, MD: Rowman & Littlefield.
Ginwright, S., & James, T. (2002). From assets to agents of change: Social justice, organizing, and youth development. *New Directions for Youth Development: Theory, Practice, Research, Winter,* 27–46.
Ginwright, S., Noguera, P., & Cammarota, J. (Eds.). (2006). *Beyond resistance: Youth activism and community change: New democratic possibilities for practice and policy for America's youth.* New York: Routledge.
Giroux, H. A. (2002). The war on the young: Corporate culture, schooling, and the politics of "Zero tolerance". In R. Strickland (Ed.), *Growing up postmodern: Neo-liberalism and the war on the young* (pp. 35–46). New York: Rowman and Littlefield Publishers, Inc.

Grossberg, L. (2005). *Caught in the crossfire: Kids, politics, and Americas future.* Boulder, CO: Paradigm Publishers.

Harris, A. (Ed.). (2008). *Next wave cultures: Feminism, sub-cultures, activism.* New York: Routledge.

Harris, A. (2004). *Future girl: Young women in the twenty-first century.* New York: Routledge.

Invernizzi, A., & Williams, J. (Eds.). (2008). *Children and citizenship.* Los Angeles: Sage Publications.

James, A. (1986). Learning to belong: The boundaries of adolescence. In A. P. Cohen (Ed.), *Symbolising boundaries: Identity and diversity in British cultures* (pp. 151–171). Manchester: Manchester University Press.

James, A., & Prout, A. (1990). *Constructing and reconstructing childhood: Contemporary issues in the sociological study of childhood.* New York: Falmer Press.

Johnson, H. B. (2001). From the Chicago school to the new sociology of children: The sociology of children and childhood in the United States, 1900–1999. In S. L. Hofferth & T. J. Owens (Eds.), *Children at the millennium: Where have we come from, where are we going* (pp. 53–93). New York: Elsevier Science Ltd.

Jones, G., & Wallace, C. (1992). *Youth, family and citizenship.* Milton Keynes: Open University Press.

Kenway, J., & Bullen, E. (2008). The global corporate curriculum and the young cyberflâuner as global citizen. In N. Dolby & F. Rizvi (Eds.), *Youth moves: Identities and education in global perspective* (pp. 17–32). New York: Routledge.

Lesko, N. (2001). *Act your age! A cultural construction of adolescence.* New York: Routledge Falmer.

Loader, B. D. (Ed.). (2007). *Young citizens in the digital age: Political engagement, young people and new media.* New York: Routledge.

Lund, D. E., & Carr, P. R. (Eds.). (2008). *Doing democracy: Striving for political literacy and social justice.* New York: Peter Lang Publishing, Inc.

Maira, S. (2005). The intimate and the imperial: South Asian Muslim immigrant youth after 9/11. In S. Maira & E. Soep (Eds.), *Youthscapes: The popular, the national, the global* (pp. 64–81). Philadelphia: University of Pennsylvania Press.

Maira, S., & Soep, E. (Eds.). (2005). *Youthscapes: The popular, the national, the global.* Philadelphia: University of Pennsylvania Press.

Miles, S. (2000). *Youth lifestyles in a changing world.* Buckingham: Open University Press.

Milner, M. (2004). *Freaks, geeks, and cool kids: American teenagers, schools and the culture of consumption.* New York: Routledge.

Mizen, P. (2004). *The changing state of youth.* New York: Palgrave.

Pole, C., Pilcher, J., & Williams, J. (Eds.). (2005). *Young people in transition becoming citizens.* New York: Palgrave Macmillan.

Quijada, D. A. (2008a). Reconciling research, rallies and citizenship: Reflections on youth led diversity workshops and intercultural alliances. *Social Justice, 35*(1), 76–90.

Quijada, D. A. (2008b). Marginalization, identity formation, and empowerment: Youth's struggles for self and social justice. In N. Dolby & F. Rizvi (Eds.), *Youth moves: Identities and education in global perspective* (pp. 207–220). New York: Routledge.

Quijada, D. A. (in press). Youth debriefing diversity workshops: Conversational contexts that forge intercultural alliances across differences. *International Journal of Qualitative Studies.*

Qvortrup, J. (Ed.). (1990). *Studies in modern childhood.* Basingstoke: Palgrave.

Robbins, C. G. (2008). *Expelling hope: The assault on youth and the militarization of schooling.* New York: State University of New York Press.

Rose, N. (1990). *Governing the soul.* London: Routledge.

Schilt, K., & Zobl, E. (2008). Connecting the dots: Riot Grrrls, Ladyfests, and the International Grrrl Zine Network. In A. Harris (Ed.), *Next wave cultures: Feminism, sub-cultures, activism* (pp. 171–192). New York: Routledge.

Schneider, B., & Stevenson, D. (1999). *The ambitious generation: America's teenagers, motivated but directionless.* New Haven, CT: Yale University Press.

Schwartzman, H. B. (2001). Introduction: Questions and challenges for a 21st-century anthropology of children. In H. B. Schwartzman (Ed.), *Children and anthropology: Perspectives for the 21st century* (pp. 1–37). Westport, CT: Bergin and Garvey.

Shepard, B., & Hayduk, R. (Eds.). (2002). *From ACT UP to the WTO: Urban protests and community building in the era of globalization.* New York: Verso.

Sibley, D. (1995). *Geographies of exclusion: Society and difference in the west.* New York: Routledge.

Smith, N., Lister, R., & Middleton, S. (2005). Young people as 'Active citizen': Towards an inclusionary view of citizenship and constructive social participation. In J. P. C. Pole & J. Williams (Eds.), *Young people in transition: Becoming citizens?* (pp. 159–177). New York: Palgrave.

Steinberg, S., & Kincheloe, J. (Eds.). (1997). *Kinderculture: The corporate construction of childhood.* Boulder, CO: Westview Press.

Strickland, R. (Ed.). (2002). *Growing up postmodern: Neo-liberalism and the war on the young.* New York: Rowman & Littlefield Publishers, INC.

Vadeboncoeur, J. A., & Patel Stevens, L. (Eds.). (2005). *Re/Constructing "the Adolescent": Sign, symbol, and body.* New York: Peter Lang.

Willis, P. (2003). Footsoldiers of modernity. *Harvard Educational Review, 73*(3), 390–415.

DARREN E. LUND AND MARYAM NABAVI

6. RENEWING YOUTH ENGAGEMENT IN SOCIAL JUSTICE ACTIVISM

INTRODUCTION

For the past several decades there has been a strong academic interest in engaging young people in promoting diversity and inclusive practices in schools. However, the current research on anti-racism education and multicultural education has included relatively few analyses of the experiences of student activism within educational settings. We undertake this study[1] as a means of analyzing how and why young people engage in existing social justice programs, and documenting some of their challenges, in their own words. For a variety of pragmatic reasons we are focusing on the Prairie region of Western Canada, which includes the provinces of Manitoba, Saskatchewan and Alberta. We seek to understand the experiences of students and teachers who form voluntary coalitions or who undertake specific school projects to address issues of racism and discrimination. This chapter focuses on findings from the youth participants in our research project, critically interrogating the neo-liberal socio-political structures that influence how social justice activism is undertaken and understood.

Research consistently reveals that many young people continue to experience racism, even in the proudly multicultural nation of Canada (Alberta Human Rights Commission, 1993; Creese & Kambere, 2003; Pruegger & Kiely, 2002; Statistics Canada, 2002). Considering young people's experiences, engaging student activists in educational research is one response to the growing conservative backlash toward youth culture. Giroux (2006) notes that "youth" as a social category is too often used as a catalyst for panic and fear. Similarly he has observed: "If not represented as a symbol of fashion or hailed as a hot niche, youth are often portrayed as a problem, a danger to adult society or, even worse, irrelevant to the future" (Giroux, 2003, p. xiv). Other than the limited data typically generated by standardized surveys of "youth attitudes" on a broad range of issues (e.g., Bibby, 2001; Griffith & Labercane, 1995) students have rarely been engaged in meaningful ways in educational research on anti-racism activism, and their understandings of the nuances of work in this area remain largely unexamined. This project engages student participants as leaders in the ongoing struggle to make schools more equitable within the limits of current neo-liberal approaches to education.

Researcher Location

This project builds on the researchers' combined expertise and experiences in anti-racism research and collaborative youth activism. We accept the complexity of gendered and racialized relations, and have conducted this research from

B. J. Porfilio and P. R. Carr (eds.), Youth Culture, Education and Resistance:
Subverting the Commercial Ordering of Life, 91–107.
© *2010 Sense Publishers. All rights reserved.*

differing subject positions. Most helpful for us has been the work of James Banks (1998) on the typology of cross-cultural researchers; we have come to better understand our roles as an "external insider" and an "indigenous insider," respectively, and the particular types of risks and benefits he notes for each role (pp. 7–9). Further, we have both strived to "conduct research that empowers marginalized communities" (p. 15). As a high school teacher, Lund formed a youth activist program, *Students and Teachers Opposing Prejudice (STOP),* which remained a collaborative anti-racism activism program for two decades (Alberta Human Rights Commission, 2000). For the past several years, he has sought a clearer understanding of the practical realities of anti-racism work among activist teachers and students (Lund, 1998, 2003, 2006), and has recently explored more specifically how his own privileges as a straight, able-bodied White male have played themselves out in his scholarly and activist work (Lund, 2008; Lund & Carr, 2007). Nabavi is a first-generation immigrant woman of color of Iranian descent. She has extensive experience working in the social justice field, has lived and worked overseas, and has been involved nationally in social justice research, policy and activism. We have been fortunate to serve on several committees together, and to have worked on a number of activist and research projects on social justice issues over the past several years. The interlocking forms of oppression are embedded in both of our personal and political work and we have found our collaboration, particularly through duoeth-nographic research approaches (e.g., Lund & Nabavi, 2008a), to be mutually rewarding.

Background/Rationale

As researchers and activists, we have an overarching goal to understand and analyze the complex nature of how students and teachers form and sustain coalitions and collaborative projects in schools. Although we see our work as emerging from the contested field of multicultural education, we also acknowledge the many problematic aspects that have been associated with this broad tradition. The word "multicultural" rarely evokes a neutral response in this country. Canada remains one of the few nations with multicultural ideals entrenched in national government policy, although it is often seen as being about preserving the status quo, viewing (non-White) immigrants as in need of assistance to assimilate to mainstream norms, taking a superficial view of culture and identity, and ignoring issues of systemic racism and intersections with other oppression. Some Canadian researchers (e.g., Ghosh, 1996; James, 2005; Moodley, 1995) have outlined approaches to multicultural education that pay some attention to issues of power and privilege but it remains a field that is viewed by many as an inadequate response to racism. Likewise, in the US, many multicultural education proponents have moved toward more critical engagement with multiple forms of oppression, with a focus on building more democratic schools and societies (Banks, 2002; Sleeter & Bernal, 2004).

A contemporary collective neo-liberal denial that ignores the abiding existence of racism in Canada is refuted by a long history of discriminatory government policies and practices. Since Europeans began arriving, systematic discrimination has been practiced against individuals and groups based on racist ideologies and ethnocentric views, beginning with the colonization of this continent's indigenous peoples. Official government policies, composed and imposed with popular public support from White European-origin citizens, served to entrench racialized segregation in schools, forced assimilation of Aboriginal Canadians, racialized immigration restrictions, promoted anti-Semitism, enabled the mistreatment of Chinese immigrant railway workers, and orchestrated the displacement and internment of Japanese-Canadians (see Boyko, 1995). For various reasons, such unsavory aspects of Canadian history have been missing or understated in current social studies school materials. Anti-racism education advocates for the close attention to these and more contemporary manifestations of racism in schools and society (e.g., Dei, 1996; Dei & Calliste, 2000).

In spite of the precarious relationship between multiculturalism and anti-racism, within the Canadian context, they cannot be explored independent of one another because the underpinnings of multiculturalism often shape anti-racism discourse in Canada. Directing specific attention to anti-racism education includes a critical and dynamic understanding of racism, refined and revised in light of emerging insights from our collaboration with research participants. Clearly, racism is just part of a larger and intertwined set of social and institutional practices and policies that create and preserve an inequitable playing field. Groups most typically affected cannot easily be categorized or described in simplistic terms, and have personal agency of their own, as clearly outlined by a growing number of cultural theorists and researchers (e.g., Giroux, 2003; McCarthy & Dimitriadis, 2005; Yon, 2000). Our approach emerges from a critical theoretical stance of "integrative anti-racism," described in greater detail in the section that follows. In our educational research we strive for solidarity with political struggles across issues of race, ethnicity, class, gender, sexual orientation and other contested elements of social identity (e.g., Dei & Calliste, 2000; Sleeter & Bernal, 2004; Solomon & Levine-Rasky, 2003). We have followed Hall's (1992) theorizing on culture and identity, a perspective that recognizes race as a social construction while acknowledging the racialized context of schooling and the pervasiveness of racism.

Many students and teachers have chosen to organize initiatives to foster acceptance in schools across North America, but relatively few sources exist for meaningful guidance in forming, sustaining, and studying school-based coalitions with a focus on eliminating all forms of oppression. A pilot project for this research sought to answer this need by developing an interactive, web-based Diversity Toolkit[2] resource for school activists based on interviews with student and teacher activists. The researchers made use of this resource as a way to focus this investigation on actual uses and understandings of how students and teachers implement social justice initiatives.

Canadian public schools are microcosms of our pluralistic society and exciting locations for studying how we might best approach living productively in a democracy with diverse social differences in this country. They can also be sites of conflict based on differences in social identity with their growing diversity mirroring Canada's recent demographic changes (Li, 2003) including dramatic increases in the foreign-born population in the past few decades (Statistics Canada, 2006). Developing proactive educational approaches to reflect the cultural diversity brought about by immigrant and refugee students needs to honour Li's reminder that integration is not simply about confining people to rigid expectations and norms; rather, "integration is about giving newcomers the right of contestation, the legitimacy of dissent, and the entitlement to be different" (p. 330).

An ever-growing body of academic literature in both Canada and the US shows promising efforts to reflect cultural sensitivity in teaching materials, training and practices (Dei & Calliste, 2000; Marx, 2004; Nieto, 2004; Sleeter, 1996; Solomon & Rezai-Rashti, 2001). Recent educational research that examines administrative and policy changes necessary to address the growing ethnocultural diversity in schools (Apple, 1999; Corson, 2000; Ghosh & Abdi, 2004) has offered numerous insights into educational reform, including the need to address non-discriminatory hiring practices, adequate representation of marginalized groups in curricular materials, culturally sensitive educational programming, respectful parent and community engagement, and other specific approaches to attaining equity and social justice for all students.

Turning to the lived experience in schools, the researchers have designed this project to examine the views of young people engaged in collaborative, school-based approaches to fostering integration as one possible response to the complexities that accompany ethno-cultural and other diversity.

Theoretical Framework

Dei's (1996) notion of "integrative anti-racism" is used as an entry point for focusing our attention on a small number of specific school-based efforts to address discrimination and inequities in collaborative ways. Integrative anti-racism addresses the "problem of discussing the social constructs of race, class, gender, ability and sexuality as exclusive and independent categories" (Dei, 1996, p. 55). Although the race, class, gender trilogy has been a focal point for social justice scholars and activists for years, integrative anti-racism builds on existing knowledge to develop a framework specifically for education. It is an activist praxis that disrupts singular, hierarchical meta-narratives as it problematizes the myriad interlocking forms of oppression. It acknowledges that different forms of oppression have different social effects, yet there is a "theoretical inadequacy of singular, exclusive constructs when it comes to explaining the diversity of human experiences of oppression" (p. 56).

Our study attended to "the social meaning of race and its intersections with other forms of social difference and oppression" (Dei, 1996, p. 19) such as the gender, ethnicity, sexuality, country of origin and migration patterns. Exploring issues of race as they intersect any of these social identities makes integrative anti-racism a valuable approach for the study of youth activism. We defined anti-racism activism for this research as direct action by a voluntary coalition of students and teachers to raise awareness or bring about social change toward eliminating racism and other forms of discrimination. Anti-racism activism can include organizing educational programs, displays, group activities, awareness events, media campaigns, and other political engagement on issues of difference and ethnicity from a critical lens that acknowledges links with other forms of oppression. Our interviews were with people who had direct involvement in any social justice initiative that tackled issues of race, gender, class, ability and sexuality. The list of guiding questions for the interviews (Appendix 1) explored what links, if any, existed in youth anti-racism involvement with other forms of oppression, as well as the level of analysis and connection made by students in their mobilization efforts.

Methology

Four long-time social justice activist colleagues collaboratively generated initial research questions for a pilot study. The researchers formulated guiding but flexible research questions generated from experiences and research in this field. Seeking a respectful and collaborative engagement with the everyday activism of the student participants, the researchers adopted features of a critical ethnography, an approach to research that addresses issues of power, inequity and hegemony (Carspecken, 1996; Creswell, 2007). While paying deliberate attention to our own values and assumptions, the researchers sought to understand participants' perspectives in their own terms, through a collaborative interview process of discovery and analysis (Fine & Weis, 1996).

Lund positioned the pilot study as a vehicle both for facilitating and evaluating anti-racism activism, and as an instrument of community-building among committed teachers and students. Rather than deny or downplay our past experiences in the field, the researchers in this study utilized their roles as "insiders" to obtain more relevant and sound data. The two main guiding research-questions were:

1. How do secondary high school students conceptualize and articulate their anti-racism activism?
2. How might these understandings, based on the lived experiences of school-based anti-racism activists, inform research, policies and programming for immigrant, refugee, and other marginalized students?
3. What, if any, are the analyses of secondary high school students in the ways that their anti-racism activities are a response to neo-liberal values and practices in formal schooling?

During the initial phase of the project, the researchers surveyed existing programs and resources, including recent research conducted on the use of specific anti-racism and diversity resources across this particular region. Then, interviews were held with 13 high school activists (students and teachers) who had recently undertaken projects to foster the acceptance of immigrant students within their schools. Field visits then ensued, which entailed meeting with activists in major cities in each of the Prairie Provinces. Activists were selected using a variation of convenience sampling methods, primarily through word-of-mouth, and contacts with community workers, teachers and other professionals, and others in the social justice field. The researchers conducted field observations and in-depth collaborative interviews with seven youth and six adult participants following protocols of critical ethnography (Carspecken, 1996). Efforts were made to sample a diverse mix of students from schools representing a range of cultural and socio-economic demographics and a balance of gender, age, and other characteristics. This chapter focuses on data from interviews with the seven student participants.

Interviews of approximately one hour in length were held in familiar and private places where interviewees felt comfortable sharing their thoughts away from other students or teachers. Insights from these few students are not meant to be representative of a larger population of activists but rather to provide insights into the specific motivations of a few student activists whose views have much to offer scholars and policy-makers in this field. The interviewers' past experiences with collaborative youth anti-racism work created an opportunity to share experiences reciprocally and to discuss at length some of the aspects of this work that are usually only shared within insular activist communities.

The interviewees ranged in age from 15–20 years old, and were either attending high school or volunteering with peers in school-based initiatives. The interviewees came from diverse range of socio-economic, cultural and ethnic backgrounds, representative of the demographics of Alberta, Saskatchewan, and Manitoba (Statistics Canada, 2006). The interviewees came from two distinct camps; the first group can be broadly characterized as privileged middle-to upper-class youth, a majority of whom are White and who were introduced to this work through supportive activist parents. For example, this was the case with Amanda[3] and Stephanie, who commented that their families' activism background and anti-racism dinner table conversation had been instrumental to their current social consciousness. Both Amada and Jason, whose father had been leading students in anti-racism initiatives for the past 30 years in his role as a teacher, reflected that their engagement in this work felt like a natural progression in their learning and development, and neither could identify an "ah-ha" moment that led them to this work. Likewise, Maya said, "My personal belief is that people are shaped by their circumstance. So my family is heavily involved in all aspects of our community… everyone in my family is really upfront about things like that, so they influenced me in taking initiative." This group of four students felt empowered and supported in all their pursuits, and in all cases they expressed that they felt a duty to the work because of their heightened social consciousness.

The other three student interviewees came from much different backgrounds; they were either first generation Canadians or had immigrated to Canada and expressed that either they or their parents had personally experienced racism. These students often wove stories of their families and immigration into the mix of reasons that they were committed to anti-racism work. Michael, who came to Canada as a refugee from Southern Africa, said that exposure to poverty in his home country has made him realize that in Canada people suffer differently, and that being Black is a major impediment in Canadian society. He broke down while recalling a conversation: "We also talked about what it's like for new immigrants when they come to the country. How others make fun of them, how they pronounce the words... [crying]." Jasmine, like Michael, immigrated to Canada with her family and commented that, because she had lived in poverty in the Philippines, her commitment to anti-racism work was simply "a way to give back."

Interview Findings

The participants' level of analysis of the concepts of racism and integration varied greatly, ranging from a grounded understanding of the multiple and complex dimensions of racism and its social and political implications for immigrant and refugee students, to an engagement in activism because of the participants' very personal, raw experiences. Although all of the students we interviewed understood that there was a need to challenge the *status quo* in terms of how racism manifests itself in Canadian society, their approaches toward school activities were wide-ranging, and roughly followed Banks' (2002) analysis of forms of multicultural education—from cultural contribution, to additive, to transformative, to social action approaches (pp. 29–32). Specifically, the students we interviewed organized school activities that ranged from traditional multicultural sharing, to creating awareness in safe and inclusive school environments, to more confrontational grassroots action.

Specific projects included formalized programs by teachers for students, such as creating a video-commercial for combating racism as part of a nation-wide competition. In this case, the students had little anti-racism awareness; through a very collaborative process, they intuitively created a powerful video depicting the emotional and psychological effects of racism. Another project included an overnight refugee simulation exercise, in which students experientially learned about some aspects of being a refugee, specifically segregation based on ethnicity, age, gender and other aspects of social identity. Interestingly in this case, racism became a catchall phrase for any form of oppression that students were experiencing. Another project included a well-established, multi-school initiative for creating awareness of multiple forms of oppression, namely racism, in which youth leaders are chosen to participate in and, with additional training, eventually lead sessions for their peers.

There were also a number of youth-initiated groups and events. The broad range included a school-wide multicultural show as an effort to build understanding of other cultures and minimize hallway racist comments to a more engaged social justice group. Here, students identified various causes they wanted to be involved in and, through their process of involvement, created awareness and engagement among other students in the school. In a different scenario, one of the participants shared that during his junior high school years, he and his friends became increasingly aware of racism in his city and took to the streets to confront racist behaviours; their involvement became more sophisticated as they went on to build websites with pertinent anti-racism information, engaged fellow students, and eventually began organizing national-level anti-racism conferences and events.

The overarching theme of the interviews was critical awareness of—and resistance to—the dominant socio-political contexts in which the interviewees found themselves. Embedded within this broader theme and pertinent to all interviewees were three themes: 1) how and why they got involved; 2) the social impact of their involvement; and 3) their success and challenges. These themes had emerged in recent social justice research with student activists (Lund, 2006), and are echoed by specific salient questions on youth agency (Giroux, 2003; Lund & Nabavi, 2008a) and literature on youth sub-cultures (Hall & Jefferson, 2003; McRobbie & Garner, 1976; Nayak, 2003; Willis, 1978).

Reasons for Involvement

There are arguably as many personal reasons for getting involved in school social justice projects as there are student activists. With this small but diverse group of student leaders, their earliest interests in equity issues ranged from painful personal experiences with racism and discrimination in Canada, to acting on global awareness of injustice, to growing up within families that encouraged and promoted anti-racism activism, to sheer accident. For Michael, immigrating to Canada after his father died, his initial drive to choose to work in a coalition to promote social justice was borne from his own lived experience:

> The drive came from my personal education. I was raised in a really poor family and we didn't have much. We had to have faith and believe in God that we'd have food. You know in South Africa people sell things on the streets; that's how we survived... But you weren't guaranteed an income. That's where my drive came from. I told my mom that there is a better life we can live.

Likewise, Jasmine, 19 years old, explained that her own experiences as an immigrant sowed the earliest seeds of her activism. Reflecting on her life in her home country in the Philippines she said, "We actually lived in poverty... so I know how hard it was. So [through my activist work I am] just trying to give back to my Mom." Jasmine also added her more self-directed motivations for engaging in activism in schools, including her own future academic and career advancement: "I think for me, it was just for myself... Maybe for me, getting involved will give me a chance to get more of the school and staff—also, to see where I'm going with my career. That's why I ran for [students' council] president, to see how far I could go with my skill." For both of these students, their experiences living in underprivileged, marginalized communities very much inspired their activist efforts in school.

Maya, a Canadian-born 17-year-old of Indian descent, offered a similar personal account of the origins of her wish to foster acceptance and promote social justice ideals: "I think the turning point for me was when I went back and visited my parents' home towns in India and you just see the people on the street begging for money. Ever since then, I've had the idea that if I can help, I will." Maya's socially conscious parents, living in a larger city on the Canadian prairies, also encouraged her to learn more about global concerns and to take action. Like Jasmine, Maya also explained that the intrinsic gratification she has received from helping is a key motivator for her:

> The other half of it is that knowledge—knowing someone out there needs help and knowing that you can help them, the smallest way possible, probably [makes] the biggest difference to me, personally—the personal benefits that I gain from it.

She added that failing to act while having knowledge of injustice would cause her to feel guilty: "You know if I never did all the things that I do, I would feel this huge cloud of guilt. Knowing that you didn't help when you could have."

For the White mainstream students—and for those students of color who came from families they described as being more affluent and upper-to middle-class—their expressed motivations for activism emerged more out of a middle-class value of wanting to help those less privileged, than by any personally experienced injustices. In many cases, family values and experiences also fostered their activism. Born and raised in a small city in Alberta in a White, middle-class home, Stephanie had travelled extensively but never to developing nations. The 20-year-old talked about what initially got her interested in social justice activism:

> My mom has always had a real interest in this type of stuff and she made me read the newspapers… We [siblings and I] always knew what was going on in the world. I wanted to do something but didn't know how to get involved; I knew what was going on in the world, but it was like, what do I do? I didn't know how to get into all those things.

Amanda, a White Canadian-born student from a city in Saskatchewan, now 20 years old and studying at university, talked of her family's strong influence on her wish to become an activist:

> I think it is mostly because of my family; my family has been activists in anti-racism so I had that support and had seen that from the time I was little. Before I became an activist myself, I'd seen and heard it and when you say about family making comments, my Dad taught in [a Canadian prairie city] for his whole career—he's a principal—and he taught mostly First Nations students so I knew them, beyond the stereotypes, from the time I was little. So I think it makes a difference when you know someone as a person and not just as a statistic.

Both of these students were made aware of suffering and injustice in the world by their families, encouraged directly by their parents to be a part of the solution, and cited this as a key motivator in their wish to become activists in school projects.

Jason, a 19-year-old from a large Alberta city, reported that he grew up in a family for whom social justice activism was a way of life. He explained, "I don't remember anything besides being involved. I don't know where the initial idea came from." For at least one other student, the activism was admittedly quite accidental, and stemmed from the filming of an anti-racist themed video commercial for a class project. Soni, 15 years old, whose affluent and well-educated parents immigrated to a large Canadian prairie city from India, said that her reasons for getting involved were almost accidental; "I think we filmed it and wanted to do well and get a good grade and that was the main initiative. But then when we won, we thought of the different possibilities. Different schools had started calling us and asked us to show it to them, so after that it started building." However, she also said she was not interested in doing further activism on this topic after graduating high school. For differing reasons, such as lived experiences, social awareness, and accessibility to initiatives, these students each showed a varying level of commitment to social justice activism, and all have taken deliberate efforts to foster inclusion and acceptance of diversity among their peers. As earlier mentioned, their experiences with school activism are varied, as are their analyzes and ability to articulate that work, but many of them share similar stories about the many challenges to undertaking social justice activism in schools.

Social Impact of Involvement

Specific challenges to the young activists' work in schools included a variety of social struggles with peers while undertaking projects that address racism and other discrimination. Throughout their interviews the students addressed the widespread apathy they noted among many of their peers toward issues of diversity. Michael said he struggled with "the students who don't really see the benefits of what we're doing. They think that it's just a waste of time and they just want to get out of school and relax and it's hard for us." Amanda remarked, "I would say the biggest challenge with dealing with anti-racism is dealing with the people who are quiet about it, so you don't get inside their head and you don't really know what they're thinking." Stephanie also encountered apathy when first trying to recruit for their school's social justice program, but only with certain segments of the student population: "Either they were into it and they were like, 'let's do something' or they didn't care. But it was all good. We actually had a few [student athletes] who were involved in it at the end. All cliques were involved in it." Talking about the same school, Samira recounted, "I guess the biggest challenge is getting [student] participation. I've actually never had trouble with people signing up; it's more getting the student body to participate."

Additionally, student participants brought up specific challenges of dealing with peers who do not seem to understand their deep commitment to social justice concerns. As Amanda recounted, taking a stand with peers on matters pertaining to racism or discrimination can come with negative consequences:

> I took a lot of harsh words from friends because they would make a joke and I'd be the one saying, "You know this isn't funny. Do you realize what you just said?" And so I think it was too much work for them; they didn't like that they couldn't just go out and have a good time because they knew that someone was listening to them. One friend in particular in high school would say, "Everyone stop talking, 'Love Everyone' is here" when I would walk into the room.

Being a young person comes with enough challenges as students make their way through secondary school, but to take on an activist concern for social justice issues added another layer to their already complex social life.

Jasmine recounted her disappointment with some students who attended an awareness-raising event about refugee issues. She had taken an active leadership role in organizing a role-play experience and found that a few students had chosen to attend the workshop for the wrong reasons:

My biggest challenge was that I heard some of the students saying, 'Oh we just wanted to come to this so we could skip school,' but I would try to get them into their roles. I was trying to get them to realize that this experience is very important. Some would say that they didn't know anything about refugees and just wanted to miss school, but at the end when I gave them letters from refugees, it was really effective.

Jasmine's perseverance and determination to educate her peers can serve as a helpful reminder of the need to persist; she is, in many ways, an admirable role model for teacher and community activists who may be tempted to give up with students they perceive as unmotivated.

Amanda said that she found that for social justice projects to be successfully implemented and sustained, there must be a certain level of peer acceptance. This often entailed efforts to "win over" the perceived student leaders. She explained how the "cool" factor can be crucial to a group's survival:

The schools where there has been a stigma to [activism] haven't been successful... and this is why the first core group of students is generally chosen. We try to get teachers to choose a couple of the "cool" kids and a couple of the "nerdy" kids that maybe are bullied, and we try to keep it so that it is fairly multicultural, so that it's not just a bunch of Caucasian people... In my school it was considered very successful, but also kind of a cool group to be a part of.

Stephanie also recounted how the first generation of her school's social justice club benefited from being seen by students as something "cool": "The original kids who started it were the cool kids, so they were in that crowd anyways. It was like 'Oh, you're in [the social justice club]? That's awesome.' It was like the basketball team." These students' candid observations shine light on the complex hierarchies that exist within schools and serve as reminders that any new school initiatives, even social justice clubs that seek to model equity and acceptance, must negotiate their own space within a school's complex social network.

For some students, their social justice efforts in school were met with overwhelmingly positive support. Erin's successful "March 21" anti-racism campaign attracted the attention of the outside media, and also her peers: "When they saw the effects that it had and that the people from 'Racism—Stop it' thought that it conveyed a good message, they felt good about it. And they were excited that it was going to be on TV!" With a similar success, Soni said that after the production of her anti-racist video project was undertaken with the cooperation of the larger school population, "they were all our friends and they were really great and supportive about participating. I think the whole school really showed a great sense of support, before and after." The recognition was also a source of pride for her parents: "They were so proud! They framed the pictures from the [newspaper]. My Dad tells his patients!"

Likewise, Maya was buoyed by the many benefits to the school community, some unplanned, that emerged from their social justice project:

> The main idea was to raise money for the grad committee, but in the end something more than that. And the kids in school, the ESL department specifically, really benefited from it because they got to showcase their talents and watch other people who had the same talents, but aren't necessarily in the same class. I think it made them feel more accepted, knowing that their culture isn't one that is going to have any racism against it. I think it really built up tolerance and a lot of people supported it and a lot of the staff supported it as well.

Maya said that she thought the acceptance she received at school for her leadership in a refugee simulation project spilled over in a positive way to her home life: "I think once you get recognition from your peers and from people at school and they let your parents know, they start to realize that it's worth it!" Some of the challenges these activists said they faced came from the adults in their community whose stereotyped or limited views on young people frustrated their activist efforts.

Successes and Challenges

There was a shared concern among our participants that youth are not being taken seriously by the adult community. Stephanie observed, "People don't take you seriously. You're a student, you don't care—they just don't take you seriously. It's actually really frustrating… I tried to do something with [an international aid agency] and they were like 'Sorry, you're not qualified' and I would think, I want to volunteer, what does it matter?" Her frustration with being marginalized or devalued due to her age was also evident in Michael's account of his experiences. He recounted trying to address a diversity issue at a meeting with teachers in his school: "I raised my hand and said that the majority of the population in the school is the students, so if you're going to talk about change, why don't you include us in the process? They looked at me and thought that I had a point." It takes moments of courage such as this for students to find and use their voices, in order to be taken seriously by adults and respected as valued collaborators in social justice activism.

When asked directly, many young people indicated that they wished to be involved in collaborative approaches to develop what Pruegger and Kiely (2002) call "youth created and directed solutions" to racism (p. v). Some young people actively seek greater involvement with an adult community that may be skeptical or unwilling to engage with young people. Stephanie noted that young people find themselves with a growing awareness of local and global injustices, but may become frustrated by what they perceive as adult indifference or inaction:

> Kids were noticing that something is going on. Things are happening in the world and they don't know what to do about it. They are growing up in a place where they were taught to something about it, even if it is racism.

So I guess the students were ready for it, to have something in place, even if everyone else wasn't... I tried to talk to adults but they were like, who cares. So it was really nice to have an outlet.

Stephanie said that she felt disillusioned by the ultra-right-wing conservative federal politician who represents her area, and expressed regret that her social justice group could not expect support from the political leadership in her region of Alberta:

I think it would be really nice to have...not so much government support, but people like [our Member of Parliament] to come out, but he's Conservative, so it wouldn't work! But anyway to have him come out and say, "Oh this is good," and to pay attention.

Her expressed desire for greater support from the adult community—particularly her teachers and the elected political leadership—serves as a clear call for more committed adults to come forward and take an active role in working collaboratively with young people in their efforts toward social justice.

For Michael, the adults within the school play a vital supporting role for student activism, and he hoped they would become motivated by the students' successes: "If we show other people the benefits of [our anti-racist program] then the teachers and principals will encourage us. I think teachers play a major role." Samira noted how helpful her adult mentors had been in organizing social justice themed events: "It's always sort of a challenge to plan these things—there is a lot of extra work and it's frustrating—but our teacher did a lot of that." Engaging students in collective efforts toward social justice in schools will entail more than having a token youth representative on a diversity committee or conducting a limited student attitude survey. Building authentic engagement and ownership involves teachers working alongside students in creating opportunities for trusting relationships to develop within respectful and reciprocal organizational structures (Lund, 2003), and confronting the forms of racism that are often imbedded in the views and experiences of White mainstream teachers (Marx, 2004; Solomon & Daniel, 2007).

Conclusion

These youth activists are excited to talk about the work they are doing and they express the importance of taking their activism work outside of their communities. Our research also revealed that they understand and are deeply committed to the ideals of social justice activism in relation to the intersections of social, cultural and political structures. However, although they did not appear to address specific intersections of race and culture with other forms of oppression in their interviews with us, we remain conscious of how our own views of an integrative anti-racism must attend to all forms of oppression. Perhaps the students felt limited by our lines of questioning, or by the nature of the specific projects on which they had worked.

Even when sharing the significant barriers and obstacles to the work, the students remained optimistic overall. As Amanda expressed it: "I think that the challenges are also the good things. I think when you confront those challenges and are able to overcome them is the best thing. If you weren't able to overcome any of the challenges, you wouldn't continue with this type of work." Amanda noted some observable improvements in her high school's climate regarding her peers accepting formerly marginalized students: "One thing we hear from kids is that people just get along better and that everyone's friends with that First Nations girl now. They're not scared to talk to her." Likewise, for Maya, it was sometimes the small changes she noticed that made her work worthwhile. She recalled the observable positive outcomes of a recent awareness raising activity: "I think it was seeing the reaction on their faces... We also got a lot of the shyer kids voicing their opinions."

Each of the emerging themes we generated from students' insights reflected our guiding ideas about how school activists initially get involved, experience and counter resistance from peers and adults, and foster acceptance and commitment among their fellow students. Together, these accounts and analyzes offer a revealing glimpse into the lived experiences of racism in a neo-liberal society, and the efforts of those who try to challenge it from within schools in communities. Following up on these initial findings with additional studies of young people engaged in activism on a broader range of oppressions and in a wider variety of school and community settings will be valuable. Further research may offer further implications for curriculum development, professional development for educators, teacher education, educational policy and government anti-racism policies, all framed within a resistance to the neo-liberal agenda and the positioning of students as consumers in a market economy.

These student activists said they were eager to talk about the anti-racism work they do and they expressed the importance of working collaboratively with adults and taking this activism outside of their communities. By acknowledging and studying their efforts we are answering Dei and James' (2002) call to educators to "enable students to use their individual collective agencies to work for change that furthers equality, thereby enriching a strengthening our social fabric" (p. 83). The strengths, limitations, opportunities and challenges expressed by our young interviewees uncovered potential areas we hope to explore more deeply as we analyze the intersections of their attitudes and practices with their adult counterparts. We look forward to sharing further findings and analyses from the teacher participants as both the research and our own ongoing activism continues to unfold.

QUESTIONS FOR REFLECTION

1. In what ways does the "integrative anti-racism" approach espoused in this study take into account the multiple and shifting identities of the participants? What aspects of identity are missing or are under-represented here?
2. Based on your reading of the youth voices in this chapter, and your understanding of how neo-liberal forces in education are shaping youth engagement, how can teachers and other non-youth allies best plan and undertake collaborative activism with students to tackle social justice issues?

3. Considering the range of responses to collaborative activism in schools—from apathetic, to dismissive, to highly positive—are there any conclusions we could reach about promising ways to encourage powerful forms of social justice activism in schools?

NOTES

[1] This research was supported by the Social Sciences and Humanities Research Council, through a research grant from the Prairie Metropolis Centre. An earlier account of this research was presented at "Immigration and Canada's Place in a Changing World," the 8th National Metropolis Conference in Vancouver, British Columbia, Canada. A revised version of the chapter appears in Lund & Nabavi (2008b) and is used with the kind permission of the publisher.
[2] The Diversity Toolkit is available for viewing at: http://www.ucalgary.ca/~dtoolkit
[3] All names used are pseudonyms.

REFERENCES

Alberta Human Rights Commission. (1993). *A survey of attitudes toward human rights and toward self in Alberta schools: Technical report.* Edmonton, Alberta, Canada: Government of Alberta.

Alberta Human Rights and Citizenship Commission. (2000, May). *Tools for transformation: Human rights education and diversity initiatives in Alberta.* Edmonton, Alberta, Canada: Government of Alberta.

Apple, M. (1999). *Power, meaning, and identity: Essays in critical educational studies.* New York: Peter Lang.

Banks, J. A. (1998). The lives and values of researchers: Implications for educating citizens in a multicultural society. *Educational Researcher, 27*(7), 4–17.

Banks, J. A. (2002). *An introduction to multicultural education* (3rd ed.). Boston: Allyn & Bacon.

Bibby, R. W. (2001). *Canada's teens: Today, yesterday, and tomorrow.* Toronto, Ontario, Canada: Stoddart.

Boyko, J. (1995). *Last steps to freedom: The evolution of Canadian racism.* Winnipeg, Manitoba, Canada: Watson & Dwyer.

Carspecken, P. F. (1996). *Critical ethnography in educational research: A theoretical and practical guide.* New York: Routledge.

Creswell, J. W. (2007). *Qualitative inquiry and research design: Choosing among five traditions.* Thousand Oaks, CA: Sage.

Corson, D. (2000). A pan-Canadian research program for more inclusive schools in Canada: The diversity and equity research background. In Y. Lenoir, W. Hunter, D. Hodgkinson, P. de Broucker, & A. Dolbec (Eds.), *A pan-Canadian education research agenda* (pp. 167–191). Ottawa, Ontario, Canada: Canadian Society for Studies in Education.

Creese, G., & Kambere, E. N. (2003). What colour is your English? *Canadian Review of Sociology and Anthropology, 40,* 565–573.

Dei, G. S. (1996). *Anti-racism education: Theory and practice.* Halifax, Nova Scotia, Canada: Fernwood.

Dei, G. S., & Calliste, A. (Eds.). (2000). *Power, knowledge and anti-racism education: A critical reader.* Toronto, Ontario, Canada: Fernwood.

Dei, G. S., & James, I. M. (2002). Beyond the rhetoric: Moving from exclusion, reaching for inclusion in Canadian schools. *Alberta Journal of Educational Research, 48,* 61–87.

Dei, G. S., James, I. M., James-Wilson, S., Karumanchery, L. L., & Zine, J. (2000). *Removing the margins: The challenges and possibilities of inclusive schooling.* Toronto, Ontario, Canada: Canadian Scholars' Press.

Fine, M., & Weis, L. (1996). Writing the "wrongs" of fieldwork: Confronting our own research/writing dilemmas in urban ethnographies. *Qualitative Inquiry, 2*, 251–274.

Ghosh, R. (1996). *Redefining multicultural education.* Toronto, Ontario, Canada: Harcourt Brace.

Ghosh, R., & Abdi, A. A. (2004). *Education and the politics of difference: Canadian perspectives.* Toronto, Ontario, Canada: Canadian Scholars' Press.

Giroux, H. A. (2003). *The abandoned generation: Democracy beyond the culture of fear.* New York: Palgrave MacMillan.

Giroux, H. A. (2006). *The Giroux reader.* Boulder, CO: Paradigm.

Griffith, B., & Labercane, G. (1995). High school students' attitudes towards racism in Canada: A report on a 1993 cross-cultural study. In K. A. McLeod (Ed.), *Multicultural education: The state of the art, Report #2* (pp. 144–151). Winnipeg, Manitoba, Canada: Canadian Association of Second Language Teachers.

Hall, S. (1992). New ethnicities. In J. Donald & A. Rattansi (Eds.), *"Race," culture, and difference* (pp. 252–259). London, UK: Sage.

Hall, S., & Jefferson, T. (2003). *Resistance through rituals: Youth sub-cultures in post-war Britain.* London, UK: Routledge.

James, C. E. (2005). Perspectives on multiculturalism in Canada. In C. E. James (Ed.), *Possibilities and limitations: Multicultural policies and programs in Canada* (pp. 12–20). Winnipeg, Manitoba, Canada: Fernwood.

Li, P. (2003). Deconstructing Canada's discourse of immigrant integration. *Journal of International Migration and Integration, 4,* 315–333.

Lund, D. E. (1998). Social justice activism in a conservative climate: Students and teachers challenging discrimination in Alberta. *Our Schools/Our Selves, 9,* 24–38.

Lund, D. E. (2003). Facing the challenges: Student anti-racist activists counter backlash and stereotyping. *Teaching Education Journal, 14,* 265–278.

Lund, D. E. (2006). Rocking the racism boat: School-based activists speak out on denial and avoidance. *Race, Ethnicity and Education, 9*(2), 203–221.

Lund, D. E. (2008). Harvesting social justice and human rights in rocky terrain. *The Ardent Anti-Racism & Decolonization Review, 1*(1), 64–67. Retrieved from http://www.arts.ualberta.ca/~aadr/contents vol1no1.htm

Lund, D. E., & Nabavi, M. (2008a). A duo-ethnographic conversation on social justice activism: Exploring issues of identity, racism, and activism with young people. *Multicultural Education, 15*(4), 29–34.

Lund, D. E., & Nabavi, M. (2008b). Understanding student anti-racism activism to foster social justice in schools. *International Journal of Multicultural Education, 10*(1), 1–20. Retrieved from http://ijme-journal.org/index.php/ ijme/issue/current

Marx, S. (2004). Regarding whiteness: Exploring and intervening in the effects of white racism in teacher education. *Equity and Excellence in Education, 37,* 31–43.

McCarthy, C., & Dimitriadis, G. (2005). Governmentality and the sociology of education: Media, educational policy, and the politics of resentment. In C. McCarthy, W. Crichlow, G. Dimitriadis, & N. Dolby (Eds.), *Race, identity, and representation in education* (2nd ed., pp. 321–335). New York: Routledge.

McRobbie, A., & Garber, J. (1976). Girls and sub-cultures: An exploration. In A. McRobbie (Ed.), *Feminism and youth culture* (pp. 112–120). London, UK: MacMillan Press.

Moodley, K. A. (1995). Multicultural education in Canada: Historical development and current status. In J. A. Banks & C. A. McGee Banks (Eds.), *Handbook of research on multicultural education* (pp. 801–820). New York: Macmillan.

Nayak, A. (2003). *Race, place, and globalization: Youth cultures in a changing world.* New York: Berg.

Nieto, S. (2004). *Affirming diversity: The sociopolitical context of multicultural education* (4th ed.). New York: Allyn & Bacon.

Pruegger, V., & Kiely, J. (2002). *Perception of racism and hate activities among youth in Calgary: Effects on the lived experience.* Calgary, Alberta, Canada: Community Strategies.

Sleeter, C. E. (1996). *Multicultural education as social activism*. Albany, NY: SUNY Press.

Sleeter, C. E., & Bernal, D. D. (2004). Critical pedagogy, critical race theory, and anti-racist education: Implications for multicultural education. In J. A. Banks & C. A. McGee Banks (Eds.), *Handbook of research on multicultural education* (2nd ed., pp. 240–258). San Francisco: Jossey-Bass.

Solomon, R. P., & Daniel, B.-J. (2007). Discourses on race and "white privilege" in the next generation of teachers. In P. R. Carr & D. E. Lund (Eds.), *The great white north? Exploring whiteness, privilege and identity in education* (pp. 161–172). Rotterdam, Netherlands: Sense.

Solomon, R. P., & Levine-Rasky, C. (2003). *Teaching for equity and diversity: Research to practice*. Toronto, Ontario, Canada: Canadian Scholars' Press.

Solomon, R. P., & Rezai-Rashti, G. (2001). Teacher candidates' racial identity development and its impact on learning to teach. *Directions, 1*(1), 52–59.

Statistics Canada. (2002). *Ethnic diversity survey*. Ottawa, Ontario, Canada: Government of Canada. Retrieved from http://www.statcan.ca/english/sdds/4508.htm

Statistics Canada. (2006). *Census trends*. Ottawa, Ontario, Canada: Government of Canada. Retrieved from http://www12.statcan.ca/english/census06/data/trends/Table_1.cfm?T=PR&PRCODE=01&GEOCODE= 01&GEOLVL=PR

Willis, P. (1978). *Learning to labour: How working-class kids get working-class jobs*. Farnborough, UK: Saxon House.

Yon, D. A. (2000). *Elusive culture: Schooling, race and identity in global times*. Albany, NY: SUNY Press.

SECTION II:
INFORMAL EDUCATION, YOUTH AND RESISTANCE

DARIUS PRIER

7. HIP-HOP AS A COUNTER-PUBLIC SPACE OF RESISTANCE FOR BLACK MALE YOUTH

INTRODUCTION

Scholars in the field of critical pedagogy suggest that youth are increasingly affirming and negotiating notions of self and identity through popular culture, in many cases in opposition to the hegemonic, neo-liberal culture of schooling (Giroux, 1996). That culture is organized around neo-liberal discourses about preparing urban youth with the "basic skills" they need for their expected role in a new globalizing labor force that is both more inequitable and more racialized. It is a culture, as Foucault (1979) would say, that is characterized by new discourses, practices, and technologies for the discipline, punishment, and surveillance of the urban student body (Carlson, 2005). Similarly, it is a culture characterized by cultural irrelevance, that is, by forms of curriculum and pedagogy that do not address the culture young people bring with them to school. All of this has resulted in a shift in identity among many urban Black males in U.S. urban contexts toward an investment in counter-spaces such as hip-hop (Dimitriadis, 2004). At the same time, this space has been shaped and negotiated out of a dialectal tension between the commodification and consumption of the hip-hop *industry* and a more "authentic," existential, critical, and empowering production of hip-hop *culture*. Tensions between the technical-rational process of education and schooling in relationship to the culture and industry of hip-hop presents new unpredictable challenges for these youth in an increasingly neo-liberal era of privatization and consolidation.

I argue that under conditions of neo-liberal hegemony in the U.S. over the past two decades or more, urban schooling has increasingly been restructured; it frequently embodies a technical-rational process of producing learning outcomes under highly-disciplined and alienating conditions, with a basic skills curriculum and a test-prep pedagogy that does not acknowledge or engage youths' everyday lived experiences, respect their culture and language, or engage them in struggles to construct empowering and self-affirming identities and to resist oppression. The technical control of the curriculum and the de-skilling of both teaching and learning in urban schools, are the latest expressions of instrumentalism and social efficiency models of schooling that have a long history in urban districts, dating back to the early Progressive era (Apple, 2001, p. 417). Carlson argues that the contemporary neo-liberal reform discourse on urban educational renewal emerged in the 1980s as economic functionalism, and a standards discourse "began to assume

B. J. Porfilio and P. R. Carr (eds.), Youth Culture, Education and Resistance:
Subverting the Commercial Ordering of Life, 111–128.
© *2010 Sense Publishers. All rights reserved.*

a more active role in shaping urban school policy and in overseeing school reform consistent with the 'bottom line' of test scores" (2005, p. 33). As teachers succumb to corporate imperatives of "banking models" in education and rote learning, how they critically engage with urban youth has become increasingly difficult. "As a result, a schism has grown between in-school and out-of-school culture, with unofficial curricula (e.g. rap music, film, etc.) and learning settings (e.g. community centers, churches, etc.) taking on increasing salience" (Dimitriadis, 2004, p. 7). In the new labor force, as the high school diploma in most urban schools has been aligned with the basic skill needs of the entrée labor, service-industry working-class, Black and Latina/o youth also begin to feel that the myth of upward mobility is just that, and that they are being oppressed and disempowered through the schooling process.

Neo-liberal corporate imperatives also play a role in the hyper-policing, surveillance, and control of Black male youths through disciplinary discursive economies that result in their disproportionate punishment in urban public schools (Carlson, 2005). "Currently the reality is that transnational capitalism plays an ever-increasing role in establishing the discursive parameters for educational policy and practice, and public schools (particularly urban public schools) are being called upon to assume a heightened role in the surveillance, policing and regulation of 'problem youth'" (Carlson, 2005, p. 22). Carlson suggests that disciplinary discourses, which circulate in and between micro-technologies of discipline, punishment, control, and surveillance, between institutions such as school systems and prisons, are rooted in a racial politics of fear that resonated from corporate boardrooms to suburban bedroom communities in the 1990s (2005, p. 36). When Black youths hung out in downtown shopping districts, waiting for buses or just meeting with friends, these public spaces also came under much tighter surveillance and policing in an effort to ease the fears of white shoppers who viewed a trip downtown as a trip into the "danger zone" (2005, p. 36).

In response to the neo-liberal cultural shift and changes in the social, economic, and political relations of urban displacement that have enlarged the private space of the corporate sector, while shrinking the public welfare state, many urban Black male youths have created and produced counter-public spaces through the cultural practices of hip-hop culture. That is, hip-hop emerged as a cultural phenomenon under conditions of economic exclusion, rampant unemployment and dead-end service jobs, along with the policing of "menacing" urban youths. From this perspective hip-hop provided at least the possibility of making a living and perhaps even the idea of getting wealthy, and it offered an outlet for play and creativity in a drab world (Kelley, 1997).

As urban youths respond to a neo-liberal culture of urban displacement, I theoretically analyze the culture of hip-hop as a way of life that emerges from the urban Black working-class community; and as a counter-public space of resistance through Stephen Haymes' critical pedagogy for Black urban struggle (1995). He focuses on the intersections between one's subjectivity and the role of culture in relationship to the politics and location of one's space and place in urban society.

This has important implications for my work on hip-hop in that, the urban space of the ghetto (or the city) has been a source of meaning for Black popular culture, and Black popular culture has been a source of meaning for the ghetto (Haymes, 1995). For urban youth, the city has been an important space and place of producing authentic meaning in hip-hop that has come to signify one's everyday lived experiences (Prier & Beachum, 2008; Rose, 1994).

For Haymes, Black popular culture is not only an important social site for the production of urban meanings, but also serves as a site of resistance, transformation, and self-actualization. The social construction of urban spaces and places are also involved in the shaping of Black subjectivity. They are spaces and places where resistance can take shape through emancipatory practices that begin with the voices, narratives, and experiences of Black people, who often struggle to construct and affirm their identities within neo-liberal urban spaces emptied of economic opportunities by neo-liberal reforms (Haymes, 1995). In addition, the reconstruction of urban public space allows Blacks to deal with the complexity and meanings of their experiences at the intersection of race, gender, class and other markers of identity and difference (Haymes, 1995, p. 135). Rap is rooted in an especially aggressive public display of counter-presence and voice (Rose, 1994, p. 59). Rose states that rap music asserted its right to inscribe one's identity on an environment that seems Teflon resistant to its young people of color (1994, p. 59).

Foregrounding these conditions, I take up the pedagogical issue of how we as critical educators might use hip-hop as a curriculum text that can energize critical dialogue with Black male youths. I illustrate how to politically mobilize the culture of hip-hop for the purpose generating a transformative praxis that helps us recognize the constitutive forces and unjust practices responsible for breeding inequity in urban public schools and in the larger society. In so doing, I locate three different discursive genres in hip-hop that have been shaped within the cultural and political terrain of rap music: Social and politically conscious rap, gangsta rap, and commercial rap music. I situate these discursive genres in relationship to Black male youths' contested and contingent identities in a neo-liberal commercial order.

I then provide examples of how hip-hop can be understood as a counter-public space of resistance through a critical ethnographic study of a hip-hop youth empowerment center. It is a study that can be useful to scholars, pre-service teachers, social activists in urban communities, and in-service teachers who work with Black male youths in urban public school settings. It shows how the politics and pedagogy of hip-hop as a form of popular culture can offer knowledge that is of necessity for teachers and students who are concerned with the moral and political ends of education and schooling in relationship to forms of injustice and inequality. It is also of importance for educators who seek alternative curricular and pedagogical spaces that open up new dialogical and material spaces for urban youth to resist oppression. In this way, I work in concert with the larger unfinished project of constructing a more democratic and liberating education for disenfranchised youth across the globe.

Discursive Genre's of Hip-hop in Context

Hip-hop culture in the U.S. has been shaped by three different genres of rap music: Postmodern Black aesthetic of social/politically conscious rap, gangsta rap, and mass-marketed commercialized rap. I mean these to be useful categories for analysis, bearing in mind at the same time that each "genre" has in part been shaped by the others, has developed in relation to the others, and has developed and changed historically. As Rose states, "an examination of how and why hip-hop arises helps us understand the logic of rap's development and links the intertextual and dialogic qualities in rap to the diverse cultural and social context within which it emerges" (1994, p. 26).

It is widely known that social and politically conscious rap music was birthed on the heels of the Civil Rights movement at a time when unemployment was the greatest source of poverty for Black males in the 1960s (Powell, 2003; Wilson, et al., 1998, p. 57). Social and politically conscious rap that shaped the genre's counter-narratives of rhetorical resistance and opposition were largely in response to U.S. President Ronald Reagan's retrenchment of hard fought Civil Rights legislation in the 1980s. Reagan's initiatives affected high unemployment and underemployment rates for Black families as well as for Black youths, a shortage in public funding for schools and community youth programs, and policies that heightened forms of surveillance, hyper-policing, discipline, control, punishment, and repression of urban youths in urban inner cities.

During the full two term presidency, 1981–1989, Reagan ushered in the neo-liberal conservative era known as "Reaganomics," which resulted in cutting back a range of public social services that exacerbated long held tensions between the urban Black working-class and a state politics of economizing the public welfare. "By Reagan's second term, over one-third of black families earned incomes below the poverty line. For black teenagers, the unemployment rate increased from 38.9 to 43.6 percent under Reagan" (Kelley, 1997, p. 47). Kelley states further that "in Midwestern cities-once the industrial heartland-black teenage unemployment rates ranged from 50 to 70 percent in 1985. Federal and state job programs for inner city youths were also wiped out at an alarming rate" (Kelley, 1997, p. 47). In addition, Reagan's "get tough on crime" policies reinforced intensive disciplinary practices that came to a climax with the beatings of Michael Stewart and Michael Griffith (Chang, 2005). The racialized beatings reflected the racial tensions and hatred that existed in New York City and in other urban contexts across the US. Therefore, the aforementioned events and circumstances, among several others, shaped hip-hop's visceral reactions and critical consciousness about social injustices that affected Black and Brown peoples in urban communities.

While groups such as the Watts Prophets, Last Poets, Amiri Baraka, and Sonia Sonchez of the Black Arts Movement (1965–1975) set the stage for rap's social and political commentary, the 1980s marked hip-hop's most powerful emergence for its uncompromising truth telling (Dyson, 2007, p. 62). Many urban youths were frustrated with the old guard of Civil Rights Leadership, and adopted a politics of confrontation and resistance to white mainstream society. The dominant group whom they felt had abandoned, neglected, and mistreated them socially, politically, and economically. Between 1987 and 1990 Grandmaster Flash and the Furious Five, Public Enemy, and KRS One, rendered social and political critique on the east coast in New York, while Ice-T, and NWA, and later solo artists of the NWA movement, Ice Cube and Dr. Dre, mapped out a more gangsta ethic on the west coast.

In terms of rap's social/political discourses, Grandmaster Flash and the Furious Five's classic, "The Message" in 1982, came up with the famous phrase, "It's like a jungle sometimes, it makes me wonder how I keep from going under." The jungle signified oppressive conditions within the post-industrial center of urban life. It was the first rap song to be promoted on MTV that spoke about the politics of ghettoized poverty and social neglect in urban America in response to de-industrialization. Soon thereafter, Public Enemy, also known as the "Black Panthers of Rap," referencing a more Black nationalist tone, came up with a name and symbol that signified the Black male as targeted under a gun stethoscope as an "enemy of the public." Two of their most monumental albums, *It Takes a Nation of Millions to Hold us Back* in 1988, and *Fear of a Black Planet* in 1990 completely changed the sonic and linguistic landscape of social and political discourses in rap music. Public Enemy's rhetorical politics of resistance involved using language as a verbal assault weapon to speak truth to power. KRS-One is widely considered as an organic intellectual who has not only attempted to preserve the cultural practices of hip-hop, but centered the elements of knowledge, critical consciousness, and political advocacy in hip-hop culture. He was particularly inspired by former gang member and one of the forefathers of hip-hop, Afrika Bambaata, who called for a meeting in 1987 at the Latin Quarter club, stating that hip-hop needed to make a commitment to stop the violence and shift toward more political advocacy in urban communities (Chang, 2005). This call from Bambaata was important: In 1987, there were "more young black men killed within the United States in a single year than had been killed abroad in the entire nine years of the Vietnam War" (Dyson, 2004, p. 139). In 1989, KRS-One responded to Bambaata's call and mobilized several hip-hop artists and came out with a song entitled "Self Destruction" of which he rapped,

Well, today's topic, self destruction
It really ain't the rap audience that's buggin
It's one or two suckas, ignorant brothers
Trying to rob and steal from one another
You get caught in the mid
So to crush the stereotype here's what we did
We got ourselves together
So that you could unite and fight for what's right
Not negative 'cause the way we live is positive
We don't kill our relatives (1989)

Since that time, there have been a number of visible social and politically conscious artists such as Nas, Talib Kweli, Dead Prez, The Roots, Common, Immortal Technique, and Mos Def who articulate critical discourses have addressed issues of systemic injustice related to matters such as education and schooling, health care, joblessness, police brutality, reparations, foreign policy, family matters, voting rights, the over representation of Black males in the prison industrial complex, and the overall politics that confront life lived at the margins of urban communities (Dyson, 2004; Kitwana, 2002). Dead Prez, for example, is generally recognized as one of the major contemporary political forces in hip-hop since Public Enemy. The song "They Schools" on their classic 2000 album, *Let's Get Free*, is perhaps one of the most potent critiques on the neo-liberal culture of education and schooling from an urban Black male perspective. For example, the group states:

> The same people who control the school system control the prison system, and the whole social system ever since slavery, nawsayin (2000)?

Dead Prez also presents us with a postmodern urban landscape marked by an aggressive militarization of ghettoized space, and by public schools that are "out of touch." In a world of institutional abandonment and social neglect, it is as if hip-hop artists are crying out that public schools should exist to serve young people, to be spaces in which they can turn to not only understand the social world around them, but engage in critical practices that make their lives more livable.

Talib Kweli recently critiqued neo-liberal state politics of the Bush Administration on a track entitled "Bushonomics" (2007) on the Cornel West & BMWMB album, *Never Forget: A Journey of Revelations*. Talib Kweli opens up the track stating,

> Revolution require participation, but sometimes people be hesitatin'. The government must respect the will of the people. The government serve the people. The people don't serve the government.

Kweli suggests that the politics of social change and transformation must emerge from below, and that the government must be held accountable to the interests of the public welfare state. He then addresses questions of equitable participatory citizenship in relationship to education; he also demystifies the traditional political lines between ideologies on the left and the right, suggesting the need for changing the United States embedded neo-liberal agenda,

> Voter registration with no scope of education. It's a waste of time with no hope, it's just frustration. It ain't no choice when you're pickin' the voice of a nation/you're just contributin' to the status quo's preservation (Kweli, 2007).

Many artists within and outside the social and political discourse have begun to translate their critical discourses into movements for social change. For example, David Banner and Master P have testified before Congress, defending hip-hop culture's free speech rights and challenged the government to be more attentive to the urban conditions of disposability that rap artists speak about, and understand how the profane language often reflects those realities. Both (along with artists such as Jay-Z and P. Diddy) have also raised millions of dollars to help clean up and rebuild New Orleans after the Hurricane Katrina disaster. Common has been a long time advocate for HIV and Aids awareness in the urban community. In 2007, Mos Def led a protest that addressed the Jena Six crisis that happened in Louisiana in 2006. He ignited a movement by sending out a viral video, which called all students to walk out of the nation's classrooms in response to the prosecution of six Black male teens that were entangled in a racial brawl with white students over a noose hanging from a tree (http://www.usatoday.com/life/music/2007-10-04-1454160090_x.htm).

Toward the latter part of the 80s and 1990s, Ice-T, followed by Ice-Cube and NWA, ushered in gangsta rap's discourses that articulated a defiant attitude and frequently, nihilistic reactions that were outgrowths of major injustices related to police brutality, low-socio-economic conditions with limited options for employment that proliferated the underground market of the crack economy, and the affects of crime on the urban scene. Themes of violence, sexism and misogyny, police brutality, and other longstanding political critiques of urban society complicate and shape discourses within gangsta rap music. The discourse of gangsta rap, rhetorically, often uses metaphors and tropes of urban street life of real and mythic proportions, ultimately rooted in vulnerable responses to a system of white patriarchal dominance that is well chronicled in the history of North American society. For example, Ice-T best captured gangsta rap's market discourses, predicated on a rugged individualism that invoked a patriarchal, misogyny in his 1990 classic hit "New Jack Hustler,"

> *I ain't got nothin' to lose, much to gain*
>
> *In my brain, I got a capitalist migraine*
>
> *I gotta get paid tonight, you muthafuckin' right*
>
> *Takin' my grip, check my bitch, keep my game tight (Ice-T, 1990)*

He later states,

> *My education is low but I got long dough*
>
> *Raised like a pit bull, my heart pumps nitro*
>
> *Sleep on silk, lie like a politician*
>
> *My Uzi's my best friend, cold as mortician (Ice-T, 1990)*

Ice-T gives a ruthless exposé of a cold calculated hustler who regulates his power and respect through monetary acquisition, while claiming his phallocentric space of male dominance over his female conquest. According to the New Jack Hustler, an inadequate education through presumably inequitable schooling practices further gives credence to the hustler's capitalist ambitions to achieve illicit cash flow of the underground street market economy. The Uzi signifies that he is ready for war and violence on urban turf if necessary. The gun, a symbolic text often used in the discourse of gangsta rap, is frequently understood, according to rap artist Killer Mike, to be that "equalizer of that feeling and not being able to exert change around them" (Matthews, 2006, p. 66).

Gangsta rap often reflects a society that has fueled high levels of anger, rage, disappointment, and disdain in urban Black male youth who feel a suffocating marginality to the larger contradictions of equality and justice in U.S. democracy. Communities that have been destabilized, who suffer the weight of oppression, often internalize it and respond inward (psychically) in complicated ways, which can result in life denying and gives consequence to the unfortunate realities of violence. However, Kelley notes that much of what gangsta rap is trying to accomplish for the audience is not advocacy but description (1994, p. 198). He states that gangsta rap is a loosely based form of street ethnography; however, the rappers who play the role of researchers are not detached observers from the scene (1994, p. 198). For example, Dr. Dre, who was formerly a part of the N.W.A. movement that significantly fomented and shaped the genre of gangsta rap in 1987, produced a track entitled, "Lil Ghetto Boy" on his 1992 classic album, the *Chronic*. The track reflects the immediacy and consequence of these realities and sentiments. On the beginning of this track Snoop states,

Murder was the case that they gave me
Dear God, I wonder can you save me
I'm only eighteen, so I'm a young buck
It's a riot, if I don't scrap, I'm getting stuck
But that's the life of a G, I guess (1992)

Snoop captures both the mentality and consequences of a society that has left him with one option: To bang, scrap, and fight to a violent end if one must. According to this narrative, there is no other option or choice if one is to survive life as a gangsta. Snoop later states:

Best, run, cause brothers is droppin quicker
Ughh, too late, damn, down goes another nigga
Bouncin off the walls, throwin them dogs
Gettin that rep, as a young hog
It ain't nuttin like the street life
You betta be strapped wit yo' shank
Cause ain't no fistfight
So I guess I gots ta handle mine
Since I did the crime, I gots ta do my time (1992)

What is being reflected here is what Freire calls a horizontal violence that is often enacted and committed amongst oppressed and subordinated groups who adopt the consciousness and mindset of the oppressor that has informed (through violent actions against marginalized groups) certain mentalities about violence and repression (2004, p. 62). This horizontal violence has contributed to the deaths of rap icons such as Biggie and Tupac, Jam Master Jay, Big L, T.I.'s assistant Philant Johnson, Busta Ryhmes' bodyguard Israel Ramirez, Eminem's fellow crew member and rap artist Proof, and a host of other unfortunate tragedies in hip-hop. These incidents were predicated on a street orientation that is rooted in an aggressive determination for respect at all costs (as cited in Anderson, 1994).

Rap music and gangsta rap in particular, cannot always be understood as literal interpretations of reality; rather as art forms they use rhetorical metaphors, similes, and tropes about committing "violence" as competitive battle expressions in the artists' performance. Phrases such as "murder all sucka' MC's," to destroy fellow rap artists through verbal competition, and microphones become symbolic as a gun; and "murdering lyrics on a track," to boast one's verbal prowess and lyrical skills are but a few of these examples (Kelley, 1996).

Sexism and misogyny have been problematic and pervasive central themes in the discourse of gangsta rap. Women in rap videos and lyrics are often symbolized as trophies and objects to be possessed by "players" in the pimp game of sexual conquest, domination, and control. Snoop Dogg, whose debut album in 1993 was entitled, *Doggy Style*, displayed this most vividly at the 2003 MTV music awards when he appeared with two women by his arms, attached to him on leashes. He has been one of the key figures that made pimp narratives in gangsta rap go mainstream in popular culture. For example, on the track, "Ain't No Fun" from the *Doggy Style* album Snoop states:

How many bitches wanna fuck this nigga named Snoop

Doggy, I'm all the above

I'm too swift on my toes to get caught up with you hoes (1993)

In this narrative, it is already assumed that women are of sexual use at his disposal, expendable for his pleasure, and on his time.

Although not considered a gangsta rap artist, Nelly's video "Tip Drill," perhaps served as a key tipping point in agitating a protest at Spelman College for rap's sexism and misogyny. The video showed a man swiping a credit card between a woman's buttocks. In response, women from Spelman College boycotted and protested his visit to their college when he was trying to raise funds and awareness for his now late sister's bone marrow cancer. On the critique of sexism and misogyny in rap Rose makes a valid and poignant point, "Perhaps these stories serve to protect young men from the reality of female rejection; maybe and more likely, tales of sexual domination falsely relieve their lack of self-worth and limited access to economic and social markers for heterosexual masculine power" (1994, p. 15).

Another major theme prominent in gangsta rap is police brutality. Gangsta rap artists' attitudes are reflexive of many urban youth attitudes toward incidents between urban police officers and urban youth. For example, NWA's song, "Fuck Tha Police," shows clearly the damaging impact that emanates from the state overpolicing urban communities and criminalizing urban youth as a matter of routine:

Fuck the police comin straight from the underground

A young nigga got it bad cause I'm brown

And not the other color so police think

they have the authority to kill a minority
Fuck that shit, cause I ain't the one
for a punk motherfucker with a badge and a gun
to be beatin on, and thrown in jail
We can go toe to toe in the middle of a cell
Fuckin with me cause I'm a teenager...

Addressing the controversy on gangsta' rap, Cube states in the 2006 edition of *The Source*, "We was getting attacked in the media, and I wanted to understand where everybody was coming from. Because of how we grew up and how we wanted to rhyme, we felt that was the only way to go. I didn't understand how people who never lived that could comment on anything" (Ford, 2006). Rap artists of the gangsta genre reflect sentiments of police departments that have generated unfair punishment practices, which collectively give consequence to racial profiling, disproportionate unjust sentencing practices in the prison industrial complex, and widespread police brutality exerted on Black males in urban society.

Given the imbalance of power for dominance and control in a white patriarchal society, many Black male youths' search for power through gangsta rap has often given way to discourses in popular culture most noted for violence, sexism and misogyny; however, as seen here, the artists at the same time evoked similar political ruminations about tense relationships with the legal and criminal justice systems. While I agree with understanding the cultural and artistic contexts which shape the complexities and symbolic nuances of gangsta' rap, I agree with Michael Eric Dyson when he states that the stakes are too high for moral neutrality in gangsta rap, particularly when speaking about the lives of urban youth.

Toward the latter part of the 1990s into the 21st century, we have the market-driven economy of commercialized rap music, which speaks more to the corporate industry of hip-hop. The music has unexpectedly become big business removed, in many ways, from the social and political concerns that emerged in the seventies and early eighties from local voices, experiences, and local practices of urban working-class communities. That is, the culture of hip-hop has become the commodity of capital that drives corporate consumption of urban youth culture. Under the neo-liberal commercial order, the culture of hip-hop is now dominated by a few media market technologies that have commodified the local practices of collective communities in urban locals. Part of this shift happened under the Telecommunications Act of 1996, which deregulated privatization of local public radio airwaves (Chang, 2005, p. 441). While the act proposed to fuel innovation and competition, it did the exact opposite: This act had effectively destroyed local community programming, standardized playlists, reduced running time for listeners, and consolidated the public airwaves under a handful of companies, namely, Clear Channel, Cumulus, Citadel and Viacom (Chang, 2005, p. 441). According to Chang, at the turn of the new millennium, five companies (Vivendi Universal, Sony, AOL Time Warner, Bertelsmann and EMI), which are mainly owned by white corporate executives, now control eighty percent of the U.S. media landscape.

Their ownership includes the music industry, movies, television, internet, video games, and magazines (2005, p. 443). Such an act allowed corporate interests to pursue global consolidation of media, while concomitantly maximizing their profit margins.

As hip-hop has become more privatized through select multinational corporations, the circulation, production, and consumption of the music's discursive texts and images became increasingly associated with constructed notions of Black masculinity. As Chuck D of Public Enemy states in Byron Hurt's documentary, *Hip-hop: Beyond Beats and Rhymes*, corporate interests of the hip-hop industry have resulted in "selling Black masculinity in a bottle." Concomitantly, the voices, images, and representations of women rappers became increasingly silenced. Even for those females in the past who had been successful, such as Missy Elliot, Raw Digga, Remi Ma, and Lady of Rage, many had to project a more masculine edge in the performance of their work. While artists such as Lil Kim and Foxy Brown projected a sexier image, they still had to prove that they were just as raw and aggressive, lyrically, as their male counterparts in their all male crews of Junior Mafia and The Firm.

Under this consolidation, performative constructions of "ghetto life" of the Black male is being sold as a commodity for global circulation. This means that much of the production of the music is being driven by record sales and profits of a few major distribution companies, rather than valuing any political or socially redeeming messages by artists who articulate more empowering discourses in hip-hop. In this regard, the commoditization of the hip-hop industry's regulated and mass production of "gangsta'"—"bling bling" identities and rap's rhetorical discourse detach "authentic meaning of the image" and inspire market ways of living (West, 2004). Subsequently, patriarchal (hooks, 1992) performance, representations, and social constructions of "Black manhood" play out "inner city" (urban centers blighted with poverty) Black male youths' desires for the maintenance of money, power, and respect to obtain self worth (Watts, 2004, p. 595).

As hip-hop music has become a billion dollar industry, the culture's influence extends beyond the local and communal discourse of the art-form into the corporate branding and media interests of multinational companies. Russell Simmons (Chairman, Def Jam Records), for example, successfully translated a blueprint for the packaging of hip-hop to mainstream American popular culture in a consumable and commodifiable form. For instance, he has played a major role in brokering the hip-hop industry into a conglomerate enterprise that includes, but is not limited to, movies (i.e. Nutty Professor), fashion (i.e. Phat Farm), music (Def Jam), soft drinks (DefCon3), and finance (i.e. RushCard). The influence of clothing lines such as Sean Jean, Roca Wear, and P. Miller, headed by hip-hop icons P. Diddy, Jay-Z, and Master P, can be traced directly back to the pioneering efforts of Simmons' shrewd business acumen. He has also been successful in facilitating the marriage between hip-hop and reality TV with the production of *Run's House* (starring Run of Run DMC) that has influenced the development of other hip-hop reality shows. Programs such as *The Flavor of Love* (starring Flavor Flav of Public Enemy), *50 Cent: The Money and the Power*, P. Diddy's *Making of the Band* and

Work for Diddy, *Snoop Dogg's Fatherhood*, *Coolio's Rules*, and Fat Man Scoop's *Man and Wife* are examples of how the commercial discourse of hip-hop has transcended rap music, and has circulated urban culture into popular culture.

In a neo-liberal commercial order, the branding in corporate America promotes spectacular images and discourses around urban life to sell a product. Corporate conglomerates have harnessed "popular" representations of urban street life and made them commodifiable and consumable to many urban Black male youths. They are the social actors who most identify with these discourses and images because they come from the same lived experiences as the artists. On the one hand, these artists represent to many urban youths powerful signifiers related to entrepreneurship and economic success without the assistance and negligence of a corporate, technical efficiency based education. For example, iconic rap artists such as Jay-Z, Biggie Smalls, Tupac Shakur, and Nas (Nas dropped out in 8th grade) were all high school drop outs, whose identities were invisible to the structures of schooling at the time. Ironically, the work of these artists' is now being studied in colleges and universities across the globe. This says something about the dialectical contradictions between knowledge rooted in urban struggle, and knowledge that has been privileged, legitimated, and valued by neo-liberal corporate interests of schooling. On the other hand, absent from these texts is the myth of overnight success. The fact is that these artists' corporate success represents the exception, rather than the contrived "rag to riches" story portrayed of the hip-hip world in dominant forms of media.

In a postmodern period, where Black males who come from low socio-economic conditions are searching for new identities outside of school, race and class identity are closely related to the products and images that these youth consume and embody the work that they perform (Apple & Carlson, 1998, p. 19). These youth consume these images at a time where joblessness remains at 50% for Black males, irrespective of having a high school diploma; poverty rates for Black families are double the national average (Giroux, 2004; Street, 2003), and are the same as when King died in 1968 (Gates, 2004); and the standardization of education is not speaking to the most pressing issues that are relevant and relational to affirming the identity of Black male youths (Dimitriadis, 2004). Subsequently, there is an ongoing negotiation between the consumption of image in relationship to everyday lived realties, where Black male youths are bereft of political and economic resource acquisition, and the contradiction between education and social mobility is apparent. As it relates to school, Willis would suggest that consumption and popular culture are relevant to existing themes of school conformism, resistance, disaffection, variations and points in between (2003, p. 405).

The genre's between the social/political, gangsta, and commercial discourses offer compelling insights into the competing and contested identities that shape the way many urban Black male youths construct their social world through the consumption of hip-hop under the neo-liberal commercial order. Their identities and sense of agency in relationship to these competing discourses are constantly being challenged and contested. What is at stake in the present moment, it seems, is how we, as critical educators, can help co-construct with students counter-public spaces of resistance to a neo-liberal culture of urban displacement that threatens radical possibilities in advancing a more democratic form of education. In the next section, I center hip-hop as a counter-public space of resistance for Black male youths that will be useful to critical educators, activists, and scholars who work in the field of urban education.

Location Hip-hop as a Counter Public Space of Resistance

As public spaces for critical citizenship have shrunk for Black male youths within the neo-liberal culture of urban public schools, there has been a need to organize counter-public spaces of resistance for social change and transformation. Situated within urban spaces of marginalization, critical discourses and movements within the art form can recover and reclaim hip-hop as a relevant, viable, counter-public, curricular and pedagogical space that resists the current neo-liberal, hegemonic, commercial order. This counter-public space allows educators, activists, and students to construct and organize political pedagogies that redefine and re-shape circumstances in the public sphere of education. These educational initiatives heighten critical awareness and enable transformative action inside and outside urban public schools. I am speaking of critical dialogic and material spaces where youths and educators alike can begin to critically analyze social constructions about what it means to be "Black" and male in this society as a way to open up new discursive terrains of struggle and transformation. Such counter-spaces also represent moments of resistance to "deficit" theories in public schooling that place the blame for underachievement on marginalized urban youths and a supposedly dysfunctional culture of poverty. In effect, public schools have participated in labeling and targeting urban youths as "public enemies" who resist educators' efforts to "uplift" them.

Hip-hop as a counter-public space also mobilizes a resistance to forms of cultural consumption of commodified discourses in the hip-hop industry that distorts the lived experiences of urban Black male youths. The dialectical tensions between Black male youths' "authentic" subjectivity within urban contexts in relationship to the power of neo-liberal, corporate interests that fuel hip-hop's mass-marketed commodified discourses presents a crucial site of critique of commercial discourses within capitalist patriarchy. These discourses have privileged North America's values of dominance, control, sexism against women, violence, misogyny, materialism, etc. Counter-public spaces of resistance in hip-hop can allow Black male youths to reclaim the power to subvert, challenge, speak and give voice to their circumstances through creative self expression and cultural practices of the art. Hip-hop as a counter-public space can open up critical, dialogic praxis that allows us to read hip-hop texts within and against the traditional texts of the critical Black History tradition, Black Power Movements of the 60s, and Civil Rights' texts. This requires that we think about how artists or texts within hip-hop culture can contextualize present moments in relationship to historical links with ideas of the past (Ladson-Billings & Donner, 2005, p. 294). In this way, we can make meaningful, relational, and intersectional connections between and across genres to better understand the continuum between the past, present, and future.

Finally, centering hip-hop as a counter-public space of resistance for Black male youths mean finding creative ways to open up more democratic spaces through non-traditional curricula and pedagogies that are in direct contrast to traditional "banking models" of education (Freire, 2004). For example, "hip-hop community centers as public spaces can be seen as sites of learning, critical reflection, and transformative knowledge production" (Prier & Beachum, 2008, p. 531). These centers serve as spaces where "students may engage in developing affirming identities in dialogue and interaction with others," and for youth empowerment and self-actualization (Prier & Beachum, 2008, p. 531). To paraphrase Freire, hip-hop may enable marginalized youths to "read the world" by naming the forces that oppress and silence them, and to thereby engage in the struggle to change their world. It opens up new opportunities for critical discursive dialogue and transformative action between urban communities and public schools.

Let me now turn to an example of "doing" hip-hop pedagogy as a counter-public space from my own research in a medium-sized, Northern rust-belt city, now largely de-industrialized and with chronic underemployment or unemployment the norm. Over the course of a year I worked with a hip-hop community center in an urban area that was established under a state grant affiliated with a school-university partnership initiative. The hip-hop youth empowerment center works specifically with socio-economically-disadvantaged Black male youths in 9th and 10th grades, and uses the cultural practices of hip-hop (i.e. DJ, emcee, graffiti, b-boy) as a way to empower and retain Black male youths in public schools. According to the director and one of the staff, many of these youths flirted with gang activity, came from homes where their family members are going through drug addiction, or participated in the underground drug market economy, or have had a family member gunned down through street violence. The director argued that given the background and history of the students', a curriculum and pedagogy organized around hip-hop culture could have a positive impact on both their achievement and retention in school. It could also, he believed, help reduce violence and incorrigibility problems by motivating students, and it could help in young people's self development, including the development of critical thinking skills and a sense of self-empowerment and self-affirmation. In all of these ways, the program staff hoped that the program would help young black men become more self-conscious and self-aware learners, active participants in their own learning, and thus gain a sense of agency that they could control their life paths, despite the harsh realities that they have faced.

In having several critical dialogues, reading popular cultural texts, and having students write out critical reflection journals on what hip-hop meant to them, the cultural practice and appreciation for the art was seen as a way of life for them, rather than a marketed form of entertainment. These students understood hip-hop as a way of life in that the art was mobilized to center "their struggles and experiences in an oppressive society," which provided them with a context for critical self-reflection to transform and subvert their reality (Prier & Beachum, 2008, p. 530). The students critically understood how the culture of a neo-liberal commercial order within the hip-hop industry has shaped the ways in which many urban youths measured and constructed their identities as Black males. They understood that many of their peers, who are marginalized economically, socially, and politically, desire and consume the corporate commercial discourse in the hip-hop industry that has sold them the myth of achieving overnight success and monetary gain to obtain the American dream. Discursive images in mass media of hip-hop icons wearing expensive clothes, seemingly unlimited access to money, and the power and respect to go along with it, can be powerful signifiers to them in how they construct what it means to be Black and male in America. Schools were seen as "fashion shows," and were contested cultural and social sites where market desires and mentalities reflected the values of neo-liberal, corporate consumption. However, the students were critically aware and self-reflected on the cultural politics of neo-liberalism that advances the myth of overnight monetary success in relationship to youths' cultural consumption practices as well as critically examined how the corporate hip-hop industry affected many vulnerable Black male youths' actions and decisions within the larger social, political, and economic contexts of urban society.

As schools represented alienating and restrictive spaces and places to be (e.g. standardized testing, disciplinary confrontations with authority, and a less than engaging curriculum), and given the undeniable power and influence that hip-hop has in shaping Black male youths' identity inside and outside schools, efforts to mobilize the culture as a counter-public space of resistance in non-commodified ways becomes crucially important. Hip-hop culture, and the physical space of the hip-hop youth empowerment center, served as material and discursive counter-public spaces of resistance to the pressures and circumstances many of them faced at home, school, or in their communities. In very concrete ways, many of them felt that the structure and dialogic space of the hip-hop youth empowerment center provided them with a way to talk about and work through very difficult realities that they felt could not be discussed in schools. The students even suggested that because they had critical discussions about life and felt comfortable in expressing themselves through the cultural practice of hip-hop, they were empowered to struggle against and resist their own perceptions about being imprisoned or dead as their destination in life. Conceptions about death or being in prison were very real for them, as many of their friends or family members had been fatal victims to the streets or were doing prison time. Thus, engaging in critical self-reflection through critical open dialogues about these experiences, and utilizing the creative cultural practices of the art reshaped their consciousness in more resilient and liberating ways.

Conclusion

Given the sense of displacement and alienation that confront Black male youths within the neo-liberal culture of urban life, educators who work in urban public school settings will need to engage in new alternative 21st century curriculia and pedagogies that recognize the powerful force of hip-hop culture as a viable democratic space for learning, social change, and transformation. Hip-hop is perhaps one of the few counter-public spaces where these youths are making sense of their everyday lived experiences and are self-fashioning identities that often contrast and compete with the traditional culture of urban public schools. In an attempt to subvert the neo-liberal commercial order of urban life alongside Black male youths, we must engage in forms of critical media literacy as a way to critique commodified texts that convey hegemonic representations and performances of black masculinity (which are both misogynistic and heterosexist) and counter-hegemonic representations and practices that are more consistent with discourses and practices of freedom and empowerment. This demands that we challenge discourses that blame youths for the social ills they encumber, and demystify the ideological asymmetrical relations of power at work in such deficit theories of the student and the students' cultural background. It also demands that we recognize that youths have agency, and resist submitting to rituals of schooling (such as high-stakes testing) that are part and parcel of their dis-empowerment. As critical pedagogues, we must work alongside these youth in mobilizing the culture of hip-hop as a political intervention for social change in their lives and communities.

QUESTIONS FOR REFLECTION

1. What is the larger pedagogical role of understanding the language, music, and culture of hip-hop in relationship to a neo-liberal culture that impacts the educational experiences of Black male youth in urban public schools?
2. How do Black males, globally, view hip-hop culture in relationship to education and schooling? Are there similarities or differences to what the author discusses here?
3. What texts within the critical Black History tradition and Civil Rights Movement would give educators some context to foreground some of the contemporary issues facing Black male youth in the hip-hop generation?

REFERENCES

Anderson, E. (1994). The code of the streets. *The Atlantic Monthly, 24*, 81–94.
Apple, M. (2001). Comparing neo-liberal projects and inequality in education. *Comparative Education, 37*(4), 409–423.
Apple, M., & Carlson, D. (1998). *Power/knowledge/pedagogy: The meaning of democratic education in unsettling times.* Boulder, CO: Westview Press.
Bynoe, Y. (2004). *Stand & deliver: Political activism, leadership, and hip-hop culture.* New York: Soft Skull Press.
Carlson, D. L. (2005). Hope without illusion: Telling the story of democratic educational renewal. *International Journal of Qualitative Studies in Education, 18*(1), 21–45.
Carlson, D., & Dimitriadis, G. (2003). *Promises to keep: Cultural studies, democratic education, and public life.* New York: Routledge Falmer.
Cornel West. (2007). *"Bushonomics." Never forget: A journey of revelations* [CD]. Santa Monica, CA: Hidden Beach.
Chang, J. (2005). *Can't stop won't stop: A history of the hip-hop generation.* New York: St. Martin's Press.
Dead Prez. (2000). "They schools." In *Let's get free.* Retrieved from http://www.ohhla.com/anonymous/deadprez/get_free/tschools.prz.txt, http://www.ohhla.com/all.html

Dr. Dre. (1992). Lil Ghetto Boy. *The Chronic*. Retrieved from http://www.ohhla.com/anonymous/dr_dre/chronic/geto_boy.dre.txt.http://www.ohhla.com/all.html

Dimitriadis, G. (2004). *Performing identity/performing culture: Hip-Hop as text, pedagogy, and lived practice*. New York: Peter Lang Publishing.

Dyson, M. E. (2007). *Know what I mean? Reflections on hip-hop*. New York: Basic Civitas Books.

Dyson, M. E. (2004). *The Michael Eric Dyson reader*. New York: Basic Civitas Books.

Dyson, M. E. (2001). *Holler if you hear me: Searching for Tupac Shakur*. New York: Basic Civitas Books.

Ford, R. (2006). G'ology. *The Source, 200*, 78–85.

Forman, M. (2004). Ain't no love in the heart of the city. In M. Forman & M. Neal (Eds.), *That's the joint!: The hip-hop studies reader* (pp. 155–157). New York: Routledge.

Foucault, M. (1979). *Discipline and punish: The birth of the prison* (A. Sheridan, Trans.). New York: Vintage Books.

Freire, P. (2004). *Pedagogy of the oppressed*. New York: Continuum.

Friedland, R. (1992). Space, place and modernity. *A Journal of Reviews: Contemporary Sociology, 21*(1).

Gates, H. (2004). *America behind the color line*. New York: Warner Books.

Giroux, H. (2004, February). Class casualties: Disappearing youth in the age of George W. Bush. *Workplace: A Journal of Academic Labor, 6*(1). Retrieved from http://www.cust.educ.ubc.ca/workplace/issue6p1/giroux04.html

Giroux, H. (1996). *Fugitive cultures: Race, violence, and youth*. New York: Routledge.

Haymes, S. (1995). *Race, culture, and the city: A pedagogy for black urban struggle*. Albany, NY: State University of New York Press.

Hip-Hop for Respect. (2000). *A tree never grown* [CD]. Los Angeles: Rawkus Records.

Hooks, B. (1992). *Black looks: Race and representation*. Boston: South End Press.

Hurt, B. (2006). *Hip-hop: Beyond beats and rhymes* [Motion picture]. Northampton, MA: Media Education Foundation.

Ice-T. (1990). *New Jack Hustler*. Retrieved from http://apps.facebook.com/lyricsdomain/artist/icet/song/new_jack_hustler

Jefferies, J. (1992). Toward a redefinition of the urban: The collision of culture. In G. Dent (Ed.), *Black popular culture* (pp. 153–163). Seattle, WA: Bay Press.

Kelley, R. D. G. (1997). *Yo' mama's disfunkional!: Fighting the culture wars in urban America*. Boston: Beacon Press.

Kelley, R. D. G. (1996). *Race rebels: Culture, politics, and the black working-class*. New York: The Free Press.

Kitwana, B. (2002). *The hip-hop generation: Young blacks and the crisis in African-American culture*. New York: Basic Civitas Books.

Ladson-Billings, G., & Donner, J. (2005). The moral activist role of critical race theory scholarship. In N. Denzin & Y. Lincoln (Eds.), *Handbook of qualitative research* (pp. 279–301). Thousand Oaks, CA: Sage.

Lazin, L. (Director). (2003). *Tupac resurrection* [Motion picture]. Hollywood, CA: MTV Networks and AMARU Entertainment, Inc.

Light, A. (1998). *Tupac Shakur*. New York: Three Rivers Press.

Matthews, A. (2006). Self destruction. *The Source, 201*, 62–68.

N.W.A. (1989). Fuck Tha Police. *Straight Outta Compton*. Retrieved from http://www.ohhla.com/anonymous/nwa/straight/fuck_tha.nwa.txt,http://www.ohhla.com/all.html

Powell, K. (2003). *Who's gonna take the weight?: Manhood, race, and power in America*. New York: Three Rivers Press.

Public Enemy. (1990). *"Fight the power." Fear of a black planet* [CD]. New York: Def Jam Records.

Public Enemy. (1988). *It takes a nation of millions to hold us back* [CD]. New York: Def Jam Records.

Prier & Beachum. (2008). Conceptualizing a critical discourse around hip-hop culture and Black male youth in educational scholarship and research. *International Journal of Qualitative Studies in Education, 21*(5), 519–535.

Prier, D. (2006). A relevant black male curriculum. *Encounter: Education for Meaning and Social Justice, 19*(3), 25–26.

Public Enemy. (1990). Retrieved from http://www.ohhla.com/anonymous/pb_enemy/fear_of/fightthe. pbe.txt http://www.ohhla.com/all_three.html

Rose, T. (1994). *Black noise: Rap music and Black culture in contemporary America*. Middletown, CT: Wesleyan University Press.

Sims, M. (2007). Retrieved from http://www.usatoday.com/life/music/2007-10-04-1454160090_x.htm

Snoop Dogg. (1993). Retrieved from http://www.ohhla.com/anonymous/snoopdog/dogstyle/aintnfun. snp.txt.http://www.ohhla.com/all.html

Stop the Violence All Stars. (1989). Self Destruction 12. *Self Destruction*. Retrieved from http://www. ohhla.com/anonymous/misc/hip-hop/self_des.stv.txt, http://www.ohhla.com/all.html

Street, P. *Deep poverty, deep deception: Facts that matter beneath the imperial helicopters*. Speech presented at The Illinois Welfare Reform Symposium, June 17, 2003, Chicago, Illinois.

Watts, E. K. (2004). An exploration of spectacular consumption: Gangsta rap as cultural commodity. In M. Forman & M. Neal (Eds.), *That's the joint!: The hip-hop studies reader* (pp. 593–609). New York: Routledge.

West, C. (2004). *Democracy matters: Winning the fight against imperialism*. New York: Penguin Press.

Willis, P. (2003). Food soldiers of modernity: The dialectics of cultural consumption and the 21st-century school. In *Harvard Educational Review* (73)3, 390–415. Cambridge, MA: The Sheridan Press.

Wilson, W., Quane, J. M., & Rankin, B. H. (1998). The new urban poverty: Consequences of the economic and social decline of inner-city neighborhoods. In F. Harris & L. Curtis (Eds.), *Locked in the Poorhouse: Cities, race, and poverty in the United States* (pp. 57–78). New York: Rowman & Littlefield Publishers, Inc.

BRADLEY J. PORFILIO AND SHANNON M. PORFILIO

8. HIP-HOP PEDAGOGUES

Youth as a Site of Critique, Resistance and Transformation in France and in the Neo-liberal Social World

With the proliferation of communication and speed technologies, there has been a ubiquitous movement of resources, corporate ideologies, and cultural practices from the First World to so-called "Third World" regions in the post-industrial era, which has allowed, according to hip-hop icon, Talib Kweli, hip-hop culture to become "the language of the children" (Runnel, 2006). On one level, hip-hop culture, like so many artistic forms produced by minoritized youth, has not only been colonized by Western political and economic leaders to exploit and profit from disaffected urban youth, but also has been procured to represent the Other in ways that "play into the racist, misogynist agenda of (W)hite supremacy" and imperialism (Keyes, 2002, as cited in Kato, 2007). In essence, the "language of the children" has become a transnational corporate configuration. White record executives have sought to manipulate the public by supporting and promoting hip-hop artists who embody a materialistic, misogynist, homophobic, and violent 'gangsta' image,' which undermines the emancipatory elements of this counterculture (Magubane, 2006; Dyson, 1996). Unlike the debilitating hegemonic characterization of the hip-hop world concocted by the corporate elite, some hip-hop artists' lyrics and their cultural activism represent a counter-hegemonic movement against the corporate, economic, and cultural status quo. Youth cultural manifestations are predicated on bringing awareness to the social and economic forces responsible for urban violence and institutional racism, on challenging neo-liberal economic, political and social arrangements responsible for human suffering and misery in other contexts, and on engendering autonomous zones through their aesthetic expression that,momentarily, give these hip-hop pedagogues the power to overcome alienation and oppression associated with growing up in blighted, militarized and impoverished communities (Kato, 2007). Consequently, the public has incorrectly blamed hip-hop and urban youths for social ills occurring in various urban contexts containing poverty, joblessness, racism, and violence, and has been prevented from seeing hip-hop intellectuals courageously emulating and building upon the cultural work of hip-hop pioneers. As an intuitive response to the unjust conditions impacting their social world in the mid-1970s, several African American youths and "the sons and daughters of immigrant youth [who] had been displaced by the movement of global capital," launched the hip-hop movement through break dancing, tagging/graffti, MCing, and DJing (Kelley, 2006, p. ix).

B. J. Porfilio and P. R. Carr (eds.), Youth Culture, Education and Resistance:
Subverting the Commercial Ordering of Life, 129–148.

The cultural manifestations and activists' agendas proffered by rap pioneers in the US also resonated with other minoritized youths whose social worlds were similarly sundered by the social and cultural conditions caused by racism, de-industrialization, over-policing, and the globalization of capital (Magubane, 2006). For example, the economic conditions and social realities that permeated the *banlieues* in France during the 1980s proved vital in sparking alienated French youths' interest in hip-hop. Specifically, the loss of permanent blue-collar work and other low-income jobs "created an atmosphere of depressed sterility," and *banlieue* youths experienced a sense of social exile when the elite in France pushed them to the margins of French society, despite the fact that many of them were French citizens (Silverstein, 2005, p. 50). They were positioned as being the "immigrant problem," which was equated to being the source of economic and social maladies permeating France (Beau, 1999). Not coincidentally, these youth identified with the messages of Afrika Bambattaa, a former gang member from New York, who visited France in 1984 in order to establish a branch of the Zulu Nation (Helenon, 2006). The message of the Zulu Nation, which was grounded in the ideals of "social responsibility, culture, and peace", was established by Bambattaa to combat gang violence (Helenon, 2006, p 153). He believed that hip-hop needed to "make a commitment to stop the violence and shift toward more political advocacy in urban communities" world-wide (Chang as cited in Prier, in this volume).

With the ascendency of the neo-liberal agenda in France as well as in former French colonies during the 1990s, the social and economic conditions deteriorated for most minoritized youth in these regions. Many disaffected youth found solace and inspiration that they could overcome their unjust realities through the lyrics and cultural work of the early French hip-hop movement, such as MC Solaar, IAM, and Suprême NTM as well as their transgressive hip-hop counterparts in the US, such as Public Enemy, NWA and Ice-T. Today, the hip-hop counterculture in France has broadened to not only reflect the local concerns and struggles of youth residing in the cities but also to provide "an immanent critique" of how neo-liberalism fosters institutional racism, classism, police corruption, Western imperialism, and environmental degradation in geographical spaces across the globe (Magubane, 2006, p. 214).

In the pages that follow, we mine the cultural manifestations of French hip-hop pedagogues to illustrate how Western colonialism, imperialism and neo-liberalism are "largely responsible for the swelling of abject poverty, suffering and misery, environmental degradation, the Western world's growing police state, the military-prison-education-industrial complex and virulent forms of racism, sexism, and homophobia" (Giroux, 2004). In particular, we uncover three recurring themes that surface in the artists' texts, which elucidate their critical insight towards what fuels injustice and oppression in France and in the wider social world: 1) life and oppression in the *banlieue*; 2) making visible the impact of Western colonialism and reconstituting and transforming self; and 3) current manifestations of neo-liberal globalization and Western imperialism. The paper also illuminates the power that the youths' cultural work has had in confronting the institutions, policies, and practices responsible for their own dark social realities and for today's increasingly morally bankrupt world. The examination begins by providing an overview of the birth of neo-liberalism followed by an explanation of how neo-liberalism gained a foothold on France's political and economic systems. Next, the lyrics of several predominant French hip-hop intellectuals are critically analyzed to illustrate the impact of neo-liberal policies and practices on life within France, the "Third-World," and in other social settings, providing a valuable critique in relation to how the latest manifestation of capitalism is hijacking humanity. Finally, this essay concludes with an examination of several hip-hop intellectuals' cultural work. It is argued that youth social activism has the potency to forge a collective, world-wide movement to subvert the corporatist and militaristic takeover of social life.

The Birth of Neo-liberalism

For the last thirty years, we have witnessed a major economic, social and political change in the Western capitalist society that has not only allowed corporate leaders to concentrate their wealth and power within the West but also to extract resources and wealth from global citizens who live in the so called "Third World." The birth of neo-liberalism can be traced to the mid-1970s, when Western political, economic, and academic leaders looked to Latin America as a site for cheap labor, an outlet to sell goods that were overproduced due to "the decline of the Post-War economic boom", and a sanctuary to reduce costs and burdens that were often part of the industrial production process in the US, such as taxes, environmental regulations, minimum wages, and workers' right to organize (Farahmandpur, 2008, p. 7). Backed by economic rhetoric generated by pro-capitalist economists such as Milton Freedman, the "Chicago Boys" at the University of Chicago, and the support of US's military forces, large-scale corporations began their virulent assault to privatize and control social life in Latin America. The assassination of Chile's President Salvador Allende in 1973 by the CIA set the trend for further Western exploitation and control of the "Third World." This allowed "Chicago Boys'" academics to freely implement their brand of "free market economics" in Chile, which equated to enacting policies that favored big business at the expense of labor and the environment (Schatan, 2001).

They "sold off state-owned companies, lowering taxes and tariffs, 'freeing' prices by eliminating government subsidies, and privatizing government social services such as health, education and social security" (Rosenfeld, 1994). International organizations, such as the International Monetary Fund (IMF), the World Bank, and the World Trade Organization (WTO), not only created a propaganda campaign to lull the public to believe that Western capitalism and technological developments will lead the world into economic prosperity and social well-being but also forced other countries throughout Latin America to adopt pro-capitalistic policies. In reality, the neo-liberal experiment was designed only to benefit the transnational capitalist class and ensure that more and more of the world's working peoples live in the throes of poverty, pollution and hopelessness (Farahmandpur, 2008; McLaren, 2005).

131

With the successful implementation of neo-liberal policies in Latin America, Western political leaders, such as Ronald Reagan and Margaret Thatcher, launched a similar neo-liberal campaign to implement policies and practices in Western social and political contexts. Particularly, these policies retrenched the role of the state from being actively involved in providing social protection for its citizens in areas such as education, health care, utilities, negotiation between labor and capital, and prisons. They also ensured the profit motive rather than the motive to meet the intellectual, social, and emotional needs of citizens who control the "public sector completely" (Said, 2000). Since this time-period, the ruling class has utilized Western military forces and the much "ballyhooed information revolution" to globalize capital, weaken organized labor, reduce taxation, open new markets to corporate conglomerates, privatize various aspects of social life, and silence critics who oppose corporate and military interests having limitless power over our social relationship and daily affairs (Martin, 2008, p. 126). Fortunately, there have been several simultaneous counterculture movements, lead by enlightened social actors who have seen past the corporate, academic and political rhetoric that neo-liberal capitalism benefits humanity. Some of this resistance is witnessed in the cultural work and aesthetic expressions of disaffected minoritized youths who have felt the deleterious impact from the latest manifestation of capital. Below, we explore some of the voices of youths living in the debilitated communities of the French *banlieues* who express their opposition, concern and doubt to the commercial and militaristic takeover of their schools, communities, and the wider society through hip-hop texts and cultural work.

Neo-liberalism Gains a Foothold in France

In France, neo-liberalism developed much more slowly than its Western counterparts, such as Britain and the US, due to three key factors: 1) France did not experience a similar economic crisis that unfolded in other countries due to high inflation and the oil crisis; 2) the country's political elite feared a backlash from the large militant working-class and electorate due to their history of rebelling against policies and practices that inhibited working-class solidarity, slashed wages, and gutted social entitlements; and 3) France feared going into debt, thus the state rather than businesses and corporations, provided low-interest loans to support economic growth (Fourcade-Gourinchas and Babb, 2002; Prasad, 2005). However, in 1984 under Francois Mitterand, the ruling elite felt pressure from France's European partners and the US to support neo-liberal policies, which were designed to integrate France into the European and international economies (Fourcade-Gourinchas and Babb, 2002). The ruling elite also used this as an opportunity to undermine the collective strength of the French working-class and French labor unions (Herrera, 2006). Gradually, neo-liberal policies rolled back workers' social gains, and allowed the ruling elite to make profit a greater priority than supporting the well-being of its citizens. Neo-liberal policies ensured that the state was not concerned with supporting the ideal of democratic equality or providing full-employment to its citizens (Fourcade-Gourinchas and Babb, 2002, p. 566).

Over the past 20 years, several policies and practices have been generated by the ruling elite to further the neo-liberal agenda. In France, the elite privatized several sectors of the economy; in fact, by the end of 2002, 80% of banking, 50% of insurance, and 12.6% of the workforce had been privatized in addition to major public services such as France Telecom, AirFrance, and Credit Lyonnais (Prasad 2005, p. 367). Furthermore, there has been a slight reduction of government spending on social welfare programs as well as an implementation of a more regressive tax structure. This is in addition to the state's attempt to thwart the public sector from providing pensions and health care for workers. Political scientist Palier, in an interview with Buchen (2007), does an excellent job articulating how the relationship between the state and businesses has been altered during the age of neo-liberalism:

> The French economy has changed a lot. It was known as a *dirigiste* economy, so the state decided a lot of things; what kind of investment you do, what kind of mergers between firms—these kinds of things. All this has vanished. Company decisions are not taken by the state anymore, they are taken by the stakeholders or the CEOs. France has become an internationalized capitalist country, as far as the economy is concerned; much more than Germany Italy or Spain, for instance. You are very close to the openness and the capitalistic machinery of the U.K. or the U.S.
>
> Industrial relations have changed a lot, too. We were living in a [confrontational] country where the unions and the employers used to negotiate at a national level after any big crisis. Now the collective negotiations over working conditions are made at the company level, not at the national level. This means less power for the confederation of the unions, and much more power locally, within the firms, which has weakened the unions.

The social groups most negatively affected by these policies and practices were, and continue to be, the unemployed, working-poor and immigrant families, who tend to inhabit the housing projects in the *banlieues* of France. "The term *banlieue* translates as 'suburb' but in fact denotes a geographical area on the periphery of major cities and made up of poor housing estates" (Gerwal, 2007, p. 41). Most of the families living in this geographical area migrated to France as a result of recruitment efforts of corporate leaders, who promised them stable employment and better living conditions. Moreover, "structural adjustment policies, state violence, and economic instability" in the former French colonies located in North and sub-Saharan Africa as well as the Caribbean were integral factors responsible for the need of immigration (Kelley, xii, 2006). Some of the families, who immigrated to the *banlieues* not only discovered how Western neo-liberal policies instituted cultural and economic oppression in the so-called "Third World" but also experienced first-hand the economic and social devastation associated with the current manifestation of neo-liberal capitalism within France due to the aforementioned policy changes. For these families as well as other working-class citizens, the implementation of corporatist and militaristic policies has resulted in job loss, high unemployment, dismantling of public services and social entitlements, and an increasing police presence within their own dislocated social worlds. This is certainly far from the prosperous picture presented by corporate conglomerates, who recruited them to be a cheap source of labor (Helenon, 2006, p. 151, 153; Silverstein 2002).

Today, the *banlieue* has become ethnicized as media outlets and government officials have captured France's popular imagination that this location is occupied by mostly Muslim youths. They are typecast as being violent, and angry, and characterized as terrorists, therefore, perceived a threat to European societies, in general, and French national identity, in particular (Grewal, 2007). According to Gerwal (2007), the ethnicisation of the *banlieue* has not only blocked the public from recognizing how neo-liberal policies have caused poverty, the 2005 riots and suffering amongst most working-class and impoverished citizens in France but has also been the impetus for the French government to implement a greater police presence and tougher measures within this 'suburb,' which will only perpetuate further suffering of its inhabitants as well as further demonizing and trivializing Arab culture.

The Hip-Hop Movement in France: Life in the Banlieue

In the early-1980s, tensions among the state and the children of immigrants and other members of the suburban underclass became heightened due to a growing police presence in the *cités* and the economic despair experienced by *banlieue* youths (Silverstein and Tetreault, 2005). Minoritized youths were frequently joining the ranks of the underemployed or working poor as industrial jobs in France were lost to de-industrialization or to the deliberate process of outsourcing labor to regions economically and socially subjugated to Western powers. Their social worlds only became further dislocated when security forces entered their communities to "extinguish theft and violence (what authorities often denounce as "delinquency") against local stores, apartments, and commercial rivals" (Silverstein, 2005, p. 50). The tensions, unfortunately, parlayed into a riot in the summer of 1981 as young men engaged in vandalism and violent encounters with security officials (Grewal, 2007). Since the 1981 riot, the conditions in the *banlieue* have continued to deteriorate and are now considered dilapidated. Within the *cités*, there is a lack of adequate public transportation, a shortage of public housing, high unemployment for youths, and gray-market institutions revolve around the drug trade and the fencing of stolen consumer items (Silverstein & Tetreault, 2005). Police and youths clash on a daily basis, and their conflicts are spawned across various media outlets, leaving French citizens from the dominant society to "reinforce the construction of the *banlieue* as a site of juvenile male delinquency and violence," and to incorrectly place blame on *banlieue* youths as the sole source for the social and economic conditions that cause their own alienation and suffering, instead of establishing corporate transnational greed as the major source of France's and the globe's social and economic problems (Grewal, 2007, p. 46).

As a result of the deterioration of social and economic conditions, being labeled as violent, aberrant or in the words of President Sarkozy "*racailles*" (scum), some youths looked to Black hip-hip pioneers' cultural work as emancipatory guideposts.

Black hip-hip pedagogues served as inspirational figures, which offered them the courage and artistic forms and expressions to denounce the state for perpetuating violence, engendering poverty and joblessness, ignoring deteriorating housing conditions and its "integrating mission," which is designed to denigrate and strip them of their culture and make them "productive and well-adjusted Frenchmen" (Silverstein & Tetreault, 2005). Even though the hip-hop movement in France in the early-1980s consisted initially of the artistic forms of graffiti and break-dancing, by 1985 French hip-hop artists began to incorporate rap into their repertoire of expressing themselves. Artists, such as Suprême NTM (Nique Ta Mère or Fuck Your Mother), Assassin, Ministère AMER, and A.L.A.R.M.E., who view themselves as "hardcore," were inspired and borrowed heavily from hip-hip pedagogues in the US, whose cultural messages displayed their opposition to the "social order and to political and economic systems," and spoke to the angst, oppression, and dislocation they encountered within often blighted, crime-ridden, and militarized urban communities across the US (Prevos, 1996, p. 716). The *raison de etre* of "hardcore" French artists was to denounce what they saw as "the social and economic exploitation of marginal groups and individuals in French society" (Bocquet and Pierre-Adolphe as cited in Prevos, 2005, p. 9).

By the early-1990s, the ideas espoused by "hardcore" French artists resonated loudly in the hearts and minds of many *banlieue* youths. They gravitated to this form of hip-hop as a conduit to voice their anger and frustrations, which were often kept silenced, towards the political and social actors, structures, and institutions fueling oppression and breeding tension between the state and their communities. Suprême NTM's song "Police" is an exemplary example of the form of critique launched by "hardcore" French pedagogues during this period. Like their US hip-hop "hardcore" counterparts, such as NWA, ICE-T, and Body Count, NTM launched a "virulent critique of police brutality against *banlieusard* (suburban) and immigrant youth" (Silverstein, 2002, p. 45). The tensions between the police and youths are demonstrated in the lyrics below:

Aussi sachez que l'air est charge d'électricité,

Alors pas de respect, pas de pitié escomptée

Vous aurez des regrets car:

Jamais par la répression vous n'obtiendrez la paix,

La paix de l'âme, le respect de l'homme.

Mais cette notion d'humanité n'existe plus quand ils passent l'uniforme

Know that the air is charged with electricity

So no respect, no pity anticipated

You will regret it because:

Never will you obtain peace with repression

Peace of the soul, respect of mankind

But this notion of humanity no longer exists when they wear the uniform.

As more and more neo-liberal policies have been implemented in France since the early-90s, the conditions continue to deteriorate for *banlieue* youths and their families. For instance, according to Debbaut (2006), in 2006, half of the inhabitants of the *banlieue* were "under 20 years old, unemployment was above 40 percent, and identity checks and police harassment occurred daily." The conditions and tensions between the state and minoritized youths constitute the vortex of violent conflicts in the cities, characterized by vandalism and confrontations between police officials and *banlieue* youths. The most noticeable conflict is the 2005 riots, which occurred after two young French teens died in Clichy-sous-Bois after being chased by police (Debbaut 2006; Grewal, 2007). The state claimed that it needed to mobilize its police forces to fight crime in working-class communities. However, according to Hajjat (2006), the actual reason the state invaded working-class communities was to thwart youths from organizing collectively to dislodge the existing social and economic systems in France. He states:

> The state of emergency was declared in order to repress a protest that was becoming more and more political—which was literally questioning the state's monopoly of violence. It was not the Republic, the nation or democracy that was being questioned, but the state as an institution of repression and subjection of the oppressed in this country.

Along with the French "hardcore" pedagogues who provided a scathing critique of the social and political order responsible for minoritized youths' oppression during the early-1990s, a new group of hip-hop pedagogues—nearly all of whom are Black or of North African-Arab origin—have made visible the social conditions and injustices generating violence and oppression in the *cités* through their music (Schofield, 2005). Groups and artists such as Sniper, Kery James, Disiz la Peste, Monsieur R, and 113 have continually identified the factors mediating economic and social disparities between minoritized citizens and dominant French society. For instance, in the video for Disiz la Peste's song "Jeune de Banlieue," the viewer sees how members of the dominant French society generally perceive the *banlieue* community, as a stereotypical White middle-class family, consisting of husband, wife, children and a luxury car, goes on an amusement park ride through what the large powers configure as "*banlieue*." The family is seen gazing at stereotypical images of the Arab "Other," who are depicted as violent, misogynistic and fanatical.

   At one level, the family is entertained by the exotic nature of the "tour." Not only do they seem to internalize the hegemonic characterization of Muslim culture rather than recognize the systemic inequalities which causes violence, oppression, and suffering in the *banlieues,* but they also seem to cling to the racist notion that their Whiteness has the power to thwart the supposedly violent, recalcitrant and exotic Muslim culture from "infiltrating" and "infecting" their Whitewashed world. At another level, a sense of fear is projected during their ride. They are left to question whether their privileged position might be challenged by an increased immigrant presence within France, which may dislodge the unjust power they garner from living in a society favoring Eurocentric ideals and privileging Western traditions.

Kery James, who was born in Guadeloupe, immigrated to France at the age of 7, and grew up in the suburbs of Paris. In his song, *Banlieusards*, Kery is more explicit in relation to how the dominant society fosters unjust power relations between themselves and minoritized citizens in the *banlieues*: He states: "it is for the discriminated, often incriminated, the innocent ones they treat as real criminals. We are viewed as predators, but we are only prey, capable but guilty and excluded from employment" (album). James also emphasizes how members of the dominant society often embrace racist and stereotypical views of the "Other" by viewing them as "potential terrorists" (album). Finally, the song illuminates how White leaders are the individuals who ultimately benefit from the fear and paranoia generated against minoritized citizens in France. Their desire to make a profit and concentrate their power are inextricably bound up in their keeping minoritized youths' "heads underwater" (album).

Hip-Hop Pedagogues' Connection to Africa: Confronting the Past, Challenging Perceptions, and Reconfiguring Themselves

Other youths in France drew upon the Afrocentric themes of Africa Bambatta and US hip-hop artists as an intuitive response to the alienation and oppression they experienced in the *cités* as well as to "[re]claim their origins, redefine their identity and challenge traditional French conceptions of race and citizenship" (Helenon, 2006 p. 151; Fourcade-Gourinchas and Babb, 2002, p. 566). For instance, the Algerian hip-hop group IAM reclaimed their African roots by adopting Egyptian stage personas. Not only did their identity performance confront the dominant society for propagating historical inaccuracies and for creating laws and policies which kept the intellectual contributions made by numerous African s/heroes to the development of Western civilization out of dominant academic discourses and structures but also it confronted the "deficit ideology" that frames African youths and their families' beliefs, values, and ideals as being the source for the social and economic maladies permeating French society (Helenon, p. 153). In the song *Tam Tam de l'Afrique*, they also pinpoint how colonialism and slavery have twinned together to denigrate and (mis)cast African and Black identity in Western societies, while concomitantly privileging the systems, values, and ideologies that structure asymmetrical relationships in the hegemonic world.

Ils leur ont inculqué que leur couleur était un crime

Il leur ont tout volé, jusqu'à leurs secrets les plus intimes

Pillé leur culture, brûlé leurs racines

De l'Afrique du Sud, jusqu'aux rives du Nil

They inculcated them to believe that their color was a crime.

They stole everything from them, even their most intimate secrets

Pillaged their culture and burned their roots

From the South of Africa to the banks of the Nile.

Other hip-hop pedagogues have shared their insights in relation to the process of, and impact from, the dominant culture denigrating, distorting, or merely excluding the experiences of Black people, who live in France or in former French colonies. The educational structures in France purposely exclude the experiences of African peoples, and fail to critically examine how Western institutions confer unearned privileges and entitlements to members of the dominant society. Monsieur R, a hip-hop artist who attended high school in Seine-Saint-Denis, an area of Paris, saw first-hand how racism pervaded his school's curricula, as his teachers failed to document how France's colonial past influences the relationship between France and many of its citizens who immigrated to France. In an interview, he states, "if kids are angry in the classroom it's because of one thing. They haven't been told the whole story about their mother county. No one ever teaches kids about France...No one taught me about French colonialism. And that's led to big problems for everyone in France" (Werman, 2006).

Some artists utilized their music to provide *banlieue* youths and communities an autonomous zone to write an unofficial curriculum of the history of how Black people impacted the development of French society (Helenon, 2006, p. 152). For instance, some artists, such as Ménélik, MC Solaar, and KDD, generated quixotic portraits of Africa's past to "counterbalance devastating impact of slavery" and to oppose values promulgated by the dominant French society (Helenon, 2006). In "Hijo De Africa," MC Solaar, who was born in Senegal and arrived in the Paris region at age six, raps about many of Africa's positive cultural aspects, which are generally over-shadowed in the Western media by sensationalized accounts of tragedies that are projected to viewers as ubiquitously taking place across the continent, such as the AIDS epidemic, war, and famine. MC Solaar wants us to "see the ancestral way, the beautiful ward robes... see the eye of the griot when he tells you our History; the village dances during ceremonies as well as the initiative rites."

Hip-Hop Intellectuals: Exposing and Subverting the Neo-liberal Agenda

There have also been several hip-hop pedagogues in France over the past 15 years who have extended their critique of what has caused oppression in their own communities, in social spaces in France, and in their place of origins. Through their music, they have illustrated how the latest manifestation of capitalism—neo-liberal globalization—is perpetuating suffering, violence, misery, and environmental degradation in their own lived worlds as well as in other social, political, and economic contexts. They have also pointed to the cultural work generated by social activists and political figures, such as Che Guevara, the Zapatistas, and the Túpac Amaru Revolutionary Movement,which provide concerned citizens and other transformative intellectuals inspiration to uproot systemic barriers and unjust policies that allow an out-of-control transnational global elite to concentrate its power and to engender more suffering, misery, and hatred across the planet (McLaren, 2005). Their actions also provide the foresight to concerned citizens for the immediate need to develop economic, political and social structures that have the potency to produce conditions where freedom, democracy, and peace can flourish.

In the early-1990s, artists, such as Suprême NTM, Assassin, and MC Solaar, began to link problems in their communities and in their various places of origin, such Africa and the Caribbean, with neo-liberal globalization. For instance, Suprême NTM's song *L'argent pourrit les gens* (Money rots people) (1991) captures how Western government officials abandoned implementing policies and practices predicated on improving the well-being of its citizens by ceding their power to CEOs and academics, who focused on amassing wealth and power through speed technologies, on controlling the agenda of international organizations, such as the IMF and WTO, on selling weapons, on conquering territories, and on controlling labor power and resources across Africa and other regions across the globe. The lyrics below highlight some of the destructive aspects of neo-liberal capitalism:

Précisément en ce moment

Tout s'achète, tout se vend

Même les gouvernements

Prêts à baisser leur froc

Pour une question d'argent...

...Apparemment l'armement

Passe largement avant

La condition de vie de chacun

Le monde est plein de bombes

Qui creuseront nos tombes

Maintenant tu sais à quoi sert le fric

Qui à lui seul pourrait stopper la famine en Afrique

L'ARGENT POURRIT LES GENS

J'EN AI LE SENTIMENT

Precisely at this moment

Everything is being bought and sold

Even governments are ready to lay down their frock

When it comes to money...

...Apparently, weaponry is more important than

The condition of our lives

The world is full of bombs, which will dig our tombs

Now you know what dough is good for
Only it could stop the famine in Africa
MONEY ROTS PEOPLE
I FEEL IT.

Furthermore, MC Solaar's song *Matière grasse contre matière grise* (1991) is indicative of hip-hop artists who placed blame on neo-liberal capitalism for problems surfacing the globe during this period when he transforms the word capitalist into *"caca-pipi-caca-pipitaliste"* (shit-piss-shit-pisstalist). He also makes clear that rap can become a transcending vehicle for the world to unite and overturn the system that oppresses humanity. In his song, he sends a message to all oppressed peoples: *"le rap est l'une des solutions pour parler des problems sans discrimination"* (rap is one of the solutions to be able to talk without discrimination).

More recently, hip-hop intellectuals, such as Skalpel, Pizko MC, Guez and E.One, have upped the radical ante by engaging in a form of "militant rap" called *Rap Conscient* or Conscious Rap. Skalpel, one of the members of the group La K-bine, defines this style of political rap as "a reflective and lucid rap, which inscribes an approach to analyze the current political situation with a strong dose of memory work and the care of being coherent with our texts in our everyday lives." Skalpel and other conscious hip-hop intellectuals detect how neo-liberal globalization is impacting social relations across the globe by first invoking a "critical pedagogy of place," which positions them to pinpoint how neo-liberalism and other historical forces infect their communities in the forms of dead-end jobs, increasing inequalities, and the repression of contestation. They also invoke an additional pedagogical approach to unpack what accounts for the oppression and misery that haunts the rest of humanity in the neo-liberal age. Through their music, they vocalize this reflexive process. They speak to the pro-social work of activists who are struggling against neo-liberal "capitalism (imperialism in its cruelest form)," and reclaim the memory of immigrants who struggled in the past so as to help minoritized groups better understand how global capitalism shapes their identities and social relationships (Bounce2dis, 2007).

In the song *Revolt*, La K-Bine makes it quite clear that the dominant society uses social activities, such as sports, to keep the masses "amused," blocked from focusing on the everyday oppressions. They state: "J'aime le foot mais je me dis que ce sport abrutis vraiment les masses. Ils parlent de modèle d'intégration, moi je te parle de lutte de classes" (I like soccer but I tell myself that this sport really numbs the masses. They talk about it being the model of integration; I talk to you about the struggle of classes.) (La K-Bine, 2006). On a macro-scale, the group, in their song *Liberez-les!!!* (Free them!!!), demands the release of revolutionary fighters and militants who have been incarcerated for their acts of transgression against the state and global capitalism. In the lyrics below, La K-Bine demonstrate how revolutionary activists are often ironically framed as terrorists by those who are actually embracing a transnational economic system that promotes terror, suffering and misrepresentation of those who challenge it. They claim:

Les gens considèrent comme terroriste

La personne qui prend arme pour lutter contre l'impérialisme.

Que pensent-ils? De ses Etats qui appliquent les méthodes de la dictature

De ses patrons qui traitent les ouvriers comme des vulgaires ordures

De ses trafiquants d'armes qui s'enrichissent sur la misère humaine

The people considered as terrorists

The person who takes up arms to fight against imperialism

What do they think? Of these States which apply methods of dictatorship

Of the corporate leaders who treat their workers as vulgar waste

Of arms traffickers who get rich of off human misery.

Another critical artist who confronts neo-liberal capitalism is Monsieur R, who was born in Belgium, moved to his parents' home country of the Congo at the age of 3, then migrated to France in 1989. This "political hip-hop soldier," in a recent album, *Le Che Guevara: Une braise qui brûle encore* (An ember that still burns) (2007), pays tribute to Che Guevara for the hope and inspiration he gives to millions of people who attempt to eradicate oppression by overturning asymmetrical economic and social relationships. In addition, he criticizes Western imperial powers in his song *Le Silence Tue* (Silence kills) (2008) for unleashing a campaign of terror against anyone who stands in the way of globalizing capital, conquering territories, garnering resources and exploiting labor power. After describing the present starkness of the world in the beginning of the song, he documents the inhumanity reflected in the detention "camps of terror" set up by US government and military officials in Guantanamo Bay, which take away fundamental civic rights of due process, attempt to silence opposition to Western imperialism and corporatism, and promote senseless violence:

Je pense que cette fois-ci, l'humanité a bien touché le fond

Persuadé qu'haut dessus de leur tête ils ont un anneau

Auréolé de leur victoire, il crée l'horrible, prison de Guantanamo

Où des hommes sont condamnés sans être jugés

I think that this time, humanity has really hit rock bottom

Persuaded that they have a halo of victory above their head

It creates the horrible prison of Guantanamo

Where men are condemned without being judged

Beyond the Music: Hip-Hop Activists Subverting the Neo-liberal Agenda

In addition to their music, many hip-hop intellectuals have joined other activists, organizations, and countercultural movements to free the globe from institutional oppression and to generate new social and economic structures that are in line with fostering the needs of humanity and respecting the ecological world. Many of the artists utilize the stage to create a sense of solidarity among minoritized peoples and activists from the dominant culture, to bring awareness to salient issues affecting French society as well as the global community, and to raise money for, and support of, political and social organizations fighting neo-liberal policies and practices. For example, in 1995, Suprême NTM and MC Solaar, along with several other French artists, held a concert to protest the mayoral victories of two National Front candidates, individuals who supported the Party's anti-immigrant, pro-capital, anti-work and anti-Semitism platform. Similarly in 1998, several artists came together to celebrate the 150th anniversary of the abolition of slavery in France, raising awareness of how the legacy of slavery and French colonial rule impact today's minoritized citizens.

Another example is Keny Arkana, a female French rap artist born in France and of Argentinean origin. Being a part of the anti-globalization collective called "*Le Rage du Peuple*" (The Rage of the People), she has used her music and concerts not only to critic neo-liberal practices but also to create solidarity and bring awareness to social issues. This is witnessed in Keny's support of demonstrators at a strike on May 4, 2008. She played her music to inspire activists, who marched to protest anti-immigration policies, and to demand the closure of immigrant retention centers (Quotidian, 2008). These detention areas keep foreign nationals "in inhumane conditions for weeks and months before expulsion to their country of origin or country of entry into the European Union" (Ria and Mabut, 2008). In fact, according to Ria and Mabut (2008), "these conditions regularly give rise to suicide attempts, self-mutilation and fights."

Many hip-hop intellectuals have added computing technology to their repertoire to build awareness and solidarity to corporate elite's desire to cement their power through education, war, the media, and policies bent on intimidation and control. The quintessential example of how technology is being used in transformative and subversive ways is the website: www.rap-conscient.com. This website has become an online hub for artists and activists alike who are able to post messages of solidarity, calls to action and protest, information about concerts and events earmarked for social justice purposes, and for creating social networks that help to support organizations, which are committed to protecting the rights of citizens and the environment in the age of disaster capitalism. Furthermore, the website provides community members links to the following categories of social justice organizations and groups: anti-publicity organizations, rap groups, militant groups, libertarian groups, media alternatives, and political prisoner organizations among others.

Hip-hop artists are also using websites, such as MySpace.com, to connect with other artists, activists and fans. Skalpel, one of the members of RapConcient, has also created a MySpace page where he posts concerts and events, responds to messages, provides links to other social justice websites, and maintains a Blog called *Mouvement Autonome des Banlieues 93* (Autonomous Movement of the Suburbs 93). In this blog, he and E.One de Eskicit, another socially conscious hip-hop artist, describe the intolerable living conditions of the *banlieue* and the "Third World" due to neo-liberal capitalism, their desire to confront the system and liberate all minoritized peoples, and the need for more people to join the revolutionary movement. One example of the critical dialogues generated in this blog is meant to remind us that capitalism—not minoritized people—are to blame for social and economic disparities. They state: "nous sommes des artistes libres qui avons choisi de résister au système voulant nous empêcher de créer...Pour certains le règne de l'injustice est supportable, pour nous il ne l'est pas. Ce n'est pas notre faute" (We are free artists who have chosen to resist the system that wants to prevent us from creating...For certain people, the rule of injustice is tolerable, for us it is not. It is not our fault) (Skalpel, 2007).

Discussion

As we have attempted to capture in this chapter, the hip-hop movement in France was formulated as an institutive response to the policies and practices emanating from neo-liberal capitalism. Through their music, hip-hop intellectuals made visible the deleterious economic and social conditions pervading their communities due to de-industrialization, to outsourcing of labor, to the slashing of social entitlements, and to social policies aimed at criminalizing, profiting from, and blaming youths for their alienation and dislocation. They also used their aesthetic expressions to challenge the state's debilitating stereotypes of the *citiés*, immigrant youths, and themselves. Several "conscious" rappers have recently documented how neo-liberal capitalism and Western military intervention are responsible for causing abject poverty, violence, (mis)representation of minoritized citizens, and repression of civil and political rights. While their cultural work has simultaneously inspired social activists, artists, and youths to work collectively to forge a new egalitarian society, and aided others in finding social networks of like-minded individuals who believe in challenging Western imperialism, corporate greed, Eurocentric ideals, and entrenched social inequalities. Despite hip-hop's power to provide hope, inspiration, and spiritual and emotional growth to the *banlieue* and minoritized youths as well as to other social activists, the question remains as to what value this counter-culture has in guiding pre-service and in-service teachers, teacher-educators, and their students to understand the impact of neo-liberal policies and practices on schools and the wider society in an effort to dismantle unjust economic and social relationships at today's socio-historical moment?

In the North American context, the cultural manifestations of French hip-hop artists have the potential to help in-service and pre-service teachers get beyond their often internalized, shortsighted view that the social structures of North American society are fair and open. The hip-hip intellectuals' texts have the power to nudge them to recognize how macro-level forces merge with unjust policies and practices in contemporary society to marginalize the vast majority of the world's population. They will also help them see that their socially mediated world is far from normal, as their skin color and class status have, thus far, shielded them from the adverse effects emanating from neo-liberal capitalism. Moreover, they may begin to see urban and minoritized youths in a newfound light. They may get beyond how government officials position urban youths as social misfits, perpetrators of violence, or even the chief source of social problems that circulates within schools and in communities to view them as intelligent individuals whose aesthetic expressions and cultural work should serve as beacons of social and economic transformation.

Holding a newfound understanding of the nature between knowledge and power, between self and Other, and an appreciation for hip-hop pedagogues and their culture, they would have the power to revolutionize their pedagogy, possessing the ability to employ the hip-hop pedagogues' cultural manifestations so that their students are able "to read the word and the world" (Friere, 2005). By revolutionizing their pedagogy, they will also have the power to guide students to channel the alienation and dislocation that they often experience in their communities, in K-12 classrooms, and other social contexts in to generating transgressive cultural work. In other worlds, K-12 teachers will provide the critical insight and emancipatory guideposts to show students how to build upon the dissent-focused projects proffered by hip-hip intellectuals to challenge entrenched policies and arrangements perpetuating suffering and social inequalities.

Certainly, we do not provide this pedagogical approach as a "magic bullet" to guide White teachers to possess the critical insight and desire to teach for personal and social transformation, as there is "no one single method" to help them understand the relationship between power and knowledge and "the extent of their privilege," especially when attempting to "meet the challenges of working with culturally diverse students" (Hill, 2007). However, we agree with Weiler (2002) that critiquing various forms of youths' cultural manifestations ought to become a central component within schools of education, as it is essential to position current and future teachers to become stewards of cultural and social transformation inside and outside of their classrooms.

Outside of the academic world, the hip-hop pedagogues' cultural manifestations can become an important ingredient in revitalizing labor education in the US, and in formulating a world-wide movement to eliminate neo-liberal capitalism. According to Bacon (2009), the US labor movement has historically been vibrant when workers have been inspired by a "real vision of social change." Currently, many US union workers are not able to "approach capitalism on an international scale" (Bacon 2009). They have been unable to link how capitalism manifests itself with military intervention and neo-liberalism.

By incorporating the spirited critique launched by French hip-hop intellectuals of Western imperialism, generally, and of US foreign policy, specifically, US workers might hold the insight and motivation to join other labor unions across the globe that have acted in solidarity against neo-liberal capitalism. For instance, they might have the motivation to join workers, students, and other residents in Guadeloupe who have been on strike and filled the streets of Pointe-à-Pitre to demand social entitlements, higher wages, better working conditions, and to stop Western imperialism. French union workers have also joined their cause because they realize that Western imperialism and neo-liberal capitalism are at the heart of all workers' suffering, and also serve to reinforce the increasing power of the transnational global elite.

Conclusion

By mining the aesthetic expressions and cultural work of hip-hop intellectuals in the French *banlieue*, we have strived to provide a richer understanding of how neo-liberal capitalism perpetrates poverty, militarism, alienation, and suffering in working-class communities in France as well as in other social contexts. We also have witnessed how youths tap their alienation and social dislocation to generate critical narratives that have the potential to provide teachers, teacher-educators, youths and other concerned citizens insight to understand the destructive path of neo-liberalism. It is hoped that this will lead to the possibility of formulating a united front to overturn globalist capital relation, in building a society predicated on the ideals of justice, hope, democracy, and peace. We now call on other transformative intellectuals to critically analyze other cultural manifestations generated by youths to lead us beyond the current social and economic malaise in order to generate a vision of hope that will take us outside the orbit of neo-liberal capitalism (McLaren, 2005).

QUESTIONS FOR REFLECTION

1. What are some other youth cultural manifestations that ought to be harnessed by teachers and teacher educators to bring awareness to the debilitating nature of neoliberalism?
2. What are some additional ways that teachers can use hip-hop intellectuals' texts and cultural work in promoting critical literacy across the K-12 curriculum?
3. What are some difference in the way in which neo-liberal globalization has impacted female hip-hop intellectuals and their male counterparts?

NOTES

[1] Despite white corporate elites supporting artists who embody a violent and misogynistic "gangsta" persona, the music and cultural work of some "gangsta" artists lend the "possibility of resisting and subverting" the social and economic systems that give rise to neo-liberalism (McLaren, 2000 p. 258) They illustrate how racism, classism and homophobia structure the lives of hip-hop artists and other marginalized youth and critique the debilitating sources behind their alienation such as white supremacy and capitalism (McLaren, 2000 p. 247).

[2] For the purpose of this essay, we define oppositional culture as everything from "extending kinship networks that function in face of harsh economic circumstances, to civil rights movements that direct the energies of the group, to legal redress of grievances, to finding expression in artistic and cultural mediums that voice or visualize cultural pride or protest and critic of the dominant culture." (Mitchell and Feagin, 1995 as cited in Martinez, 1997, 268)

[3] Milton Freedman and pro-capitalists economics espoused the idea that free market economics would ameliorate poverty, promote peace and usher prosperity across the globe. In reality, free market economics were never embraced by Western political leaders. They used their control of international organizations such as the IMF (International Monetary Fund), the World Bank and the World Trade Organization (1999) to enact policies (such as NAFTA (1994) and CAFTA) that supported the interests of large scale corporations at the expense of the world's population.

[4] According to Silverstein and Tetreault (2005), "by the early 1990s, youth unemployment nationwide was as high as 20 percent—twice the average among all age groups. In certain cités, the figures have been even higher, with unemployment among young residents on average above 30 percent, and as high as 85 percent."

[5] Please see in this volume to examine further the importance of developing a critical pedagogy of place to bring awareness to how neo-liberal policies and practices generate social and economic inequalities at today' historical moment.

REFERENCES

Al-Jadda, S. (2005, November 8). In French riots, a lesson for Europe. *USA Today*.

Bacon, D. (2009, February). A radical vision for today's labor movement: The importance of internationalism and civil rights. *Monthly Review*.

Basu, D., & Sidney, J. L. (Eds.). (2006). *The vinyl ain't final: Hip-hop and the globalization of Black popular culture*. Ann Harbor, MI: Pluto Press.

Beau, M. A. (1999). *Hip-hop and rap in Eurpoe: The culture of the urban ghettos*. Retrieved from http://www.icce.rug.nl/~soundscapes/DATABASES/MIE/Part2_chapter08.shtml

Bounce2dis. (2007, December 6). [Interview with Skalpel]. Retrieved from http://blogs.myspace.com/index.cfm?fuseaction=blog.ListAll&friendId=98933060&page=2

Bruce, D. (2007). *France and Germany: The impact of globalization on society and culture*. University of Waterloo. Retrieved from http://www.wcgs.ca/events/bruce_paper.pdf

Buchen, C. (2007). *Rough cut: France: The precarious generation changing France*. Interview with Bruno Palier. Retrieved from http://www.pbs.org/frontlineworld/rough/2007/04/france_the_precint.html

Debbaut, K. (December 2005/January 2006). Riots and repression, and more neo-liberalism in France. *Socialism Today*. Retrieved from http://www.socialismtoday.org/97/france.html

Dyson, M. E. (1996). *Race rules: Navigating the color line*. Reading, MA: Addison Wesley.

Durand, A. P. (Ed.). (2002). *Black, Blanc, Beur: Rap music and hip-hop culture in the Francophone world*. Maryland, MD: The Scarecrow Press.

Farahmandpur, R. (2008). Imperialism, global capitalism, and neoliberlism: Critical pedagogy in the age of empire. In B. Porfilio & C. Malott's (Eds.), *The destructive path of neo-liberalism: An international examination of urban education* (pp. 3–22). Rotterdam: Sense Publishers.

Fourcade-Gourinchas, M., & Sarah, L. B (2002). The rebirth of the liberal creed: Paths to neo-liberalism in four countries. *American Journal of Sociology, 108*(3), 533–579.

Giroux, H. A. (2004b). Class causalities: Disappearing youth in the age of George Bush. *A Journal of Academic Labor, 6*(1). Retrieved from http://www.henryagiroux.com/online_articles.htm

Green, A. M. (2005). Social stakes and new musical styles: Rap music and hip-hop cultures. In A. P. Durand's (Ed.), *Black, Blanc, Beur: Rap music and hip-hop culture in the Francophone world* (pp. 76–86). Maryland, MD: The Scarecrow Press.

Grewal, K. (2007). The threat from within representations of the Banlieue in French popular discourse. In *Europe: New voices, new perspectives*. Proceedings from the Contemporary Europe Research Centre Postgraduate Conference (pp. 41–67).

Helenon, V. (2006). Africa on their mind: Rap, blackness, and citizenship. In D. Basu & S. J. Lemelle's (Eds.), *The Vinyl ain't final: Hip-hop and the globalization of Black popular culture* (pp. 151–166). Ann Harbor, MI: Pluto Press.

Hill, S. J. (2007). Drop it like it's hot! Hip-hop in the Twenty-First-Century classroom. *Diversity Digest*, *10*(2). Retrieved from http://www.diversityweb.org/digest/vol10no2/hill.cfm

Hajjat, A. (2006). The riots did not take place in a 'political desert.' *International Socialism: A Quarterly Journal of Socialist Theory, 109.* Retrieved from http://www.isj.org.uk/index.php4?id=157&issue=109

Herrera, R. (2006, June). Three moments of the French revolt. *Monthly Review.*

Kato, M. T. (2007). *From kung fu to hip-hop: Globalization, revolution, and popular culture.* Albany, NY: SUNY Press.

Kelley, R. (2006). Forward. In D. Basu & S. J. Lemelle's (Eds.), *The vinyl ain't final: Hip-hop and the globalization of Black popular culture* (pp. xi–xvii). Ann Harbor, MI: Pluto Press.

Keyes, C. L. (2002). *Rap music and street consciousness.* Chicago: University of Illinois Press.

Magubane, Z. (2006). Globalization and gangster rap: Hip-hop in the post-apartheid city. In D. Basu & S. J. Lemelle's (Eds.), *The vinyl ain't final: Hip-hop and the globalization of Black popular culture* (pp. 208–229). Ann Harbor, MI: Pluto Press.

Martin, G. (2008). Neoliberlism, education, and cost-effectiveness in state terror in Australia. In B. Porfilio & C. Malott's (Eds.), *The destructive path of neo-liberalism: An international examination of urban education* (pp. 123–140). Rotterdam: Sense Publishers.

Martinez, T. A. (1997). Popular culture as oppositional culture: Rap as resistance. *Sociological Perspectives, 40*(2), 265–286.

McLaren, P. L. (2000). Gangsta pedagogy and ghettocentricity: The hip-hop nation as counterpublic sphere. In K. A. McClafferty & C. A. Torres (Eds.), *Challenges of urban education: Sociological perspectives for the next century* (pp. 227–270). Albany, NY: SUNY Press.

McLaren, P. L. (2005). *Capitalists and conquerors: A critical pedagogy against empire.* New York: Rowman & Littlefield Publishers.

Poggioli, S. (2005, December 14). French rap musicians blamed for violence. *NPR.*

Prasad, M. (2005, September). Why is France So French? Culture, institutions, and neo-liberalism, 1974–1981. *American Journal of Sociology, 111*(2), 357–407.

Prevos, A. J. M. (1996). The evolution of French rap music and hip-hop culture in the 1980s and 1990s. *The French Review, 69*(5), 713–725.

Prévos, A. J. M. (2002). Two decades of rap in France: Emergence, developments, prospects. In A. P. Durand's (Ed.), *Black, Blanc, Beur: Rap music and hip-hop culture in the Francophone world* (pp. 1–12). Maryland, MD: The Scarecrow Press.

Prévos, A. J. M. (2001, April). Le business du rap en France. *The French Review, 74*(5), 900–921. Quotidien des Sans-papiers. Dimanche le 4 mai, tous à Vincennes. Dans le bulletin d'information et d'alerte. Retrieved from http://parisseveille.info/dimanche-4-mai-tous-a-vincennes,1350.html

Ria, C., & Mabut, P. (2008, June 28). *France: Immigrant retention centre burnt down following the death of inmate.* Retrieved from www.wsws.org

Rap Conscient. (2008). Retrieved August 4, 2008, from http://www.rap-conscient.com

Rosenfeld, S. (1994). The myth of the Chilean miracle. *The MultiNational Monitor, 8.* Retrieved from www.multinationalmonitor.org/hyper/issues/1994/08/mm0894_12.html

Runnel, M. (2006, September 16). Hip-hop Education 101. *VIBE.* Retrieved from http://www.vibe.com/news/online_exclusives/2006/09/hip_hop_education_101/

Saïd, E. (2008, September). The problems of neo-liberalism. *Al-Ahram Weekly, 7*, 13.

Schatan, J. (2001). Poverty and inequality in Chile: Offspring of 25 Years of neo-liberalism. *Development and Society, 30*(2), 57–77.

Schofield, H. (2005, December 2). Rappers prophecies come true. *BBC News.* Retrieved from http://politicalpalace.yuku.com/forum/viewtopic/id/4228

Silverstein, P. (2002). "Why are we waiting to start the fire?": French gangsta rap and the critique of state capitalism. In A. P. Durand (Ed.), *Black, Blanc, Beur: Rap music and hip-hop culture in the Francophone world* (pp. 45–67). Maryland, MD: The Scarecrow Press.

Silverstein, P., & Tetreault, C. (2005, November). Urban violence in France. *Middle East Report Online.* Retrieved from http://www.merip.org/mero/interventions/silverstein_tetreault_interv.htm

Skapel. (2007). *Autonomous movement of the suburbs 93*. Retrieved from http://www.myspace.com/skalpeleltupa

Weiler, K. (2002, Fall). Teacher education and social justice-introduction. *Racial Teacher*. Retrieved from http://findarticles.com/p/articles/mi_m0JVP/is_2002_Fall/?tag=content;col1

Werman, M. (2006, March 13). Interview with Monsieur R. Retrieved from http://www.pri.org/theworld/?q=month/2006/03&page=10

TOUROUZOU HERVER SOME

9. POPULAR MUSIC AND NEO-LIBERAL GLOBALIZATION IN BURKINA FASO

Counter-Hegemoic Possibilities and Limits of a Youth Movement

INTRODUCTION

Through the analysis of lyrics of artists from Burkina Faso, this chapter seeks to capture the ways youth construe neo-liberal globalization. While modern music in Burkina, former Upper Volta—especially hip-hop—, has become increasingly more articulate about the political and economic situation prevailing in the country, I argue that not all popular music forms produced by youth are in a position to challenge the behemoth of globalization and the local socio-political order. Some forms, like the Takiborsé, may even partake in the entrenchment of the global and local hegemony and the de-politicization of youth, positioning them for political illiteracy and apathy.

The purpose of this chapter is to analyze the practices and discourses in three moments of the musical development in Burkina Faso: Blacksomania, Takiborsé (or interchangeably, for Takborsé), and the hip-hop movement. What potential does popular music hold in the education of the youth of Burkina Faso within the ravages of neo-liberal globalization? To what extent does this music challenge the hegemonic discourse geared towards entrenching consent through the establishment of commonsense? What are the limits of the musical movement that is taking place in Burkina Faso with regard to progressive social and political change?

With the advent of globalization, African societies have been pillaried by the impact of the weak state and the deification of the private sector. The privatization of thriving public companies has become the new economic and political mantra with structural adjustment programs (SAPs) being implemented in most African countries. As a result, thousands of workers have been laid off in Africa, Burkina Faso being no exception (Some, 2008; Some & Barrel, 2008). Goehr (1994) argues that the quintessence of musical understanding is best appraised if one takes into account "the extra-conditioning of music" (p. 101) that helps us "… capture the social dynamics generated through music" (Somé, 2007, p. 4). This is best achieved through the exploration of lyrics, rather than just paying attention to the aesthetics, of the music.

Overview of Modern Music in Burkina Faso

There is a dearth of empirical research on the history of modern music in Burkina Faso. Presumably, however, "the formation of this modern music in Burkina followed the same path as in the other national instances of modern music development in

B. J. Porfilio and P. R. Carr (eds.), Youth Culture, Education and Resistance:
Subverting the Commercial Ordering of Life, 149–164.

Africa" (Somé, 2006, p. 6). Erlmann (1991) maintains that "the early phases of popular musical history everywhere in Africa are primarily the product of the continent's increasing integration into the world economy and political order since the late nineteenth century" (p.176). As for McNee (1998), "West African youth culture entered the era of globalization long ago, as youth reappropriated and recontextualized arts and musics imported from the African Diasporas as well as other parts of the world" (p. 231).

Kaboret and Kabore (2004) report that modern music hails back to the 1940s, with the birth of a few bands in Ouagadougou, the capital city, and Bobo-Dioulasso, the second most important city. These orchestras would play to a White patronage and colonial civil servants in pubs and casinos. The lyrics drew primarily on the themes of romance, friendship, morality, and the difficulties of life. While *l' Harmonie Voltaïque* saw the light of day in 1948 in Ouagadougou, the first true orchestra, called *Le Rossignol* (The Nightingale), was brought to the baptismal fonts in Bobo-Dioulasso early on in 1945.

Since the mid-1990s, more than one hundred hip-hop music groups have been formed in Ouagadougou. Other musical genres, such as the one developed by Black So Man and the Takiborsé, may direct the observer's attention to the lived realities of the youths who stand to suffer more from the neo-liberal project.

Method

I have selected three musical "trends" which are evident nationally, and even at the level of the West African sub-region to some extent: Blacksomania, Takiborsé, and hip-hop. Black So Man (black is also a man), artist Bintogoma Traoré, was one of the rare local artists to sell out the emblematic Maison du Peuple of Ouagadougou for his concert, on December 31, 1997. He used his music to castigate the bankruptcy of the process to commodify social life. Although his entrée to the national music scene was short-lived because of an ill-fated accident, he left a definite imprint on Burkinabé music and any serious musical analysis could not bypass him. As for hip-hop music, it started timidly in the 1990s, and did not sit very well with the public, who saw it as rubbish produced by thugs and not worthy of being labelled as art.

The search for national identity is all the more urgent as countries in the sub-sahara region have developed sonorities of their own. Mali has its own musical stamp embodied by the emblematic Salif Keita, Oumou Koita, Amy Sangaré and others. Ghanaian High-life is known internationally. The musical scene in Ivory Coast is steaming with racy sounds that perpetually reinvent themselves: Ziglibity, Zoblazo, Zogoda-Dance, Zouglou, Coupé-décalé, etc., did not need to look toward the Congos, the hub of African music, for any respectability. I have deliberately excluded Reggae music—many readers might expect the contrary—simply because this music that was "highly prized by the youth for nearly over two decades (arguably because of its apparent simplicity of execution) has started a slight decline in favor of rap..." (Kaboret & Kaboré, 2004, pp. 108–109). Youth have seemed to have found national pride in the Takiborsé concept, a genre of music that emerged in 2005.

I have listened to more than sixty songs and selected twenty-five based on their connection with neo-liberalism, consumerism and youth resistance, or lack thereof. Several of these songs could be found on Youtube, and it was helpful to see artists "on live" as it provided insights that I would not have gathered otherwise. I listened to the songs several times, and transcribed them in their French version, then translated them into English for data analysis. With the help of Google, I was able to locate the lyrics of many of the songs. I coded my data into categories that I later collapsed into emergent themes, continually referencing my background knowledge of the country and its social and political dynamics. An outsider may have missed many of the subtleties of these songs.

Social Critique as a Musical Comedy

In 2005, Ahmed Smani produced Zalissa, his album in the Takiborsé mode. Zalissa is a compilation of songs stigmatizing such social flaws as the growing irresponsibility of youth andthe erosion of friendship. The album also magnifies the virtue of hard work and the centrality of the family in a collectivist culture.

The Takiborsé, a musical style as well as a style of dance, was a response to the deterioration of the quality of life in the country. This led a group of rappers in the K-Ravane Band to release a record entitled Viim yaa kanga—it means life is hard—in Mooré, a language spoken by nearly 50% of the population in Burkina Faso. Implicitly, the concept of Takiborsé was geared toward boosting the morale of a populace that had plummeted to an all-time low.

After Zalissa, Takiborsé, quite serendipitously, became a musical movement in its own right. Le Gouvernement (The Government), three different groups of hip-hop musicians (Faso Kombat, Yeleen, Smokey) and Madson Junior came together, and presented the public with a promotional album (Somé, 2007). Le Gouvernement is a mockery of a retrogressive government in an African country, the type that could never lead the people down the road to sustainable development. Le Gouvernement joined with this musical comedy to sustain the imagined community (Anderson, 2003) of the people; yet the glimmer of critique was there, although subdued in the general philosophy of the founding father of Takiborsé, Ahmed Smani, that is, "faire le malin", to show off.

In response to Le Gouvernement, two other artists, Ali Veruthey and El Tafa Siboné, alongside Hamed Smani, formed another band called Le Pouvoir, or Power, to the effect that without power there could be no government. They went on to establish in the popular psyche the concept of "faire le malin", the underpinning philosophy behind Takiborsé—in spite, or because of the adverse socio-economic conditions. This philosophy is articulated in one of their songs,

Le Malin:

Every morning as I get out of bed, I show off
As I am ready for my breakfast, you can feel it in me, I show off
When I feel like expressing my love for you
My love, in a song, I always show off

151

So, brother, sister, go ahead, show off
Refrain: This is showing off
Wake up, citizens from Burkina Faso, show off!
Burkinabé citizens, show off!

A third group, called La Cour Suprême (The Supreme Court), weighed in, scandalized by the boasting of Le Pouvoir at a moment when the people are suffering. In their musical prank, they find it unconscionable that Le Pouvoir is showing off when "[t]o even find food to eat is hard". In *La Sentence* (The Sentence), they launch a scathing attack on behaviors at odds with the current economic situations in Burkina Faso:

There is fire in your home
There is fire, there is fire in your house
The gents are angry
'Cause there is no food
The ladies have not done the cooking
They [men] preferred to go showing off
Now no gas in the tank of their cars
They are pushing their cars
Children are crying everywhere
Cause there's nothing to eat

Three ladies, Kadie Jolie, Aïcha Junior, and Magui Leslie, forming Les Premières Dames, clashed with Le Pouvoir, voicing concerns aimed at improving life in society, in general, and the well-being of women, in particular. They make it clear that forced labor, female genital circumcision, and violence directed at women should be elements eradicated. They call for women to be emancipated, and for more women to hold positions within the country's political structures. For them, the future belongs to women, who are the first ladies, arguing that even God proposes more justice for women.

Tak Tak, it's nothing
To show off, it's no use
Le Pouvoir, it's no use, Le Gouvernement, it's no use
La Court Suprême, it's no use
For they have nothing and they are the ones to show off
They have no money but they are the ones to form a government
There is no building and they are the ones to form a Supreme Court.

These "first ladies" also clashed with the "Supreme Court", who believed that women should live up to hegemonic constructions of femininity, such as getting married. They call on "old girls", who they feel should not soil the name of the real First Lady in the country. The political limitations of this musical genre are discussed later.

An Interpretation of Neo-liberal Globalization from a More Miliant Perspective

As hinted to earlier, a more combative socio-political critique was articulated by Black So Man towards the end of the 1990s in his album, *Tout le monde et Personne* (*Everyone and Nobody at the Same Time*). This unfinished, albeit bold, business of social denunciation, owing to a fatal car accident, will be continued through the hip-hop movement anchored in several local groups such as Yeleen, Faso Kombat, La Censure, Clepto Gang, Koumankan, Sofaa, 2Kas, K-Ravane, KTA, and Mick K Panga, as well as individual artists, such as Smokey, Smarty, Mawndoe, Wed Hyack. Today, hip-hop is a powerful movement in Burkina. Rap, more generally hip-hop, is shaping a new destiny for the Burkinabé music. In Ouagadougou, Bobo-Dioulasso, Fada-N' Gourma, to mention these towns only, "youth were queuing up during hip-hop shows" (Kaboret & Kaboré, 2004, p. 109). It is arguably the case that hip-hop music speaks to the idiom of their daily lives. The socio-economic conditions in the late 1990s had not attained the degree of squalor, which now prevails as neo-liberal globalization gains have commodified life in Burkina Faso.

Black So Man, this iconic figure in the musical landscape of Burkina Faso, was one of the first artists to elect himself as the voice of the down-trodden in an inequitable system that makes life highly fragile for ordinary people. Black So Man depicts a dog-eat-dog society in his song "Le Système du Vampire", or "The Vampire system". The song castigates the propensity of individuals to get rich quick through the frenzied accumulation of goods, irrespective of the consequences for ordinary people. The vampire motive seems to be a recurrent them cherished by committed artists in Burkina in their musical orchestration. In another song entitled "Système Vampire", Faso Kombat shows how "[t]hey are [the human predators] intent on feeding us like sheep...", cows, or chickens. Ultimately, the ties that bind us together as a community of human beings have dissolved.

In "Le Système du Vampire", Black So Man's lyrics were smart and subtle. He speaks in metaphors and poetry, yet his message is clear: the "vampire" system of corruption at both international and national levels is causing massive and unnecessary suffering (Sassan, 2005, p. 7). Black So Man draws people to the mode of accumulation by dispossession (Harvey, 2005) that is simply insane, if not inhuman. In the wake of this depredation, human beings are no longer an ends justifying means, but are just disposable objects in the service of material and financial goals. In *Le truc qui rend digne* (The stuff that makes you worthy of dignity), Smokey (2005b), one of the leaders of the hip-hop movement in Africa today, ironically warns that "[m] oney is not everything. Money is the only thing." That is why many business people and other leaders have their hands stained with the blood of defenseless people. Whenever an employer has a backlog of wages to pay, he or she partakes in the system of the vampire that never tired of sucking the blood from its victims. Refusing to pay workers' wages in Burkina Faso is common, which has wrought deleterious effects for workers. It is a scary world, and Black So Man puts it vividly in "On s'en fout (Who cares?)":

My grandfather is scared of today's world...
To survive, punches below the belt are ok

153

Oh, God!
A father sells his son
A mother sells her daughter
Monopolization of public goods
The cfa franc has been devaluated
Workers are not well-paid
Health care is privatized
Public goods are not well managed
Privatization on your right
Laying off on your left
In this state of vampire man no longer knows what to do to survive.

In general, neo-liberal globalization has wrought havoc on social networks, with education and health care being the epicenter. Yeleen provides a gripping account of the consequences of liberalization, or not to put too fine a point on it, the selling off of health care to private providers for those who can pay. The lack of vital vaccines, such as those against deadly strains of meningitis, and the lack of equipment in hospitals in Burkina Faso is stultifying. Yet, based on the norms of the private sector, heath care is said to be more responsive to the consumer and more respectful of good management. This is illustrative of the notion that the quasi-market is efficient and equitable.

The song chronicling the woes of young *Maxime,* who was taken to the emergency ward of the hospital after an accident, is telling in this regard:

Who is to blame? Men, science, or destiny?
No! The lack of vocation of our doctors
who always let people die for lack of care
Without money, you are left to rot alone in your corner
Anarchy reigns supreme
Our hospitals have lost their notion of hospitality

When Maxime's father was informed of the accident of his only son, he rushed to the hospital only to find him dumped by the ambulance in front of the emergency department. He was lying on the ground like a beggar, soaking in his own blood. No first aid was given to him; yet, his father was obliged to pay 2,500 cfa francs (around 5 US. dollars) for a rotten mattress for him but it would not take long before he lost his "bed" to the benefit of somebody richer who was ready to pay more:

Nobody takes care of him because he [the father] did not have the money,
after a vain attempt to borrow something from his co-workers
That's how Maxime died

in the premises of the Yalgado Hospital

under the helpless eyes of his father

The capacity to pay that entitles people to health care has reached a critical point where many doctors function as bounty hunters who seize every opportunity to prescribe as many medical treatments as possible. This raises the question of the collusion between medical doctors and the pharmaceutical industry. One might think that the Hippocratic oath has wryly turned into a hypocritical one. Smokey (2005d) suggests, through the witty alteration of the French word "pharmacie" (pharmacy) into "pharma-scie" (the particle "scie" in French is the equivalent of "a saw"), that the pharmaceutical industry is sawing the people, in which case it might not be acting differently from plunderers of a former mercantile epoch. The metaphor of the cavalry provides a lead into the exploitative nature of neo-liberal globalization:

That is why it is suspected that behind the vicious virus

There is always an anti-virus

When comes the cavalry of the pharmaceutical industry

Thus, one ends up wondering

Whether in making the medicine they don't also make the disease

Education has also deteriorated with the advent of neo-liberal globalization. Children have been damaged by the dire economic climate impacting their households. Instead of attending school, youth often wind up living on the streets and fending for themselves. There has also been an increase in gang activity, as youth engage in illicit activities to procure food as well as to gain support in facing the dire conditions impacting their lives. In a mock trial of youth for allegedly causing trouble, Black So Man makes the defendant drop a bombshell:

Thank you, your honor, for the opportunity to me given

To talk about the educational derailment and the betrayal of politicking

How many are they, my brothers and sisters, who at an early age

Are kicked out of their homes by their parents

Who pretend that they can now fend for themselves?

The acquired immune deficiency?

They don't give a damn

Also, that's why you can see adolescents being gangsters because they have been brought up in the street

Yeleen captures this dire state of education in the *Génération Sacrifiée (The Lost Generation)*:

From 1960 [the independence year for many African countries] until now, what to remember?

Nothing

On the school desks nobody could explain to me the real history of my
country, what to remember?
Nothing
If it's not the metaphors of Shakespeare
Christopher Columbus, Louis XIV
Napoleon
These names stained my notebooks.
....You see
Independence, my son, is still an illusion
The ghost of the colonialist is still blurring our perception.

The youth are well aware that the educational system leaves them nearly nowhere. Indeed, there is a mismatch between the curriculum and students' lived experiences. In *Confessions*, Yeleen observes that:

Around us, nothing works
The pen that we hold in our hands leads us nowhere
Scribbled note books, crumpled sheets of paper
All our lives are wasted leaning on school benches
I watch these fingers which to me are only being overzealous.

There is a strong sense in which the youth are not going to be better off even if they graduate, unemployment being rife.

The Critique of "Local" Political Establishments

Putting their physical integrity at stake with varying degrees of effectiveness, artists have used their voices to critique the political system in place. *J'étais au procès* (At the Trial) by Black So Man, with regard to its allegorical tone, can be read a scathing indictment of the 4th Republic in Burkina Faso. While the political stability in the country along with the political maturity of the Burkinabé people are due, in large part, to the country's current political arrangements, the situation is less bright when it comes to economic democracy. The country is still among the poorest in the world, according to the UNDP annual ranking. Moreover, there are issues of impunity that remain to be addressed, stemming, in part, from the lack of separation of powers between the executive, the judiciary, and the legislature:

He promised us the sun...
From democracy to autocracy
Students are persecuted
The unemployment rate increases day by day
The public treasury is privatized
Health is no longer for all.

In *Roodwoko*, Smokey (2005e) admonishes the powers that be. Confrontational, he castigates the mockery of democracy in many African countries through the impersonation of a political tyrant who has no vision for his people. In *Votez pour moi* (Vote for me), he solicits the votes of his people based on demagogic promises:

No wonder that he is going to
do better in one term than Mobutu in ten.

In *Daar-Es-Salam*, Yeleen goes a step further in his critique of the political landscape in Burkina Faso. He audaciously sends an open letter to President Blaise Compaoré of Burkina Faso in the name of underdogs whose voices cannot reach him simply because they just have no voice in public affairs. Yeleen clearly states the purpose of the endevour:

This song is not meant to please
It is meant for a more equitable world

The Ubiquitousness of Big Capital and the Reification of Life

The pervasive effect of neo-liberalism is far-reaching and touches upon fundamental human rights. K. Djoba, featuring Yeleen, in *La traite*, or *human trafficking*, blasted the shameful human exploitation of the weakest segments of the populations, such as children forced into hard labor, and little girls lured into prostitution:

Picture these children ages 10 in the plantations
In Ghana or Ivory Coast carrying bags weighing 50 kilograms
Very often, after this hard work deprived of food and water
Living in worse conditions than a detainee in Guatanamo
You dig? It's just like in the 16th century
Where blacks...
Girls are very often raped and placed in prostitution rings
History is unequivocal about that
You parents and governments are all a party to this

Human suffering is probably the price to pay for the world to enjoy chocolate (Ivory Coast is the largest producer of cocoa). The same certainly goes for other raw materials in other countries in the South but they do not benefit these countries as much. This is partly due to the so called First World establishing inequitable terms of trade with the South. In any case, Smokey (2005d) attempts to clarify in *Pharma-scie:*

In the Middle Age
there was a medical practice that was systematically applied to the sick
It was called bleeding
Today, nothing has changed

As we are all bled through our wallets

Whether they are the pharmaceutical industries or the arms industries

They are the same monopolies that refuse to comply with the norms

Preoccupied as they are with big profits

Of course, globalization offers corporate conglomerates the possibility to relocate in tax havens, in countries with tax legislation or corrupt institutions, where it is easy to commit tax evasion or even tax fraud.

Locally, human beings are reduced to a basic monetary value. Justice has become a travesty as "several court cases have been smothered," as denounced by Smokey (2005a) in *Alerte (Alert)*:

The rule of the law becomes the law of the powerful and

the powerful apply the law of the dominos

to make sure that they always remain the powerful

Smokey points here to the national judiciary, which has lost much of its credibility. Several judges have been suspected to be in collaboration with individuals, businesspeople, and companies in court cases. At a global level, the logic of the market has shown that corruption is no longer the preserve of developing countries. Powerful western corporations have also been smeared by corruption scandals. Neo-liberalism seems to thrive on the breeding-ground of corruption, which easily accommodates itself with denial of justice. Another variant on the theme of the reification of life, the preference of profit over people, to paraphrase Chomsky (1999), is the belligerent nature of neo-liberalism that poses a threat to global peace. This does not go unnoticed with socially and globally conscious artists.

The Neo-liberal Globalization, Enemy of Global Peace

The government of George W. Bush has exacerbated the nefarious effects of neo-liberalism with his attempt to "[c]ontrol the earth as if it was [his] domain;" thus "pushing a certain people in its last retrenchment", just for the sake of grabbing its minerals (Faso Kombat, in *Et ça continue*, And the beat goes on).

The grassroots in Burkina Faso, not unlike those in many other countries in the South, have seen their living conditions plummet below the level of the 1960s. Neo-liberalism has further led to the global division of labor whereby developing countries, such as Burkina Faso, are still playing the role of providers of raw materials and agricultural products. Thus, "a new form of slavery" has replaced a former one:

For today, who grows cotton, coffee, sugar cane or cocoa?..

The slave trade has ended but its scars are far from healed" (Smokey, in Code Noir, Black Code).

This takes place on a tilted playing-surface, as the World Trade Organization's regulations are being flouted by countries of the North. The US is subsidizing its agriculture, namely its cotton producers, ignoring the principle of comparative advantages for weak countries like Burkina Faso. The only major export [in Burkina Faso] is cotton (50% of all exports). Despite the good quality of the cotton, the country has difficulty in selling crops to the world market because of the high agricultural subsidies in western industrialized countries (http://www. cotton-made-in-africa.com). The European Union is intent on dumping its agricultural products in African countries through the Accord de Partenariat Economique (APE), or the Agreement for Economic Partnership. It begs another name: It is a de facto "Accord de Pillage Economique", an Agreement for Economic Plunder, as most of the African agricultural products will barely make a dent in the European consumer market. It is a fool's bargain, and, as it were, the African civil society can smell a rat. African governments are now reluctant to sign another fair treaty.

The group Yeleen, among others, was very active in increasing people's awareness to the danger of this dubious deal. During the Pan-African Cinema and Television Festival (FESPACO) in 2005, the artist collected thousands of signatures to protest the subsidization of Western agriculture, which is stifling cotton and rice production in Africa (Künzler, 2006). Such policies, according to Faso Kombat in *Et ça continue*:

Just set up

The context that has begotten assistance for us

And the substance for the North

Still today by dint of genetically modified organisms

The rules of the game are being changed

We are pushed into crisis

Tell me, is it safe for an African farmer

To look for his seeds in America?

From a simply moral stand-point, it is unacceptable to impose upon poor countries genetically modified organisms that have not proven to be safe for the environment or for human health. Just because they might yield more crops—again, profit over people—is a poor excuse. This has led Smokey (2005c) to complain in *Ma Dignité* (My Dignity) in these terms:

Imported religion, imported policy, imported economy conditioned by WTO

I hope we'll not import our sperms in order to continue to live

Neo-liberalism expresses its aggressiveness, leaving destruction and desolation in its wake. Ardiess Posse, and Yeleen in *La Guerre des Mondes* (The War of the Worlds), recalls that this era is a dangerous one as the war of the worlds has set in. The conflict is "strictly commercial" because "they wanna gain mo'", laying off people without any consideration for "what they mucked up", delocating "their factories, "f***ck"[ing] workers' families and their future. Yet, the greatest suffering is yet to come:

Hée, haa

We are in for the war of the worlds

Blood is flowing, tears inundate us
And in the hearts hatred is fertile

As can be seen, pre-revolutionary Burkina musical productions dealt predominantly with romance, friendship, morality, and the hardships of life (Somé 2007). If the younger generation of musicians is more antagonistic and less conciliatory in general, one can hardly say that popular music in Burkina Faso has become a weapon for critical awareness and socio-political change all across the board.

Limits of a Musical Movement

The current generation takes a more confrontational stance, expressing their discontent about their material conditions that have been adversely affected by neo-liberal globalization. McNee (1998) equates the latter to modern Babylon.

> Although the images [of enslaved peoples of Israel weeping on the banks of the River Babylon] are local, fixed in a specific time and place, youth around the world attempt to "chant down Babylon"—white controlled, westernized capitalism-by creatively re-imagining the confrontation between oppressor and victim in song and art. (p. 231)

Yet, there is reason for a cautionary note here. Barber (1997) cautions us against believing that discourse of popular culture only contains counter-hegemonic elements. Rather, our aim is to distinguish "between what is 'truly' popular, and what is contaminated by hegemonic ideological infiltrations from above" (p. 3). As stated earlier, the people, understandably, were desperately in need of their own national rhythm, and may be very much inclined to anesthetize their critical thinking in the face of a musical genre that ultimately furthers the interests of materialism and neo-liberal capitalism.

The aim of Takiborsé is hedonism and feel-goodism through its elaborate, conscious attempt "to display classiness, not only through the singing but also the sartorial elegance of the singer and the gracefulness of the dancer as well" (Somé, 2007, p. 15). In a typical Takiborsé attire, the founding father of the beat, Hamed Smani, poses like a dandy, with a dark costume, a white shirt, a vintage hat on, and a pipe in his mouth (Somé, 2007). This is reminiscent of the Congolese in Paris in *Money Has No Smell* by MacGaffey and Bazenguissa-Ganga (2000), who are overly concerned with their "look", funneling fortunes into fashionable clothing. Somé (2007) excludes Takiborsé from street culture altogether. "Takiboronsé is not only a style of music and a dance. It is a style of behavior that suggests excellence, neatness, and gracefulness in everything one does..." (p. 15).

Perhaps, the most serious indictment of Takiborsé is its superficial promotion of materialism that boils down to advancing uncritical consumerism. A new trend observed in Burkina Faso is the conspicuous exhibition of luxury items, from high fashion, clothing, glittering jewelry, and super-expensive personal effects, items that are totally out of reach to the commoner. Such a commitment to hyper consumerism obviously impacts the national economy (Somé, 2007, p. 20).

Gills (2000), in an attempt to offer a serious alternative to the globalization characterized above, proposes a change of strategy.

> The analytical focus of the study of the globalization phenomena must therefore shift from the technical to the political. It is no longer sufficient for critics of globalization simply to "document transnational neo-liberalism". There is a profound need for re-thinking the question of what social practices now constitute viable political strategies in the world economy. (p. 4)

Of what logic is it to "show off" when one lives in the midst of a desert of squalor when one's basic needs are far from met? Takiborsé exhorts people not to cave in to the hardships of life but his call makes little attempt to raise the level of consciousness and critical thinking of the population. Rather, they deserve to understand the science of their misery. They need to unpack hwo the country has became dispossessed. What are the macro-structural forces that constrain the leaders, and what is their responsibility in the present socio-economic bankruptcy? By refusing to historicize the fate of the people through problematizing the lack of socio-economic development, Takiborsé is suspected of being a tool in the service of hegemonic forces.

C. Wright Mills (1958) called for the (re-)invention of a sociological imagination. It is the duty of the social scientist—and here, I beg the question that the artist is one—to provide a common thread between the individual problems of people. People are struggling individually with their problems, forgetting that they are not isolated ones but are interrelated social phenomena. If they are made to see the inter-connectedness between their problems, they will gain political consciousness, and take the necessary action to change their situation. One would expect the pioneers of Takiborsé to extol the virtues of producing what we consume, and also consuming what we produce. This is a viable alternative to the extraverted consumer mentality. This mentality is no longer tenable within the experience of the hike in the price of foodstuffs in 2008. The government of Burkina Faso seems to have perceived the necessity to promote an endogenous development, a movement that starts with food self-sufficiency through the promotion of subsistence farming.

Redecker (2008) makes a perceptive analysis of the concept of culture. It deserves further elaboration if only because it problematizes Takiborsé's interpretation. This musical style born out of the need to improve a national self-concept conceals the history of the people's hardships. It also socializes the youth to global and local government hegemony (Williams, 1978) by papering over serious issues, frittering away such values as simplicity, humility and integrity that have become the hallmark of the Burkinabe people. In fact, Takiborsé has been adept at building consent. Redecker makes a distinction between culture and the cultural. His cautionary stance is going to be made explicit in the following lines. As a young boy, Redecker thought that culture and revolution (read any progressive change, not necessarily a violent one) were inseparable. He has been disillusioned as

> Culture has become the orphan of politics and its battles, of the great evenings and bright morrows....The contemporary usage of culture is rather

shown through the break of its link—which, for more than a century, from Hugo to Lamartine to Aragon, seemed indestructible—with the political transformation of human-kind and society.

Redecker bemoans the multiple attempts in contemporary society to void the political animal—in the Aristotelian sense—that inhabits human-kind in order to produce an "inoffensive" person incapable of challenging the status quo. He argues that this stems from the fact that the cultural has succeeded in "phagocytosing" culture. In the beginning, human culture was revolutionary because it was a principle of transformation of self: "Through culture, I become somebody else".

The hip-hop movement, if it still has to hone a collective strategy in order to redeem the commons (Esteva & Prakash,1998) being lost to neo-liberal globalization, seems to have got a sound interpretation of history and of the responsibility of youth in these troubled times. As Smokey puts it: There is no breakfast for those who will not wake up. This is not to say that hip-hop is irreversibly free from the grips of the market materialism as evidenced by *Le Gouvernement*. This group of rappers joined the bandwagon of the Takiborsé movement for apparently the good cause: To give a soul to a national music, and make a whole nation feel good about itself in the way others might perceive it. As Künzler has put it rightly, "[y]outh cultures very often have contradictory relations to commodification and capitalism and hip-hop makes no exception" (Künzler, 2006, p. 24). This is not to say that hip-hop has lost its critical edge. Rather, it emphasizes the fact that one musical art form does not have any inscribed entitlement to progressivism that would be valid forever.

Conclusion

In this chapter, I reviewed the relationship between youth and neo-liberal globalization as mediated by popular music in Burkina Faso. In a culture of oral-aural tradition, music has the potential to de-colonize the conscience from a mental slavery that manufactures unreflective zombie consumers, people ignorant of their political rights and the implications of their apparently most benign behavioral choices. Modern music in Burkina Faso has the potential to talk back to neo-liberal globalization from a counter-hegemonic standpoint. Yet, while it can be used as a locus for raising youths' awareness about the ravages of neo-liberal globalization, regressive forms of art like the Takiborsé only further a commercial, ahistorical and "apolitical" ethos, and thus have the potential to dwarf the generational consciousness of the youth. This could postpone *sine die* any transformational possibility. Ultimately, it might mean chanting a requiem for the regeneration of a whole nation, the youth being the burning spear of the future.

QUESTIONS FOR REFLECTION

1. It is said that with the development of information and communication technologies that no frontier or sovereignty can prevent the circulation of musical messages that pursue a social reproduction function, and subjugate

youth to thoughtless consumption of goods. How do you perceive the contribution of politically and socially conscious musicians in Burkina Faso? To what extent can they succeed in raising the awareness of youth as to the necessity to fight the commercial ordering of life?

2. What does Künzler mean when he maintains that "youth cultures very often have contradictory relations to commodification and capitalism? Do you agree with him?

3. How might music be used to advance the cause of universal design in education in a low-literate culture?

REFERENCES

Anderson, B. (2003). *Imagined communities: Reflections on the origin and spread of nationalism.* New York: Verso.

Apple, W. M. (2001). *Educating the "Right" way: Markets, standards, God and inequality.* New York: Routledge.

Ardiess Posse & Yeleen. (n.d.). *La guerre des mondes.* Retrieved from http://www.youtube.com/watch?v=jKAhj355Wfc

Black So Man. (1998). *Le système du vampire.* Retrieved from http://www.youtube.com/results?search_type=&search_query=Black+ So+ Man+aq=f

Black So Man. (1998). *On s'en fout. Le système du vampire.* Retrieved from http://www.youtube.com/results?search_type =&search_query=Black+ So+ Man+aq=f

Black So Man. (1998). *J'étais au procès. Le système du vampire.* Retrieved from http://www.youtube.com/results?search _type=&search_query=Black+ So+ Man+aq=f

Chomsky, N. (1999). *Profit over people: Neo-liberalism and global order.* New York: Seven Stories Press.

Cotton made in Africa: Portraits of cotton producers in Zambia, Benin and Burkina Faso. Retrieved from http://www.cotton-made-in-africa.com

Erlmann, V. (1991). *African Stars: Studies in Black South African Performance.* Chicago: The University of Chicago Press.

Esteva, G., & Prakash, M. S. (1998). *Grassroots postmodernism: Remaking the soil of cultures.* London: Zed Books.

Faso Kombat. (n.d.). *Retour aux sources.* Ouagadougou: Seydoni Production [Tape, Burkina].

Faso Kombat. (n.d). *Konscientization.* Ouagadougou: Seydoni Production [Tape, Burkina].

Faso Kombat. (n.d.). *Système vampire.* Ouagadougou: Seydoni Production [Tape, Burkina].

Gills, K. B. (2000). Introduction. In B. K. Gills (Ed.), *Globalization and the politics of resistance* (pp. 1–18). New York: St Martins' Press.

Goehr, L. (1994). The philosophy of music. *The Journal of Aesthetics and Art Criticism, 52*(1), 99–112.

Harvey, D. (2007). *A brief history of neo-liberalism.* New York: Oxford University Press.

Kaboret, A. F., & Kaboré, O. (2004). *Histoire de la musique moderne du Burkina Faso: genèse, évolution et perspectives.* Ouagadougou: EDIPAP International [History of Modern Music of Burkina Faso: Genesis, Evolution and Prospects].

Djoba, K. (n.d.). *La traite.* Retrieved from http://www.youtube.com/watch?v=3GSIDOd55xg

Ravane, K. (n.d.). *Viima yaa kanga.* Retrieved from http://.youtube.com/watch?v=MyGZt2y

Künzler, D. (2006, July 27). *Hip-hop-movements in Mali and Burkina Faso: The local adaptation of a global culture.* Paper presented at the XVI International Sociological Association, World of Sociology, Durban (pp. 1–27).

La Cour Suprême. (n.d.). *La sentence.* Retrieved from www.youtube.com/watch?v=IAZZnGa2y1w

La Cour Suprême. (n.d.). *Il y a feu.* Retrieved from http://www.youtube.com/watch?v=iAazmGDiqgs& feature

Le Pouvoir. (n.d.). *Le malin*. Retrieved from http://www.youtube.com/watch?v=qiLx2hLLlm8&
feature=related

Les Premières dames. (n.d.). Retrieved from http:// www.youtube.com/watch?v=YImbOoSTKOy

MacGaffey, J., & Bazenguissa-Ganga, R. (2000). *Congo-Paris: Transnational Traders on the Margins of the Law*. Bloomington, IN: Indiana University Press.

McLuhan, M. (1994). *Understanding the media: The extensions of man*. Cambridge: The MIT Press.

McNee, L. (2005). Back from Babylon: Popular musical cultures of the diaspora, youth culture and identity in Francophone West Africa. In R. A. Young (Ed.), *Music, popular culture, identities* (pp. 231–247). Amsterdam: Rodopi.

Mills, C. (2000). *The sociological imagination*. New York: Oxford University Press.

Redecker, R. (2008). *Le culturel contre la culture ou comment en finir avec la possibilité de la révolution*. Passant Ordinaire. Retrieved from http://www.passant-ordinaire.com/revue/31-52.asp, [The cultural against culture, or how to put to death the possibility of revolution]

Sassan, A. (2005, Spring). *Conspiracies of resistance: Singer-revolutionaries in `Burkina Faso*. Africa on Campus: The Newsletter of the Institute of African Studies at Columbia University.

Smokey. (2005a). *Alerte*. Ougadougou: Studio Abazon [Tape, Burkina].Smokey. (2005b). *Le truc qui rend digne*. Ougadougou: Studio Abazon [Tape, Burkina].

Smokey. (2005c). *Ma dignité*. Ougadougou: Studio Abazon [Tape, Burkina].

Smokey. (2005d). *Pharma-scie*. Ougadougou: Studio Abazon [Tape, Burkina].

Smokey. (2005e). *Roodwooko*. Ougadougou: Studio Abazon [Tape, Burkina].

Somé, B. (2007, March 29–April 1). *Singing, dancing and acting at home. The Takiboronse effect in Burkina Faso's popular culture*. Paper presented at the 7th Africa Conference on Popular Culture, University of Texas, Austin.

Some, T. H. (2008). Global and neo-liberal forces in education: The struggle of education workers in Burkina Faso. In D. Hill & E. Rosskam (Eds.), *The developing world and state education: Neo-liberal depradation and egalitarian alternatives* (pp. 170–203). New York: Routledge.

Some, T. H., & Gueye, B. (2008). Neo-liberalism and education in Senegal and Burkina Faso: Silencing the African mind. In C. Malott & B. Porfilio (Eds.), *The destructive path of neo-liberalism: An international examination of education* (pp. 141–157). New York: Sense Publication.

Williams, R. (1978). *Marxism and literature*. London: Oxford University Press.

Yeleen. (2001). *Confessions*. Ouagadougou: Seydoni Production [Tape, Burkina].

Yeleen. (2006). *Dar Es Salaam*. Ouagadougou: Waga N'djam.

Yeleen. (2001). *Génération sacrifiée*. Ouagadougou: Seydoni Production [Tape, Burkina].

Yeleen. (2001). *Juste 1 peu de lumière*. Ouagadougou: Seydoni Production [Tape, Burkina].

Yeleen. (2001). *Maxime*. Ouagadougou: Seydoni Production [Tape, Burkina].

CURRY MALOTT

10. USING GOD TO TURN OFF THE RADIO

Punk Rock and the Complexities of Youth Resistance

...Religion is not simply a topic among topics but the driving force of American history, that without close attention to Protestant Christianity it is impossible to make sense of our past...The Protestant Passion, the insatiable desire to redeem mankind from sin and error...has been manifest in a variety of forms...While the great majority of professing Christians belonged to particular sects or denominations...many were stoutly and sometimes stridently opposed to the churches. This was perhaps most strikingly the case with the abolitionists...Generally speaking, however, their weight fell on the side of political and social conservatism. The theological emphasis was on personal piety, good works, and individual salvation. The tendency was to ratify the existing order and support, without qualification, the sanctity of private property. (Smith, 1984, pp. 554–555)

As alluded to in the above quote, Smith (1984) locates the primary difference between competing approaches to American Christianity in the way the nature of sin is articulated, which demonstrates the difference between a democratic perspective and one based on hierarchical mysticism. That is, are those in poverty simply suffering the wrath of God by paying for their inherent weakness and bad habits, or are they "more sinned against than sinning" (p. 562)? Following Smith (1984), I begin with the recognition that religion has been put to use as a tool of coercion as well as a vehicle for (in)justice. However, the object of critique here is the hegemonic tendencies within the contemporary fundamentalist movement. This chapter focuses on one moment of the relatively recent Christian fundamentalist censorship movement, which began in the late-1960s and continues to the present. I analyze the use of Christian fundamentalist "values" by conservative right-wing politicians in the creation of a reactionary politics of intolerance, a political platform earmarked to silence dissent in music—a decidedly Western European approach. This happened, supposedly, because the leaders of the Christian right arguably began their holy cultural war against punk rockers, who were most outside the control of corporate influence and regulation. This chapter looks at not only the attempts by those in power to silence the spaces of youth underground and transgressive culture but also, more importantly, the way in which youth opened up democratized cultural spaces to critique the debilitating perspectives offered by Christian fundamentalists.

B. J. Porfilio and P. R. Carr (eds.), Youth Culture, Education and Resistance:
Subverting the Commercial Ordering of Life, 165–181.
© 2010 Sense Publishers. All rights reserved.

I first briefly outline the concrete context that gave way to the current wave of fundamentalism. This contextualization leads into a discussion of the 1980s punk rock band the Dead Kennedy's being taken to court for a record, one of the most important examples of music censorship spearheaded by Tipper Gore and the Christian conservative right. The remainder of the chapter examines the music that emerged within this atmosphere of Christian intolerance.

The Larger Context

During the United States' formative years, between the mid- and late-eighteenth century, when its leaders were seeking frequent council from the Iroquois, many experts on large-scale democratic governance, Ben Franklin and the like, were warned that if their many anti-democratic contradictions were not resolved, such as the enslaving of Africans, and a democratically-unaccountable, hierarchical system of income distribution more generally, they should expect serious problems in their future (Lyons & Mohawk, 1992). For example, it is therefore not surprising that at the height of the U.S.'s post-World War II global economic hegemony that peaked during the 1960s, a time when the US was the envy of the world, the African-American community created a civil rights movement demanding a fair share of the pie. The civil rights movement in the US became a leading force of revolutionary struggle against a system that seemed unable or unwilling to resolve its own contradictions at the expense of millions of people of color and working people as a whole (Jones & Jefferies, 1998; Lusane, 1998).

Convinced the reform-based, non-violent initiatives of the civil rights movement were a dead-end, in 1969 Huey P. Newton and Bobby Seale started the Black Panther Party (BPP) for Self Defence, which was designed to go beyond the traditional goal of gaining equal opportunity within the system that exists. They wanted to transgress it entirely and build an egalitarian society. While the BPP and the many movements it inspired, such as the American Indian Movement and the Young Lords, were certainly not free from hegemonic contradictions as their members and leaders dealt or failed to deal with their own internalized oppressions, they were able to spawn a crisis in the U.S. capitalist system. It was marked by the breakdown of the Nation's ability to garner its own population's consent. (Cleaver & Katsiaficas, 2001). The second, and ongoing, phase of this crisis has included the ruling elite/class attempt to regain social control through restricting access to resources. The political theory behind the policies that were created in this vain has been dubbed neo-liberalism (Porfilio & Malott, 2008). As a result, the wealthiest country in the world, the United States, has the largest gap between the rich and the poor of any industrialized nation, which, in the international community, is common knowledge. The basic structures of power within the US are maintained, in part, by ensuring that these class analyses are not included in the standard school-based curriculum. Instead, schools promote a bootstrap ontology that argues poverty comes not from structural inequality, but from personal flaws such as laziness and intellectual inadequacy. Accompanying this economic disempowerment has been a refocused propaganda campaign to indoctrinate the youth whose belief in the system has been continuing to erode. Central to these efforts has been the use of religion.

In her classic text, *Religion: The Social Context*, McGuire (1992) situates the emergence of the most recent surge of Christian fundamentalism in the United States as a direct response *by the bosses* to the "social and political turmoil of the 1960s and 1970s" (p. 218) that led to civil rights legislature and the desegregation of schools (Marsden, 2006). As the bosses consciously devised new methods of plundering the earth, and extracting value from human labor power, an increasing number of the world's people have been entering the ranks of the poor, the impoverished and the pissed off. Scared of the swelling tides of discontent, the ruling class continues to draw on whatever tactics they have at their disposal to keep the masses in line, such as fear. What has proven especially effective in keeping people scared and in line? Religion. The war launched by US Vice Presidential Second Lady Tipper Gore under President Bill Clinton, and continued by US Senator Joe Lieberman and US Vice Presidential Second Lady under Bush II, Lynne Cheney, for example, against transgressive youth cultures not only reflects how scared elites are of their own populations but also illustrates the extent to which fundamentalism has influenced mainstream politics.

What is the source of the ruling class' fear? They are threatened of what billions of people around the world have done, and are doing to end their own suffering. Again, this is not a new fear. It is not a secret to the powers that be that people are not as ignorant as they are characterized by our corporate and political leaders in mass media outlets. In the United States, the ruling elites can only wish working people were as dumb as the schools are designed to make them, paraphrasing Jello Biafra (1991). Contextualizing the ruling class's cultural attack on the poor and oppressed in the US, Biafra (1998) argues that, ultimately, this campaign, outlined below, is an attempt to silence the spokespersons of an increasingly disgruntled populous.

The Attack

Before we proceed with our discussion on censorship, what I have dubbed for the purposes of this chapter "the attack," let us pause for a moment and consider how fundamentalism has been defined and characterized by leading scholars in the field of religious studies. According to Marsden (1991) in *Understanding Fundamentalism and Evangelicalism:*

> An American fundamentalist is an evangelical who is militant in opposition to liberal theology in the churches or to changes in cultural values or mores, such as those associated with secular "humanism..." Fundamentalists are a subtype of evangelicals and militancy is crucial to their outlook. Fundamentalists are not just religious conservatives; they are conservatives who are willing to take a stand and fight. (p. 1)

Marsden (1991) places special emphasis on the militancy of fundamentalists. It is precisely this militancy, what we might refer to as right-wing activism that has made fundamentalism such a powerful tool for mobilizing against those proclaimed to be enemies of God. However, the relative success of the fundamentalists cannot be attributed solely to their militancy. Such militancy would be useless if it were not for their anti-intellectualism. Many fundamentalists embrace absurd propositions, such as blaming teen suicide and gang violence on rock n' roll and rap/hip-hop music. Anti-intellectualism has also been a defining characteristic of fundamentalism throughout its history. According to Marsden (2006) in his critically acclaimed *Fundamentalism and American Culture*, since at least the first half of the twentieth century, fundamentalists have been accused of being ignoramuses, bigots, against reason, over-emphasizing emotion, and motivated by a desire to support, without question, the status quo.

As a result, the right-wing fundamentalist religious movement has been widely critiqued as nothing more than a ruse to foster civil obedience among an increasingly impoverished, mis-educated, alienated, and disgruntled citizenry. Commenting on the irony within this use of Christianity, Mumia Abu-Jamal (1997), himself a victim of severe state-censorship, comments:

> Isn't it odd that Christendom—that huge body of human-kind that claims spiritual descent from the Jewish carpenter of Nazareth—claims to pray to and adore a being who was a prisoner of Roman power, an inmate on the empire's death row? That the one it considers the personification of the Creator of the Universe was tortured, humiliated, beaten, and crucified on a barren scrap of land on the imperial periphery, at Golgatha, the place of the skull? That the majority of its adherents strenuously support the State's execution of thousands of imprisoned citizens? That the overwhelming majority of its judges, prosecutors, and lawyers—those who condemn, prosecute, and sell out the condemned—claim to be followers of the fettered, spat-upon, naked God? (Abu-Jamal, 1997, p. 39)

Is it not also odd that an increasing number of American Christian leaders, most notably TV-evangelical fundamentalists, such as Billy Graham, Jerry Falwell and Pat Robertson, support the usage of their God to not only silence the condemned (as noted above) but also to condemn those who deviate from their own set of beliefs? Perhaps this phenomena is not so much "odd," but, again, indicative of the tendency within contemporary right-wing Christian fundamentalism, according to the late prominent theologian, Vine Deloria (1994), among many others, to not be informed by the "actual scholarly knowledge of Jesus and his times, the nature of the Roman world, and the movement of the early church" (p. 231), but by their own "traditional mythologies of American life" (Deloria, 1994, p. 226)—in a word, their anti-intellectualism. Such mythologies tend to be informed by a version of the Protestant work ethic that explains the accumulation of wealth as God's reward for those who have been *good* Christians—and a good Christian in this context is one who uncritically works hard for the bosses and is intolerant of any ideas or values that differ from those held by the conservative right. The absence of historical knowledge and the perspective it offers has enabled today's leading fundamentalists to remain secure in their ideology "because it is the idealized, law-abiding, goody-goody projections of themselves, which they call Jesus, that forms the object of their devotion" (Deloria, 1994, p. 231).

As alluded to above, what distinguishes this contemporary fundamentalism from the movement of the 1920s "...is its deep involvement in mainstream national politics" whose adherents have currently been estimated to be in the hundreds of millions (Marsden, 2006, p. 232). Most significantly signalling the political rise of fundamentalism in the contemporary era was Ronald Reagan's successful campaign for governor of California in 1966. Regan became governor due the overwhelmingly support of the religious right (Marsden, 2006). President Reagan ushered in a new wave of fundamentalist-elected presidents, and in so doing marked an era of national, militant anti-intellectualism that has remained very much alive and well into the present moment. As a primary influence of Tipper Gore's campaign against popular music—a campaign based on the laughable assumption that rock music is responsible for social problems, such as teen suicide, teen pregnancy and drug use—the Reagan/Bush era has had deep ramifications with long-lasting implications.

In her book, *Raising PG Kids in an X-Rated Society*, Tipper Gore (1987) notes that "President Reagan, in announcing plans for a new national strategy against illegal drugs, pointed directly to the influence of rock music on drug use" (p. 133). In making her case, Gore (1987) quotes Reagan, who, essentially, has argued that rock musicians have rendered drug use socially acceptable by making their own usage public and part of their persona thereby contributing to the increase in teen consumption and, paradoxically, to both suicide and sex. Nowhere in this discourse of sin and temptation are structural factors mentioned, such as the alienating and exploitative nature of capitalist work, racism, homophobia, sexism, and consumer society, for possible explanations as to why youth might find appealing the temporary relief from the daily reality of their lives offered by mind-altering substances. The Conservatives also deny any possible benefits, such as a critical perspective on material reality, offered by a temporary change in consciousness. Rather, it is the assumed *immoral* aspects of popular culture that supposedly account for what is considered to be the deviant behavior of easily influenced youth. It therefore follows that popular culture must be regulated to protect children. What could be better suited for this work in an American context than the anti-intellectualism and militancy of right-wing Christian fundamentalism?

However, while Tipper Gore and her gang, like Reagan before them, tended not to be openly avid fundamentalists, they were firmly aligned and have been described as serving as a political front for this contemporary Christian inquisition under the guise of "protecting the children" (Biafra, 1998). One need only browse through her book, *Raising PG Kids in an X-Rated Society*, to begin to notice Gore's connection to fundamentalism. For example, in describing the early development of the Parent Music Resource Center (PMRC), which turned out to be one of the most influential strong arms of the early anti-rock censorship movement, Gore (1987) notes that:

In May of 1985, we set out to alert other parents in our community [of porn rock]. [We]...arranged for Jeff Ling...a youth minister at a suburban Virginia church, to give a slide presentation graphically illustrating the worst excesses in rock music...aimed at the teenage market. We invited the public, community leaders, our friends (some of whom hold public office), and representatives of the music industry. (p. 19)

From the beginning, therefore, the PMRC can be understood as a form of covert fundamentalist activism—that is, anti-intellectual militancy. What came from these first engagements was an attempt to get the large music publishers, such as Warner Brothers, Capitol, and RCA, to include lyrics with their albums so radio stations could more efficiently detect sexual and violent content inappropriate for their audience. Gore (1987) notes that record companies "were not so excited" referring to Lenny Waronker's comment that it "smells of censorship" (p. 21). Dedicated in their cause and unwilling to give up, Gore and the PMRC then turned to Stan Gortikov for advice, who was president of the recording industry's trade group, the Recording Industry Association of America (RIAA). What emerged was a "strategy" Gore (1987) characterized as "simple," which included building "a consumer movement to put pressure on the industry" (Gore, 1987, p. 22). While Gore and the fundamentalists come from the ruling class and are staunch supporters of capitalism, they have not hesitated to punish capitalists who profit from dangerous ideas, such as ideas that are deemed a threat to the existing social order. For example, a popular 1980s Prince song, "Darling Nikki", was deemed to be morally and/or culturally deviant by fundamentalists because it alluded to masturbating in public. Tipper seems to have had a difficult time appreciating this song. Gore (1987) writes:

> I couldn't believe my ears! The vulgar lyrics [masturbating with a magazine] embarrassed both of us. At first I was stunned—then I got mad! Millions of Americans were buying *Purple Rain* with no idea what to expect. Thousands of parents were giving the album to their children... (p. 17)

There *is* substantial evidence pointing to the existence of a *real* crisis disproportionately effecting children that is indeed cause for alarm. However, contrary to the story told by Gore (1987) and other conservative elites, the source is primarily economic, not cultural. The attack on social programs and the driving down of wages that defined the 1980s have resulted in children, especially children of color, comprising the most impoverished group in the United States (Albelda, et al, 1988). Nowhere in her book does Gore mention the trickle-down, neo-liberal economic policies that have caused real and measurable damages to children since at least the 1980s (see Ackerman, 1982), but rather hysterically points the finger at Prince (and others) for singing about a girl *rubbing herself* in a hotel lobby. In their campaign to define the parameters of public discourse concerning the wellbeing of children, Gore and the PMRC fundamentalists turned to public school organizations for support.

Publicly aligned with the National Congress of Parents and Teachers (PTA), the PMRC was determined to force the music industry into a "solution" that was "palatable" to their particular right-wing, fundamentalist sensibilities. The PMRC's media blitz designed to expose "the dangers" of "porn rock" was wildly successful as they drew national attention from radio, television, magazine, and newspaper media outlets (Gore, 1987). The success of this campaign has been attributed to the fact that the architects of the PMRC were the wives of powerful legislators and politicians, such as Tipper's husband, former democratic vice president Al Gore, who was a senator during the height of the PMRC (Fischer, 2003).

Responding to critics who contend the PMRC's movement against music violates artists First Amendment rights, Gore (1987) argued that they did not advocate the banning "of even the most offensive" records, but rather, sought to inform consumers of the content of their musical purchases through a labelling system designed to "protect...children from explicit messages that they are not mature enough to understand or deal with" (pp. 26–27). The "Explicit Lyrics—Parental Advisory" labels that came out of this campaign have been dubbed "Tipper Stickers" by proponents of the independent music scene. Gore (1987) has commented that the success of this labelling system has provided an invaluable tool in assisting parents in "avoid[ing] the twisted tyranny of explicitness in the public domain" propagated by "a few warped artists [and] their brand of rock music [that] has become a Trojan Horse, rolling explicit sex and violence into our homes" (pp. 28–29). The result of this labelling system, as we will see below, has limited the ability of small independent record labels to get their albums into the large chain stores. Thus this has kept them out of the hands of the majority of Americans who live outside the large urban centers.

Independent and Critical: The Best of Punk Rock

The view of the world endorsed by Christian fundamentalism, its axiology and ontology, for example, by definition, has made itself personally responsible for eradicating all competing philosophical perspectives. In the realm of popular music the fundamentalist axiology (what is good and bad) is based on the assumption that Paul McCartney of the Beatles and Mike Love of the Beach Boys are *good* because they, like Tipper, are "disturbed by the entertainment industry's penchant for the violent and explicit," and that the Dead Kennedys and Prince, for example, are *bad* because they represent the "moral and artistic decline of American entertainment" (Gore, 1987, p. 167). The ontological (the nature of the universe) perspective behind these axiological assumptions is that God is the center of the universe and the white middle-class puritanical culture of many fundamentalist leaders represents the highest level of moral development, rendering its adherents responsible for forcing it on the rest of humanity. However, this work of God has not proven too glamorous to be mediated by market mechanisms.

Because the independent record labels tend to be far less economically endowed compared to the major labels (that are parts of much larger international multimedia empires), it has been deemed more efficient, economically, to go after the fiscally-impaired smaller companies first, as it has been assumed that they are easier to bankrupt and thus silence. In the early days of the contemporary censorship movement during the late-1980s, its leaders publicly despised artists such as Ozzy Ozbourne and Prince (Gore, 1987). However, these widely popular employees of some of the world's largest corporations were often too expensive as cultural targets. The fundamentalists would have to settle with Jello Biafra, original Dead Kennedys front man and founder of Alternative Tentacles Records (Biafra, 1991).

On April 15th, 1986, Biafra received a group of unexpected visitors at his San Francisco flat—nine San Francisco and Los Angeles police officers searching for the "harmful matter" he was suspected of distributing. That harmful matter included a record, Frankenchrist by Biafra's band, the Dead Kennedys. In the album was a reproduction of a painting by Swiss artist H.R. Giger, entitled "Penis Landscape." In their search of his apartment, they came across a number of Alternative Tentacles releases, including an album by the Butthole Surfers. After the discovery Biafra reported that the police inquired, "are you involved with them too?" (Biafra, 1989). After two and half hours of interrogation and tearing apart his house, the police left with three copies of the Frankenchrist record, a few extra copies of the Giger poster, Biafra's personal mail, and some legal documents. This left Jello suspicious that the state had been conducting surveillance and gathering intelligence on the underground music scene for a long time.

A few months later Biafra and four other people were charged with one count each by the Los Angeles City Attorney's Office with the distribution of harmful matter to minors, which held the maximum penalty of one year in jail and a two thousand dollar fine (Biafra, 1987, 1989, 1991, 1998). The PMRC's "truth in packaging laws" were in effect and it was, therefore, argued that the Dead Kennedys record, *Frankenchrist*, was in violation because copies were not fitted with the required "Parental Advisory" sticker at time of purchase. Instead, the records were adorned with the mockingly sarcastic label that made fun of the "Tipper Sticker." The evening these charges were made public the prosecuting attorney (the City Attorney from LA) went on the news arguing that "we feel this is a cost-effective way of sending a message that we are going to prosecute offenders" (Biafra, 1989). Again, targeting the Dead Kennedys was deemed "cost-effective" because they were small and relatively powerless. What was the message being sent? According to Biafra, the state was telling record stores that if they wanted to avoid problems with the police, they should not carry Dead Kennedys' records, which effectively blackballed their music for years to come. Even though the charges were eventually dropped after a lengthy trial, Biafra and his co-conspirators nevertheless paid a high price. They spent eighty thousand dollars and expended a year and a half of their lives in court. The chain store that sold the record not only took the *Frankenchrist* album off the shelf, it took all the records the Dead Kennedys ever made off all its selves throughout the United States. The damage, as it were, had been done (Biafra, 1989).

Not only have the fundamentalists gone after music and oppositional youth culture through laws and legislature, but also they continue to use media in an attempt to scare kids away from the evils of devil music such as heavy metal, punk rock and rap/hip-hop. The recent "Hell House" phenomenon stands as a scary example. The roughly thirty-year old "Hell House" phenomenon, popularized by Jerry Falwell, illustrates how fundamentalists use scare tactics to foster a strict dogma of behavior and belief. At hundreds of active "Hell Houses" in service around Halloween in North America "customers" are led through a number of scenes, acted out by real people in full drama right before your very eyes. They are designed to highlight the consequences (which is always going to hell and suffering for eternity) of abortion, gay-marriage, homosexuality in general, teaching of evolution in school, and listening to rap, heavy metal and punk music, for example.

The Push Back

As we will see below, these outrageous claims by fundamentalists have provided the underground punk music scene's *push back* with a seemingly unlimited supply of material for sarcastic songs. Central to this discussion is the direction Biafra has taken Alternative Tentacles since 1979–1980 as a form of transformative, cultural-resistance, which, at its core, has been philosophical.

One of the consequences of the "distribution of harmful matter to minors" charges and the subsequent court case outlined above was the breakup of the Dead Kennedys. However, over the years Jello Biafra has continued to make music with a number of bands, many of which have been signed with his label, Alternative Tentacles, such as Nomeansno. As a result of the trial, Biafra also began a long career making records and touring as a spoken word artist informing the public of the Christian fundamentalist campaign against counter cultural formations based on his personal experience. His first spoken word record, *No More Cocoons*, came out in 1987. Since then he has published hours and hours of lively, hilarious, fact-filled commentary on the nature of power and how it is exercised. Shedding light on his method of collecting, organizing and analyzing information, which is the stuff of his spoken word performances, Biafra comments in an interview with V. Vale (2001)

> A lot of what I know comes from articles or anecdotes people send me or tell me...I read commercial mags and daily papers...it's important to analyze what they want you to think. Noam Chomsky reads the Wall Street Journal and a lot of the business magazines because they are much more open with each other about what their dirty plans and visions are. (p. 183)

The publication of Biafra's first spoken word album marked the beginning of a new kind of punk record—the lecture/commentary. This deepened the democratic impulses of Alternative Tentacles and the punk movement more generally. Milagros Peña and I (2004) document the development of these trends in our book *Punk Rockers' Revolution: A Pedagogy of Race, Class, and Gender* where we analyze message trends over time on three record labels, Alternative Tentacles, SST, and Epitaph. What follows is an updated, summative version of our findings focusing on Alternative Tentacles, which underscores the contemporary relevance of punk as a force of counter-hegemony.

Theoretically, our study rejected a commonly held belief among Frankfurt School theorists such as Theodor Adorno (1998) who argued that popular culture is an embodiment of the ideas, values and beliefs of the dominant culture and therefore has no redeeming qualities. We were equally dissatisfied with the romantic idea that sub-cultures such as punk rock are not affected by the hegemony that permeates the dominant society and therefore manifest themselves as pure forms of counter-hegemony. What drew our attention were more complex understandings of cultural reproduction and production in the theories of youth resistance. We found these understandings in the work of critical scholars such as Paul Willis (1977) and Angela McRobbie (2000).

After analyzing message trends, I can say with confidence that Alternative Tentacles has become more counter-hegemonic over time. While the amount of content coded as counter-hegemonic remained relatively consistent between the 1980s and 1990s (around 80%), the message presenters became less white and less male. As a result of these findings, we suggested that punk rock should not be so much as defined by a particular musical style or aesthetic, but be viewed as an increasingly democratized cultural space. The spoken word record has opened up new possibilities within spaces created by punk rockers. Alternative Tentacles, in collaboration with AK Press, has published dozens of such records by revolutionaries from all walks of life from Earth First! activist Judi Bari to former Black Panther Party and Community Party USA member Angela Davis. The spoken word phenomenon has been an important development for Alternative Tentacles, which Biafra himself has used to expose the new and old Tippers and their PMRCs in his many "Talk[s] on Censorship" over the years, and in so doing, demonstrating the connection between the fundamentalists and the White House. What follows is a look at some recent song lyrics that serve a similar function.

Sarcastically referring to the prominent Christian leader Billy Graham's questionable professional training and subsequent theological praxis Deloria (1994) comments, "having never attended a seminary, he did not have the opportunity to study Christian history or doctrine and had no chance to be led astray by the facts" (p. 226). Similarly, the recent sarcasm within the song "Leaving Jesusland" (2006), by legendary punk rock band, NOFX, can be contextualized within the preceding analysis offered by Deloria (1994). In his opening verse, "Fat Mike," NOFX lead vocalist and bass player, sings

We call the heartland, not very smart land
IQ's generally low and threat levels are high
They got a mandate, they don't want man-dates
They got so many hates and people to despise...

While the message transmitted though Jesusland is clear and, as indicated above, relatively accurate, as critical educators we are compelled to mention, if only as a side note, that associating IQ with intelligence uncritically legitimizes the often racist biases built into the tests themselves. However, the anti-intellectualism within the fundamentalist movement is well-documented (Marsden, 2006), and NOFX's intended message and critique therefore remain relevant. Not only does the analysis offered by NOFX extend our understanding of fundamentalism, but it also demonstrates the widespread opposition to restrictive dogmas within organic, cultural spaces such as those created and recreated by punk rockers—the object of attack by prominent right-wing Christian fundamentalists. At its finer moments punk rock therefore acts as a keeper of hope, an ontological human need (Freire, 1992).

In "Jesus was a terrorist" by Jello Biafra with Nomeansno (1991), Biafra echoes the irony that surrounds the fundamentalist movement:

Jesus was a terrorist
Enemy of the state…
Today bible-thumping cannibals
Reap money from his name…

Again, such lyrics point to the hypocrisy of right-wing Christian fundamentalists who claim to be followers of the rebel-leader Jesus while simultaneously persecuting contemporary revolutionaries. Biafra (1987, 1989, 1991, 2000) has also consistently used this critique through his spoken word performances. Echoing this sentiment in "Christian? Christ-like?," another Alternative Tentacles spoken word artist, Mumia Abu-Jamal (1997), speaking from Pennsylvania's death-row, notes that "Christianity became, in America, the faith of the slavemaster, the alleged belief of the rich, the protector of the propertied. For the slave, though, it was more farce than faith; in his eyes what was truly worshipped by all was wealth" (p. 45).

Another relatively recent Alternative Tentacles release, *New Dark Age Parade* (2006) by one of Canada's most influential punk bands of the late 1970s and early 1980s, the Subhumans (not to be confused with the UK Subhumans), offer yet another voice critiquing propensity for violence. In their hard-hitting song "I Got Religion" the Subhumans sarcastically speak from the perspective of a "born again" shedding light into their understanding of the mind of the converted under the influence of white-supremacist, war-mongering fundamentalist doctrine. In their opening verse musician and political activist Gerry Hannah writes, "I've been born again and now I'm lily-white. I want to prove my faith and get into a fight." Bringing the collective implications of this white-God-laden-violence into clear focus, the song, reaching a crescendo, indignantly continues

I want to start a war and show my master's wrath
I want to leave a bloody ruined aftermath
I'm always free from guilt whatever I may do
I can always tell them it was god who told me to

In another track, "Clash of the Intransigents," which again takes aim at the violence that often surrounds religious fundamentalism, in both Christian and Islamic manifestations, the Subhumans (2006) offer a faith-centered analysis of the United States' invasion of the Middle-East

Killing a family won't get you to heaven
Saluting a flag won't make your country secure
It's time to say no to this unholy destruction
I question your theology

Following this verse the first two lines of the "Clash of the Intransigents" chorus, "Is an act divine when it's written in blood? Are a people free when they're dead in the mud?," capture the essence of this genuinely old-school sounding (harsh and aggressive with the harmonic smoothness of pop) punk album, "New Dark Age Parade," as a whole. The record's artwork contributes significantly to the album's message. The cover displays an image embodying the signifiers of a white, nuclear, middle-class family taken from a 1950s magazine. The father, mother, and son (holding the family dog), standing arm-in-arm, are all smiling adorning cheeks bright with redness. This essentialist image of the white American family is situated in the context of a sky filled with the silhouettes of World War II United States fighter plains. The backdrop of these images is alternating bright yellow and light yellow sunrays contributing to the sense of uneasy happiness the cover art engenders. Adding a final layer of contrast, the header bears a bold black and white "SUBHUMANS," the accompanying footer similarly reads "NEW DARK AGE PARADE," so as not to leave any doubt in the viewer's minds the meaning of title of the album.

While the Subhumans' record draws on the use of cleaver irony—a shallow, manufactured happiness in the context of the death and destruction indicative of war, all cloaked in the essentialist anti-intellectualism of religious fundamentalism— Nausea, another Alternative Tentacles band, transmits similar messages but contributes to a slightly different tradition, or sub-genre, within the punk movement. One of Nausea's (2006) recent AT re-issues, "The Punk Terrorist Anthology Vol. 1," draws on the gritty and grimy, harshness of hardcore punk rock in their images, lyrics, and sound.

The cover of "The Punk Terrorist Anthology Vol. 1" makes no attempt at subtlety. The background displays a torn and tattered US flag held together with safety pins. Placed on top of this stained and corroding symbol of patriotism is an upside-down, white, crucified, and bloodied Jesus figure. Nausea is written across the top in a font we might aptly dub *electrocuted*. Emblazoned along the bottom of the composition in a font that looks like jagged handwriting is the name of the album, "The Punk Terrorist Anthology Vol. 1." As a whole this hardcore cover art would surely offend any patriotic Christian—clearly the intended effect. The song titles and lyrics are represented well by the record's artwork. Of particular interest here are the songs "Cybergod," "Body of Christ," and "Godless." In "Cybergod" (2006), for example, lyricists "Al" and "Amy" spew out the following lyrics over a grinding guitar and driving drum beat

His omnipresent power is felt in every home…

You know without his guidance you surely would be lost…

Praise the Cybergod for the fools you put in power…

Praise the Cybergod for a world of misery

The message is clear: TV evangelicals serve hegemonic interests by equating happiness with "money and fast cars" and by defining religiosity as unquestioning obedience to the self-appointed representatives of God. In short, like other critics, punk rock and otherwise, Nausea takes aim at the exploitative and destructive nature of mindless anti-intellectual fundamentalist Christianity. In "Godless" Nausea (2006) offers not just a critique of right-wing Christian fundamentalism, but also a personal rejection of its attempt to control all of social life. Again, Al and Amy unleash the following lyrical assault

Take your religious chains

You don't own my soul

You've...blessed us with this living hell

Your pious solve their problems with their guns

A chorus that warns mainstream religious leaders to "beware" of their "Godhood" because "they will rebel" accompanies these straightforward verses. Nausea's uncompromising in-your-face attitude and unmistakable agency are not uncommon characteristics within the Do It Yourself (DIY) punk movement. Providing one of the most interesting responses to "the faith of the slavemaster," the self-identified fundamentalist Christian punk rockers, the Knights of the New Crusade, who are signed with Alternative Tentacles, represent a wildly complex and contradictory manifestation of Christotainment.

As a result, their songs cover a wide rang of topics, each one written from the philosophical perspective of their reading of Christian religious texts, which, at times, challenge mainstream forms of Christianity, while, at other times, accommodating it. For example, The Knights sing about kicking big-money fundamentalists out of the church for using the Good Word to get rich. Their two releases, "My God is Alive! Sorry About Yours" (2005) and "A Challenge to the Cowards of Christendom" (2006), together, offer over twenty tracks of the most comprehensive critique of Christian hypocrisy in musical form to date. However, their subject matter, in other ways, is little different from contemporary Christian fundamentalism and Christian rock in particular. For example, "Ain't No Monkey's in My Family Tree," on their 2005 release, offers a challenge to the science of evolution not dissimilar to current fundamentalist doctrine. The song, situated in the white supremacist context of the dominant society, can too easily be interpreted as transmitting anti-Black, racist messages. For example, in the opening verse, vocalist, Leaky states "there's monkeys in the jungle, there's monkeys in the zoo, you'll even find monkeys in some of our schools."

Another example of their lyrics from the Cowards of Christendom (2006) include, "some of the people who get on our case for being Knights are under the influence of the same war-mongering demons as the politicians who ignore the commandments that Jesus affirmed." The Knights' lyrics, such as these, are sung over a garage punk sound that is about as raw as it comes, while their appearance is designed to be a Knights Templar's taken right out of a movie about the middle-ages.

The Knights have seemed to have left most of their reviewers—reviewers who typically review AT releases—utterly confused. Are they for real, or are they a joke gone too far? No one seems to know for sure, but the consensus seems to be that they may actually mean what they say, and say what they mean, while simultaneously making fun of the idea of the Christian fundamentalist crusader. They have stated that their own personal mission is to "take Christianity back from the powerful hypocrites who have hijacked it and to make Christian rock that actually rocks." While their critiques of right-wing Christian fundamentalism are not uncommon within the cultural spaces of left-wing/counter-hegemonic punk rock, their positionality as white-Christian-fundamentalists against greed and war, as far as I know, is one hundred percent original. Again, employing the sounds of 1960s US garage band rock n' roll and 1980s skate punk rock, and the image of the European Dark Age Christian Crusader, fused with moments of a Left-politics seen through the eyes of a contemporary Christian fanatic, their very existence have sparked a whole debate centered around the question: Is this real or a parody?

In one of the premier punk rock journals/magazines, Razorcake, in a "Staff" written review of 'The Knights' (2005) *My God is Alive, Sorry About Yours* (2005) the editors argue that "if this is, in fact, a joke" then it should be counted as some of "the best" works of "pointed parody," but if it is not a joke, "then Jesus' army is in sorry shape" (Razorcake, 2007). The authors point to The Knights' appearance, which include Crusader helmets, that is, "buckets on their heads," as evidence for why they are not taken seriously. While their attire makes for an interesting visual experience, in my judgment, it is the extreme complexity and deep contradictions that can be found within their lyrics that leaves listeners confused; they simultaneously resemble both liberation theology radicals *and* conservative self-righteous fundamentalists, and therefore, it is not clear whether or not they are real or a joke. For example, The Knights attack warmongering and pro-death penalty Christians for ignoring the commandments of Jesus, while, at the same time, attacking science for evolution.

Debates on sites such as *punknews.org* surrounding these issues are not uncommon. For example, a Review of The Knights 2006 release, *A Challenge to the Cowards of Christendom*, by FuckYouO iO iO (2008), notes that the Knights are so over-the-top that one must wonder if they are being serious. FuckYou's reflections sparked a lengthy debate drawing the attention of punk rock bloggers. The discussion started with people just assuming that The Knights are a joke making statements such as "there is no way this is not a joke." However, not all listeners are convinced the band is a parody noting that the band members themselves state their mission is to basically expose mainstream Christians as frauds. Another poster theorizes that The Knights are a joke to those who think they have comedic value. Attempting to end the discussion, situating the issue of authenticity in the context of their label, Alternative Tentacles (AT), another discussant rants, "its on AT!!! Anyone who sees that and still thinks it's serious knows nothing." The Knights themselves have been quoted as saying that their band is *both* real *and* a joke. Others joined the discussion, it seems, to just express that they like the band. One blogger wrote "I don't care if it is joke or not, I love these guys." Another similar observer notes, "I love this band, they're so nuts and they actually play some really good rock n' roll."

As if the lyrics weren't enough, one need only examine a few of The Knights' live performances on You Tube to begin to understand why they would be described as "nuts." While all the members wear crusader metal mesh and the traditional cotton shirt over their old school skate shorts and vans, only the singer, Leaky, waves a four-foot battle sword around the stage as he sings. However, through any given performance Leaky can be observed waving around not a sword, but a bottle of beer, stumbling with intoxication, reassuring the audience that "beer is not evil, it is proof that God loves us and wants us to be happy." Another aspect of their theatre is conducting an informal holy communion where Leaky and an assistant pass small paper cups to a few members of the front of the audience and distribute wine and crackers while the band moans on in the background. The audience, "every freak, faggot and bull dyke" as Leaky addresses them, is continuously reminded that no matter what they have done in their lives God will always love them and will forgive them, but on judgment day, when the trumpets sound in the sky, they will have to move, that is change. This rant leads into the bluesy punk rock n' roll song, "you gotta move." The drunk stumbling punk rock Leaky moving in and out of sarcasm and genuine critique, and simultaneously blurring the line between reality and imagination does come across as genuinely "nuts."

However, even though the conceptual ground from which punk rock has been built is tension and paradox, the contradiction between identifying with the Crusading Christians of the Middle Ages that created Christopher Columbus and his lasting spirit of conquest and plunder and their simultaneous call for peace and democracy, might be a bit unsettling for those on the Left not fluent in punk rock, regardless of The Knights' original intentions. Again, it cannot be overstressed that The Knights of the New Crusade are an aberration in the punk scene. While it is a common practice for punk rockers to call themselves what they are protesting, such as the left-wing, activist punk band Riot Cop who sing about their own experiences battling riot police in the streets as part of the struggle against the capitalist system of dehumanization and exploitation, The Knights of the New Crusade argue that they are re-appropriating Christianity from corruption. In other words, as Riot Cop resist what they call themselves; The Knights also resist what they call themselves while simultaneously embracing what they call themselves through a process of re-appropriation and sarcasm. It is much easier to "get" Riot Cop because they do not dress up like riot cops. They dress like the punk rock anarchist riot cop street fighters they are and portray themselves as being.

Conclusion

Punk rock, at its finer moments, has served the interests of radical democracy by fighting oppression and abuse, such as those examples from the Christian conservative backlash against alternative cultural formations. That is, punk rock has proven to be an effective vehicle through which people can explore and develop their creative endowments in the humanization of the world against human suffering and epistemological intolerance. Effective because punk rock, by definition, is experimental, and when it succeeds at transgressing dogma and rigidity, it is particularly conducive to empowerment. What we are discussing here is culture—youth culture in particular—and culture might be understood as the essence of the human statement endowing it with a great deal of emotional significance. It is as cultural beings that we engage the world and construct knowledge about that world and ourselves in it. It is therefore not surprising that culture has historically been a highly contested terrain.

QUESTIONS FOR REFLECTION

1. How can cultural studies be used counter-hegemonically in the classroom?
2. How can other forms of youth culture, such as hip-hop, enhance the epistemological diversity of such pedagogical and curricular approaches?
3. Why do youth cultures sometimes fail to operate counter-hegemonically?

REFERENCES

Abu-Jamal, M. (1997). *Death blossoms: Reflections from a prisoner of conscious.* Farmington, PA: Plough Publishing House.

Ackerman, F. (1982). *Reaganomics: Rhetoric vs. Reality.* New York: South End Press.

Adorno, T. W. (1998). On the Fetish character in music and the regression of listening. In A. Arato & E. Gebhardt (Eds.), *The essential Frankfurt school reader* (pp. 270–300). New York: Continuum.

Albelda, R., McCrate, E., Melendez, E., Lapidus, J., & The Center for Popular Economics. (1988). *Mink coats don't trickle down: The economic attack on women and people of color.* New York: South End Press.

Biafra, J. (1987). *No more cocoons: Spoken word album #1.* San Francisco: Alternative Tentacles, Virus 59.

Biafra, J. (1989). *High priest of harmful matter: Tales from the trial: Spoken word album #2.* San Francisco: Alternative Tentacles, Virus 59.

Biafra, J. (1991). *I blow minds for a living: Spoken word album #3.* San Francisco: Alternative Tentacles, Virus 94.

Biafra, J. (1998). *If evolution is outlawed, then only outlaws will evolve: Spoken word album #5.* San Francisco: Alternative Tentacles, Virus 201.

Biafra, J. (2000). *Become the media.* San Francisco, CA: Alternative Tentacles, Virus 260.

Biafra, J. with Nomeansno. (1991). *The sky is falling and I want my Mommy.* San Francisco: Alternative Tentacles, Virus 85.

Cleaver, K., & Katsiaficas, G. (2001). *Liberation, imagination, and the black panther party: A new look at the panthers and their legacy.* New York: Routledge.

Deloria, V. (1994). *God is red: A native view of religion.* Golden, CO: Fulcrum.

Fischer, P. (2003). Challenging music as expression in the United States. In M. Cloonan & R. Garofalo (Eds.), *PolicingPop* (pp. 221–238). Philadelphia: Temple University Press.

Freire, P. (1999). *Pedagogy of hope: Reliving pedagogy of the oppressed.* New York: Continuum.

Freire, P. (2005). *Teachers as cultural workers: Letters to those who dare teach.* New York: Continuum.

FuckYouO iO iO i. (2008, May 4). A review of the knights of the new crusade. *A challenge to the cowards of Christendom.* Retrieved from http://www.punknews.org/review/5454

Gore, T. (1987). *Raising PG kids in an X-Rated society.* Nashville, TN: Abingdon Press.

Jones, C., & Jefferies, J. (1998). "Don't believe the hype": Debunking the Panther mythology. In C. E. Jones (Ed.), *The Black Panther party reconsidered* (pp. 25–56). Baltimore: Black Classic Press.

Knights of the New Crusade. (2005). *My god is alive! Sorry about yours!* San Francisco: Alternative Tentacles, Virus 350.

Knights of the New Crusade. (2006). *A challenge to the cowards of christendom.* San Francisco: Alternative Tentacles, Virus 352.

Lusane, C. (1998). To fight for the people: The Black Panther party and Black politics in the 1990s. In C. E. Jones (Ed.), *The Black Panther party reconsidered* (pp. 443–468). Baltimore: Black Classic Press.

Lyons, O., & Mohawk, J. (1992). *Exiled in the land of the free: Democracy, Indian nations, and the U.S. constitution.* Santa Fe, NM: Clear Light Publishers.

Malott, C., & Peña, M. (2004). *Punk rockers' revolution: A pedagogy of race, class, and gender.* New York: Peter Lang.

Marsden, G. (1991). *Understanding fundamentalism and evangelicalism.* Grand Rapids, MI: Eerdmans.

Marsden, G. (2006). *Fundamentalism and American culture, second addition.* New York: Oxford University Press.

McGuire, M. (1992). *Religion: The social context.* Belmont, CA: Wadsworth.

McRobbie, A. (2000). *Feminism and youth culture* (2nd ed.). New York: Routledge.

Nausea. (2006). *The punk terrorist anthology* (Vol. 1). San Francisco: Alternative Tentacles, Virus 348.

NOFX. (2006). *Wolves in Wolves' clothing.* San Francisco: Fat Wreck Chords.

Porfilio, B., & Malott, C. (2008). *The destructive path of neo-liberalism: An international examination of urban education.* Rotterdam: Sense Publishers.

Razorcake. (2007). *Record reviews that didn't fit in issue 21.* Retrieved from http://www.razorcake.org/site/modules.php ?name=News&file=article&sid=402

Smith, P. (1984). *The rise of industrial America: A people's history of the post-reconstruction era* (Vol. 6). New York: Penguin Books.

Subhumans. (2006). *New dark age parade.* San Francisco: Alternative Tentacles, Virus 366.

Vale, V. (2001). *Real conversations no. 1: Rollins, Childish, Biafra, Ferlinghetti.* San Francisco: Re/Search Publications.

Willis, P. (1977). *Learning to labour: How working-class kids get working-class jobs.* New York: Columbia University Press.

ROBERT HAWORTH

11. ANARCHO-PUNK

Radical Experimentations in Informal Learning Spaces

INTRODUCTION

In this chapter I argue that youth involved in contemporary anarcho-punk movements are creating what I call "transformative possibilities." These transformative efforts are not deterministic or fixed political and cultural spaces but are occurring through on-going efforts by anarcho-punk youth who attempt to drill holes within the totalizing efforts of neo-liberalism and global capitalism (Day, 2005). Within these holes, anarcho-punk continues to play an important role in developing an ethics based in mutual and voluntary relationships that undermine and resist authoritative and hierarchical structures. As I reflect on my own experiences in punk as well as my continued efforts to live within some of its political and cultural practices, I believe it is important to have conversations about punk's ability to be reflexive. Just as many current social movements have come to new realizations about organizing against oppressive state and corporate structures, punk, and specifically anarcho-punk, has learned, grown and transformed through complex and sometimes painful experiences. I find it important to continue the conversation about punk, not out of nostalgia, but because it highlights opportunities for youth to experiment in radical politics and sub-cultural practices in spite of the restructuring of public spaces. Through their own agency, these spaces offer youth unique and diverse experiences where critical knowledge is produced, and in some cases, acted upon. Thus, I argue that these spaces create possibilities, or the potential, for youth to disrupt traditional routines of market-place logic, as well as offering alternatives in how we act and communicate in differing communities.

Anarchy in the O.C.: The Beginnings of a Middle-Class Punk

> *Big A, little A, bouncing B*
> *The system might have got you but it won't get me*
> *1 -2 -3—4*
> *(Crass, 1982)*

I remember when I was around ten or eleven (sometime around 1983) when my brother started to bring home music that completely rattled and transformed our mundane, White, middle-class lifestyle. Power chords, grinding distortion, lyrical

B. J. Porfilio and P. R. Carr (eds.), Youth Culture, Education and Resistance:
Subverting the Commercial Ordering of Life, 183–196.

screams and chanting choruses left me in political and cultural shock. It was interesting: here I was, a young boy in the middle of Orange County, California, living a privileged life with regards to race, class and gender, and listening to driving music and the relentless lyrics that called on youth to expose and resist the fallacies of political conservatism and traditional cultural practices.

During the 1980s, punk expanded internationally. Although it is has been considered a predominantly White middle and working-class sub-cultural practice, punk can be found in Mexico, South America and other countries, as well as within other cultural groups in the United States, albeit in new and differing forms. Most of my own initial experiences in what was considered "punk rock" were through the English punk scene (Thompson, 2004). The Exploited, The Partisans, Conflict and of course, the notorious anarcho-punk band Crass comprised my daily listening habits. I was also supportive of bands from the local area: Wasted Youth, Bad Religion, Social Distortion, and others. I soon became attracted to San Francisco's punk scene. This became prevalent when I picked up the vinyl compilation entitled *Not So Quiet on the Western Front* (1982). Contributing artists, Capital Punishment, Crucifix and Social Unrest, all played an important part in developing my sense of radical politics. For example, I learned about political movements in El Salvador, Reaganomics and the ill effects of trickle-down economics explicitly through punk lyrics. Punk songs became stories or vignettes of the ugliness of capitalism and US imperialism. Similar to the radical folk songs of Woody Gutherie, Utah Phillips and Phil Ochs, punk rock supports diverse narratives that attempt to name the world outside the comforts of privilege, and advocate for actions against oppressive structures.

My brother was older, and had more disposable income. He would frequently come home with more records, flyers from local gigs, and other punk paraphernalia from the local record store. His room was plastered with these texts. Most of Crass' intense artwork caught my eye because of Gee Vaucher's (1999) unique style of black and white collage art, as well as its striking political critiques of religion, war, politics and consumer culture during Reagan and Thatchers rule.

For many punk bands, the music did not stand-alone. Zines and sleeve inserts became important supplements in purchasing records. Moreover, supplements became ways in which punk artists were able to emphasize the radical political context of their lyrics. They not only gave a visual representation of the lyrics and album concept but were also used to support other political artists in the local scene (such as Gee Vaucher). Additionally, punk records enabled others outside of the local scene to engage in conversations about differing cultural practices around the country. In other words, records, zines and sleeve inserts were independent productions that were explicitly and implicitly utilized to disseminate and publicize punk politics. Zines were a means of communication with individuals in the local scene as well as other punks internationally. Moreover, these cultural productions enabled punks from differing geographical locations to get a sense of what was happening outside their own backyard. From interviews with touring artists to letters challenging and defining punk culture and politics, zines supported the ongoing discussions (and at times, debates) about the everyday practices and future of punk.

The punk zine *Maximum Rock n Roll* made some of the largest impacts on punk movements all over the US as well as other parts of the world. I agree with Stephen Duncombe (1997) that *Maximum Rock n Roll* supported multiple conversations by "continually defining and re-defining what is punk" (p. 61). Equally important to point out is that *Maximum Rock n Roll* and other zines created active networks that exchanged ideas, information, as well as a particular anarchist politics and cultural practices. Discussions surrounding direct action, police brutality, costs of all ages shows, vegetarianism, temporary autonomous zones (TAZ), and other aspects of punk ethics became transparent within these conversations. Although these exchanges were often intense and at times, divisive, the active communication gave youth a way to connect and become responsive to the problems and politics of different punk scenes or movements.

A Young Naïve Punk Moves to Northern California

During my middle-school years, I moved to a small town in Northern California. Most youth were interested in mainstream heavy metal and country music, and were definitely not interested in punk. With my plaid thrift-store pants and spiked hair, most of the students called me a "faggot", and I occasionally received a beating from the "rednecks." I had a few friends who I skated with but they were much older. I went to a few shows in San Francisco at the *Rock on Broadway* and *the Farm* but still felt isolated from what was happening in some of the larger music scenes. I soon sifted through more issues of *Maximum Rock n Roll*, and began communicating with others who were going through similar struggles.

We wrote letters to one another, traded tapes, and gained deeper understandings of what was occurring in other punk spaces, including scenes in Europe. I learned about squatting in abandoned buildings and of the disparaging economic restructuring that privatised and deregulated public structures. Moreover, zines supported a particular way of producing knowledge. Many of us were listening to the bands' raw political lyrics and reading more information within the sleeve inserts. This gave us the insight to discuss and critique the artistic and poetic attributes with others at shows and other sub-cultural hang-outs.

Reflecting on these experiences, I ask myself if there were concrete political actions occurring from these cultural productions? Not always. In fact, similar to contemporary political and cultural spaces, I would argue that punk and, particularly, anarcho-punk spaces share affinity with notions of "transformative possibilities." They had spontaneity and, at times, temporary characteristics, which ought to characterize them more as radical experiments or as Paulo Freire and Miles Horton describe in their dialogical exchange, "making the road by walking" (Bell, Gaventa & Peters, 1990). Similar to other youth involved in resisting contemporary neo-liberal values, anarcho-punk continues to re-imagine radical politics which are non-deterministic, yet grounded in anti-capitalism, collectivity, anti-authoritarianism and building mutual relationships. Moreover, I would argue that anarcho-punk should be considered within the Freirian (1970) context of "always becoming" because youth are creating radical spaces through ongoing experimentations in and around the complex policies and structures of neo-liberalism.

It would be naïve to think that these spaces are not immune to many of the hegemonic discourses of the marketplace, but certain punk movements have been able to engage in reflexive practices; thus, they find ways to confront and expose the barrage of marketplace intrusions within our everyday lives. Therefore, to define and name "punk" as a singular political and cultural practice is problematic. Chicano punks in Los Angeles, Afro-punks in New York, as well as those living in Mexico and Spain, have defined punk through differing complex narratives and political struggles (Fexia, 2006; Lipsitz, 2001; O'Conner, 2003). While many sub-cultures can be sold in malls and its music listened to on corporate radio stations, the supremacy of the marketplace has, in many instances, sanitized punk. This is evident by putting consumers at ease, and even invigorating youth in purchasing rebellion (Clark, 2003). However, the anti-capitalist politics of anarcho-punk offers something beyond the buying and selling of style and certain musical tastes. In actuality, youth involved in anarcho-punk engage directly with differing components or experiences within punk, where subjects participate in continuous political and cultural projects that attempt to experiment in life beyond capitalism.

Contemporary Anarchism: Why Punk Still Matters

Punk had to die so that it could live. *(Dylan Clark, 2003; p. 234)*

I would agree with many who have stated that certain aspects of punk have died. But I would also argue that within its death, punk has re-imagined itself in differing forms, particularly in the resurgence of anarchism and the movements against neo-liberalism (Clark, 2003; Holtzman, Hughes and Van Meter, 2007). In other words, punk still matters. The radical political undertones and cultural practices within anarchist movements have evolved in many differing situated spaces. Although corporate hipsters and embedded industry rebels have made extreme efforts in commodifing many sub-genres of punk, I would argue that anarcho-punk has taken on more fluid political and cultural identities to keep it out of the hands of global capitalists. According to Clark (2003), many people involved in punk movements "disavow an orthodox name, costume or music; yet in many ways they continue to live, or perhaps squat, within the classical structure of sub-culture" (p. 233). Youth who are involved in movements against neo-liberalism have found it more and more difficult to navigate through the privatizing efforts of corporate culture and market fundamentalism (Giroux, 2004); yet rather than naming oneself as punk, individuals have engaged in the process of praxis. Where youth once had made efforts to focus on identity politics and accepted sub-cultural styles, contemporary anarcho-punk movements concern themselves more with how they are acting and reflecting in differing communities. In other words, the rapid movements of neo-liberalism to open up markets have forced youth to construct spaces where they have the ability to learn and act with one another collectively, while at the same time, having to negotiate in and through the oppressive structures of global capitalism. This becomes more like a balancing act of trying to live and operate in radically different spaces, while having to navigate through the dominant market forces that either reject differences or attempt to commodify them. These reflexive processes bring important and complex issues regarding punk ethics to the forefront of many conversations within anarcho-punk movements.

Although punk ethics differ through informal negotiations and within certain situated locales, many underlying ethical practices in punk have crossed geographical, philosophical and historical borders. Punk ethics engage in a political and cultural critique of capitalism and a willingness to develop non-statist communication and actions that take place and evolve in situated and sometimes temporary communities. Punk, and explicitly anarcho-punk, is rooted in anti-capitalism. As stated earlier, punk lyrics have exposed many youth to the ill effects of U.S. imperialism, corporate dominance, class struggles, racism and many other inequities capitalist structures perpetuate. According to Nicolas Rombes (2005);

> From Crass' 'Do They Owe Us a Living?' ('Do they owe us a living? /Of course they fucking do!' [1978: n.p.]) to Fugazi's 'Merchandise' (Merchandise keeps us in line / Common sense says it's by design' [1990: n.p.]) to the thousands of zines and webpages outlining, sometimes crudely and sometimes with great subtlety, the social, ecological and moral dangers of exploitation, commodification and corporatisation, punks have always opposed capitalism as a perceived evil. (p. 23–24)

Additionally, anarcho-punk continues these anti-capitalist efforts through engaging in differing political and cultural projects. One of the major concerns anarcho-punks and anarchists have with capitalism and corporate structures is the issue of hierarchical decision-making. In confronting oppressive hierarchical structures, anarchists make concerted attempts to produce collective decision-making processes, drawing on direct democracy and other creative forms of consensus. Moreover, anarchists see representative democracy as problematic, since it relies on majority rule and undermines individuals' ability to self-organize and respond to immediate concerns in their daily lives. Anarcho-punk and anarchist collectives in general attempt to develop these non-hierarchal and anti-authoritarian processes in many differing spaces and for multiple purposes (O'Connor, 1999). Some spaces that utilize direct democratic or consensus models may include: communal houses, store fronts/info shops, and worker-owned collectives. What these political and cultural projects offer are alternatives to capitalism, hierarchy and the state. However, these projects are not deterministic or fixed, but are experimentations in possible communities beyond privatisation, hyper-competition and economic rationalism. For example, Alan O'Connor's (1999) research explores the difficulties in participating in the creation of a storefront (Whos Emma) in Canada, based in collective and non-hierarchical decision-making. His insightful reflections demonstrate the difficulties and sometimes limitations of "creating collectives and working in/with uncertainty. He suggests:

> Differences in aims and goals can often be expressed as personal conflicts: 'you don't respect me.' How these issues are handled will have important consequences for the future of the whole project. So the limits are real: finances

and dealing with legal matters; creating an organizational culture in which people can work together; and developing a collective project that of necessity excludes some people and ideas. (p. 695)

The importance of O'Connor's' work exemplifies the need for a thorough and honest analysis of how individuals participate and interact within collective spaces. Whether the discussion surrounds how certain voices are excluded in decision-making or the everyday realities in how collectives operate, an open and transparent process does not always equate with inclusion or a respect for differences. Although these experiments in participatory spaces are difficult, they are still important facets to the anarcho-punk landscape. This is especially pertinent for anarcho-punks who advocate for having autonomy or certain control over the production of goods and services provided to the community.

Although many international figures and collectives dispute the definition of the term, *Do-it-Yourself* (DIY) has had major influences in anarcho-punk ethics. DIY is a political and cultural practice that encourages punks to take control and create their own record labels, book their own concert tours, and distribute their own zines, activities that were "normally reserved for the realm of capitalist production" (Holtzman, Hughes & Van Meter, 2007). It is important to note that DIY culture is not just a different way of presenting capitalism. What differs under DIY culture is the way individuals organize and produce "use-value commodities rather than an exchange-value products" (p. 45). DIY efforts are not just symbols of changing one type of capitalism for another. Instead, they also involve "active construction of counter-relationships and the organization against and beyond capitalism" (p. 45). For example, many punk youth are explicitly involved in organizing gigs or concert events. These events are usually put on in community centres, veteran halls and other venues that accept "all ages" shows and low entrance fees. When those spaces are unavailable, gigs are moved to public parks, warehouses, garages and storage sheds. Many of these shows are free or sustain themselves through donations. In most cases, these are temporary venues because cops and other bureaucratic city officials shut many of these cultural spaces down. Often local bands and artists come together collectively, pool their money to rent a venue, borrow equipment from other contacts, and photocopy flyers at school in order to create mutual spaces that are normally discouraged or viewed as a threat in many towns and cities. While DIY spaces continue to emerge and become more prevalent in differing locations, they are also growing within other decentralized locations.

Anarcho-punk and the Re-working of Technology

Before communication technologies expanded, anarcho-punks utilized mailings, traded mixed tapes and 7 inches and communicated differing radical politics through zines, flyers and info shops. Most of these practices either "broke even" or were economically running on a deficit. Unfortunately, due to many of the collectives' voluntary and unpaid labor force, many of these political and cultural spaces did not survive (Thompson, 2004). More recently, the introduction of new technologies, has given anarcho-punk collectives the ability to distribute music and political information to both local networks and to a much broader audience without the high costs of production. In many cases, information is not only able to reach urban and suburban areas, but it has the ability to be disseminated to differing communities and at times, reinterpreted within other spaces and locales. However, having access to these new technologies is not always easy or affordable. Carles Feixa's (2006) work offers an important example of the differences amongst punk movements. Although global participants in punk movements across geographical borders have similarities, these unique spaces should not be described as "imitative or homogenous" (p. 164). According to Feixa (2006, p. 164) "local appropriations of global youth style like punk produce different cultural expressions in different places at different times". Thus, globally, punk movements differ with regards to local and national contexts in how certain political cultural practices are created and expressed. These differences are particularly important with reference to the use of technology.

Although many anarchists are critical of the techno-romanticism of the 21st century, many anarcho-punk movements have transformed the way technology is used, especially in how information is circulated through multiple platforms including open source and publishing software. Parallel to the *Zapatista* uprising in Southern Mexico and their use of technology, anarcho-punk movements utilize similar methods and tactics to distribute information and build networks of support across international borders. An important example was during *N30*, when over fifty thousand people marched against the undemocratic practices of the World Trade Organization (WTO). *Indymedia* utilized open source software to publish independent news that countered dominant corporate viewpoints. Activists and independent journalist were able to write or capture video of what was happening on the ground during the protest and then upload it for immediate release. Rather than attempting to get a short sound bite or blurb in the corporate media outlets, activists were able to freely disseminate information and become actively involved in online discussions regarding their stories or videos.

Differing communicative technologies have also enabled youth who are involved in anarcho-punk movements to develop online communities where individuals are able to discuss radical politics, engage in organizing actions or find out about an upcoming show. Nicolas Burbulas (2006) has described online interactions between individuals and groups as "self-directed learning communities." Self-directed learning communities produce knowledge that is active and freely distributed through other affinity spaces or community networks (Day, 2005). According to Burbulas (2006), individuals within these communities have a "strong ethos" where individuals are rarely acknowledged for their labour and contributions, yet are connected through informal and decentralized networks. This means punk cyber-networks produce and distribute knowledge freely across multiple sites and in most instances, not exclusive to one website. Uri Gordon (2008) describes many of these anarchist collectives including online networks, as having parallels to Delueze and Guatarri's (1987) rhizomatic networks that are highly decentralized and have complex inter-relationships with one another.

Again, I cannot discuss connections between the Internet and current social movements without bringing up the *Zapatista* movement. The *Zapatistas* provide an important example of how information is produced, translated, circulated and reflected on through differing political online networks. Through differing listservs, the *Zapatistas* are able to distribute information freely to other supporters around the world. In turn, many of these organizations and in some cases, individuals, translated and circulated the new information. As the listserv grew, international support and assistance expanded for the *Zapatistas*. Moreover, these international networks, including many anarcho-punk collectives, became integral contributors in pressuring the Mexican government to stop its military incursions on the indigenous people of Chiapas (Porta, Andretta, et al., 2006).

Contesting Neo-liberalism and Resisting the State Through Multiple Fronts

Although critical pedagogies, anarchism and punk are connected together through similar interests and have similar understandings in relationship to what causes injustice in our social world, there are also some differing understandings across these intellectual and cultural domains. A major difference resides in the notions of revolution and the state. This has been an extremely important historical debate, and I do not believe that it has been resolved within Marxian or anarchist camps and, quite frankly, will always be an area of contestation. Although some Neo-Marxists and autonomous Marxists have engaged in rigorous re-readings and interpretations of Marx, anarchists are still sceptical of movements that focus specifically on economic and material conditions. Within the current movements against neo-liberalism this scepticism offers differing and expansive strategies to interrupt certain power dynamics. Giorel Curran (2006) suggests, that anarchists are, "heartened to see the critique of domination extend beyond the social relations of capitalism to include the politics of race, gender, culture and nature" (p. 32). Furthermore, this "broadening of critique" enables anarchism to expose and contest power at varying levels of society from the nation-state to our everyday communication and personal/public interactions.

Additionally, youth involved in anarcho-punk movements have been able to navigate in and through these complex political and cultural terrains. Interestingly, Richard Day (2005) chronicles those subjects who navigate in and around these spaces as *autonomous smiths*. According to Deleuze and Guatarri (1987) the *smith's* characteristics differ from how the *nomad* and *citizen* operate. Where the citizen stays on particular traditional pathways, the nomad consistently destroys sedentary roads, the smith offers a unique position. According to Day (2005),

> Where the practice of the citizen is oriented to 'staying on the road', as it were, and that of the nomad to destroying all roads, the smith is guided by an alchemical, metallurgical will to the 'involuntary invention' of new strategies and tactics. Rather than attempting to dominate by imposing all-encompassing norms, the smith seeks to innovate by tracking and exploring opportunities in and around existing structures. (p. 174)

Anarcho-punk offers an important relationship to Day's concept surrounding the *smith*. While youth involved in anarchist struggles continue to intervene in neo-liberal policies and undemocratic movements to uphold global capitalism, they do so while having to negotiate those oppressive spaces. Many youth associated with anarchist movements still attend public schools, have jobs, and interact with the dominant culture, but what is important to understand is their ability to broker borders even within these enormously complex and, at times, contradictory political and cultural environments. Part of what this entails is the ability to act within what Foucault (1973; 1980) describes as, "micro-politics" or being able to contest power at multiple fronts. Moving outside of the vanguardist and economic determinism of past movements, Foucault looks at power and transforming society differently. More specifically, Foucault calls for a "plurality of autonomous struggles...where numerous local groups contest, diffuse and decenter forms of power spreading" (Best & Kellner, 1991; 56). With regards to anarcho-punk, micro-politics enables youth to intervene in dominant power dynamics through multiple locations. For example, anarcho-punks utilize the Internet to create political zines, blogs and discussion boards to share ideas, events and actions. At the same time, they are personally involved in face-to-face activities through organizing direct actions, creating local info shops, and contributing to independent media outlets. All these struggles take on certain forms of 'micro-politics' where these spaces not only contest the larger neo-liberal and global capitalist agendas, but are experimenting in complex ways of living outside these oppressive structures in more local contexts (Day, 2005; May, 1994; Morland, 2004).

Anarcho-punk movements have also concomitantly evolved significantly in the past few decades, where they have incorporated differing political strategies to eradicate hegemonic power dynamics within their own lived worlds and in the wider society. While these radical experimentations tend to be criticized as temporary and sporadic, anarcho-punk continues to renew itself both politically and culturally. Thus enabling subjects to engage in multiple political projects and create what Pickerill and Chatterton (2006) describe as, "*autonomous geographies*—those spaces where people desire to constitute non-capitalist, egalitarian and solidaristic forms of political, social and economic organization through a combination of resistance and creation" (p. 730).

I have argued that youth involved in anarcho-punk are conducting ongoing experiments in radical politics. But I would like to extend these discussions to ask how critical educators and researchers in formal public structures may begin to recognize and support these ongoing political and cultural projects. Not offering support as guides or dominant influences, but as mutual participants; thus building potential affinities or critical intersections with youth outside of the classroom.

Critical Intersections Between Public Schools and Informal Learning

Punks are right: the world is fucked up, and we need to do something about it
(Dunn, 2008; p. 179).

I have argued that anarcho-punk and informal learning spaces are important in how youth participate in learning environments outside of the formal school setting. As I mentioned in my earlier narrative, I grew up in a punk culture. It had its ethical roots in a DIY culture and resistance to traditional conservative values. But what is interesting is how these political and cultural experiences unfolded differently in different spaces. From my own experiences in punk, it is clear that one of these structures involves public schools. Because of educational institutions' tendencies to uphold traditional and conservative values, it is no wonder that punk youth continue to be ridiculed and marginalized within the classroom and school culture. This is not surprising since punk has predominantly operated in the peripheries of society. However, there have been occurrences where anarchism attempts to cross political and cultural borders, particularly within public schools. It is here that important questions and concerns arise, especially when anarchism's anti-authoritarian and non-hierarchical processes come up against extremely centralized and bureaucratic structures. Can critical educators take part in supporting these radical spaces even when much of their work resides in traditional public schools and state run universities? Can they do this through differing forms of participatory and activist research without imposing on youth's autonomy?

Just as youth are working in diverse contexts, I would argue that critical educators have the ability to work *in* and interact *with* youth in multiple locations as well. Recent developments in activist research and ethnographic studies have called for building multisited research in areas of education (Dimitriadis & Weis, 2008). These research opportunities enable critical educators and researchers to view education beyond the borders of classrooms. They also support mutual and authentic relationships that make concerted efforts to connect or develop affinity with youth in these complex-learning sites. Anarcho-punk offers just one of many outside informal learning spaces where youth engage in discussions about the world beyond capitalism. More importantly, these spaces create moments where subjects may communicate and act within these re-imagined communities. According to Dimitriadis & Weis (2008);

> Today…education is an increasingly emergent phenomenon, unfolding across numerous sites and settings with and in-between multiple texts. It is the "in-between"—the moving back and forth between sites and texts—that increasingly defines our children's lives and cultural landscapes and must, therefore, define our research agenda. (p. 335)

As neo-liberalism forces youth to create meaningful learning experiences outside of the classroom, it is important for critical educators and researchers to recognize these "in-between" spaces that youth inhabit. These radical experimentations are valuable sites for youth to construct ways of communicating, learning and acting (if only temporary) outside of the constraints and limitations of neo-liberalism and global capitalism. Thus, giving a glimpse of how we may live and learn differently. However, this is not a call to utilize political and cultural aspects of anarcho-punk in the classroom. What I am advocating for is that critical educators and researchers recognize and actively support these youth generated spaces in varying capacities (affinity groups) and in their own sub-cultural contexts. For example, when I taught year 12 government and economics at a semi-rural school in Northern California several of my students, who identified themselves as "punk" refused to stand during a 9/11 commemoration ceremony. Many of the other students became angered by the fact they were protesting the war and the vice-principal decided to suspend the individuals for "safety reasons." It was not until I was approached by the several students who were involved in the incident that I advocated on their behalf. At that point the students and I attempted to open up a dialogue with administrators regarding freedom of speech and reclaiming public spaces. Unfortunately, our attempt to dialogue was met with an unwillingness to formulate a meaningful conversation surrounding these issues; students became frustrated and suspicious of public schooling and its prevailing authoritarian structure.

At the same time, on the other side of the country, Katie Sierra, a fifteen-year old, self-identified anarchist was suspended for a t-shirt she wore in opposition to the war in Afghanistan. The principal made the excuse of suspending Katie due to "student safety" as well as "disrupting school activity" (www.democracynow.org, 2001; http://www.courttv.com). Prior to Katie's suspension, she also wrote a proposal to the principal to create an "anarchist club." Part of the club's manifesto encouraged students and teachers to "see beyond commonly held beliefs to discover the basic freedoms that anarchy presents to the world" (http://www. courttv.com). The proposal was later denied by the principal and, coupled with the t-shirt incident, led to her suspension. Later, Katie sued the school district and won on one account of being "improperly denied" the right to start an anarchist club, but the original verdict upheld the right for the principal to suspend her for wearing a political t-shirt.

What these two examples demonstrate are the tensions that arise between formal (traditional public school) and informal (anarchism) educative practices. Part of this stems from the political and cultural climate in post-9/11 schools, as well as in the larger society (Giroux, 2003). Extreme and reactionary conservatism magnifies oppositional and "unpatriotic" behaviour and then attempts to silence those dissenting voices. It is clear that dissenting youth have also become targets for government officials to vilify voices of resistance. For example, during the *Republican National Convention* (RNC) held for presidential candidate John McCain, local government officials in collusion with paid informants, arrested over 400 people (many of them anarchist youth) during "crash the convention" protests (www.democracynow.org, 2008). Eight of the protesters were held under the states' version of the *Patriot Act*, which can carry a sentence up to seven and half years. One of the eight held was 19 year-old, Elliot Hughes and according to his testimony, was tortured for being disruptive while imprisoned (www.democracynow.org, 2008). I agree with Giroux (2003; 2004) that these are not isolated instances. There has been an extremely reactionary shift in how youth are perceived and treated in the United States. According to Giroux's (2004) research on the "disappearing youth" in the age of George W. Bush,

> Rather than being cherished as a symbol of the future, youth are now seen as a threat to be feared and a problem to be contained. A seismic change has taken place in which youth are now being framed as both a generation of suspects and a threat to public life. If youth once symbolized the moral

necessity to address a range of social and economic ills, they are now largely portrayed as the source of most of society's problems. Hence, youth now constitute a crisis that has less to do with improving the future than with denying it. (http://www.cust.educ.ubc.ca/workplace /issue6p1/giroux04.html)

Even within the criminal and undemocratic behaviour behind neo-liberal policies and the state, I am hopeful about the capacity for youth to self-organize and become more reflective subjects. Through radical experimentations within cyber-networks, info shops, storefront collectives and other sub-cultural spaces, anarcho-punk has the ability to challenge many of the ill affects of restructuring capital. More importantly, youth-driven communities should not be patronized or taken lightly. Many of these diverse collectives continue to engage in unique informal learning practices where subjects work and communicate through voluntary, non-hierarchical and non-authoritarian processes. It is not only important for critical educators to acknowledge youth for their creativity and willingness to experiment in differing political and cultural practices, but for us to build, what Day (2005) describes as "affinity" with these autonomous networks. While neo-liberalism has the ability to transform globally in differing situated spaces, it is important to contest these ill transformations from differing fronts. Therefore, I agree with Day in developing a "multidimensional analysis of oppression...[in order to] subvert or offer alternatives to neo-liberalism" (Day, 2005, p. 184). I believe that anarcho-punk offers particular critiques of neo-liberalism, yet because of its relationship to praxis, has the ability to create transformative possibilities in how subjects might live and communicate in differing communities outside the limitations and oppressive nature of global capitalism.

QUESTIONS FOR REFLECTION

1. As anarchism continues to play a significant role in organizing, how can critical educators and researchers begin to include and value anarchism's critiques of the state and hierarchical structures as well as its "new dimensions" with regards to theory and practice?

2. Without a particular blueprint for transforming society, what are the limitations that anarcho-punk and other sub-cultural practices have in terms of creating alternatives to dominant capitalist structures?

3. Within a similar framework, what are the opportunities or "transformative possibilities" that anarho-punk and other sub-cultures may provide for future discussions in how we learn, reflect and act in differing communities?

REFERENCES

Best, S., & Kellner, D. (1991). *Postmodern theory: Critical interrogations.* New York: Guilford Press.

Bell, B., Gaventa, J., & Peters, J. M. (1990). *We make the road by walking: Conversations on education and social change.* Philadelphia: Temple University Press.

Burbulas, N. (2006). Self-educating communities: Collaboration and learning through the internet. In Z. Bekerman, N. Burbules, & D. Silberman-Keller (Eds.), *Learning in places: The informal education reader* (pp. 273–284). New York: Peter Lang.

Clark, D. (2003). The death and life of punk, the last sub-culture. In D. Muggleton & R. Weinzierl (Eds.), *The Post-sub-cultures reader* (pp. 223–236). Oxford: Berg Publishers.

Cohn, J. (2006). *Anarchism and the crisis of representation.* Selinsgrove, PA: Susquehanna University Press.

Conway, J. (2006). *Praxis and politics: Knowledge production in social movements.* New York: Routledge.

Courttv.com. (2002). *Teen anarchist sues school principal.* Retrieved from www.courttv.com/trials/taped/sierra/verdict.html

Crass. (Writers and Performers). (1978). [sound recording] Do they owe us a living? In *On feeding of the 5000.* UK: Crass Records.

Crass. (Writers and Performers). (1982). [sound recording] Big a, little a. In *On Christ the album.* UK: Crass Records.

Curran, G. (2006). *21st century dissent: Anarchism, anti-globalization and environmentalism.* New York: Palgrave.

Day, R. J. F. (2005). *Gramsci is dead: Anarchist currents in the newest social movements.* Toronto: Between the Lines.

DeLeon, A. P. (2006). The Time for action is now! Anarchist theory, critical pedagogy, and radical possibilities. *Journal for Critical Education Policy Studies, 4*(2). Retrieved from http://www.jceps.com/?pageID =article&articleID=67

Deleuze, G., & Guattari, F. (1987). *A thousand plateaus: Capitalism and schizophrenia* (B. Massumi, Trans.). Minnesota, MN: University of Minnesota Press.

Democracynow.org. (2001). *"When I saw the dead and dying Afghani children on TV, I felt a newly recovered sense of national security. God Bless America": High school suspends a 15-Year-old student for anti-war t-shirt.* Retrieved from www.democracynow.org/2001/12/11/when_i_saw_the_dead_and

Democracynow.org. (2008). *"We Are not terrorists": Activists with the RNC Welcoming Committee speak out against police crackdown & terrorism charges.* Retrieved from http://www.democracynow.org/2008/9/5/we_are_not _terrorists_members_of

Dimitriadis, G., & Weis, L. (2008). Globalization and multi-sited ethnographic approaches. In C. McCarthy, A. S. Durham, L. C. Engel, A. A. Filme, & M. D. Giardina (Eds.), *Globalizing cultural studies: Ethnographic interventions in theory, method, and policy* (pp. 323–342). New York: Peter Lang.

Duncombe, S. (1997). *Notes from underground: Zines and the politics of alternative culture.* New York: Verso.

Dunn, K. C. (2008). Never mind the bollocks: The punk rock politics of global communication. *Review of International Studies, 34,* 193–210.

Fexia, C. Tribus urbanas and chavos banda: Being a punk in Catalonia and Mexico. In P. Nilan & C. Feixa (Eds.), *Global youth?: Hybrid identities, plural worlds* (pp. 149–166). New York: Routledge.

Foucault, M. (1973). *The order of things.* New York: Vintage.

Foucault, M. (1980). *Power/knowledge: Selected interviews and other writings, 1972–1977.* New York: Pantheon.

Freire, P. (1970). *Pedagogy of the oppressed.* New York: Continuum.

Giroux, H. (2003). *The abandoned generation: Democracy beyond the culture of fear.* New York: Palgrave-Macmillan.

Giroux, H. (2004). Class casualties: Disappearing youth in the age of George W. Bush. *Workplace: A Journal of Academic Labor, 6.1*(11). Retrieved from http://www.cust.educ.ubc.ca/workplace/

Gordon, U. (2008). *Anarchy alive: Anti-authoritarian politics from theory to practice.* Ann Arbor, MI: Pluto Press.

Graeber, D. (2004). *Fragments of an anarchist anthropology.* Chicago: Prickly Paradigm Press.

Graeber, D. (2007). *Possibilities: Essays on hierarchy, rebellion and desire.* AK Press.

Holtzman, B., Hughes, C., & Meter, K. V. (2007). Do it yourself... and the movement beyond capitalism. In S. Shukaitis, D. Graeber, & E. Biddle (Eds.), *Constituent imagination: Militant investigations collective theorization* (pp. 44–61). Oakland, CA: AK Press.

Lipsitz, G. (2001). *American studies in a moment of danger.* Minnesota, MN: University of Minnesota Press.

Livingstone, D. W. (2006). Informal learning: Conceptual distinctions and preliminary findings. In Z. Bekerman, N. Burbules, & D. Silberman-Keller (Eds.), *Learning in places: The informal education reader* (pp. 203–227). New York: Peter Lang.

May, T. (1994). *The political philosophy of poststructuralist anarchism.* Pennsylvania, PA: Pennsylvania State University Press.

Moreland, D. (2004). Anti-capitalism and poststructuralist anarchism. In J. Purkis & J. Bowen (Eds.), *Changing anarchism: Anarchist theory and practice in a global age* (pp. 23–38). Manchester: Manchester University Press. *Not so quiet on the western front* (music compilation). (1982). [Sound recording] San Francisco: Alternative Tentacles.

O'Connor, A. (1999). Whos Emma and the limits of cultural studies. *Cultural Studies, 13*(4), 691–702.

O'Connor, A. (2003). 'Punk sub-culture in Mexico and the anti-globalization movement: A report from the front. *New Political Science, 25*(1), 43–53.

Pickerill, J., & Chatterton, P. (2006). Notes towards autonomous geographies: Creation, resistance and self-management as survival tactics. *Progess in Human Geography, 30*(6), 730–746.

Porta, D., Andretta, M., Mosca, L., & Reiter, H. (2006). *Globalization from below: Transnational activists and protest networks.* Minneapolis, MN: University of Minnesota Press.

Rombes, N. (2005). *New punk cinema.* Edinburgh: Edinburgh University Press.

Spring, J. (2008). *Wheels in the head: Educational philosophies of authority, freedom and culture from confucianism to human rights* (3rd ed.). New York: Lawrence Erlbaum Associates.

Thompson, S. (2004). *Punk productions: Unfinished business.* Albany, NY: State University of New York Press.

Vaucher, G. (1999). *Crass art and other pre post-modernist monsters.* UK: Existencil Press.

Ward, C. (1973). *Anarchy in action.* London: Freedom Press.

KATIE JOHNSTON-GOODSTAR, ALMA M.O. TRINIDAD,
AND ASTER S. TECLE

12. CRITICAL PEDAGOGY THROUGH THE
REINVENTION OF PLACE:

Two Cases of Youth Resistance

Globalization is simply the new metaphor for imperialism

-Sandy Grande (2000, pg. 469)

INTRODUCTION

Rhetorical distinctions between projects of colonialism, Manifest Destiny, territorial annexation and neo-liberal globalization obfuscate the steady agenda of imperialism that has assailed the political, cultural and economic diversity of Indigenous peoples for centuries. For those on the receiving end, superfluous distinctions are but a distraction from the striking social conditions created across time, people and place; conditions of genocide, health disparity, discrimination, forced migration, loss of land, and the decimation of traditional knowledge systems, ecologies, and economies (Benham & Heck, 1998; Deloria & Lytle, 1998; Evans-Campbell & Walters, 2006; Kanahele, 1986; LaDuke, 1999; Smith, 1999; Trask, 1993; Walters & Simoni, 2002). Presenting these projects as discrete historical events not only fails to recognize their common ideological foundations but also serves to diffuse burgeoning critiques and community practices of reinvention and resistance.

Minoritized youth and their communities are particularly affected by the consequences of neo-liberal policies, and, yet, they are rarely provided educative opportunities to examine and engage with the forces that so devastate their communities. Instead, these youth often attend schools that are struggling to stay afloat amidst growing segregation and poverty (Kozol, 2006), the increasing influence of 'learn to earn' and neo-liberal ideologies (Giroux, 2001; McLaren & Kinchloe, 2007; McLaren, 2006) as well as a preoccupation with standardized testing (Hursh & Martina, 2003), and "standardized, placeless curriculum" (Gruenewald, 2003, p. 8). There are schools where local and tribal knowledge is dismissed and minoritized students see themselves, at best, represented in electives or extracurricular activities.

In this chapter, we argue that critical pedagogy *can* provide minoritized youth, particularly Indigenous youth, with educational engagement that positions them as change-agents for social transformation. Critical pedagogy is generally referred to as the encounter between critical theory and education. Its adherents have played an instrumental role in engaging youth in exploration of, and resistance to, neo-liberal

B. J. Porfilio and P. R. Carr (eds.), Youth Culture, Education and Resistance:
Subverting the Commercial Ordering of Life, 197–216.
© *2010 Sense Publishers. All rights reserved.*

forces (Giroux, 2001; McLaren & Kincheloe, 2007; McLaren, 2006). Critical pedagogy however, *can and has* been critiqued on a number of fronts; its anthropocentric neglect of place (Gruenewald, 2003, p. 3), its retention of hegemonic notions of social justice, democracy and identity (Grande, 2000), its focus on individual, rather than community, liberation (Lee, 2006), and its reliance on Western epistemological and ontological views that displace Indigenous understandings (Ball, 2002; Bowers, 2005; 2006).

So while critical pedagogy is exceptionally suited to serve as a conduit to social action amongst minoritized youth (Duncan-Andrade & Morrell, 2008), it must adhere to Freire's epistemological curiosity and be open to modification by Indigenous contexts (Kincheloe, 2008, vii). With this in mind, we introduce two community-based, critical Indigenous pedagogies that center Indigenous theories of place, education and justice (Alfred, 1999; Barnhardt & Kawagley, 2005; Cajete, 1994; Deloria & Wildcat, 2001; Grande, 2004; Kanahele, 1986; Meyer, 2003) to catalyze Indigenous youth engagement with and against exclusionary social forces that contribute to inequalities in their communities. The first project, located in a Pacific Northwest metropolitan area, is for urban, Native American youth, and uses a critical Indigenous pedagogy of place coupled with the Photovoice method (Wang, 1997) to transform youth into investigators of environmental injustice and protagonists of change. The second project, located in Hawai'i, is a youth-led organic farm that addresses food insecurity, reduces chronic diseases, and mobilizes Native Hawaiian youth leadership for social transformation. These projects, while developed independent of one another, present parallel findings that reveal the powerful role that critical pedagogies of place can and do play in the development of Indigenous youth consciousness and engagement in the struggle for social justice.

Critical Pedagogy of Place

> A critical pedagogy must be a pedagogy of place, that is, it must address the specificities of the experiences, problems, languages, and histories that communities rely upon to construct a narrative of collective identity and possible transformation.
>
> *McLaren & Giroux (1990, p. 263)*

Critical pedagogies of place (CPP) attempt to identify and engage the intersections between place-based education and critical pedagogy. Place-based educators often use constructs associated with critical pedagogy, and, likewise, Freirian inspired cultural workers and community organizers frequently engage with environmental inequalities and neighborhood conditions. Nevertheless, critical pedagogy's general neglect of place, combined with the place-based tradition's acquiescence to dominant culture and oppression, has left the two disciplines somewhat like ships passing in the night.

Sobel (1999) states that children need to be able to love the natural world before being asked to save it. Critical pedagogues of place, while in clear agreement with this statement, believe that both critical pedagogy and place-based education can, and in many cases must, exist harmoniously. They claim that 'place' can be a catalyst for social transformation (Brandt, 2004) especially for communities who have experienced colonization, displacement and other forms of disruption or injury to their 'places' (Lee, 2006). For example, in Stephen Haymes' pedagogy of place for the Black urban struggle, Gruenewald (2003) finds "the importance of people telling their own stories (reading the world) in a place where people may be both affirmed and challenged to see how individual stories are connected in communities to larger patterns of domination and resistance" (p. 5). From the standpoint of CPP, the urgency to address neo-liberal and neocolonial policies and consequences make a *connection to place* and a *praxis for place* inseparable from one another.

A critical pedagogy of place then is the "conscious synthesis" (Gruenewald, 2003, p. 3) of critical pedagogy and place-based education. Kahn states (of the similar *ecopedagogy*) that it not only synthesizes, but also consciously speaks to both disciplines in the way "third world feminism attempted to critique both patriarchy and feminism as unresponsive and totalizing vis-à-vis marginal needs" (2007, p. 5). Critical pedagogies of place, such as those above, emphasize the critical analysis of ecological, rather than solely human relationships. In doing so, they have potential to address some of the typical critiques of critical pedagogy for example-its tendency toward anthropocentrism and general neglect of place (Bowers, 2003, 2005, 2006; Kahn, 2003; Gruenewald, 2003).

Gruenewald's critical pedagogy of place proposes two interrelated objectives entitled *decolonization* and *reinhabitation*, which "mirror the thematic emphases of critical pedagogy and ecological, place-based education respectively" (2003, p. 9). It is the most comprehensive description of *critical pedagogy of place* that we were able to locate. The objectives of CPP are to: (a) "identify, recover, and create material spaces and places that teach us how to live well in our total environments (*reinhabitation*)"; and (b) "identify and change ways of thinking that injure and exploit other people and places (*decolonization*)" (p. 9).

Because it is found at the crossroads of place and liberation from oppression, CPP is a form of critical pedagogy exceptionally relevant to Indigenous communities. However the language of Gruenewald's definitions, and the scholarly genealogy of his CPP, indicate, in many ways, that it centers a non-Indigenous audience. For example, the definition of *reinhabitation* foregrounds the *identification and recovery of spaces and places* but fails to mention active efforts to *preserve, sustain and strengthen* these places and tribal connections to them. His definition of decolonization is also distancing; while critical *to identify and change ways of thinking that injure and exploit **other** people and places* it is just as imperative, if not more so for Indigenous peoples, *to identify and change ways in which they and their sacred places have been/are being injured and exploited.*

While CPP attends to some of the critiques of critical pedagogy, its limited engagement with Indigenous studies leaves it inadequately situated to attend to the remaining concerns such as its retention of hegemonic notions of social justice, democracy and identity (Grande, 2000, 2004), Western epistemological and ontological leanings (Ball, 2002) and focus on individual, rather than community liberation (Lee, 2006). Gruenewald's definitions are no doubt vital contributions, but they speak from a fundamentally different standpoint. His pedagogical objectives are essential to challenging the dominant culture, but their applicability for the Indigenous struggle is limited and CPP's lack of engagement with Indigenous theory signals a need for reflection and modification.

An Indigenous praxis for place looks different; it is focused on self-determination, sovereignty and the critical reclamation of ancestral knowledge. Just as Grande (2004) called critical pedagogy to task, we believe an *indigenization* of critical pedagogies of place is necessary. Places that teach Native communities are well identified; they are embedded in tribal tradition and knowledge. Connections to these places continue to be practiced and responsibilities nurtured. Therefore, centering Indigenous' worldviews is essential. A critical Indigenous pedagogy of place (CIPP) thus involves identifying and engaging the intersections between place-based education, critical pedagogy and Indigenous studies. That said; it is in the spirit of Freirian reflective praxis that we identify these divergences and attempt to contribute to, rather than depart from, the critical pedagogical tradition.

Critical Indigenous Pedagogy of Place

Critical Indigenous pedagogies of place (CIPP) have a long tradition of community-based practice. Not always formally named as such, they have been discussed at length by Indigenous scholars (Barnhardt & Kawagley, 2005; Cajete, 1994; Deloria & Wildcat, 2001; Denzin, Lincoln & Smith, 2008; Grande, 2004; Kanahele, 1986; Kanai'aupuni & Malone, 2006; Meyer, 2003, 2001; Smith, 1999; Welchman-Gegeo & Watson-Gegeo, 2001, p. 59). CIPPs are direct extensions of Indigenous identity and ways of *knowing* and *being* in place over countless generations. Rooted in tribal cosmology, these pedagogies of place were forced underground and, at times, even destroyed by centuries of colonization and policies of compulsory assimilation. Efforts to remember, reclaim, and strengthen these pedagogies are then, efforts for Indigenous justice and self-determination. Kahnawá:ke scholar Taiaiake Alfred (1999, p. 42) makes this clear in his definition of Indigenous justice as the "perpetual process of maintaining that crucial balance and demonstrating true respect for the power and dignity of each part of the circle of interdependency". In other words, place is fundamentally linked to Indigenous justice, knowledge and identity and it is inseparable from the goals of an Indigenous critical pedagogy.

Grande (2000, p. 483) articulates this centrality of place in her critique of critical theory when she says, "where they ground their vision in Western conceptions of democracy and justice that presume a 'liberated' self, American Indian intellectuals ground their vision in conceptions of sovereignty that presume a sacred connection to place and land". In her development of Red Pedagogy, Grande (2004) contends that critical pedagogy retains heavily Western hegemonic notions of social justice, democracy and identity. Ball (2002) similarly cautions that Western epistemologies and ontologies of place continue to obfuscate Indigenous philosophies. Mindful of these tensions, rather than simply encouraging youth to embrace an "oppositional identity" and pursue social justice in a Western sense, CIPPs *indigenize* or fortify a positive subjectivity (Young, 2000, p. 45) of Indigenous identity, knowledge and tradition (Meyer, 2001).

Our pedagogies, rooted in the context of Indigenous worldviews and the afore-mentioned history, began with a simple proposition-'place' has always been a critical point of encounter for Indigenous youth. However, 'place' is additionally relevant to helping youth explore the complexities of neo-liberal injustice, to pursuing Indigenous justice and to critically evaluate, defend and reinvent community. The two case examples described below will present the ability of these critical Indigenous pedagogies of place to: 1) engage in a cycle of critical praxis that creates knowledge-action-reflection and, 2) develop critical indigenous consciousness through the exploration of the complexity of systemic inequalities and injustices, and 3) develop critical indigenous consciousness by the promotion of cultural identity through connection and service to community and the strengthening of a "sense of place."

Case One: 'Picture This' Photovoice Project

'Picture This' was a collaborative research project started in 2006 at the request of members of a community-university research collaborative. Community members had become interested in the Photovoice method (Wang, 1997) following its use in a nearby neighborhood and sought to develop a project for the youth of their community. The first author proposed to incorporate Photovoice as a method to critically investigate place and an initial plan was developed. A collaborative agreement between the first author, community volunteers (including two peer volunteers) and a local middle school was obtained. In conjunction with a Native American teacher at the school, participants were recruited. Recruitment was open to all youth who self-identified as Native American students of the partner school.

The community reflects many of the challenges to well-being faced by Native Americans across the United States: Intergenerational trauma, higher rates of poverty, chronic illness, low-income households and exposure to environmental risk (Evans-Campbell & Walters, 2006; Walters & Simoni, 2002; LaDuke, 1999). The school itself is located in an area facing high levels of poverty, unemployment and violence. It is in a predominantly minority school with a slightly higher than average Native American student body (~2% in comparison to the ~1% statewide average). The school district in which it is located has a free-reduced lunch rate higher, and a graduation rate significantly lower, than state averages. That said, while inequitable levels of risk and disparity are most certainly present, the community is a politically, intellectually and spiritually active, urban Native American community known for producing innovative opportunities for its youth.

The project pedagogy centered place. More specifically, it investigated environ-mental injustice in an urban community with Native youth. We engaged a baseline of topical knowledge including a review of current media, analysis of historical environ-mental injustices, documentary films on topics such as sacred places, medicinal plants, the Indigenous environmental justice movement and land disputes with local governments. Also included were guided field trips with and the personal stories of local elders. Careful attention was paid to include Indigenous representations of injustice, land ethics, relationships and epistemologies of 'place'. Youth participated in talking circle discussions and personal reflection to process the various perspectives presented. In effect, the pedagogy established the collective as a space where both critical inquiry and alterNative, decolonized knowledge was welcome.

The final piece of our pedagogy was praxis-oriented and included the completion of a Photovoice project. Photovoice is a "participatory-action research methodology based on the understanding that people are experts on their own lives" (Wang, Samuels, Hutchison, Bell, and Robert, 2004, p. 911). Explicitly situated in Freireian critical education theory, Photovoice uses the camera as a tool for investigation. It also encourages individuals to take pictures of their world, to tell the stories of their visual investigation through narratives and to critically engage those stories, in praxis for social change (Wang, 1997). Photovoice has been used as a method in the investigation of survival and change in post-war societies (Lykes, Blanche, & Hamber, 2003), community organizing in contexts of poverty (Davis, 2003), the development of critical consciousness and community research engagement (Carlson, Engebretson, & Chamberlin, 2006), community violence in Latino neighborhoods (Angulo, personal communication, 2007) and community building with youth and adults (Wang et al., 2004). For this exploration, youth used cameras to investigate environmental and place-based justice issues. Youth were provided training in photographic equipment, technique and Photovoice ethics (Wang & Redwood-Jones, 2001) and were positioned as investigators of injustice. Youth were given the task of identifying injustices/risks as well as justice/strengths in three social sites—community-school, neighborhood and their Native American community.

Data Collection Methods and Analysis

Data for this project were collected via a "cycle of critical praxis" (Duncan-Andrade & Morrell, 2008): A continual process of issue identification, data collection, analysis and social action. Final participants of the project included the author, community volunteers (adult and peer) and seven female students of the aforementioned middle school. The students ranged in age from twelve to thirteen and descended from various Northwest coastal and Plains region tribes. All had previously been involved in the school's Native American culture club and were familiar with one another. This cyclical, participatory analysis began with talking circle discussions about curriculum presentations and continued through the Photovoice segment as youth selected their favorite photos, presented them for group discussion and prepared individual photographic narratives for chosen photos. Throughout the project, further data were gathered through the compilation of in-depth participant observation notes by the author, these included notes from photo-discussions and pre and post-project interviews and author reflections. Notes were documented following most project meetings over the course of two years. Photo-discussion and interview notes were documented at the time of conduct. Ongoing community feedback and media coverage of the project was also collected. These multiple sources of data constitute a triangulated or multiple methods data collection technique (Fine, et al., 2000, p. 126) and contributed to a fuller understanding of the research foci. Preliminary findings from a theoretical thematic analysis (Braun & Clarke, 2006) are presented as they intersect with the findings of the second case study.

Themes: Towards CIPP

Theme #1: Cycle of Critical Praxis (Knowledge-action-reflection). As youth participated in the Photovoice project, they wrote narratives for selected photos and created a traveling photographic exhibit, which they used to increase public awareness of identified injustices. This praxis also had an impact on the youth as they began to think of themselves as investigators engaging in a social dialogue. They participated in numerous public exhibitions of their photography including community-based, policy focused and academic orientation. These planned engagements allowed the participants to reflect on their investigations individually and dialectically. This praxis holds promise for dialectic youth engagement as can be seen in the following exhibition encounter:

   Visitor: So this project says it is about environmental justice

   Participant: Yeah it is. It's about all kinds of justice though....

   Visitor: So what would you do, would you fix the school, what do you plan to do?

   Participant: We want to fix our school but we also want to fix our neighborhood and we want to learn more about our tribes and the medicines and stuff because that is important too.

   Visitor: So that is your idea of what would make things better?

   Participant: Yeah that's justice, all of it!

Their photographs and narratives were also showcased in exhibitions and a local magazine. The artifacts increased their awareness of identified injustices in the larger community. When participants found out about these opportunities, they were excited to have a public forum to voice their opinions and engage in counter-dialogue:

   Andrea: Wow I can't believe it. We are in a magazine!

   Twyla: Everyone has to listen to us now.

The praxis also provided opportunities to reflect on the self as investigator and participant in counter-dialogue. This impact was difficult to capture in the text; instead, it was most profoundly evident on the participants' faces, in their growing confidence and increasing ease with public speaking. It can also be felt in the following quotes:

   Renee: He [a visitor to an exhibition] really thinks our photo show is important

   Andrea: That [the first exhibition] wasn't bad, it was really cool. They all liked my stories....a lot! [And at a later exhibition] I needed to be here, it makes me feel better.

As the project progressed, youth requested and received training in media justice, internet blogging and documentary film production in order to further their storytelling and advocacy skills. While some activities were unable to be sustained due to a lack of financial resources, the experiences and skills gained will be beneficial for a lifetime of engagement.

Theme #2: Developing critical indigenous consciousness through the exploration of the complexity of systemic inequalities and injustices. Youth clearly exhibited a developing critical consciousness. Not only were they able to identify specific environmental injustices, they were also able to connect these injustices directly to practices and policies of capitalist businesses and government institutions. As peer volunteer Victoria stated,

> Sometimes I drive by a place and I see a clear cut and it makes me feel like the whole world is changing in a very bad way.

Others indicated,

> Twyla: This is junk [junkyard and tire dumping in the neighborhood] laying around....what is this about, it's not right! We don't want this stuff and neither does anyone else. We need to confront people about this junk"

> Andrea: This is dangerous [pollution] but it is also about the space, it takes up space where there could be a grocery store or a restaurant or something.

> Renee: These bars and this sign, send mixed messages, one of them talks about quitting smoking like they [public health officials] care about your health and behind it are all these bars, like its obviously not a safe place.

Participants exhibited a keen awareness not only of the polluting and over-development of land, but also of the practice of taking land by force, coercion or political act. In reference to a documentary film scene where a woman was being evicted from her house and the police were removing her by threatening to take her infant if she did not leave the property, Melissa pointed out the coercion often present in these situations of injustice,

> That's not really a choice huh...they [the police under orders of the state government] kind of gave her the only choice that would just make her go away.

Renee stated,

> I'd choose the baby of course but that's not fair!

Melissa commented,

> That [the taking of land] makes me sad and hecka mad. The government is like a 5 year old, greedy, demanding; they just take it [the land].

Their growing ability to connect environmental injustices to the loss of Indigenous communities and life ways was also profound. In a group dialogue the following was expressed,

Twyla: That isn't right, they destroyed a whole community

Melissa: They flooded them out of their village [to build] a dam?

Georgina: That is sad, all those people had to move and couldn't fish for their salmon anymore!

Youth also identified an awareness of the contemporary structural discrimination that their urban community faced. The urban area that their families now occupied was often disparaged with stereotypes as Andrea, Georgina, Melissa, Twyla and Renee noted,

Andrea, Twyla and Melissa: People think our community is ghetto, they always think welfare and food stamps and that it sucks.

Twyla: But it's not safe or unsafe…sort of in the middle.

Renee and Melissa: It has tiny stores and awesome friends!

Georgina: There are good things and bad things about our community.

In addition to inequitable environmental conditions, the taking of land and its direct impact on culture, and contemporary stereotypes, youth participants mentioned a continued loss of Indigenous knowledge and cultural traditions because the mentors and elders who have this knowledge are often focused on economic survival. Their elders face challenges and have limited time and ability to pass on knowledge. Youth frequently reported that their relatives have to "work" to earn money, to "pay the rent", "to buy" things that their families need. At times, some of our participants were prevented from attending our activities because they provided childcare to younger relatives so that family members could work. Material inequalities served as a barrier to desired knowledge and are noted in the following quotes:

Georgina: [My grandma] teaches me about plants and medicines like Native Band-aid but she can't teach very often because she is way to busy working and helping with the family kids and things.

Melissa: I had to leave this beautiful place [the reservation garden] and I was sad because of the fact that I had to go outside of my community to see a place like this [a field trip that participants would not have been able to access].

Theme# 3: Promotion of cultural identity through connection and service to community, and the strengthening of a "sense of place." Because connection and commitment to community and a "sense of place" are distinguishing aspects of a critical Indigenous consciousness, (Lee, 2006) the project also sought to develop these elements. Youth participants as expected possessed varying levels of knowledge of traditional practices but regardless, all youth showed a keen interest in increasing their awareness of, connection and commitment to their Indigenous community. At levels outmatching their solid identification of risks and injustice, youth demonstrated an eager ability to identify and learn more about Indigenous knowledge and cultural tradition.

Youth participants were especially catalyzed by a sense of place, e.g., sacred sites, relationships with land, medicinal plants, and the knowledge that stems from ancestral interaction with the places. In reference to the sacred connection to land, participants noted,

> Georgina: Those sacred places are true you know.... you don't have to believe it but its true!

> Brenda: Why is it a crime to climb Mt. Rushmore and not a sacred place? [These are] the traditions of our ancestors, you should be able to pray there without people climbing around you.....How about we go climb their church?

Intergenerational and medicinal knowledge extending from place were mentioned frequently as ways through which one is made aware of deeper cultural, moral and spiritual lessons. The intensity of the participant's awareness and connection to this knowledge is felt in their following words:

> Brenda: Your ancestors pass that [knowledge about sacred places] to you, you can't just make it.

> Georgina: This plant is called Native band-aid. When you have a wound, you can use this to help stop the bleeding and heal it. My traditions are really important!

> Twyla: The elder who made this garden brought in lavender. Lavender is from another culture but he believed every culture had something good in it and he wanted to bring the good things all together. To me, this means that we could all get along; we don't have to have wars, we can along get along like these plants.

> Andrea: It [a traditional Native garden] was built for Native youth to remember their culture. This is a place where people can get better if they are sick. It has medicine and it helps people. It exists because people take the time to remember Native traditions.

> Melissa: These stairs are all messed up [and] rusty but these are the stairs to the Native Club.

Youth also expressed ongoing commitments to community. Toward the conclusion of the project, they explored possibilities of continued engagement, such as the creation of a community garden and attending indigenous medicinal knowledge classes. Their commitment to the preservation, defense and promulgation of these knowledge and places were evident in the following quotes:

> Twyla: This [traditional medicinal knowledge] ...THIS is what I want to learn about!

> Melissa: I could make a garden of my own, or a community garden.

> Renee: I want to learn more about mint and grow it!

Andrea: This is a lodge pole pine. This was an important tree; it provided building material for tipis. I think it is important to keep planting these trees so that this tradition can continue.

Georgina: [On reaching out to elders to learn about Native knowledge] This is important and food for the culture to survive.

Brenda and Josie exchange their commitments to community in the following,

Josie: It's not that hard really, not that hard to figure it out [sacred places].... I mean they wouldn't expect us to climb a church would they?

Brenda: How about we go climb their church....I'm gonna do that even if I'm like 60 or 70 or something, I'm gonna do that!

Georgina adds,

How about political action like protesting?

In summary, through a combination of critical Indigenous pedagogies of place and the praxis-oriented method of Photovoice, the 'Picture This' project proved successful in increasing a critical awareness and articulation of place-based injustices and of community strengths by centering Indigenous theories of place, education and justice. It also served to connect youth participants and encourage commitment and action on behalf of their communities and knowledges.

CASE TWO: THE YOUTH ORGANIC FARM

Background Information, Community History, and Project Description

The Youth Organic Farm is part of a community-based, non-government, non-profit organization. It fulfills its food security initiative. Its goal is to empower the community to move towards self-sufficiency. It is a social movement to develop a comprehensive plan and sustainable local food system by educating youth, fighting hunger, improving health and nutrition, and being part of the growing organic agriculture industry. To meet its mission, interconnected economic development and educational projects were developed. They include the following activities:

- The Organic Farm: a 5-acre certified farm, producing and selling over 25 different varieties of high quality organic fruits and vegetables
- School-based Workshops: hands-on, culturally based programs at the intermediate school that nurture youth and families through traditional Hawaiian agricultural and food practices
- Partnership with the High School: hands-on, learning organic garden at the high school that studies contemporary agricultural science in the context of traditional Hawaiian culture and knowledge
- Youth Leadership Training: hands-on, entrepreneurial, agricultural, educational leadership experience in which participants earn an Associate of Arts degree from the community college
- The Community Organic Agricultural Center: a partnership with a community college and U.S. Department of Housing and Urban Department (HUD) to establish and expand expertise in the fields of tropical organic agriculture.

The Organic Farm impacts five critical areas of need: Out-of-school youth, sustainable economic development, agricultural, health, and Native Hawaiian culture. Youth leadership and social enterprise development became the priorities of the program. The Organic Farm builds a localized movement to put the value of *aloha 'aina (love for the land)* into action.

The rural town in which the program is located mirrors the political, economic, social, and cultural barriers facing today's minoritized, rural families and youth. Over the years, its residents have seen the gradual overdevelopment and abuse of its natural resources such as land and water, the negative impact of urbanization, and the disconnect of Native Hawaiian youth and families from the *'aina (land)*. It was the *'aina* that once nurtured a strong and cohesive cultural community. The revival of the *'aina* is the utmost importance of the program.

Furthermore, many youth from this geographic area, like other rural communities in Hawai'i, struggle to achieve self-sufficiency and self-determination. Native Hawaiian youth have the highest rates of teen pregnancy, school suspensions, incidence of substance abuse and juvenile arrests (Gao & Perrone, 2004; Pearson, 2004). Additionally, the community is recognized as a high risk for food insecurity in Hawai'i (Baker, et al., 2001). Difficulties for Native Hawaiians are exacerbated because they have the highest rates of preventable diseases such as diabetes, heart disease, and some cancers (U.S. DHHS, 1989, 2001; as cited in Else, 2004). Despite these struggles, the community strives to maintain a rural vision, a willingness to perpetuate its "country" values, and a commitment to offering hope and validation to their youths' personal and cultural identities.

Data Collection Method and Analysis

The case study of the Organic Farm was part of a larger national study of youth programs across the United States funded by the Ford Foundation in 2005. Individual interviews were conducted that lasted one to two hours. The interview guide for the case study generally covered the following issues: the youth program and different types of activities of youth involvement; the neighborhood and community and the role they play in the youth program; and what youth take away from their involvement in the program. Utilizing a critical Indigenous, interpretive methodology (Charmaz, 2006; Denzin, Lincoln, & Smith, 2008; Harvey, 1992; Hollander & Howard, 2000; Stryker, 1987), the interviews were transcribed, and content analyzes were conducted based on past literature on theories of critical pedagogies and community youth organizing.

The Organic Farm case study included seventeen participants: Four youth staff members, two parents, one board member, one person who was both a parent and a board member, one community advocate/*kupuna (elder)* who eventually became a board member, and eight youth. Among the youth, all were males except one, and ranged 18–21 years old. All identified as part-Hawaiian except one, who identified himself as Samoan. The presentation of the findings provided here for this book chapter was drawn from data provided by youth participants and a twenty-eight years old youth staff member who was a former youth participant. Pseudonyms were used to distinguish these individuals.

Themes: Towards CIPP

Theme #1: Cycle of Critical Praxis (Knowledge-action-reflection). The Organic Farm provided a range of activities to engage in critical praxis. Examples included testifying at political events, attending to the daily tasks of running the organic farm, and carrying on discussions between youth and the local community at a cafe, which were pertinent to meeting the community needs and political agendas. The impact of youth participating in these activities not only provided the youth with a political "voice," but allowed them to reflect how their actions may have impacted the decision-making process.

The Organic Farm was a place for youth to develop leadership skills as a result of engaging in critical praxis. They became more confident and aware of their environment and community as they developed a sense of *kuleana* (responsibility). A male young adult, Kamalu, shared how participating in critical praxis encouraged him to be actively involved with community issues,

> For me personally, the Organic Farm has given me a different outlook on things—on subjects. We always have heated discussions on the politics of the Organic Farm.....The program does help me learn to get involved, because through the program, there were a couple of times where we went, as a group, to the Senate to see bills being voted on by the Senate. One of the bills we went to observe was the bill on making genetic food legal in Hawai'i. We saw how that process went. It was pretty fun. It was also educational. We found out some of the views of the public and how a lot of people really don't want it, but on the flip side we see how it could be beneficial.

In general, critical praxis taught youth that they need to be knowledgeable about issues impacting their community if they want to become stewards of social and personal transformation.

Theme #2: Developing critical indigenous consciousness through the exploration of the complexity of systemic inequalities and injustices. Youth in the Organic Farm have the opportunity to gain awareness of the injustices that exist in their community. Many youth found an outlet to talk about these injustices through their weekly workshops or side conversations as they worked in the field. A female young adult, Leilani, observed,

> There's a lot of trouble going on. A lot of drugs, abuse, [and] hunger going on. A lot of sickness, because of the food that has been put out.... The community has potential, because there's a lot of land, fish, and veggies and livestock. Our community should be sustainable, but it's not because there's imported stuff. The question is why. The community needs a lot of education.

Another male young adult, Kawika, commented,

> Now people need to be educated, because people drop out of school at a young age. It's pretty bad here. Here, there's lots of crime. Drugs are a big power over here. The cops try their best, but they can't do that much. The social

structure is not good here. The program has showed me that there's more stuff out there. It has taught me how to talk to people and that there's good things—being healthy, being respectful to others—and that there's more to what we see.

Some youth identified the inequalities and injustices related to land and abuse of it and its natural resources by others (e.g., military),

> Kai (male): [Our community is] surrounded by the military. Seventy-five percent of what surrounds this valley is owned by military and less than 15% is actually farmland in production. When the wind is blowing, you could hear them bombing the mountains. We used to have fresh water flowing through the land, but now the military is rerouting it and we don't have access to fresh water anymore, except water from the tap.

> Noa (male, 28 years old): Where we live is either fast food [restaurants], convenience stores, or the military. But we have land. So the solution is to create more opportunities for local markets and cooperatives.

Many young adults also became aware of the structural inequalities (e.g., stereotypes and prejudices about the community). The program not only permitted a space to unpack such issues and their complexity, but also provided ways to ameliorate them. A communication class was an example of such space. A female young adult, Leilani, shared more specifically how oppression played out in the hiring process,

> If you go to a place where the guys who are hiring are from [other more privileged communities] and all that, and you tell them that you're from [this community], they'll think, "I don't know if he is really dependable."

Another male young adult, Kawika, added,

> I've been out to jobs where I applied in [down]town [in the city of Honolulu]. And "You from the homestead, huh?" I'm like, "Yup." So they think, "If I hire this guy, I'm taking a particular risk. He might steal from me. He's from the homestead, and he might not show up at work, because he lives on the homestead."

A space was provided to discuss these sensitive issues, and move on to critique the existence of inequalities and oppression. Twenty-eight years old young adult male, Noa, indicated his thoughts about the media's role in diverting youth attention from critical issues,

> Well, I think a big part is that the media has a lot to do with distracting young people from important things in life... The media doesn't put value on food and the sacredness of food in the way we promote it.

He pointed out how working with others in the program helped youth, including himself, to be more enlightened or aware,

> But after working with a lot of students, they become much more aware. Because of our discussions that we have—political or philosophical—a lot of students become enlightened. They get exposed to a lot of ideas... we talk

about a lot of other things. Mainstream media's ongoing narrative is pretty self-centered, and that doesn't really work on the farm. It's the diversity and shared effort that is the value we promote.

Theme #3: Promotion of cultural identity through connection and service to community, and the strengthening of a "sense of place." The Organic Farm provided youth with the opportunities to develop an identity of resistance, but the utilization of a critical indigenous pedagogy of place also encouraged youth to commit to their community and be responsible for their place. Being grounded in one's roots has helped youth develop their self-esteem, the responsibility to stand up for their community and advocate for important issues. Many youth expressed how knowing about their community and the socio-political climate led them to understand their cultural identity. As a Samoan male youth, Ronnie, shared,

I think it's very important for the youth to understand where they're coming from. It's always good to know good points and also bad points of the community to work on them. Youth should understand where they're coming from. If they understand about their community, they'll grow up with confidence and self-esteem and they'll be able to work.

By participating in the Organic Farm's activities, not only did the youth learn how to make a difference, but grew a sense of attachment to the community. The Organic Farm also provided opportunities for youth to take part in a larger social movement of resistance—promoting food security, community health, and self-sufficiency. A male youth, Kamuela, summed it up,

Being in the program helps me to care more about the community. I learn small things like recycling, etc. ....Being in the farmers market helps the population with knowledge about health, selling the produce. They also take the knowledge to the family and help the family out. It's also about the community and helping the community to be healthier. [Lastly,] I'd say the one thing I want to see improved is to have youth see a bigger picture, not see this just as a normal job. It's not all about making money, but about helping the community, providing the community with food security, helping the community become self-sufficient and healthy.

Most youth indicated that the Organic Farm has impacted their thinking about their community. Although it may appear that youth may initially not do so, the seed planted was evident in Leilani's testimony,

[The program director] would teach us about the Organic Farm and all that, but he would also teach us about all kinds of political stuff. Like we would talk about stuff in the newspaper a few times, oh yeah, like when they voted for whatever. Whatever affects us, he would tell us: "why aren't you guys getting into this, or why aren't you guys stepping in. It's going to affect you guys more than me." And us, personally, we don't really think about it. But when someone puts it bluntly like that, you think, "Oh, okay. Maybe we should do something." The classes opened our eyes a bit. I admit that most of the time if you were to ask [the program director] personally, he probably thought I was sleeping. But I heard some of the stuff he was saying.

In general, the Organic Farm helped youth feel connected on the inside, to other youth, and to the earth. With the opportunities made possible by the Organic Farm, they have the tremendous potential to restore, rejuvenate, care, and take care of the earth and each other.

Discussion/Implications

Through two place-based Indigenous youth projects, we have attempted to demonstrate and argue that: (1) incorporating Indigenous ways of knowing and place-based education into critical pedagogy extend the field towards recognizing and engaging Indigenous knowledges on their own terms; and (2) that Indigenous youth explorations and reflections upon historical, social, cultural and environmental injustices, allow them to become agents of change who critically respond to and resist neo-liberalism and cultural hegemony from an Indigenous standpoint.

Both projects are based on and placed in *place*. The urban, Native youth project used a CIPP and Photovoice to transform youth into investigators of place-based injustice. Through action and critical reflection, their narratives presented the injustices, knowledge and experiences of Indigenous peoples; they informed how place-based justice is conceived amongst Indigenous youth and provided hopeful directions toward community reinvention. In the second project, the Hawaiian youth group recreated and utilized place to reclaim Indigenous land, culture and the wisdom within, through which food security, health and environmentally safe places could be ensured. Both projects demonstrated place as a marker of the past and future, endurance and change, and therefore a critical component of critical pedagogy.

In addition to youth critical reflections, keeping Indigenous values central to both projects reflects how, despite their marginality, Indigenous youth engage in re-imagining what it means to be Indigenous. Yearning for intergenerational knowledge they undertook measures to transform the encounters from within their marginal spaces to the beyond. As one of the youth quotations informs, youth are open to people as much as they are to nature, "The elder who made this garden brought in lavender. Lavender is from another culture but he believed every culture had something good in it and he wanted to bring the good things all together. To me, this means that we could all get along; we don't have to have wars, we can along get along like these plants," a unique venue that needs to globally be pursued.

While these two case studies contribute to existing critical pedagogy literature, there are also further implications that need to be considered, including:

– Theory of place, and Indigenous knowledge of place in particular, are catalysts for critical pedagogy, including how to think beyond Western frameworks.
– Further development of critical Indigenous pedagogy of place is needed.

Youth, as agents of social transformation, can lead this pedagogy forward. The current trend of youth political involvement, in Obama's presidential election for instance, is an indication of existing satiety for change and how youth perceive the change they aspire that goes beyond social categorizations.

– Youth have and will continue to play "an instrumental role in the struggle to subvert the corporate ascendancy of our social world"
– Critical Indigenous Pedagogy of Place can be an individual and community empowerment tool through solidarity and global collaboration of youth to investigate injustices and expand resistance to neo-liberalism and corporate expansionism.

QUESTIONS FOR REFLECTION

1. The two projects inform youth resistance in relation to neo-liberalism at micro levels. How might such youth-initiated exploration of exclusionary and discriminatory sites, and the proactively created culture of resistance, be sustained and extended to challenge consumerist cultures, globalization and global food systems?
2. As indicated in the two projects, youth are reinventing and giving life to their communities by challenging yet simultaneously preserving the environments they inhabit. These case studies speak to the reality for Indigenous youth who struggle between two fundamentally different worldviews. Discuss other innovative ways and means that indigenous youth could re-enforce their position against neo-liberal policies and the capitalist system, and center their cultural identity.
3. Youth are usually represented as controlled by the media, which typifies them as culturally-tamed and consumption-obsessed individuals. However, youth can deflect this representation and replace it with their own representations through the use of media-related tools such as Photovoice. Discuss how the media can be used to portray youth resistance to mass information, mass culture and mass consumption.

NOTES

[1] We acknowledge the scholarly debate between C.A. Bowers and critical pedagogues Peter McLaren and Donna Houston as well as the subsequent contributions made by Martusewicz, Gruenewald and Kahn. We admire the contributions of all involved. Given our limitations in space, the critiques are too numerous to discuss at length. Any particular absence is not intended to imply agreement or disagreement but rather the need to focus on, what we identified as the most pressing concerns to our projects in specific.

REFERENCES

Alfred, T. (1999). *Peace, power and righteousness: An Indigenous manifesto*. Canada: Oxford University Press.

Baker, K., Derrickson, J., Derrickson, S., Reyes-Salvail, T., Onaka, A., Horiuchi, B., et al. (2001). *Hunger and food insecurity in Hawai'i: Baseline estimates 1999–2000, Hawai'i health Survey (HHS)*. Honolulu, HI: Hawai'i State Department of Health, Office of Health Status Monitoring.

Ball, M. W. (2002). People speaking silently to themselves": An examination of Keith Basso's philosophical speculations on "Sense of place" in apache cultures. *American Indian Quarterly, 26*, 460–478.

Barnhardt, R., & Kawagley, A. O. (2005). Indigenous knowledge systems and Alaska native ways of knowing. *Anthropology and Education Quarterly, 36*(1), 8–23.

Benham, M. K. P., & Heck, R. H. (1998). *Culture and educational policy in Hawai'i: The silencing of native voices.* Mahwah, NJ: Lawrence Erlbaum Associates, Publishers.

Bowers, C. A. (2006). Silences and double binds: Why the theories of John Dewey and Paulo Freire cannot contribute to revitalizing the commons. *Capitalism Nature Socialism, 17*(3), 71–87.

Bowers, C. A. (2005). How Peter McLaren and Donna Houston, and Other"Green" Marxists contribute to the globalization of the west's industrial culture. *Educational Studies, 37*(2), 185–195.

Bowers, C. A. (2003). Can critical pedagogy be greened? *Educational Studies, 34*(1), 11–21.

Brandt, C. B. (2004). A thirst for justice in the arid Southwest: The role of epistemology and place in higher education. *Educational Studies, 36*(1), 93–107.

Braun, V., & Clarke, V. (2006). Using thematic analysis in psychology. *Qualitative Research in Psychology, 3*, 77–100.

Cajete, G. (1994). *Look to the mountain: An ecology of Indigenous education.* Durango, CO: Kivaki Press.

Carlson, E. D., Engebretson, J., & Chamberlain, R. M. (2006). Photovoice as a social process of critical consciousness. *Qualitative Health Research, 16*(6), 836–852.

Charmaz, K. (2006). *Constructing grounded theory: A practical guide through qualitative analysis.* Thousand Oaks, CA: Sage Publications, Inc.

Davis, D.-A. (2003). What did you do today: Notes from a politically engaged anthropologist. *Urban Anthropology, 32*(2).

Deloria, V., Jr., & Lytle, C. M. (1998). *The nations within: The past and future of American Indian sovereignty.* Austin, TX: University of Texas Press.

Deloria, V., Jr., & Wildcat, D. (2001). *Power and place: Indian education in America.* Golden, CO: Fulcrum Resources.

Denzin, K., Lincoln, Y., & Smith, L. (2008). *Handbook of critical & indigenous methodologies.* Thousand Oaks, CA: Sage Publications, Inc.

Duncan-Andrade, J., & Morrell, E. (2008). *The art of critical pedagogy: Possibilities for moving from theory to practice in urban schools.* New York: Peter Lang Publishing.

Else, I. (2004). The breakdown of the Kapu system & its effect on Native Hawaiian health & diet. *Hulili: Multidisciplinary Research on Hawaiian Well-Being, 1*(1), 241–255.

Evans-Campbell, T., & Walters, K. L. (2006). Catching our breath: A decolonization framework for healing indigenous families. In R. Fong & R. McRoy (Eds.), *Intersecting child welfare, substance abuse, and family violence: Culturally competent approaches* (pp. 266–290). Alexandria, VA: CSWE Publications.

Fine, M., Weis, L., & Wong, L. (2000). For Whom? Qualitative research, representations, and social responsibilities. In N. Denzin & Y. Lincoln (Eds.), *The landscape of qualitative research: Theories and issues* (pp. 107–131). Thousand Oaks, CA: Sage Publications, Inc.

Gao, G., & Perrone, P. (2004). *Crime in Hawai'i 2003: A review of uniform crime reports.* Honolulu, HI: Hawai'i State Attorney General, Research & Statistics Branch, Crime & Justice Assistance Division.

Giroux, H. (2001). *Theory and resistance in education: Toward a pedagogy for the opposition.* Westport, CT: Bergin and Garvey.

Grande, S. (2000). American Indian geographies of identity and power: At the crossroads Indigena and Mestizaje. *Harvard Educational Review, 70*(4), 467–498.

Grande, S. (2004). *Red pedagogy: Native American social and political thought.* Lanham, MD: Rowman and Littlefield Publishers.

Gruenewald, D. (2003). The best of both worlds: A critical pedagogy of place. *Educational Researcher, 32*(4), 3–12.

Harvey, L. (1992). *Critical social research*. Boston: Unwin Hyman.

Hollander, J. A., & Howard, J. A. (2000). Social psychological theories on social inequalities. *Social Psychology Quarterly, 63*(4), 338–351.

Hursh, D., & Martina, C. (2003). Neo-liberalism and schooling in the U.S.: How state and federal government education policies perpetuate inequality. *Journal for Critical Education Policy Studies, 1*(2). Retrieved from http://www.jceps.com/index.php?pageID=home&issueID=2 1740-2743

Kahn, R. (2003). Paulo Freire and eco-Justice: Updating pedagogy of the oppressed for the age of ecological calamity. *Freire Online: A Journal of the Paulo Freire Institute/UCLA*. Retrieved from http://www.paulofreireinstitute.org/freireonline/

Kahn, R. (2007). *Questions on ecopedagogy*. Retrieved from http://richardkahn.org/writings/ecopedagogy/questionsonecopedagogy.pdf

Kanahele, G. (1986). *Ku Kanaka stand tall: A search for Hawaiian values*. Honolulu, HI: University of Hawai'i Press.

Kana'iaupuni, S., & Malone, N. (2006). This land is my land: the role of place in Native Hawaiian identity. In J. W. Frazier & E. L. Tuttey-Fio (Eds.), *Race, ethnicity, and place in a changing America* (pp. 287–300). Binghamton, NY: Binghamton University Global Academic Publishing.

Kincheloe, J. (2008). *Knowledge and critical pedagog: An introduction*. New York: Springer Publishing.

Kozol, J. (2006). *The shame of the nation: The restoration of apartheid schooling in America*. New York: Three Rivers Press.

LaDuke, W. (1999). *All my relations: Native struggles for land and life*. Cambridge, MA: South End Press.

Lee, T. S. (2006). "I came here to learn how to be a leader": An intersection of critical pedagogy and Indigenous education. *InterActions: UCLA Journal of Education and Information Studies, 2*(1), Article 3.

Lykes, M. B., Blanche, M., & Hamber, B. (2003). Narrating survival and change in Guatemala and South Africa: The politics of representation and a liberatory community psychology. *American Journal of Community Psychology, 31*(1/2), 79–90.

McLaren, P., & Giroux, H. (1990). Critical pedagogy and rural education: A challenge from Poland. *Peabody Journal of Education, 67*(4), 154–165.

McLaren, P. (2006). *Life in schools: An introduction to critical pedagogy in the foundations of education* (5th ed.). Boston: Allyn & Bacon.

McLaren, P., & Kincheloe, J. (2007). *Critical pedagogy: Where are we now?* New York: Peter Lang Publishing.

Meyer, M. (2003). *Ho'oulu: Our time of becoming Hawaiian epistemology and early writings*. Honolulu, HI: Ai Pohaku Press.

Meyer, M. A. (2001). Our own liberation; reflections on Hawaiian epistemology. *The Contemporary Pacific, 13*(1), 125.

Pearson, R. S. (2004). *Ka Leo O Na Keiki: The 2003 Hawaii state alcohol, tobacco, and other drug use study*. Kapolei, HI: Hawai'i Dept. of Health, Alcohol & Drug Abuse Division.

Smith, L. T. (1999). *Decolonizing methodologies*. London, UK: Zed Books Ltd.

Sobel, D. (1999). *Beyond ecophobia, Yes magazine*. Retrieved from http://www.yesmagazine.org/article.asp?ID=803

Stryker, S. (1987). The vitalization of symbolic interactionism. *Social Psychology Quarterly, 50*(1), 83–94.

Trask, H. (1993). *From a native daughter: Colonialism and sovereignty in Hawai'i*. Honolulu, HI: University of Hawai'i Press.

Walters, K., & Simoni, J. (2002). Re-conceptualizing native women's health: An indigenist stress-coping model. *American Journal of Public Health, 20*(4), 520–524.

Young, I. (2000). Five faces of oppression. In Adams, et al. (Eds.), *Readings for diversity and social justice* (pp. 35–49). New York: Routledge.

Wang, C., & Redwood-Jones, Y. A. (2001). Photovoice ethics. *Health Education and Behavior, 28*(5), 560–572.

Wang, C., & Burris, M. A. (1997). Photovoice: Concept, methodology, and use for participatory needs assessment. *Health Education and Behavior, 24*(3), 369–387.

Wang, C., Samuels, S. M., Hutchison, P. M., Bell, L., & Robert, M. (2004). Flint photovoice: Community building among youths, adults, and policymakers. *American Journal of Public Health, 94*(6), 911.

Welchman-Gegeo, D., & Watson-Gegeo, K. (2001). How we know: Kwara'ae rural villagers doing epistemology. *The Contemporary Pacific, 13*(1), 55–88.

SECTION III:
POST-NEO-LIBERALISM, YOUTH AND RESISTANCE

MICHAEL O'SULLIVAN

13. SUPPORTING YOUTH IN THE PURSUIT OF A POST-NEO-LIBERAL VISION

Transitioning From Soft to Critical Pedagogy in a Time of Possibility

"When there is an alternative, the political landscape will look very different"

(Marginson, 2006, p. 218).

INTRODUCTION

Critical pedagogues have long advocated that teachers have a key role to play in relation to encouraging students to develop a transformative, social justice-oriented social vision in opposition to the dominant neo-liberal ideology (Freire, 1970; McLaren, 2003; Shor, 1987). Recognizing that change will not occur simply because people have a critique of the socio-economic and ecological impact of neo-liberalism, critical pedagogues assign teachers the role of social change agent (Freire, 1970, 1985; Giroux, 1988, 1995, 1997, 2001; McLaren, 2003). This role involves encouraging students, as they develop critical insights and critical consciousness, to become politically engaged through organizations committed to social change. Critical transformative educators also encourage teachers to extend their influence beyond classrooms, and play the role of public intellectuals in community organizations (Aronowitz & Giroux, 1991; Lingard, Hayes, & Mills, 2003). Engagement by educators in the community is important because it provides teachers with the possibility to become familiar with a lived reality that, while very different than their own, is frequently found in their classrooms.

The Collapse of Neo-liberalism and the Emergence of Transformative Opportunities

The literature that assigns such roles to teachers has been written during, and, thus, has been shaped by, the era of global neo-liberalism. History will record that this era, at least in the particular form it has taken for the past three decades, ended with the crisis that occurred over the space of several years but which culminated with the dramatic meltdown of the global financial system in 2008. We might now be living in a period of transition to post-neo-liberalism, and a new literature is appearing that theorizes critical pedagogical practices, both in classrooms and beyond, shaped by the quickly changing realities of this new historical period. Critical educators, whose views were dismissed by so many of their mainstream

B. J. Porfilio and P. R. Carr (eds.), Youth Culture, Education and Resistance: Subverting the Commercial Ordering of Life, 219–231.

colleagues (Schweifurth, 2006), now have the opportunity to emerge from the shadows of the pedagogical periphery and engage with more receptive audiences, including their colleagues and youth in their classrooms.

Capitalism has, with the recent collapse of the global financial system and the simultaneous discrediting of neo-liberal ideology, entered into one of its reoccurring deep crises. Even *The Economist* (2009), the business magazine that is the authoritative voice of neo-liberal globalization, recognizes that "the global economy is under threat" (p. 9). *The Economist* suggests that this threat to the global economy is due to the rise, in response to the crash of financial markets, of economic nationalism. Its editors urge President Obama to work to resolve the crisis in a way that ensures the "open border" policies associated with neo-liberalism. In order to protect the global economy, *The Economist* called on the President to veto the $787 billion "stimulus" bill passed in mid-February, 2009, if Congress did not delete the "Buy American" provisions contained in it. Congress did not delete those provisions, and Obama did not veto the bill; however, on the same day he signed the bill into law, in an interview on Canadian television, he assured Canadians, whose country is America's largest trading partner, that he did not think Canadians had to be "too concerned" about these provisions (Whitten, 2009). Not surprisingly, the commentary from Canadian observers following the interview focused on what not being "too concerned" might actually mean in practice. These economic nationalist provisions are seen as an example of anti-global isolationism and protectionism, and are, by definition, contrary to the very essence of the neo-liberal doctrine. In the same interview, with an eye on calming the nerves of neo-liberal lobbyists, Obama reiterated his belief in the importance of global trade, and assured listeners that the US would stand by its World Trade Organization and NAFTA obligations "as we always have" (Whitten, 2009).

As the beneficiaries of globalized capitalism struggle to preserve essential elements of the system that has served them so well, critical-transformative opponents of neo-liberalism have been provided with an opening to offer a fundamental challenge to the policies, practices, and ideologies of contemporary globalized consumer capitalism. Youth in the US, many of whom recently participated in the massive political movement that led to Obama's election, are particularly well positioned to make a significant contribution to such a challenge. If the millions of people, young and not-so-young, who came together to support the Obama candidacy, were to use their political, organizational and ICT (Information and Communication Technology) skills to pressure the President to devise progressive, indeed transformative, solutions to the troubled economy, and to the equally troubled social fabric of American life, such a development would represent a sea-change in American political culture. The "we can be the change" optimism, and the political movement that gave organizational expression to that optimism, could now be re-oriented to send Obama a strong message—American youth and workers want their government to adopt progressive post-neo-liberal policies, a platform to serve the interests of the social base that elected him and not reward, as the administration is doing with its multibillion dollar bailout (AKA stimulus) packages, the financiers and corporate executives who created the mess that is negatively impacting citizens across the globe.

There is a precedent for such a mass movement. During the 1930s, the unemployed organized and created a political movement pressured governments to take decisive action to address the social and economic hardship resulting from the Depression (Beito, 1989; Cohen, 1990). This movement pressured politicians from the city to the national level, including President Roosevelt who was under constant pressure from the unemployed to strengthen the provisions of the New Deal. Anti-globalization activist and author Naomi Klein argues that this "history of resistance, struggle and community organizing needs to be replicated [today]" (Klein, cited in Siddiqui, 2009, p. A19).

Unfortunately, rather than being transformed to operate in the post-election period, this dynamic political movement has been demobilized. While letting the politicians act in the name of the electorate between elections is a central tenet and practice of liberal-democracies, it serves to reduce the role of citizens to that of mere observers of the political process. It is, therefore, not at all surprising that this socio-political retreat is happening. Critical pedagogues advocate for a participatory and deliberative democratic engagement by citizen activists (Giroux, 1988; Shor, 1987). Faced with this situation, activists, like Klein, are calling for a reactivation of this movement to apply pressure on Obama and his administration. She writes "that just at the very moment when that kind of grassroots organizing and mobilization could have an impact, we are demobilizing and waiting for the good acts to be handed down from on high, whether it is withdrawal from Iraq or the perfect economic stimulus package" (Klein, cited in Siddiqui, 2009, p. A19).

As urgent as the need to articulate a new political consensus is—after all, political openings such as that created by the recent global financial meltdown rarely last long—framing such a consensus is not something that will happen overnight. Nonetheless, this opening exists, and it provides an opportunity for the US public to rethink core values in a way that has not been seen in decades. This opportunity is suggested by economist David Kotz (2009), who writes "as neo-liberal capitalism enters a period of crisis, we can see the rapid loss of legitimacy of the previously reigning dominant 'free market' ideology" (p. 1). He likens this to "the sudden demise of the previously dominant Keynesian ideology of regulated capitalism in the 1970s" (p. 1). This reference to Keynesianism recalls the fact that the form of capitalism which supposedly served the interests of capital accumulation well in the post World War II period, after a quarter century of growth and legitimacy, stumbled on its own contradictions, and was displaced by its neo-liberal successor (Kotz, p. 1). Kotz presumes that, as in the past, capitalism will find its feet and "be restructured, in the United States and globally, during the coming years [however] the outcome of this restructuring process ... is not pre-determined" (p. 1). The lack of clarity about what form this restructuring will take is evidenced by the difference of opinion between the editors of *The Economist* (2009) and the Obama administration over the stimulus package. These contrasting perspectives are indicative of the issues that divide ideologically hard-core neo-liberals from others, such as the President, whose views, while still very much constrained by the logic of global capitalism, are arguably less beholden to a particular formula of what the solution must look like. This crisis, as with past crises, does indeed provide the opportunity for capitalism to restructure itself and, as the concerns of *The Economist* suggest, powerful forces are at work to ensure that the restructuring is consistent with their particular views. The clash of these warring neo-liberal perspectives provides the framework within which social movements enter the fray. One of the tasks of these movements will be to pressure President Obama to not give in to the neo-liberals, while, at the same time, attempting to articulate a social vision that resonates with a broad social base, attempting to diminish the logic of the present US political and social-economic system.

What social sectors are likely to take up the challenge of mounting a vigorous movement that will give expression to a very different, transformative, post-neo-liberal vision? It is reasonable to expect that youth, both those who have, in recent years, developed their political skills in the wide range of social movements and organizations as well as new recruits motivated by a new sense of possibility, will form the base of such a movement. It is also likely that youth will be joined in this post-neo-liberal political movement by workers who have been extremely hard hit by the crisis.

Worker participation in such a social movement is anticipated in the labor press. Canadian labor economist Jim Stanford (2008), writing on the website of the Canadian Auto Workers, a union whose membership, like that of its US counterpart, is threatened with decimation, argues that the situation created by "the failure of neo-liberalism" opens up the possibility of advancing "a very fundamental critique ... of the very essence of its economic project" (p. 5). He suggests that the popular movement could now "be thinking very big thoughts indeed about how to change, and ultimately replace it" (p. 5).

The Role of Youth in the Post-Neo-liberal Era and the Challenge for Teachers

In her Preface to *Contemporary Youth Culture: An International Encyclopedia*, Shirley Steinberg (2006) reminds us that:

> Youth does not float in some timeless space, above and beyond the influence of historical and social forces. Like any other human dynamic, youth is shaped by macro-social forces such as ideology. Although individual response to such forces may be unique and self-directed, it is not simply free to operate outside the boundaries drawn by such social influences. (p. xiii)

She then analyses the forces that are influencing the social construction we call youth, and comments on two essential characteristics that are significant to our analysis: youth have unprecedented access to information, and, as a result of acquiring a broad knowledge base, they have significant influence within their families, and contribute to the formation of shared ideas and values.

On the issue of access to information about "topics traditionally viewed as the province of adults," Steinberg (2006) observes that

> [s]ome scholars have argued that youth often have more information than adults in these domains because of the time many have to access TV, radio, the Internet, music, and other media. One of the traditional ways suggested to

differentiate between youth and adults has involved knowledge of the world. In light of recent changes in information access it is safe to conclude that traditional distinctions between youth and adulthood may no longer be relevant. (p. xiv)

Steinberg suggests that such privileged access to information has consequences for the relationship between youth and adults, notably between young people and their parents, and, of course, their teachers. With respect to the relationship with their parents, she notes, "evidence indicates that many youth have gained more influence in the life of the family. In such families, negotiation, engagement, and more open and egalitarian forms of interaction have replaced authoritarian, hierarchical parent-child relationships" (p. xiv). This observation surely has implications for the role of youth in dialoguing with family members over a range of topics, including political discussions on issues that directly and indirectly impact family life. That is, what kids learn on the Web, from radio and TV, in the street, and at school, will form part of family discussions in which young people have growing influence. As youth become more politically engaged, and as their parents feel the effects of the economic crisis, the possibility is greatly enhanced of formulating a cross-generational consensus on a variety of issues, including on a post-neo-liberal social vision. Analytical and communication skills possessed by youth not only will help them play an influential role in the family but will also serve them well as they engage with older generations of activists with whom they must make alliances if the movement is to foster social justice in schools and in society.

Of course, what young people learn from these multiple sources will be understood by them within the ideological frame of reference of these sources of information—that is, unless teachers guide them to develop their own critical and autonomous understanding of the world and how it works. Teachers have privileged access to young people, and have the opportunity to help them interpret the conflicting messages that daily bombard them. This responsibility brings us directly to the importance of critical-transformative pedagogies, which have as their goal bringing students to *critical consciousness* (Connolly, n.d.; Freire, 1970). This requires teachers to adopt pedagogies which are designed, first and foremost, to bring students (and, not unimportantly, their teachers) to the recognition that their worldviews and their values are socially constructed. Of course, any alternative understanding of the world they adopt will also be socially constructed; the difference being that the influences on the latter will be transparent, and worked out in the community, be that community the classroom or a social change organization within, or beyond, schools. To achieve this critical consciousness and resulting alternative understandings of how the world works requires a conscious effort by teachers because, as Daniel Schugurensky (2003) points out, young people are not born with the habits of mind associated with the kind of engagement required to form a part of a democratic movement for social change. Such habits of mind and practices have to be nurtured. Consequently, teachers have an essential role to play in supporting the emergence of a youth movement based on the values essential to a democratic politics of social justice and equity.

This constitutes a tremendous challenge for teachers. The socially constructed youth that will emerge from the shaping of the post-neo-liberal times will be different than the youth of the present and recent past because the world that will shape them will be different. The politically demobilizing trope of TINA (the "there is no alternative" mantra of the advocates of neo-liberalism in its ever-so-recent heyday) has, as detailed above, been called into question by politicians, workers, and educators in recent months. According to labor economist Stanford (2008), a space now exists to flesh out new ideas and social practices that have the potency to end neo-liberal globalization.

Classroom Practices for Critical Educators in the Post-neo-liberal Age

It is one thing for critical pedagogues to assign the role of a social change agent to teachers; it is entirely another thing for teachers, other than a small minority operating, to paraphrase Schweifurth (2006), on the periphery, to feel comfortable in that role. There is literature documenting how teachers feel nervous about teaching controversial issues (Davies, 2005; Larsen & Faden, 2008; Robbins, Francis, & Elliot, 2003). There is also an emerging literature about transitions to successful critical classroom practices (Davies, 2005; Larsen & Faden, 2008; O'Sullivan & Vetter, 2007). Despite some breakthroughs reported in these and other studies, two issues keep coming up as being at the core of teacher reticence to teach critically: one is that teachers feel they do not have sufficient support from school administrators, colleagues, and parents to take the risk; the other is that they do not feel that they know enough to teach controversial issues or to teach from a critical perspective. Ironically, with respect to the first point—perceived lack of support—there is a push by senior educational administrators in the US and elsewhere to promote teaching from a critical perspective. In fact, if we are to believe the Crick Report, the English policy paper that gave rise to that country's global citizenship education curriculum, permission is even being granted to teach transformatively. Despite this official sanctioning, or mainstreaming (Ibrahim, 2005) of criticality, the results have not lived up to the expectations. In England, the impact of new critical expectations, such as those defined by Crick, has been studied, and explanations offered for the disappointing results. Harber (2002) identified the cause of these disappointing results as lying with the academic preparation of most teachers which, in England, he suggests, does not include enough emphasis on the social sciences. A spokesperson for the Citizenship Foundation stated that this situation constitutes "… a significant issue which seems to weaken the whole capacity of schools to deliver a sound social education" (cited in Harber, p. 228).

I do not want to disagree with either teacher perceptions of lack of support—a perspective, as noted above, which is deeply felt and widely reported by classroom teachers—or with the observation that a solid formation in the social sciences is an important professional preparation to effectively teach what are perceived as controversial and critical issues. I am convinced, however, that there is a prior, but not entirely unrelated, issue which might well explain both the academic choices made by pre-service teachers that steer them away from the social sciences as well as their nervousness about teaching those issues. I am referring to the class and racial composition of the teaching profession. Teachers are, by and large, white, middle-class professionals whose untroubled life experiences are such that they have never had to confront the challenges posed by poverty, race, and dislocation, which constitute the reality of so many of their students (O'Sullivan, 2008).

This issue of the racial and class composition of the teaching profession poses one of the most significant dilemmas faced by critical pedagogues who advocate that teachers are, in and out of schools, transformative intellectuals, individuals who are committed to eliminating social and economic inequalities. Given these circumstances, can more than a small minority of teachers be expected to assume such a role? This dilemma is rendered all the more complex if, to be considered social change agents, educators must teach from an explicitly critical and transformative perspective. Such a perspective is often presumed to be sharply demarcated from other *soft* perspectives (Andreotti, 2006), which, while they are broadly progressive, are, nonetheless, not viewed by critical pedagogues as being legitimately critical. This raises several questions: How should critical pedagogues engage with those colleagues who teach from what they consider to be a liberal-humanitarian perspective? Can their efforts be seen as being part of an opening of the critical potential of students or do these "non critical" pedagogies constitute a brake from such transformative learning?

I am not convinced that these approaches are somehow inherently antithetical to each other. When educators encourage their students to consider the impact of war, poverty, racism, sexism, and so forth—even if they do not do so from an explicitly critical-transformative perspective—, are they not creating space for an important classroom dialogue with critical potential?

Bridging the Gap between Humanitarian Pedagogies and Criticality

The proposition that pedagogies viewed as "soft" (Andreotti, 2006) or liberal-humanitarian have the potency to lead teachers and students to greater levels of criticality has both a theoretical and an empirical base. Theoretically, this proposition is based on Freire's (1974) concept of consciousness, and the distinction he makes between superstitious (or what I chose to call *conventional*) consciousness and critical consciousness.

(i) Freire's Concept of Consciousness: A Theoretical Bridge

For Freire, the form of consciousness that empowers people to engage in transformative practices is critical consciousness. Critical consciousness "recognizes that cultural institutions are created and sustained by human purpose and [that] action and language both shape and reflect people's perceptions of cultural institutions" (Finlay & Faith, 1987, cited by Connolly, n.d., p. 6). This is the level of consciousness which recognizes that "culture ... can, theoretically, be changed or acted upon" (Connolly, p. 5) by human intervention. Connolly's use of the term "theoretically" implies that, yes, such change is possible but only with many preconditions.

Conventional consciousness (Freire's *superstitious* consciousness) is "characterized by a recognition of cultural options but a concomitant sense of powerlessness to do anything about those options" (Connolly, n.d., p. 5). People who live at the conventional level of consciousness recognize that many of our institutions, including schools, corporations, government ministries, and the media, are the products of human endeavor but they also accept the permanence of these socially constructed institutions in their present form even though a social constructivist perspective clearly shows that any institution created by humans can be modified or abolished by humans. Freire labeled this form of consciousness as superstitious consciousness because it attributes near mystical and unchanging powers to such institutions. I would argue that this level of consciousness characterizes the worldview of most US citizens, including most teachers, and, thus, my decision to label it *conventional* consciousness.

Freire's categories of consciousness are not water-tight, and this allows us to consider the relationship between critical pedagogic practice and the practice of those who, while wanting to instill critical thinking into their classroom practice, are not doing so from an explicitly critical pedagogic perspective. For example, individuals who, for the most part, operate at the conventional level of consciousness will neither always exhibit a sense of powerlessness in the face of dominant institutions, nor will they always shy away from the prospect of engaging in social change. The constrained sense of empowerment experienced by people at the level of conventional consciousness may not fundamentally challenge established beliefs, practices, or institutions (a characteristic of the empowerment arising from critical consciousness) but, at the same time, we should not underestimate the significance of change that can emerge from citizens who are still very much influenced by conventional consciousness. The impact of such partial empowerment is attested to, and helps explain why and how, in the U.S., attitudes and values have shifted to the point that a Black man was elected president and a woman was a serious contender, a situation that would have been unimaginable a very few years ago.

(ii) Those "Ah-ha" Moments: The Empirical Bridge

My contention that teachers and students can make the transition from humanistic worldviews and the practice of non-critical "soft" pedagogies is also based on my empirical observations of classroom teachers, pre-service teachers, and students who have experienced "ah ha" moments, which have constituted the first important step in their transition from liberal-humanitarian worldviews to critical and transformative perspectives. Anecdotally, I do not recall having ever seen a hard-line traditional liberal or conservative teacher make this transition. On the other hand, resistant students can, over time and with proper teacher support, be won to criticality. Among teachers, it is those who come to these issues with an open mind and from a liberal-humanitarian perspective who are more likely to accept a move to criticality. They are, after all, genuinely attempting to understand the root causes of the inequities, injustice, and ecological degradation that they see all around them. Furthermore, not to include this possibility, leaves one open to a static and unhelpful analysis that transformations in social consciousness are either impossible or inexplicable. This said, I am perfectly aware that there are teachers and students whose educational experiences—including, in some cases, field trips to countries in the developing world—do not move them beyond a firmly entrenched "lucky us/poor them" duality which, at best (if, indeed, *at best* is the appropriate term) does not lead them beyond a desire "to help the poor" through occasional individual acts of charity.

Andreotti (2006) observed the phenomenon of educational practices that lead students to the charitable stance of wanting to "help the poor." She raises the concern that if pedagogical practices are not critical, then the classroom experience may become the ideological justification for a new generation of privileged, global North youth taking up "the 'burden' of saving/educating/civilizing the world" (p. 1). In effect, she asks, how can we move students (and teachers) to an "ah-ha" moment, and get them beyond a charitable helping response? To address this challenge she provides a pedagogy and an epistemology.

(iii) A Pedagogy that Bridges Critical and "Non Critical" but Progressive Educators: Critical Literacy

The pedagogy that Andreotti (2006) proposes is critical literacy. Critical literacy addresses issues "of power, voice, and difference" (p. 7). This pedagogy has the advantage of being a classroom practice with which teachers operating from a range of perspectives are familiar. Critical literacy is well-known and widely practiced in K-12 schools. Critical literacy also has the potential to be a far more radical pedagogy. Andreotti defines critical literacy:

> ... as a level of reading the word and the world that involves the development of skills of critical engagement and reflexivity: the analysis and critique of the relationships among perspectives, language, power, social groups and social practices by the learners. Criticality, in this context, does not refer to the dominant opinion that something is right or wrong, biased or unbiased, true or false. It is an attempt to understand origins of assumptions and implications. In this sense, critical literacy is not about 'unveiling' the 'truth' for the learners, but about providing the space for them to reflect on their context and their own and others' epistemological and ontological assumptions: how we came to think/be/feel/act the way we do and the implications of our systems of belief in local/global terms in relation to power, social relationships and the distribution of labor and resources. (p. 7)

This understanding of critical literacy helps students (and educators) understand that their world-views are socially constructed and, therefore, they can be deconstructed and reconstructed. The present historical moment provides an opening for this to happen. There is, of course, no alternative ideological "package" that teachers should be trying to convince young people to accept. Rather, using the skills and perspectives associated with critical literacy and the values of participatory democracy, social justice, and ecological balance, teachers have an opportunity to work with young people to transform their "views/ identities/relationships" and to take political action, should they choose, "after a careful analysis of the context of the intervention, of different views, of power relations (especially the position of who is intervening) and of short and long term ... implications of goals and strategies" (Andreotti, p. 7).

The practice of critical literacy, conceived of in this way, has all the elements common to the various schools of thought that I have grouped under the general heading of critical pedagogy, and it has the advantage that, because it is so widely promoted, it can be introduced into the classrooms of teachers who might well be nervous about teaching controversial or political topics. This conception of critical literacy combined, for example, with Selby's (2004) concepts developed in *Global education as transformative education*, provide a bridge between "soft" and critically transformative pedagogies.

(iv) An Epistemology that Bridges Critical and "Non Critical" but Progressive Educators: Critically Interrogating Our Place in the World

With respect to the epistemology required to move students and their teachers toward greater criticality, Andreotti's (2006) suggestions (pp. 2–4) include the need to:

- interrogate and work to move beyond the "common humanity" assumptions of "soft pedagogies" and the notion of 'global citizen' both of which fail to address issues of unequal power. She notes that the concept of global citizen requires critical examination as it is frequently based on a "local and parochial, interest which has been globalized through the scope of its reach" (p. 3);
- understand the "chains of cause and effect that promote obligations of justice rather than sympathy, pity or beneficence" (p. 2); in the case of global poverty, the chains of cause and effect involve understanding that poverty is created and some people, including many of the advocates of critical pedagogy, benefit materially from the global division of labor that results in the creation of poverty at home and abroad; and, closely related to this,
- understand that a sense of solidarity must be built, not as a result of a moral (i.e., humanitarian) obligation, but arising from our analysis of the causes of poverty including the recognition that our well-being is generated by the same processes that generate the poverty that upsets us so (p. 2).

The essential message here is that students and teachers in the global North must be made aware that our privilege emerges from the same processes that generate "their" poverty (and, importantly, that "they" may very well not live all that far away, and may even be found in our classrooms). Rather than seeing problems as being "out there" (e.g., the South African AIDS problem; the First Nations' poverty problem), these problems have to be understood as being socially constructed by processes of capital accumulation in which we are implicated and for which we bear a measure of responsibility.

Conclusion

The global crisis—both institutional and ideological—of neo-liberal capitalism provoked by the meltdown of world financial markets in 2008 has created an opening for popular movements to make, in the words of labor economist Stanford (2008), "a very fundamental critique" of neo-liberalism's economic project and to "be thinking very big thoughts indeed, about how to change and ultimately replace it" (p. 5). At the same time, even though their system is shaken, neo-liberals are regrouping, blaming the crash on the irresponsible actions of individual companies, not on the neo-liberal capitalist system itself, and are attempting to convince those in power to see the future in neo-liberal terms, encouraging them to adopt policies that move things in this direction.

Activists from all walks of life as well as progressive interest groups, including and especially young people, need to move quickly to take advantage of this opening and the receptiveness of the public to a new political message and a more enticing sicual vision. This should take the form of a two-pronged strategy stressing short-and long-term goals. The former involves pressuring the Obama government to cede as little relief as possible to those responsible for the crisis through the bailout/stimulus packages, and demand that the government provide programs to assist ordinary US citizens over the hump created by the crisis; the latter involves growing the movement and articulating a coherent post-neo-liberal vision for America and America's role in the world based on the values associated with the globalization from below movement (Singh, Kenway, & Apple, 2005, p. 7): democracy, equity, social justice, and ecological balance.

Meanwhile, critical pedagogues in our schools need to create opportunities for students to develop critical faculties and encourage them to become agents of social transformation inside and beyond schools. Creating such opportunities constitute recognition that students will not spontaneously acquire either the social perspectives, the motivation for engagement, or the requisite skills for effective involvement in this post-neo-liberal social movement on their own.

Furthermore, because it is essential that there be more teachers preparing students for such critical engagement, critical pedagogues need to identify and mentor allies from among their colleagues, and win them over to increasingly critical perspectives. I have argued that such allies are to be found among those liberal-humanitarian colleagues who teach progressively but "non critically," not because of consolidated opposition to such criticality but rather because, at this time, they occupy an ideological space which is characterized by a sense of justice/injustice. While their perspective does not meet the criteria of Freire's critical consciousness, nevertheless, it does constitute a good starting-point from which to move, with the encouragement of a supportive colleague, to a pedagogical position characterized by greater criticality. Pedagogical sectarianism in the staffroom is as counter-productive to the increase in educators teaching critically as political sectarianism in the social movements is to broadening those social movements. When a political opening occurs, such as the one that has recently occurred, our collective capacity to capitalize on that possibility will be determined by our ability to set aside small differences for a common good, whether that common good is defined in classroom-level critical pedagogic terms or in broader social movement terms. This approach could, undoubtedly, provide support and relief to youth seeking to resist the nefarious efforts of neo-liberalism.

QUESTIONS FOR REFLECTION

1. Youth are frequently radicalized by the school experience but not in the way envisioned by critical pedagogues. Black, Latino, working-class youth, and others who frequently find themselves marginalized in the school setting often adopt a hostile relationship to schools and teachers (Dei, Mazzuco, McIsaac, & Zine, 1997; Solomon, 1992). How can critical pedagogues take this rebelliousness into account, and work with such youth to develop critical consciousness and a sense of the possibility of collective political action?

2. TINA, the neo-liberal mantra that "there is no alternative," has been replaced by Marginson's (2006) prediction that "when there is an alternative, the political landscape will look very different" (p. 218). How has this landscape changed since 2008 and how will that affect the formation of new social movements and their ability to advance an agenda of deep political, cultural, and socio-economic change?

3. Critical pedagogy will get into mainstream classes in a significant way only when there are effective demands from beyond the school system to ensure that it happens. How can teachers and teacher-educators become part of broad postliberal social movements that make such demands on educational authorities?

REFERENCES

Andreotti, V. (2006). Soft versus critical global citizenship education. *Policy and Practice, 3.* Centre for Global Education, Belfast. Retrieved from http//www.osdemethodology.org.uk/texts/softcritical van.pdf

Aronowitz, S., & Giroux, H. (1991). *Postmodern education: Politics, culture cnd social criticism.* Minneapolis, MN: University of Minnesota Press.

Beito, D. (1989). *Taxpayers in revolt; Tax resistance during the great depression.* Chapel Hill, NC: University of North Carolina Press.

Cohen, L. (1990). *Making a new deal: Industrial workers in Chicago.* Cambridge, UK: Cambridge University Press.

Connolly, M. (n.d.). *Freire in the (post-modern) classroom: A post colonial tale.* Unpublished paper.

Davies, L. (2005). Teaching about conflict through citizenship education. *International Journal of Citizenship and Teacher Education, 1*(2), 17–34.

Dei, G., Mazzuco, J., McIsaac, E., & Zine, J. (1997). *Reconstructing drop out: A critical ethnography of the dynamics of Black students' disengagement from school.* Toronto, ON: University of Toronto Press.

Freire, P. (1970). *Pedagogy of the oppressed.* New York: Seabury.

Freire, P. (1974). *Education for critical consciousness.* London: Continuum.

Freire, P. (1985). *The politics of education: Culture, power, and liberation.* South Hadley, MA: Bergin & Garvey.

Giroux, H. A. (1988). *Teachers as intellectuals: Toward a critical pedagogy of learning.* South Hadley, MA: Bergin & Garvey.

Giroux, H. A. (1995). *Academics as public intellectuals: Rethinking global politics.* New York: Routledge.

Giroux, H. A. (1997). *Pedagogy and the politics of hope: Theory, culture, and schooling.* Boulder, CO: Westview.

Giroux, H. A. (2001). *Public spaces, private lives: Beyond the culture of cynicism.* Lanham, MD: Rowman & Littlefield.

Harber, C. (2002). Not quite the revolution: Citizenship education in England. In M. Schweisfurth, L. Davies, & C. Harber (Eds.), *Learning democracy and citizenship: International experience* (pp. 225–239). Oxford, UK: Symposium Books.

Ibrahim, T. (2005). Global citizenship education: Mainstreaming the curriculum? *Cambridge Journal of Education, 35*(2), 177–194.

Klein, N. (2007). *The shock doctrine: The rise of disaster capitalism.* Toronto, ON: A. A. Knopf.

Kotz, D. (2009). *Crisis and neo-liberal capitalism.* Retrieved from http://www.dollarsandsense.org/archives/2008/1108kotz.html

Larsen, M., & Faden, L. (2008). Supporting the growth of global citizenship educators. In M. O'Sullivan & K. Pashby (Eds.), *Citizenship education in the era of globalization: Canadian Perspectives* (pp. 91–104). Rotterdam: Sense Publishers.

Lingard, B., Hayes, D., & Mills, M. (2003). Teachers and productive pedagogies: Contextualizing, conceptualizing, and utilizing. *Pedagogy, Culture & Society, 11*(3), 399–424.

Marginson, S. (2006). Engaging democratic education in the neo-liberal age. *Educational Theory, 56*(2), 205–219.

McLaren, P. (2003). *Life in schools: An introduction to critical pedagogy in the foundations of education* (4th ed.). Toronto, ON: Pearson Education.

O'Sullivan, M. (2008). You can't criticize what you can't understand: Teachers as social change agents in neo liberal times. In M. O'Sullivan & K. Pashby (Eds.), *Citizenship education in the era of globalization: Canadian perspective* (pp. 113–126). Rotterdam: Sense Publishers.

O'Sullivan, M., & Vetter, D. (2007). Teacher-initiated, student-centered global education in a K to 8 school. *Journal of Teaching and Learning, 4*(2), 13–28. The return of economic nationalism. (2009, February 7–13). *The Economist, 390*, p. 9.

Robbins, M., Francis, L., & Elliot, E. (2003). Attitudes toward education for global citizenship among trainee teachers. *Research in Education, 69*, 93–98.

Schugurensky, D. (2003). *Three theses on citizenship learning and participatory democracy.* Retrieved from http://fcis.oise.utoronto.ca/~daniel_schugurensky/lclp/lclp_intro.html

Schweifurth, M. (2006). Education for global citizenship: Teacher agency and curricular structure in Ontario schools. *Educational Review, 5*(1), 41–50.

Selby, D. (2004). *Global education as transformative education.* Retrieved from http://www.citizens4change.lrg/global/intro/global_introduce.htm

Shor, I. (1987). *Empowering education: Critical teaching for social change.* Chicago: University of Chicago Press.

Siddiqui, H. (2009, February 15). Canada's star left-winger. *Toronto Star*, p. A 19.

Singh, M., Kenway, J., & Apple, M. (2005). Globalizing education: Perspectives from above and below. In M. Apple, J. Kenway, & M. Singh (Eds.), *Globalizing education: Policies, pedagogies, & politics* (pp. 1–29). New York: Peter Lang.

Solomon, P. (1992). *Black resistance in a high school: Forging a separatist culture.* New York: NUNY Press.

Stanford, J. (2008). *The global financial crisis for beginners—No. 165.* Retrieved from http://www.caw.ca/en/news-events-newsletters-facts-from-the-fringe-the-global-financial-crisis-for-beginners.htm

Steinberg, S. (2006). Preface. In S. Steinberg, P. Parmar, & B. Richard (Eds.), *Contemporary youth culture: An international encyclopedia* (pp. xii–xviii). Westport, CT: Greenwood Press.

Whitten, J., & Executive Producer. (2009, February 17). *The National* [Television Broadcast]. Toronto, ON: Canadian Broadcasting Corporation.

PAUL R. CARR AND GINA THÉSÉE

14. POLITICAL (IL)LITERACY

Confrontingthe Neo-liberal Agenda[1]

INTRODUCTION

As is evident in the various chapters contained in this book, neo-liberalism is a concept, philosophy, and operating system which serve as a template for the world's political-economy (Tabb, 2001; Treanor, 2005). In some quarters, globalization has been reduced to a series of inexpensive "midnight-madness" sales at Walmart without any meaningful socio-cultural inter-change. Economics, within the energized neo-liberal era that makes little attempt to mask the rawness of the capitalist under-belly, rules the day, at least that is the way politics is presented in the current quest for democracy in the West and around the world (Hoffman, 2006). McLaren (2007) defines this neo-liberal economic quagmire as

> a corporate domination of society that supports state enforcement of the unregulated market, (which) engages in the oppression of nonmarket forces and antimarket policies, guts free public services, eliminates social subsidies, offers limitless concessions to transnational corporations, enthrones a neomer-cantilist public policy agenda, establishes the market as the patron of educational reform, and permits private interests to control most of social life in the pursuit of profits for the few (i.e., through lowering taxes on the wealthy, scrapping environmental regulations, and dismantling public education and social welfare programs) (p. 27).

There is an implicit underlying residue to the neo-liberal agenda stressing that the collective is much less important than the individual, which poses an obvious and not so delicate problem of how we are to consider social justice, especially within the educational context (Hill, 2003). If we are all individuals, can we then bear collective responsibility for such realities as racism, sexism, classism, homophobia, xenophobia, etc. (Dei, Karumanchery, & Karumanchery-Luik, 2004)? An important backdrop to this chapter is an obvious and viscerally entrenched socio-economic system that blends inequities, marginalization and vastly differential experiences (i.e., employment, housing, education, wealth accumulation, crime rates, travel, etc.) alongside a pervasive belief that there is hope, freedom and fairness in our society (see Smiley, 2006, and McLaren, 2007, for summaries of the numerous ways that race and class, in particular, are important predictors of marginalization). Critical, political literacy can become an indispensable tool for citizens outside of

B. J. Porfilio and P. R. Carr (eds.), Youth Culture, Education and Resistance:
Subverting the Commercial Ordering of Life, 233–255.

elite-circles to counter hegemonic oppression. Moreover, critical political literacy, in line with Frere's (1973) concept of conscientization, can also be an emancipatory disposition in support of youth resistance to neo-liberalism.

Public education (K-12) is pivotal in this discussion because this fundamental period of formal learning in young peoples' lives can help them critique, deconstruct and become engaged in society, or, conversely, it can make them passive consumers, patriotic supporters of war, and enthusiastic adherents of the "market-place" (Westheimer & Kahne, 2004; Westheimer, 2006). The process of teaching and learning is critical to supporting or diminishing the drive toward the complete marketization of society (Dermaine, 2004; Hill, 2003). The disenfranchisement of large portions of society in and through the education process beckons the call for greater political literacy as a counter-measure to pre-packaged curriculum and evaluation reforms that emphasize conformity and underplay the importance of social justice (Carr, 2006a; Holm & Farber, 2002; Hursh & Martina, 2003). Understanding identity, marginalization and social justice (Vincent, 2003), therefore, becomes a critical feature to the leveling of the proverbial playing-field for students and others who are not privy to the decision-making processes that shape and control public education. Similarly, it is imperative that the prevailing notion of color-blindness be challenged (Carr, 2006b), especially since "racism and racial inequality undermine democracy in any form, especially in its radical and inclusive versions," and, further, "neither racism nor racial inequality can be systemically contested or transformed unless the power of neo-liberalism is simultaneously contested" (Robbins, 2004, p. 1).

This chapter attempts to make the connection between neo-liberalism and political literacy in education (Rossatto, 2005), focusing, in particular, on social justice in education. Some of the questions that will be addressed include: Do we teach for political literacy (Schugurensky, 2000)? What are the considerations for teaching, or not, political literacy (Giroux, 1988)? How does political literacy relate to neo-liberalism (McLaren, 2007)? How are educators and students engaged in political literacy to construct their roles in shaping democracy, and how does this democracy relate to social justice (Carr, 2006a)? Must political literacy be taught in an explicit way, or can it be learned through osmosis (Davies & Hogarth, 2004)? What are the implications for society of neglecting political literacy in education (Parker, 2003)? Political literacy is a critical component to this discussion because of the lurking danger of neo-liberal education to further destabilize marginalized groups and re-entrench vastly inequitable power relations, which would have obvious consequences for a democratic society (Westheimer and Kahne, 2004; Parker, 2002, 2003).

Building on the work of Paulo Freire (1973), Giroux (1988) has been one of the most prolific writers arguing for "critical literacy as a precondition for self- and social-empowerment", as well as "literacy as a form of cultural politics". Almost twenty years ago, Giroux (1988) framed the context for how literacy has been re-formulated in a narrow, functionalist way, compatible with what we now know as neo-liberalism:

the language of literacy is almost exclusively linked to popular forms of liberal and right-wing discourse that reduce it to either a functional perspective tied to narrowly coerced economic interests or to a logic designed to initiate the poor, the underprivileged, and minorities into the ideology of a unitary, dominant cultural tradition. In the first instance, the crisis in literacy is predicated on the need to train more workers for occupational jobs that demand "functional" reading and writing skills.... In the second instance, literacy becomes the ideological vehicle through which to legitimate schooling as a site for character development; in this case, literacy is associated with the transmission and mastery of a unitary Western tradition based on the virtues of hard work, industry, respect for family, institutional authority, and an unquestioning respect for the nation (p. 61).

The incessant and all-encompassing ideology pushing the working classes to believe that K-12 public education is a meritocratic, transformative enterprise is evident in schools at several levels. What may seem obvious is often obscured with neo-liberal arguments in favor of competition and high standards. Kozol (2005) has long advocated for a more critical approach to understanding the organization and structure of schools, how resources are allocated, the relevancy (and control) of the curriculum, and the redundancy of accountability measures that effectively constrain teachers from teaching and students from learning. Kozol has been particularly effective in underscoring the marginalization of minority groups within the broader society, questioning the perceived *sagesse* of avoiding tackling basic issues, such as the availability and quality of the environmental and physical infrastructure housing students, including the technological, library, physical education, cafeteria, and other fundamental services. Kozol makes the case in a compelling manner that minority and socio-economically marginalized groups have long lost out in receiving a just and equitable share of the required and available resources. Accordingly, the public mantra of equal opportunity within a neo-liberal context serves to dissuade many young people from achieving the very standards decisionmakers proclaim are the goal for all students. Our perspective, therefore, reflects the need for critical and emancipatory engagement (Freire, 1973; Giroux, 1988; McLaren, 2007; Rossatto, 2004), surpassing the basic reading, writing and numeracy skills so often trumpeted in contemporary curriculum standards, and is, additionanly, inextricably connected to democracy and social justice in the broadest terms (Vincent, 2003; Carr, 2006a, in press; Gross & Shapiro, 2005).

There are three sections to this chapter: first, some of the primary tenets of neo-liberalism, as they relate, primarily, to the US context, are presented so as to frame the following sections as well as elucidating why political literacy in education, including at the post-secondary levels, is imperative; second, the question of political literacy in education, especially in relation to social justice and accountability, is contextualized, making linkages with diverse concepts such as democracy and citizenship; and the concluding section offers an analysis of some of the vantage-points that could constructively shape the discussion, and also presents two proposals for establishing a politically literate education system that is more holistic and embracing of difference, all the while being critical of the neo-liberal model of education. Our experience and research in the areas of anti-racism, anti-colonial and democratic education augment the analysis and illustrations throughout.

Neo-liberalism and the Human Condition

Decrying the role of US hegemony in the new mania for globalization, Hoffman (2006) defines the neo-liberal agenda as broad, encompassing and extremely divisive in terms of the center and the periphery. The mixture of fundamentalist ideology combined with a "permanent war on terror" (McLaren, 2007) buttresses the fanatical drive to maximize profits. Part of this re-restructuring involves relinquishing unprecedented leverage and rights to transnational corporations, eliminating large swaths of the economy in developing countries, reducing other sectors to intolerable conditions and highly uncompetitive wages, and becoming submissive economically to international bodies, such as the International Monetary Fund, the World Bank, and the World Trade Organization, which do not prioritize socio-cultural development or a genuine respect for the world's environment (Martinez and Garcia, 1996).

Hoffman (2006) effectively summarizes the world's reaction to this new US hegemony after 2001 as follows:

> the US and much of the rest of the world fell out over America's new unilateralism and its refusal to accept the International Criminal Court, the Kyoto Protocol (on the environment), and arms control generally. Most nations were appalled by America's flaunting of it dominance; its use of preventive war, particularly the invasion of Iraq, was wisely seen as proof of a will to reshape and dominate the Arab world. America's new mixture of patriotism and religiosity annoyed many secularists at home and abroad, and the American way of fighting terrorism by bombing and torturing Iraqis and mistreating Afghans shocked many previously well-disposed allies (p. 60).

Hoffman (2006) goes on to critique the rather flimsy notion of the "free market" economy that will bring peace and prosperity to all corners of the globe, as proposed by the US, which subsidizes some sectors while concurrently abolishing the social safety net. The astronomical number of US citizens who have no health-care coverage while a small minority of individuals reaps untold profits, often in an illegal manner (i.e., Enron, World.com, the savings and loans banking crisis) is a case in point.

The contradiction inherent in US foreign policy, as well as domestic policy, belies the polished veneer proudly presented as American meritocracy.

> The most flagrant and widely deplored contradiction is between American's self image as a force of democracy and human rights and a reality in which many rights at home are sharply limited, the death penalty continues along with torture of "enemy combatants," while the US repudiates the international laws of war. Abroad the US support of dictators and its failure to protect victims of genocide in Rwanda and Darfur have contributed greatly to anti-Americanism. Foreigners can observe for themselves, on the one hand, the weakness of public services throughout the US, the cult of low taxes, and the distrust of any redistributive role of government and,

on the other hand, the formidable apparatus of American military and intelligence services throughout the world and in the US itself (Hoffman, 2006, p. 60).

There are visible signs of anti-Americanism cresting throughout the four corners of the globe, epitomized by the rejection of the US dollar in favor of the Euro, reduced numbers of foreign students to the US, a wave of countries opting for a less than friendly approach to the US in Latin America (in the last few years, Venezuela, Argentina, Brazil, Chile, Bolivia, Nicaragua and others have elected left-wing governments critical of the US), and a general decline in American prestige in cultural terms, in large part owing to the American intervention in Iraq and elsewhere.

Ultimately, neo-liberalism is an all-encompassing mind-set that is predicated on having no permanent physical infrastructure since capital and free-market capitalism are encouraged to shift into and out of local, regional, national and international economies, seeking endless profit while downplaying the relevance of the environment, social justice and the basic needs of the masses (Hill, 2003). It is, therefore, not surprising to witness social policy predicated on the basis of maximizing economic gain, as is the case evident in such policies as workfare for welfare recipients, and the emphasis on business and "employability" in education. This can be juxtaposed with the limited emphasis placed on the social aspect of the human condition in education, including the capacity to participate in and influence society, to appropriate mechanisms in place to ensure that discrimination, poverty and civil strife are addressed at all levels, and, significantly, to ensure that democracy, social justice and equity resonate with all sectors in society, not just those able to financially find a place at the decision-making table (Westheimer & Kahne, 2004).

While neo-liberalism seems to be focused on the macro-level political and economic issues framing society, it is, importantly, appreciably intertwined with the culture and daily living conditions of the people in each respective society. How could neo-liberalism be sustained if people did not support it? Are people led to the proverbial well, as Herman and Chomsky (2002) suggest, to sing and dance but not to think and act owing to sophisticated and systemic media manipulation that they characterize as "manufacturing consent"? In other words, would people not naturally resist something which they consider to not be in their best interests, as some of the more visible parts of neo-liberalism have clearly demonstrated? Or, rather, are people even aware of their rights and interests in a society that discourages them to organize to fight for social justice? Are teachers able to engage themselves and their students in the struggle for an education that will be liberating and decisive for society, as articulated by Freire (1973)? Why are the numerous groups and movements at the local and international levels (for example, those focused on human rights, development, peace, fighting the spread of AIDS, and racism) not more broadly incorporated into the formal learning process in schools? Thus, the potential of a politically literate population, supported and nourished through public education, is a key consideration in the discussion on neo-liberalism (Davies & Hogarth, 2004; Giroux, 1988).

Perspectives for a more Politically Literate Education

Tabb (2001) identifies the key threads of neo-liberalism as being a driving-force behind the disintegration of education as a public good in the turbulent waters of the market-place, emphasizing three key factors:

> making the provision of education more cost-efficient by commodifying the product; testing performance by standardizing the experience in a way that allows for multiple-choice testing of results; and focusing on marketable skills. The three elements are combined in different policies—cutbacks in the public sector, closing "inefficient" programs that don't directly meet business needs for a trained workforce, and the use of computers and distance learning, in which courses and degrees are packaged for delivery over the Internet by for-profit corporations.

Lopez (2000) highlights that neo-liberalism aims specifically to promote the privatization of education services. This tendency to make education a commodity involves increasing "user fees and private contributions to educational costs", creating "more flexible hiring methods and teachers salaries, and at the same time develop(ing) centralised state evaluation systems", and striving to enhance "the productivity of teachers by augmenting the number of students per class" (Lopez, 2000).

The ideological tendency of neo-liberal supporters is to over-emphasize that the education system is broken and "bankrupt", and also to argue that only radical profit-oriented, business practices can restore integrity and support for public education. It is telling that with the election of a decidedly pro-market, conservative government in Ontario, Canada, in 1995, after five years of a moderately left-wing social-democratic government, the new Minister of Education immediately pronounced that he intended to "create a crisis in education", and, consequently, the educational climate for the next several years was known for an abrupt and radical elimination of any commitment to equity and social justice (McCaskell, 2005; Carr, 2006b).

The neo-liberal model of education is, therefore, characterized by severe rationalization and cost-cutting, reduced investments, more students in fewer programs (for example, it is not uncommon to witness the elimination of music, physical education and arts programs), privatization, expanded school choice (the No Child Left Behind [NCLB] legislation in the US is a classic example), which diminishes the strength and integrity of the public education system, and an attack on teachers, both at the effectiveness (quality of teaching) and efficiency (costs) levels (Hill, 2003; Torres, 2005). Hursh and Martina (2003) stress how "this testing and accountability system (NCLB) has resulted in increased inequality", buttressed by an untenable situation in which the federal government is responsible for funding only a small portion of education but "has determined what subject areas take precedence, limits the ways in which they may be taught, and designates what reform options are available to schools and districts that fail to improve sufficiently their test scores" (pp. 1–2), all of which diminishes the role and capacity of local jurisdictions to manage education. Clearly, social justice and political literacy are not central components to these broad and far-reaching reforms.

Referring to the infiltration of neo-liberalism in education in the US, Torres (2005) points out that the two principal political parties, the Republicans and Democrats, essentially share the same values and orientation, and, in relation to NCLB, are not at odds. To this end, it is worth questioning how schools present and inculcate political literacy so that students are able to effectively dissect what bipartisanship actually means, and whether two political parties functioning in the same socio-economic landscape and mindset can actually relate and respond to the needs of the entire population, including those traditionally not involved in power-sharing. Further, Torres (2005) documents other significant shortcomings and contradictions in NCLB, including the inadequate funding levels, the sanctions on schools in poorer communities that do not meet standards, the lack of prescribed scientifically-based instructional practices, the support of vouchers and charter schools, and "provisions that try to push prayer, military recruiters, and homophobia into schools while pushing multiculturalism, teacher innovation, and creative curriculum reform out".

Morse (2006) unearths several social justice problems with NCLB, which relate specifically to the marginalization of disadvantaged children and minorities. A case in point is how many children are not counted in Annual Yearly Progress (AYP) reports simply because they were asked to stay home on the day of testing, a measure that is surprisingly common in those schools striving to reflect high performance standards without having to contend with potentially low scores from disadvantaged or minority children. Further, she notes that "the tests which are designed to measure AYP are based on a naïve realist assumption that the 'knowledge worth having' is easily identifiable and can be validly and reliably tested in a multiple choice format" (Morse, 2006).

NCLB has effectively reduced the ability of teachers to provide students with intrinsically motivated curricula, replacing it with formalized programs from commercial developers (Hoover & Shook, 2003). As teachers and administrators prepare for the standardized testing required for compliance with NCLB, the need for scripted materials appears to be increasing. However, most teachers decry the use of such materials as not representing the true needs of their students, especially in the urban areas, claiming that there is too much attention on obedience to authority as well as on rote memorization. In advancing a neo-liberal agenda antithetical to the needs and concerns of teachers, NCLB "assumes that the capitalistic model of businesses competing for market share is appropriate for public education, although there are many ways in which public education is unlike the capitalist model of business" (Morse, 2006).

In sum, there are many deficiencies in the new and enhanced interpretation of the role of education in the twenty-first century, and it is increasingly questionable how the neo-liberal hegemony will provide for social justice and democracy during and after the formal education experience. As Hill (2003, p. 2) notes, "the capitalist class in Britain and the USA have:"

1. a Business Plan for Education: this centres on socially producing labour-power (people's capacity to labour) for capitalist enterprises,

2. a Business Plan in Education: this centres on setting business 'free' in education for profit-making,

3. a Business Plan for Educational Businesses: this is a plan for British and US based Edubusinesses to profit from international privatizing activities (p. 2).

The issue of formal accountability, therefore, seems to focus on spread-sheets and budget-items more than the actual educational experience of the students, while students' understanding and engagement with the structures, processes and manifestation of power is increasingly an isolated but critical feature to educational attainment for all students.

What do We Learn, and What should We Learn?

Rather than simply considering education as a means of euphemistically achieving "higher standards" and a "qualified workforce", it is necessary to interrogate the foundation of education. Some of the questions we feel relevant in this regard include: How do we teach and train teachers for education (Davies & Hogarth, 2004)? What are the specific aims or purposes of education in society (McLaren, 2007)? What are the implications of emphasizing employment skills over citizenship (Schugurensky, 2000)? Can we have education without focusing on society's problems and the lived experiences of the students (Carr, in press)? How do we measure what we are learning, especially in relation to political literacy (Parker, 2002)?

The US National Institute for Literacy (2006), for example, produces reams of data and research on literacy but does not delve into the area of political literacy. In our individual and collective research, we have found that there is a purposeful de-emphasis on political literacy, the explicit and implicit processes of engaging in critical thinking and action to shape and influence one's environment. For some decision-makers, curriculum developers and educators, there should be no place for, what some perceive to be, "indoctrination" in education (Carr, 2006a). For others, the main feature of education should be helping students to become workers or employees in a market-based economy. For this group, the key is learning the skills and knowledge required for the workplace through a re-jigged curriculum emphasizing business skills, comfortably woven into a framework referred to as employability. However, there is evidence that greater political literacy can improve academic outcomes, improve the educational culture and experience, and reduce unacceptably high drop-out rates, especially for marginalized groups, that have plagued the education system for generations (Dei, Karumanchery, & Karumanchery-Luik, 2004; Ryan, 2006).

In examining the issue of indoctrination in relation to citizenship education, Sears and Hughes (2006) are critical of the present trend in Western countries to superficially respond to concerns about citizenship development, denouncing the "promotion of single, assailable views, and the shunning of evidence" (p. 4). This closed discourse buttressing indoctrination is characterized by:

creating false crises, sloganeering, setting up false dichotomies, grossly over simplifying both problems and solutions, and the demonizing of opponents and alternatives. The cult-like mantras that sometimes dominate our discourses are consistent with an indoctrination approach to citizenship education in that they are much more focused on creating true believers than on listening to alternatives or making substantive arguments (Sears and Hughes, 2006, p. 5).

Sears and Hughes (2006) conclude their analysis by exposing how measures, when they are evident, taken by governments to develop citizenship education curriculum and programs are lacking at several levels, and there is virtually no empirical evidence to demonstrate success. Demaine (2004) further echoes the problematic nature of developing meaningful citizenship education programs that seek political understanding and engagement.

To "do" democracy in education, as Westheimer and Kahne (2004) have articulated in their research, it is necessary to formally connect tangible learning experiences in a political way to the educational experience. They provide evidence that not making explicit linkages with the political side of civic engagement can serve to reinforce and undermine democracy. The example of Ontario's 40-hour mandatory voluntary experience component (Ontario, 2002) required to meet graduation requirements is pertinent in this regard because it is not explicitly linked to the learning experience, is not funded nor supervised by educators, and leaves the impression that doing anything is sufficient to meet the rigors of developing a well-rounded student (Westheimer and Kahne, 2002). This raises the important question of the place of citizenship and civic engagement in the formative years of students. An important part of this learning necessarily involves engaging students in discussions about politics in a process that entices, encourages and challenges youth to listen, argue and become effectively part of the process of understanding and taking action on controversial issues (Hess, 2004; Parker, 2003). Therefore, it is incumbent to have some formalization to the process of fostering and legitimating political literacy within a formal context, notwithstanding the concerns of trivialization and cooptation that will arise when some educational and political leaders may wish to simply fabricate a policy-response in order to placate enunciated concerns for change.

Perspectives, Opportunities and Challenges for Political Literacy in Education

Having presented some of the principal trends, obstacles and factors framing the way education is presently conceptualized, we now turn to our own research to underscore how marginalized groups are becoming increasingly disenfranchised through inequitable power relations. We briefly profile some of our research, attempting to solidify our argument for the need for greater political literary in education. Although we have centrally focused on the issue of race in our individual and collective research, we both acknowledge the powerful and direct relationship between issues of social justice and economic decisionmaking and control within the context of neo-liberalism.

Anti-racism and Leadership

Carr (1996) examined the state of anti-racism education in the Toronto Board of Education in the 1970–1995 period, focusing on the institutional culture and the representation of race as well as the formulation of educational policy in the Ontario government during the 1990s when there was in effect an anti-racism education policy (Carr, 2006b). He found an intricate and sophisticated labyrinth of systems, processes and mechanisms that reinforced systemic discrimination and marginalization of non-White individuals and groups (Carr, 1999, 2006b; Carr & Klassen, 1997). This is not to say that all Whites accrue the same advantages, nor that all racial minorities suffer from the same disadvantages. However, over time, there is an inherent, although manifestly subtle at certain levels, power imbalance (Carr, 1999, 2008; Carr & Lund, 2007). How decisions are made, how resources are distributed, how teachers are trained, how students learn, who is able to access the system, how accountability is determined, and other similarly important questions all constitute a framework for diagnosing the issue of anti-racism and social justice in education (Carr, 2007, 2008).

Focusing more on the pedagogical implications, Thésée (2003) found that Black students in Montreal encountered a range of individual and systemic barriers in relation to their relationship to, and success in, science education, a key gateway subject to advanced university studies, which paralleled findings from Carr's research. Her study (Thésée, 2003) underscored the lack of role models and teachers in education as well as a general incompatibility with guidance counselling and leadership, in particular, which served to further marginalize some students of colour.

The education system could be considered to be democratically racist (Henry & Tator, 2005), in that there is a consensus on the world view, which is overwhelming White, not to mention male, European, Christian and heterosexual. Thésée (2006) questions identity and power from an epistemological vantage-point, surmising that our notion of knowledge in itself must be problematized in order for there to be the appropriate conditions to resist neo-liberalism. Similarly, Carr and Klassen (1997) found that White and racial minority teachers in the Toronto Board viewed and experienced race issues quite differently, with the former devaluating its salience and the latter feeling that race was an extremely important factor in defining one's lived experience. Elsewhere, Carr and Thésée (2006) have also illustrated how even the usage of the terminology related to race can be highly contentious. The importance of racial minority teachers in diverse, as well as non-diverse, contexts is immeasurable, yet there are a number of obstacles to recruiting, integrating, retaining and promoting racial minority teachers (Carr & Klassen, 1996; Carr, 1995). The issue of Whiteness (Carr, 2006b), therefore, requires understanding how education systems have favored a Eurocentric vision, how meritocracy is not necessarily firmly anchored into our conception of democracy, and significantly, how Whites may have the power and privilege to avoid considering the lived experiences of non-Whites. It may be easy for some to affirm that 'we are all individuals' but less comfortable in acknowledging that most Whites do not have to represent their race, let alone be publicly affiliated with it. Carr and Lund (in press) have compiled a vast collection of works on Whiteness in education, concluding that avoiding a deeper analysis of the historical, sociological, political and pedagogical can only further marginalize and diminish the quality of the educational experience required by all students, those with and without advantage and privilege (Carr, 2006b).

Ultimately, leadership becomes a pivotal issue in ensuring any meaningful change or reform in relation to anti-racism and social justice (Carr, 1997, 1999, 2006b, 2008). The willingness of educational leaders, who are largely White, to embrace diversity, including the plurality of issues, concerns and identities intersecting with race (gender, class, sexual orientation, religion, language, etc.), is limited, yet the risk of not doing so is substantial (Ryan, 2006). If educational leaders do not experience nor understand the issues related to social justice, and they are reluctant to be out of step with the over-arching discourse which profoundly de-emphasizes the social conditions from which students originate, how can progressive change be made (McLaren, 2007)?. In sum, political literacy can become an indispensable lever for ensuring that public education is not simply reduced to the reproduction of social relations (Freire, 1973).

Democracy, Citizenship and Educational Experience

The issue of democracy and citizenship in education is pivotal in that how students are engaged in these areas during their formative education years will impact on their commitment to, and engagement in, society afterwards. Diamond (1997) discusses educating for democracy, emphasizing that "To improve democracy and make it work, citizens must have not only democratic knowledge and values but also skills and propensities to organize with one another for common ends, to stir one another to action, and to voice their concerns in speech and writing." Understanding and working against intolerance, marginalization, injustice, and prejudice are key to preventing people from feeling unworthy and less deserving of a place in society, and, therefore, a more explicitly political approach to learning is considered beneficial for all students (Giroux, 1988).

Strama (1998), in analyzing youth participation and electoral politics, states that low voter turnout among youth is countered by more youth engaging in community service: "The wiring of American democracy is disconnected. Americans no longer believe that ours is a government of, by, and for the people." Strama (1998) points to the influence of money in the formal political process as being one of the key alienating factors in diminishing youth involvement in elections. Therefore, it is critical to dissect the formal propensity to reduce political education to the knowledge of elections and political parties in favor of a broader and more developed understanding of how everything has a political dimension, and that, moreover, students and citizens can "do" something to shape their environment.

Schugurensky (2000) examined adult citizenship education, particularly regarding the connections between citizenship learning and the redistribution of political power, focusing particularly on knowledge, skills, attitudes, closeness to power, and resources. He claims that these areas are inter-related but that average citizens may not have a high-level capacity in more than one of them (Schugurensky, 2000). This analysis speaks to the cultural capital that students bring to their educational experience, and the concomitant need to equip all students with insight into the intricate workings of power so as to de-mystify the notion of a color-blind, meritocratic society Delpit (1988).

In his research into democracy and education, Carr (2006a; Lund & Carr, 2008) found that College of Education students (teachers and future teachers) had a relatively low level of political engagement in relation to their own educational experience and that of their students, and that the majority do not make a direct linkage between democracy and social justice in education. Concerned about "indoctrination", most of the education students surveyed were reluctant to address controversial issues, such as the war in Iraq, in their classes. There was also the obstacle of not having the training nor the support, not to mention the fact that the NCLB context marginalized such important learning, all of which serve to dissuade teachers from becoming engaged in democratic education. The need for a more inclusive and explicit approach to political literacy in education is, therefore, supported by our research.

Discussion

This chapter has sought to situate the problematic nature of neo-liberalism within the context of an increasing need for political literacy in education. Greater political literacy can be the starting-point for more dialogue, partnerships, solidarity, and, ultimately, action to re-define the supposed meritocracy, color-blindness and democracy under-pinning society. Critical thinking and engagement require thoughtful, well-resourced and inclusive decision-making (Carr, in press). There are many ways of understanding political literacy—epistemology, institutional culture, curriculum, and student engagement—, all of which were alluded to in our analysis. Is there a place for political literacy in the neo-liberal education agenda? How will this be developed and effectuated?

Dudley and Gitelson (2002) present a number of salient, as well as cautionary, points concerning political literacy in education, stressing the merits of service learning (Westheimer & Kahne, 2002, 2004) being connected to the curriculum, acknowledging the hidden curriculum (Apple, 1996), as well as the need for research about how political knowledge underpins civic engagement. Building on this research, O'Toole, Marsh and Jones (2003) highlight the concern that decision-makers and researchers often have a narrow view of youth (non-)participation, which does adequately consider how young people define politics and political engagement, "non-participation is not problematised," and "there are insufficient youth-specific explanations for declining participation among young people" (pp.349–350). Their research found that young people feel marginalized and disconnected from mainstream politics, especially decision-making processes, and, similarly, that they did not sense that they are encouraged to participate in political life, nor are they appropriately represented. However, O'Toole, Marsh and

Jones (2003) conclude that young people are not apathetic, nor are they disinterested in politics, but they are discouraged from the way the present system seems to present issues: interestingly, they note that "politics is something that is done to them, not something they can influence," and "inequalities based on class, gender, ethnicity and age are crucial features of the lives of our respondents: they are not variables, they are lived experiences" (p. 359). In sum, the present neo-liberal configuration of educational curricula, standards, expectations and testing concurrently isolates political literacy and places a premium on learning that disenfranchises many students.

Davies and Hogarth (2004) argue that political literacy must be re-situated as the focal-point of citizenship education. Their vision of political literacy surpasses the "compound of knowledge, skills and procedural values" to also include "such areas as respect for truth and reasoning and toleration as opposed to substantive values which could mean that pupils would be told what to think about particular issues" (p. 182). They reject previous political literacy models such as the "civics" model centered on "factual knowledge and a didactic teaching methodology" as the modus operandi (p. 182), and the "big issues" model in which adversarial political debates take place in class. For this latter approach, there is concern that issues will only be examined at a superficial level without serious follow-up. Rather, they favor the "public discourse model", which "seeks to induct pupils into the language, concepts, forms of arguments and skills required to think and talk about life from a political point of view, emphasizing both process and product. Factual knowledge is important but is made subservient to other aspects that are centrally important to political literacy" (p. 183).

Demaine (2004) examines the subject of citizenship education and globalization, highlighting that, *de facto*, the world is confronted with interdependent economic (and, therefore, political) relations, which have been an area of inquiry and concern since the writing of the *Manifesto of the Communist Party* by Karl Marx and Frederick Engels in 1848 (p. 202). While both concepts—citizenship education and globalization—are problematic, and need to be problematized, there is significant concern about how to teach about and for the international changes and machinations that are shaping local realities. Teachers, therefore, have a substantial role in preparing and engaging students for a world that is increasingly less focused on uniquely local and/or national concerns (Portelli & Solomon, 2001).

Santora (2006) examined why cooperative learning often failed to promote democratic behavior among culturally diverse students, and found that students reacted to knowledge provided by the teacher in multiple ways, including finding avenues to dispute or complement such knowledge with the knowledge acquired in/from their families, the environment, and the media. Her study demonstrates how power, as it affects knowledge construction, is locally reproduced or re-constituted through classroom interaction: "Controversial issues relevant to students' lives considered within the groupwork structure can, depending on the type of dialogue and student engagement within its 'disturbing spaces,' silence some students while empowering others." This analysis reflects Delpit's (1998) work on how minorities are systemically excluded from the decision-making process in the classroom as well as in the broader society through myriad processes, which codify the implicit and explicit ways that power works. Ogbus' (1991) educational inquiry also questions the interpretation of black student underachievement, challenging the notion that the education-system is neutral and, further, that individuals can succeed if the requisite effort is exercised, which, in effect, avoids dealing with the power-imbalance issue. The case of a segment of the young black male population, in particular, arguing that the formal educational experience does not speak to their reality, and that it is not "cool" to succeed at school, speaks to the institutional culture in education vis-à-vis those who contest inequitable power relations, thus highlighting the need for a re-invigorated approach to political literacy. Such questions that might be raised include: Why is there exclusion, who defines it, how do we measure it, and what can be done to remedy it? What are the implications of sustained marginalization? What formal and informal processes are in place to effectively bring together and to ensure constructive engagement between peoples from different races, social classes, ethnicities, religions, etc.? What is the responsibility of those who have access to power and decision-making?

We are interested in understanding why the general public does not demand a more holistic, inclusive, politically literate education, one that would help remedy some of the debilitating systemic problems that have plagued society for generations. We understand that the present education system does not encourage such reflection, nor does the media (Herman and Chomsky, 2002) support critical engagement. The need for boisterous patriotism (Westheimer, 2006) collides with the obvious particularities of an increasingly closed education system while the US government preaches for a market-based globalization. To this end, it is noteworthy to highlight that the US clearly lags behind other nations in the teaching/learning of languages, exchanges with other countries, and travel to other lands, underscored by the relatively low number of American passport-holders (Holm & Farber, 2002). If students were to know other languages, cultures, and people, and have a stronger sense of the inter-connections and inter-dependence between groups and nations, would we then see less conflict and a reduction in discrimination, conflict and other problems in the long-run?

From our analysis, we propose two models for addressing, rectifying and challenging neo-liberalism. Each involves political as well as educational engagement, and each concerns itself with broad considerations about how society has privileged some issues, relations and people over others. Carr's model of social justice accountability seeks to restructure how educational systems produce, define, legitimize and demonstrate social justice whereas Thésée's model of resistance to hegemonic oppression focuses on reconstructing and challenging Eurocentricity and entrenched racism. Both models attempt to better understand and soften, if not abolish, inequitable power relations, and, importantly, to enhance political literary in, through and with education. The two models, together, seek to provide a framework for assisting marginalized groups and those interested in transformational change in education to introduce processes, structures and proposals to ensure greater accountability and empowerment throughout the intricate formal and informal machinations and sectors constituting educational systems. Lastly, as the far-reaching implications of neo-liberalism cannot be countered with individual, punctual efforts, these two models together strive to reinforce political literacy and transformational change in education in a sustained, systemic and liberating way.

Carr's Model of a Social Justice Accountability Framework

Carr's Social Justice Accountability Framework can be visualized and operationalized in the form of a matrix (Figure 1). On one side, there are eight substantive content components (strategic policy; leadership; curriculum; extra-curricular; service-learning; community involvement; training; and evaluation), complemented by eight functional criteria along the top of the matrix (inclusion; representation; decisionmaking process; communications; funding; data-collection and analysis; accountability mechanism; and monitoring and review). This Framework need not give the perception of being too complex or unattainable, especially in light of highly sophisticated formulae and strategies already in place, which could be considered disconnected and ineffective in addressing social justice considerations. Moreover, governments already have at their disposal enormous power and resources that continue to over-look social justice in the name of neo-liberal ideology and the quest for greater accountability.

How is the Framework operationalized? If we are able to set targets for graduation rates, literacy levels, academic achievement, class size and spending, why should we not be more dedicated to establishing formal measures and procedures to guide us in achieving social justice in education? This framework

	1. Inclusion	2. Representation	3. Decision Making Process	4. Communication	5. Funding	6. Data-Collection Processes	7. Accountability	8. Monitoring/Review
1. Strategic Policy								
2. Leadership								
3. Curriculum								
4. Extra-Curricular								
5. Service-Learning								
6. Community Involvement								
7. Training								
8. Evaluation								

Figure 1. Social Justice Accountability Framework.

provides a means for education-systems, from schools through to the highest decision-making bodies, to plan for meaningful social justice in education. Rather than avoid the numerous issues necessary to achieving a progressive and receptive institutional culture apt to cultivate change in the educational experience and decision-making processes fundamental to structuring social relations, this Framework requires inclusive and comprehensive collaborative work to develop, implement, monitor and review standards, targets and processes for each of the components in the matrix.

In practical terms, to use the example of the curriculum (the third item on the left side of the matrix), this would mean determining how inclusive the curriculum is, how representative it is, whether or not the decision-making process employed to formulate and develop the content of the curriculum was mindful of social justice considerations, if the communications around the development and implementation were appropriate, whether the funding required was allocated to ensure that there would be an engaging social justice core to the content, how data around curriculum issues were collected, managed and analyzed in support of social justice, what accountability mechanisms permeate the entire curriculum process to enable high quality as well as critical teaching and learning, and, finally, what monitoring and review mechanisms are in place and are used. Unlike the present configuration in traditional educational planning, this Framework would focus on various research methodologies and approaches to develop, implement and measure *bone fide* social justice progress. In dissecting each of the components in the Framework, the objective would be to cultivate a meaningful citizenship-based educational experience focused on social justice, one that strives to meet high academic standards for all students that transcend the contemporary fixation with prescribed, standardized, neo-liberal expectations.

Thésée's Model of Resistance to Hegemonic Oppression

Thésée (2006) has argued against the positivistic nature of science and science education, seeking to re-distribute the way scientific thought is constituted and presented (Reiss, 2003). She is particularly concerned with the marginalization of Blacks in the world of science, how their inventions, innovations and participation in advancing and preserving cultures has been devalued. She also questions the way colonialism and neo-colonialism, a hybrid and segway to the neo-liberal era, have served to pillage indigenous cultures, ravaging the environment, coercing innocent peoples into military and pharmaceutical research, and resulting in the "enslavement of the mind" (p. 33).

There are four components to Thésée's (2006) model to resisting colonial hegemony:

1. *Refuse*: Globally, this strategy is used to address the different discourses which are infused into the mind continuously in everyday life. These discourses present strong symbolic, implicit and explicit content. The symbolic content includes images, styles, attitudes or relations which fill the ordinary social environment with, for example, media and artistic productions.

2. *Re-questioning*: This strategy relates to new forms of questions to address issues of scientific knowledge. Re-questioning is similar to de-construction: the de-construction of the technocratic world, which asks mostly "how much?", seeking the measurable goals in various situations. Re-questioning the "How?", therefore, shatters the certainty and rigidity of methodologies by daring to structure procedures differently.

3. *Re-define*: There must be a re-definition of knowledge in all its dimensions that is social in nature: formal traits, aesthetics, choices, ethical values, and collective rituals. The formal traits of knowledge include concepts, basic principles, rules, laws and theories which have been formalized through periods of inert-subjectivity and broad consensus.

4. *Reaffirm*: To reaffirm the self is necessary in order to deviate from the pervasive Eurocentric view of others that one is inferior. Going further in the resistance process is supposed to affirm the collective self supported by all actors at all levels (societal, community, family and individuals of all ages) (pp. 38–40).

Thésée (2006) concludes by emphasizing that:

> The most important factor associated with the resilience of the persons in post-traumatic syndrome, as well as in school, is the positive support offered by a nurturing social environment which can buffer the trauma. Despite the impregnation of colonization through scientific knowledge, and despite the erosion of vernacular cultures (re)generated by people and nations, the hope for a meaningful resistance and resiliency is situated within the framework of understanding, meaning and empowering, which can be only achieved within a strong and supportive communitarian-based experience, and a strong racial socialization and identity (p. 40).

Thus, the pivotal concern of who determines what knowledge is deemed relevant within the political context of educational policymaking and teaching and learning is highlighted by Thésée's (2006) insistence on resistance to oppression.

Concluding Thoughts

Writing about confronting and undoing neo-liberalism is a daunting, cathartic, destabilizing proposition. We live in a society shaped by myriad contradictions and ethical quagmires: how do you talk to people about peace when you are simultaneously accused of 'not supporting the troops' and being 'non-patriotic'? Can we seek the truth in our teaching, knowing that the process of attaining the truth lies in process of endless interrogation, reflection and dialectical, critical thought? Yet, there is a cultural ethos supporting simplistic answers and sloganeering. Popular culture is full of get-rich-quick schemes, with a plethora of mind-numbing (supposed) reality shows preoccupying the minds of large portions of society. People, and students, are focused on their economic livelihood, and questioning is sometimes misconstrued as being hostile to the social environment (a common refrain to prevent critical thought is to label someone as being *cynical*). This is not to say that we need to dismiss the cultural manifestations of the various groups constituting society, only that we need to be critically aware and *conscious* of how power works to socially construct reality. For instance, we are concerned about a woman who steals food for her children, and learn about her insidious shortcomings through sound-bites and trivial comments in the media but we often do not learn of or question the poverty in which she lives, nor the broader, more significant issues around how infinite resources can be found for a war in a country that most Americans cannot identify on a map; similarly, we do not question why schools are under-funded, or how it is that there are intolerable levels of violence in schools and neighborhoods, especially in racialized, poorer areas, which does not excuse individual acts but does provide important context and background to how power is formulated. Thus, our concern for political literacy involves many intricate components. Would poverty, racism, war, disproportionate wealth accumulation and other manifestations incompatible with a democratic society be effectively remedied with more political literacy in schools (Lund & Carr, 2008)? Our conclusion is that the *process* of and *support* for becoming engaged would undoubtedly work toward more dynamic and meaningful participation in the identification and resolution of problems. Politics must be considered more than an economic equation, and the multiple inter-connections between peoples and nations requires a more extensive, lucid and critical examination in schools (Kincheloe, 2008).

We are challenged by students who reject the notion that society may not be as fair and balanced as they were led to believe. One student told Carr at the end of an undergraduate course in the Bachelor of Education program: "Why did no one tell us about this (racism, and how our education system can reproduce inequities) before?" Other students proclaimed that they were unaware that the social construction of identity had such a huge influence on how we are educated. Surprisingly for Carr (a Canadian teaching at a mid-sized US city in Ohio), many students have not overly considered their own implication in racism, nor do they (the majority are White students) consider it a priority to become engaged in improving the situation. Many are of good faith and believe in the sanctity of fairness as the basis of US values, which complicates their 'shock and awe', to embolden the terminology used by the US government to describe its military assault on Baghdad, of how the myriad stories of those who have not benefited from integration into American society have been systemically downplayed throughout their lives. Some students are openly hostile to the point of claiming that one might be disrespectful to even talk about the war in Iraq. The epistemo-logical starting-point for many is not considered: the important questions about who is an immigrant, how the working-class has been treated, the complicity in suffering abroad, and the not-so-cushy inner-lining of the esteemed 'market-place' are rarely subjected to critical discussion.

Thésée, in an urban university in Montreal, has also faced challenges about her place in society, especially when issues about discrimination are raised. While teaching courses on science education, she constantly faces the dilemma of some students wanting the one and only correct answer, a positivistic approach that conforms to neo-liberalism's mania for high standards, discounting what the knowledge means, how we teach about it, why some groups are absent, and, importantly, whether the correct answer is relevant. In one dramatic example attesting to the power of the academy to silence and trivialize this quest for critical thought, Thésée, a Black, female (and, at the time) untenured professor, was (literally) confronted by a White male, tenured professor at a conference, who demonstrated his control, power and disdain by standing, insulting, gesticulating in a violent manner, and denouncing, then leaving the lecture hall, slamming the door for effect because he did not agree with her critique of the place of technology in science education. This was an academic conference, where the expression of critical thought is paramount, and the attack on Thésée's person and intellectual concepts dealing with the hegemonic nature of science and science education exemplified the severe sensitivity and threatening nature of discussion aimed at challenging traditional views of the truth. Most telling in this anecdote is that no one in the lecture hall formally came to the defence of Thésée, although afterward people mentioned to her that it was unfortunate and that she should not worry about it. Why did this man feel as though he could do what he did, and why did no one immediately seek to discredit either the form or content of his intervention? What might this vignette say about political literacy in elementary and secondary schools and among teachers?

Crow (2006) argues that "Social justice in a global and knowledge society is not only important in schools but in our educational leadership departments. After all, if diversity is critical for the work of our students, is it any less important for our own work? Increasing racial, ethnic, gender, sexual, ability, and intellectual diversity is not only an ethical response, it is also an effective way to develop our own skills and dispositions to work in a changing, complex, and global environment". Gross and Shapiro (2005), in their analysis of Democratic Ethical Educational Leadership (DEEL), aim to create an action-oriented partnership, privileging open dialogue, free speech, community involvement, and participation toward the common good, and call for a more direct approach to political literacy in education: "upon reflection colleagues around the nation and around the world are coming to a different conclusion: there is no democracy without social justice, no social justice without democracy and that these mutually inclusive concepts are indispensable ingredients to school improvement worthy of the name". Ultimately, for there to be meaningful change in education at the social justice and political literacy levels, several inter-twined actions and processes are required, including an enlightened leadership (Carr's model) as well as an orchestrated push from below (Thésée's model). In the neo-liberal context, it is questionable whether there is room for educational policymaking that is original, progressive and in touch with a holistic, humanistic approach to education, which is open to constructively including a range of interests, groups and research that would effectively advance an agenda more aligned with the needs of society as opposed to the market.

We, therefore, argue for an education system that is more open to difference, not in a passive, superficial way, but in a dramatic, enforced, formal way. As Giroux (1988) reminds us, this emancipatory and political literacy we are advocating must also include the empowerment of teachers, who have long been discouraged and prevented from doing progressive work in their classrooms. Thus, we conclude that there is a pressing and indispensable need for a re-configured vision and framework for accountability for political literacy, and this process must consider how and why we teach and learn what we do in schools, something at the core of critical pedagogy (Freire, 1973; Kincheloe, 2008; McLaren, 2007).

QUESTIONS FOR REFLECTION

1. Although neo-liberalism is so pervasive, shaping the context and form of education, it is not readily critiqued by educators. What strategies can you think that could challenge a non-critical assessment of neo-liberalism in education, especially with regard to minoritized, racialized and marginalized youth?
2. Do the two models or approaches presented in this chapter by Carr and Thésée make sense, and could they make a difference in achieving greater political literacy?
3. How important is it to seek change from the inside (in schools) and the outside (in the community) concurrently? Is the formalized intransigence and non-progressive nature typically associated with the public school system an impediment to facilitating change among progressive forces and youth interested in cultivating resistance to neo-liberalism?

NOTES

[1] This chapter is a version of a previously published work: Carr, Paul R. & Thésée, Gina. (2008). The quest for political (il)literacy: Responding to, and attempting to counter, the neo-liberal agenda. In Porfilio, B. and Malott, C. (eds.), *An International Examination of Urban Education: The Destructive Path of Neo-liberalism* (pp. 173–194). Rotterdam: Sense Publishers.

REFERENCES

Apple, M. (1996) The Hidden curriculum and the nature of conflict. In W. C. Parker (Ed.), *Educating the democratic mind* (pp. 173–199). Albany, NY: State University of New York Press.

Carr, P. (2008). The "Equity Waltz" in Canada: Whiteness and the informal realities of racism in education. *Journal of Contemporary Issues in Education, 3*(2), 4–23. Retrieved from http://ejournals.library.ualberta.ca/index.php/JCIE/article/view/4575/3735

Carr, P. (2007). Educational policy and the social justice dilemma. In H. Claire & C. Holden (Eds.), *Controversial issues in education.* London: Trentham.

Carr, P. (2006a). Democracy in the classroom? *Academic Exchange Quarterly, 10*(2).

Carr, P. (2006b). Social justice and whiteness in education: Color-blind policymaking and racism. *Journal for Critical Education Policy Studies, 4,*2. Retrieved from http://www.jceps.com/index.php?pageID=article&articleID=77

Carr, P. (1999). Transforming the institution, or institutionalizing the transformation? Racial diversity and anti-racism in education in Toronto. *McGill Journal of Education, 34*(1), 49–77.

Carr, P. (1997). Stuck in the middle?: A case study of how principals manage equity-related change in education. *Education Canada, 35*(1), 42–49.

Carr, P. (1996). *Anti-racist education, institutional culture and the search for educational transformation.* Doctoral dissertation at the Ontario Institute for Studies in Education at the University of Toronto.

Carr, P. (1995). Employment equity for racial minorities in the teaching profession. *Multicultural Education Journal, 13*(1), 28–42.

Carr, P., & Lund, D. (2007). *The great White north? Exploring whiteness, privilege and identity in education.* Rotterdam: Sense Publishers.

Carr, P., & Klassen, T. (1997). Institutional barriers to the implementation of anti-racist education: A case study of the secondary system in a large, racially diverse, urban school board. *Canadian Journal of Educational Administration and Foundations, 12*(1), 46–68.

Carr, P., & Klassen, T. (1997). Different perceptions of race in education: Racial minority and white teachers. *Canadian Journal of Education, 1*(Winter), 68–81.

Carr, P., & Klassen, T. (1996). The role of racial minority teachers in anti-racist education. *Canadian Ethnic Studies, 28*(2), 126–138.

Carr, P., & Thésée, G. (2006). Race and identity in education in Quebec. *DIRECTIONS: Research and Policy on Eliminating Racism.*

Crow, G. (2006). Democracy and educational work in an age of complexity. *UCEA Review*, Winter, 1–5.

Davies, I., & Hogarth, S. (2004). Political literacy: Issues for teachers and learners. In J. Demaine (Ed.), *Citizenship and political education today* (pp. 181–199). Hampshire, England: Palgrave MacMillan.

Dei, G., Karumanchery, L., & Karumanchery-Luik, N. (2004). *Playing the race card: Exposing white power and privilege.* New York: Peter Lang.

Delpit, L. (1996). *Other people's children: Cultural conflict in the classroom.* New York: The New Press.

Demaine, J. (2004). *Citizenship and political education today.* Hampshire, England: Palgrave MacMillan.

Diamond, L. (1997, November/December). *Cultivating democratic leadership.* Excerpts from an address at a 1996 Buenos Aires Conference, Buenos Aires.

Dudley, R. L., & Gitelson, A. R. (2002). Political literacy, civic education, and civic engagement: A return to political socialization? *Applied Developmental Science, 6*(4), 175–182.

Freire, P. (1973). *Pedagogy of the oppressed.* New York: Continuum.

Giroux, H. (1988). Literacy and the pedagogy of voice and political empowerment. *Educational Theory, 38*(1), 61–75.

Gross, S., & Shapiro, J. (2005). Our new era requires a new DEEL: Towards a democratic ethical educational leadership. *UCEA Review*, Fall, 1–4.

Herman, E., & Chomsky, N. (2002). *Manufacturing consent: The political economy of the mass media.* New York: Pantheon.

Hess, D. (2004). Discussion in social studies: Is it worth the trouble? *Social Education, 68*(2), 151–155.

Hill, D. (2003). Global neo-liberalism, the deformation of education and resistance. *Journal for Critical Education Policy Studies, 1*, 1. Retrieved from www.jceps.com/?pageID=article&articleID=7

Holm, G., & Farber, P. (2002). Teaching in the dark: The geopolitical knowledge and global awareness of the next generation of American teachers. *International Studies in Sociology of Education, 12*(2), 129–144.

Hoover, R., & Shook, K. (2003). School reform and accountability: Some implications and issues for democracy and fair play. *Democracy and Education, 14*(4).

Hursh, D., & Martina, C. (2003). Neo-liberalism and schooling in the U.S.: How state and federal government education policies perpetuate inequality. *Journal of Critical Education Policy Studies, 1*, 2. Retrieved from www.jceps.com/?pageID=article&articleID=12

Hoffman, S. (2006, August 10). The foreign policy the US needs. *The New York Review of Books, LIII*, 13, 60–64.

Kincheloe, J. L. (2008a). *Critical pedagogy: Primer.* New York: Peter Lang.

Kozol, J. (2005). *The shame of the nation: The restoration of apartheid schooling in America.* New York: Crown Publishers.

Lopez, C. (2000). *Neo-liberalism and teachers.* Retrieved from http://www.vcn.bc.ca/idea/neolib.htm

Lund, D. E., & Carr, P. R. (Eds.). (2008a). *"Doing" democracy: Striving for political literacy and social justice.* New York: Peter Lang Publishing.

Martinez, E., & Garcia, A. (1996). *What is neo-liberalism? A brief definition for activists.* Retrieved from http://www. corpwatch.org/article.php?id=376

McLaren, P. (2007). *Life in schools: An introduction to critical pedagogy and the foundations of education.* Boston: Allyn and Bacon.

Morse, J. (2006, April). *Social justice and federal intervention in education.* Paper presented at an international conference on America's least wanted: Urban children and urban youth, Buffalo, NY.

National Institute for Literacy (US). (2006). *Facts and statistics.* Retrieved from www.nifl.gov/nifl/facts/facts.html

Ogbu, J. (1991). *Immigrant and involuntary minorities in comparative perspective.* In M. Gibson & J. Ogbu (Eds.), *Minority status and schooling: A comparative study of immigrant and involuntary minorities* (pp. 3–33). New York: Garland.

Ontario Ministry of Education. (2002). *Ontario secondary school diploma requirement: Community involvement activities in English-Language schools* (Policy/Program Memorandum No. 124a). Toronto: Ontario Ministry of Education. Retrieved from http://www.edu.gov.on.ca/extra/eng/ppm/124a.html

O'Toole, T., Marsh, D., & Jones, S. (2003). Political literacy cuts both ways: The politics of non-participation among young people. *Political Quarterly, 74*(3), 349–360.

Parker, W. (2003). *Teaching democracy: Unity and diversity in public life.* New York: Teachers College Press.

Parker, W. (2002). *Education for democracy: Contexts, curricula, assessments.* Greenwich, CT: Information Age.

Portelli, J., & Solomon, P. (2001). *The erosion of democracy in education: From critique to possibilities.* Calgary: Detselig Enterprises Ltd.

Reiss, M. (2003). Science education for social justice. In C. Vincent (Ed.), *Social justice, education and identity* (pp. 153–165). London: RoutledgeFalmer.

Robbins, C. (2003). Racism and the authority of neo-liberalism: A review of three new books on the persistence of racial inequality in a color-blind era. *Journal of Critical Education Policy Studies, 2,* 2. Retrieved November 23, 2006, from www.jceps.com/?pageID=article&aticleID=35

Ryan, J. (2006). *Inclusive leadership.* Toronto: Jossey-Bass.

Santora, E. (2006). *"Disturbing spaces": Struggling for identity and democracy in culturally diverse collaborative groups.* Paper presented at the Second Annual Symposium: Urban Education and Intercultural Learning, Buffalo, NY.

Schugurensky, D. (2000). *Citizenship learning and democratic engagement: Political capital revisited.* Retrieved from http://www.edst.educ.ubc.ca/aerc/2000/schugurenskyd1-web.htm

Sears, A., & Hughes, A. (2006). Citizenship: Education or indoctrination? *Citizenship and Teacher Education, 2*(1), 3–17.

Smiley, T. (2006). *The covenant with Black America.* Chicago: Third World Press.

Strama, M. (1998). Overcoming cynicism: Youth participation and electoral politics. *National Civic Review, 87*(1), 71–77.

Tabb, W. (2001). Essay: Globalization and education as a commodity. *Clarion.* Retrieved from http://www.psc-cuny.org/jcglobalization.htm

Thésée, G. (2006). A tool of massive erosion: Scientific knowledge in the neo-colonial enterprise. In G. L. Sefa Dei & A. Kempf (Eds.), *Anti-colonialism and education: The politics of resistance* (pp. 25–42). Rotterdam: Sense Publishers.

Thésée, G. (2003). *Le rapport au savoir scientifique en contexte d'acculturation. Application à l'étude de l'expérience scolaire en sciences d'élèves d'origine haïtienne.* Doctoral dissertation at the Université du Québec à Montréal.

Torres, C. (2005). No child left behind: A brainchild of neo-liberalism and American politics. *New Politics, X,* 2. Retrieved from http://www.wpunj.edu/newpol/issue38/torres38.htm

Treanor, P. (2005). *Neo-liberalism: Origins, theory, definition.* Retrieved from http://web.inter.nl.net/users/Paul.Treanor/neo-liberalism.html

Reiss, M. (2003). Science education for social justice. In C. Vincent (Ed.), *Social justice, education and identity* (pp. 153–165). London: RoutledgeFalmer.

Ryan, J. (2006). *Inclusive leadership.* Toronto: Jossey-Bass.

Vincent, C. (2003). *Social justice, education and identity*. London: RoutledgeFalmer.

Westheimer, J., & Kahne, J. (2002). Education for action: Preparing youth for participatory democracy. In R. Hayduk & K. Mattson (Eds.), *Democracy's movement: Reforming the American political system for the 21st century* (pp. 91–107). Lanman, MD: Rowman and Littlefield.

Westheimer, J., & Kahne, J. (2003). Reconnecting education to democracy: Democratic dialogues. *Phi Delta Kappan, 85*(1), 9–14.

Westheimer, J., & Kahne, J. (2004). What kind of citizen?: The politics of educating for democracy. *American Educational Research Journal, 41*(2), 237–269.

Westheimer, J. (2006). Patriotism and education: An introduction. *Phi Delta Kappan, 87*(8), 569–572.

GREG DIMITRIADIS

AFTERWORD

Youth Culture, Education and Resistance by Brad Porfilio and Paul Carr is a timely and powerful intervention in contemporary literature on youth, education, and neo-liberalism. Collectively, these essays register the urgency of our moment—the massive world economic realignment that has so brutally worked to marginalize the most vulnerable among us. Indeed, this global realignment (what the authors call neo-liberalism) has worked to sort youth in increasingly stark ways—with particularly virulent implications for education. While elite youth are being "set up" for success in all kinds of explicit and not-so-explicit ways, an increasingly large group of youth is struggling to find their footing. These youth are increasingly treated as a problem to be monitored and managed—for example, through high stakes testing and new forms of school surveillance and discipline—before entering a workplace that has increasingly rendered them (at best) cheap labor and (at worst) irrelevant. The economy today clearly draws sharp lines of distinction between economic winners and losers—and the implications for youth are profound.

Of course, several generations of scholars have taken up the question of youth culture, particularly in moments of great social, cultural, and material transition. I am thinking here of movements within the U.S. (such as those associated with the Chicago School of Sociology) as well as in the U.K. (such as those associated with the Birmingham School of Cultural Studies). This work has usefully focused on the everyday practices of young people. In particular, work in Cultural Studies has provided us a language to talk about the ways young people resist their interpellation into dominant culture through everyday resistant practices. This work focused on the autonomy of culture itself—as not reducible to the economic dictates of Marx and Marxism. As this work began to travel widely starting in the late 1970s—in particular, as in landed in the U.S.—a focus on popular culture emerged.

One result of this stress on (perhaps even conflation between) young people and popular culture was a loss of focus on the material contexts that so clearly circumscribed their lives. Culture was forced to bear a large burden here—often treated outside of the economic shifts, pressures, and constraints that so dramatically bore down on youth. The fear of "economic reductionism," it is fairly clear now, precluded years of serious work on political economy. The rise of deregulated financial interests—supra-national institutions no longer bound by national limits and dictates—effectively worked to re-orient the lives and aspirations of young people in ways that are becoming all-too evident. Critical scholars, I believe, were left with an impoverished set of tools to address the moment—binary distinctions between inequality and privilege that often mapped too easily onto constructs such as urban and suburban, black and white, public and private, etc. All the while, the world was being realigned in complex ways not evidenced since the turn on the century.

Youth Culture, Education and Resistance is a powerful intervention here. Collectively, the authors and editors open up the discussion around young people today, offering us a new and richer language to think about the specific kinds of inequalities young people face today—and how they are being resisted. The topics are as broad as the treatments are deep. We are asked to look beyond an (exclusive) focus on "urban education" towards rural settings as new loci of inequality. We turn our gaze towards white working-class youth in first ring suburbs in the US. We are pushed to de-link questions of nation and culture, turning towards the range of ways young people around the world—from Arab youth in France to young people in the West African country of Burkina-Faso—pick up and deploy hip-hop music to address local concerns. And, of course, we look at the ways young people are resisting their place in this new, brutally realigned world—not only at the level of style and everyday culture, but in more formal and organized ways.

This is, of course, only a brief afterword. Yet, I offer it in the spirit of this text—as a starting-point. The editors and authors have provided us a rich set of resources to begin to think in more complex ways about inequality, to revisit the methods and (especially) the questions that have structured discussion around youth over the last several decades. *Youth Culture, Education and Resistance* is a vibrant and generative text. With you, I hope to explore its implications for years to come.

CONTRIBUTOR BIOGRAPHIES

Paul R. Carr is Associate Professor in Foundations of Education at Youngstown State University, Ohio, where he conducts research on critical pedagogy, social justice, democracy, and political sociology. He recently co-edited two books with Darren Lund, and has written a single-author manuscript entitled *Does your vote count? Critical pedagogy and democracy*, which will be published in 2010 by Peter Lang.

Greg Dimitriadas is Professor of sociology of education at the University of Buffalo, The State University of New York. He is author or editor (alone and with others) of over ten books and 50 articles and book chapters. His *Studying urban youth culture* was published by Peter Lang in 2008.

Julie Gorlewski earned her Ph.D. from the State University of New York at Buffalo in 2008. Julie teaches English, and directs the learning center at a public high school serving an inner-ring suburb of Buffalo. Her research focuses on the social context of education from a critical theoretical perspective, exploring the influences of social class on teachers and students, particularly when they share other salient, more visible characteristics such as race, locality, and national language.

Kevin Gosine is an Assistant Professor in the Department of Sociology at Brock University in St. Catherines, Ontario, Canada. He holds a Ph.D from York University in Toronto. His primary areas of research include ethnicity and racialization, social identity construction, social inequality, the sociology of education, social welfare, and cultural studies. In his recent published work he has explored processes of multiple identity construction and cultural negotiation among highly educated and upwardly mobile Black Canadians. He is presently part of a collaborative study of racial bias in Toronto's child welfare system.

Robert Haworth is an Associate Professor in Multicultural Education at the University of Wisconsin-La Crosse. He received his Ph.D from New Mexico State University with an emphasis on critical pedagogies and social studies education. He teaches courses in schooling and globalization and multicultural education, and is currently interested in research surrounding radical literacies, youth culture and informal learning spaces. His interests in these areas stem from being involved in punk/hardcore sub-cultural practices as well as from working in collective and autonomous spaces. Currently, he is developing an edited book on anarchist pedagogies.

Carl E. James teaches in the Faculty of Education as well as in the graduate program in Sociology at York University, Toronto, Canada, and is the Director of the York Centre for Education and Community. He teaches courses in urban education, adolescence, and the foundations of Education. His research explores issues of identity/identification in terms of race, ethnicity, gender, class as well as citizenship/immigrant status; sports in the schooling and educational attainments of racialized students; and the practices and implications of multiculturalism as a state policy in addressing racism/discrimination. His publications include *Race in Play: The Socio-Cultural Worlds of Student Athletes* (2005) and *Seeing Ourselves: Exploring Race, Ethnicity and Culture* (2003).

Katie Johnston-GoodStar currently works with the Indigenous Wellness Research Institute at the University of Washington's School of Social Work. In 2006 and 2007 she received a Roadmap traineeship for her research entitled 'Picture This': Native Youth Look at Their Environment, a Photovoice project using a critical pedagogy of place, youth photography and narrative to explore environmental justice with Native American teens in the Seattle area. Katie's research focus on: 1) environmentally focused Social Work policy and practice, 2) establishing place-centered pedagogies, research and interventions for Indigenous community wellness and 3) maintaining the vitality of Indigenous sociopolitical movements through community-based endeavors.

Darren E. Lund earned his Ph.D in anti-racism education at the University of British Columbia, in Vancouver, Canada, in 2002. He has published widely in the field of social justice activism and teacher education, with a focus on collaborative student and teacher projects. For 16 years Darren taught high school and founded the award-winning *Students and Teachers Opposing Prejudice* (STOP) Program. Darren has won a number of national and international honors for his work, including *Exemplary Multicultural Educator of the Year*, and a *Reader's Digest National Leader in Education*. Darren is co-editor *The great white north? Exploring whiteness, privilege and identity in education* (Sense, 2007), and *Doing democracy: Striving for political literacy and social justice* (Peter Lang, 2008). He is currently an Associate Professor at the University of Calgary in Calgary, Alberta.

Curry S. Malott is an Assistant Professor of Education at D'Youville College. He has published numerous peer-reviewed manuscripts. Curry's most recent books are *Punk rockers' revolution: A pedagogy of race, class and gender* (2004 Peter Lang), *A call to action: An introduction to education, philosophy, and Native North America* (Peter Lang 2008), *The destructive path of neo-liberalism: An international examination of urban education*, edited with Bradley Porfilio (Sense 2008), and *Teaching Native America across the curriculum: A critical inquiry* (Peter Lang 2009) (with Lisa Waukau and Lauren Waukau-Villagomez). He is also series editor of Critical Constructions: Studies on Education and Society (Information Age Publishing).

Peter McLaren is a Professor at the Graduate School of Education and Information Studies, University of California, Los Angelos. He is the author, coauthor, editor, and coeditor of approxiamtely forty books and mongraphs. Several hundred of his articles, chapters, interviews, reviews, commentaries, and columns have appeared in dozens of scholarly journals and professional magazines since the publication of his first book, *Cries from the corridor*, in 1980. His work has been translated into seventeen languages, and he lectures internationally.

Maryam Nabavi is currently a doctoral student in Educational Studies at the University of British Columbia. She uses a cultural studies approach in her research on first-generation immigrant youth's social and political learning. She has a Master's degree from the Ontario Institute for Studies in Education/University of Toronto. Maryam was a board member with the National Youth Antiracism Network of the Canadian Race Relations Foundation, and was a Youth Antiracism Facilitator with the Youth Reach Out Against Racism (ROAR) program of the Committee on Race Relations and Cross-Cultural Understanding in Calgary, Alberta, from 2002–2003.

Michael O'Sullivan is a faculty-member of the Department of Graduate and Undergraduate Studies of the Faculty of Education at Brock University, Ontario, Canada. Michael studied political science as an undergraduate student at Saint Mary's University in Halifax, where he was elected president of the student council. Shortly after graduation he was elected vice-president of the Canadian Union of Students, a national student organization. Subsequently, he continued his studies in political science at the University of Regina where he earned his master's degree. Michael has published numerous peer-reviewed manuscripts on the topics of global citizenship education, neo-liberalism, and democracy and education.

Brad J. Porfilio is Assistant Professor of Education in the Educational Leadership for Teaching and Learning Doctoral Program at Lewis University, Chicago. He teaches courses on Globalization and Education, History of Education, Curriculum Theory, Qualitative Research, Critical Pedagogy, and Multicultural Education. He also held appointments as Assistant Professor at Saint Louis University and The Richard Stockton College of NJ. He received his Ph.D. in Sociology of Education in 2005 at the University at Buffalo. His research interests include urban education, neo-liberalism and schooling, transformative education, gender and technology, and cultural studies. He has published numerous peer-reviewed articles, book chapters, and conference presentations.

Shannon M. Porfilio is currently a lecturer and graduate student in the department of Modern and Classical Languages at Saint Louis University. After completing her Master's degree in Foreign Language Education at the University at Buffalo, she taught French language and culture courses at the secondary level for 8 years while concomitantly teaching Foreign Language Methods at the graduate level for D'Youville College. Her research interests include: youth culture, language pedagogy and curricula, identity formation and marginalized youth in the Francophone world. Her latest manuscript will be published in the *French Review*.

Darius Prier received his Ph.D. in Educational Leadership from Miami University, Oxford, Ohio. His work incorporates discourses within critical pedagogy, cultural studies, critical race theory, popular culture, and social justice education. He has taught courses in socio-cultural studies of education in a teacher education program. Prier recently developed a special focus course on hip-hop in Miami's Cultural Studies and Public Life Thematic Sequence on Youth Subculture, Popular Culture, and Non-formal Education for undergraduate majors. He is a visiting faculty member of Miami University's Department of Educational Leadership.

David Alberto Quijada Cerecer holds a joint Assistant Professor position in the department of Education, Culture, and Society and in the Ethnic Studies program at the University of Utah. His research interests include: inter-cultural/ethnic youth alliances; cultural citizenship and identity formations; community coalition-building projects; feminist ethnographic methods; youth participatory action research and critical discourse analysis. Quijada was named the "2008/09 Community Scholar in Residence" by University of Utah's Neighborhood Partners. With his colleagues he also co-directs Mestizo Arts and Activism, a participatory youth research collective that supports youth in developing and researching social change projects.

David Requa has served as the Superintendent of the Rantoul Township High School District #193 since 2005, and works toward an activist agenda to provide greater equity for all students. He holds a law degree, and practiced law for 20 years before returning to public education. He is working to complete his Ph.D in Educational Administration and Leadership at the University of Illinois at Urbana Champaign under the direction of Dr. Carolyn Shields.

Carolyn M. Shields is Professor and Head of the Department of Educational Organization and Leadership at the University of Illinois Urbana-Champaign. She holds a Ph.D in Educational Administration from the University of Saskatchewan, Canada. She has recently served on several ministerial advisory boards and completed terms as president of the Canadian Association for Studies in Educational Administration and as a Board member for the Commonwealth Council for Educational Administration and Management. Her research relates to leadership for academic excellence and social justice in diverse settings. She has published five books and over 90 articles.

Aster Solomon Tecle is currently a doctoral student in Social Welfare at the University of Washington, Seattle, School of Social Work. She earned a Master's degree there (2008) as well as a Master's in Sustainable International Development from The Heller School for Social Policy and Management, Brandeis University. Before that she worked with the Ministry of Education and the National Union of Eritrean Women (NUEW) in Eritrea as an educator. Her research interest includes girls' education, adult literacy; single mothers and the informal economy; international social work; and globalization and social welfare issues.

Gina Thésée is Professor of Education at the Université du Québec à Montréal, where she also completed her doctorate. She teaches course in science education, research methods and epistemology. She has published several articles on critical pedagogy, knowledge construction and de-colonization, and environmental education. She has participated in numerous community development and research projects pertaining to the Haitian community in Montreal, and has also been a keynote speaker at a number of events in Quebec in relation to intercultural relations. Gina is also a board-member of the international *Association pour la recherche interculturelle.*

Alma M.O. Trinidad is a doctoral candidate in Social Welfare at the University of Washington, Seattle, School of Social Work. She earned her MSW from the University of Michigan in 1999 with a concentration in community organization and social policy. Alma's research interests concern positionalities, mental health promotion, and community among Asian Pacific Islander adolescents and emerging adults. Her dissertation examines how critical pedagogy, community contribution, and community epistemology serve as venues for empowerment, collective consciousness, and health and mental health promotion. Alma is a former Council of Social Work Education fellow, and a current NIMH Prevention Research Trainee.

Touorouzou Hervé Somé was a Fulbright scholar (2000), and holds a Ph.D. in the Social Foundations of Education from the University of Buffalo at New York. He is currently an assistant professor in the Teacher Education Department at the College of Education and Human Services of the University of Southern Maine. He has taught the sociological and philosophical foundations of education, critical issues in education, multicultural education, and research in education, as well as supervising student teachers in Africa and in the USA. His research interests include comparative and international education, the education of African children in the USA, and culturally responsive pedagogy.

INDEX

CPSIA information can be obtained
at www.ICGtesting.com
Printed in the USA
FFOW01n1648061215
19252FF